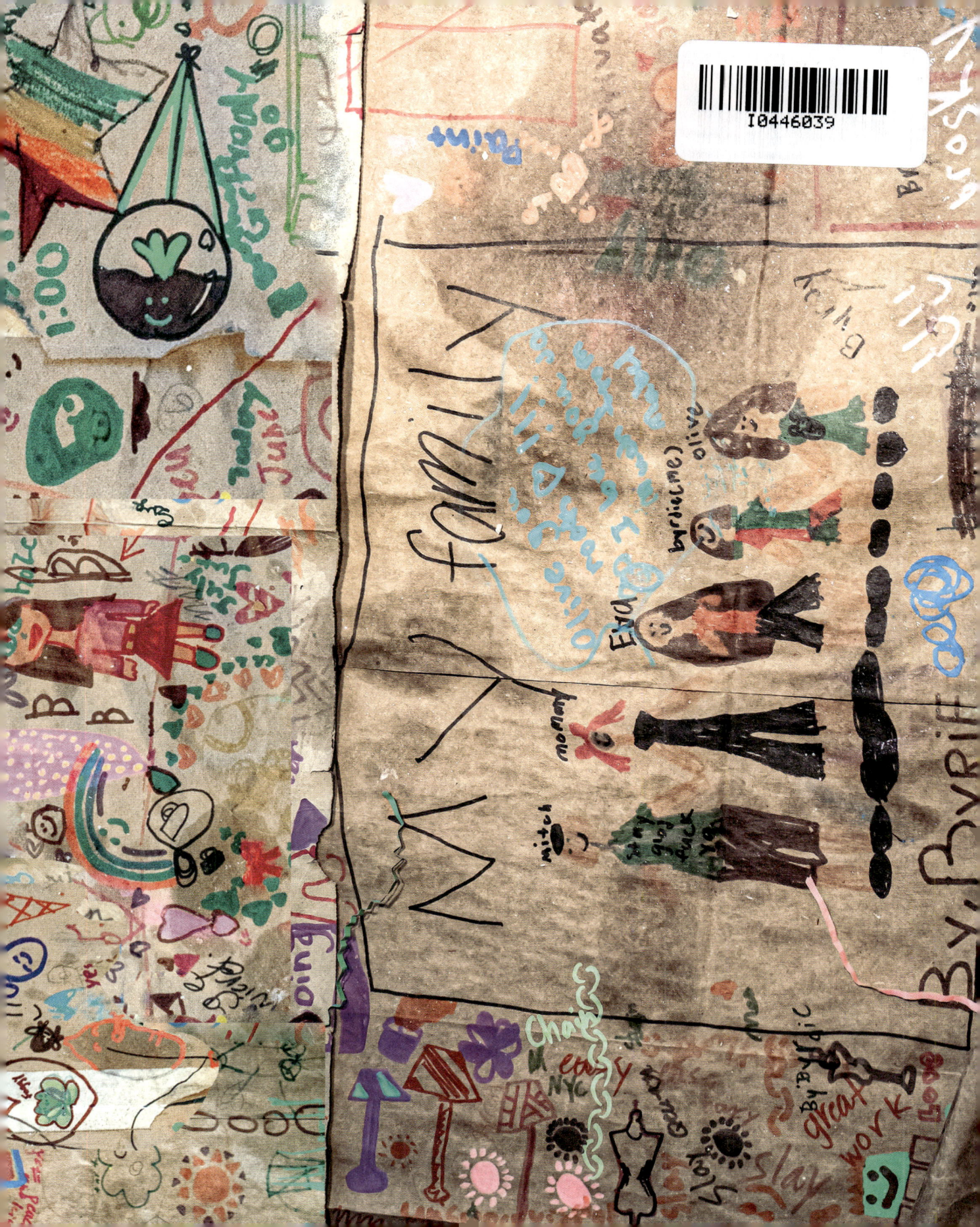

un•super•vised, adjective

: not watched or under constant observation by someone in authority

Imagine a world where families felt safe enough to live their lives free from the fear of judgment, criticism, and inadequacy. To live a life unsupervised. *Unsupervised* is an intimate look at the modern family. My curiosity regarding the everyday routine of raising children is what led me to begin spending anywhere between 24 and 72 hours simply documenting a family's unscripted life. With the birth of social media came the ability for anyone to present a highly curated version of themselves and their life, oftentimes under the social pressures to appear "perfect." I have watched this directly affect how parents, especially mothers, share their life with the outside virtual world. Ultimately, this creates a feeling of isolation and loneliness, as parents are completely disconnected from the reality of their life and their tailored life online. This photographic exploration is an attempt to reveal the similarities I have witnessed by photographing my subjects' vulnerability, challenges, joy, hardships, and humorous moments of raising a family. It is my hope that this project helps parents feel less alone, realizing that their experience is a shared one with the global community of parents around the world, to remind us all of how much more we are connected than divided.

Cofounder: Michael Itkoff
Creative Director: Ursula Damm
Copy Editor: Gabrielle Fastman

© 2025 Daylight Community Arts Foundation

Photographs © 2011–2024 by Kirsten Lewis
Text © 2024 by Kirsten Lewis
"Letter to Mabel" © 2024 by Brett Magdovitz

ISBN: 978-1-954119-39-0

Printed by Ofset Yapimevi, Turkey

Daylight Books
E-mail: info@daylightbooks.org
Web: www.daylightbooks.org

Kirsten Lewis

unsupervised

Daylight

Dedicated to my Byrdie Mae.

My most favorite creation, you are the reason I continue to dream. I am so lucky I get to be your bridge between the unknown world and this world and beyond.

In memory of Sara.

Oh how I wish you could hold this book in your hands, for you are the guiding light that led me to this life I have right now. Thank you for the most beautiful present I have ever been given; I am grateful each and every moment.

Nothing is better than real life.

—Kirsten Lewis

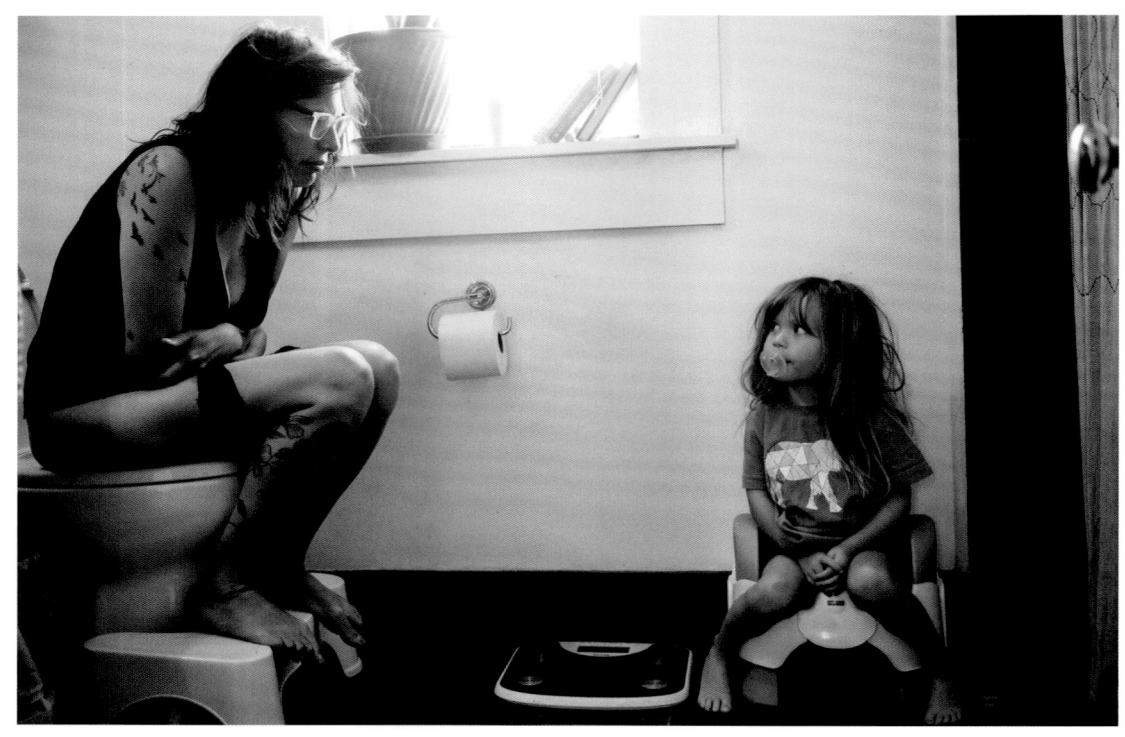

Promises to my seventeen-week-pregnant self:

1. Wooden toys only.

2. I will not have a picky eater.

3. No technology until middle school.

4. My kid will sleep in her own bed once she is done nursing.

5. I will always stay calm and in control during conflict.

6. I will not allow outside judgment to influence how I parent or how I feel about my own parenting.

Sincerely,
First-Time Old Mom

My seven-year-old just fell asleep in my bed watching *Is It Cake?* on her iPad after eating pasta, butter, and 5 mg of melatonin for dinner, for the sixth night in a row. I can barely stretch far enough to grab my bedroom-nightstand readers because I have, once again, pulled out my neck by . . . yes, you guessed it . . . breathing. After chugging the last of my much-needed iced coffee, I carefully lean over the snoring child to grab my laptop. If I am not going to have sex due to my "no kids in the bed" boundaries, I might as well work. That being said, despite the 9 p.m. caffeine charge, my eyes are heavier than a pool diaper on a Sunday afternoon in August.

Today. Today was hard.

I started the morning hitting my snooze button every two minutes for an hour straight before crawling out of my sheetless, crumb-dusted, broken pillow fort of a bed.

"SHIT!" I whisper yelled, remembering that I needed to pack not one but three lunches because yesterday our youngest decided she was officially a vegetarian, despite *never* expressing interest in it before. The oldest had a field trip to who knows where, and the middle one, well, she only eats seven things total, so I am the mom who will be packing lunches for the next 3,650 days. Somehow, miraculously, I managed to get all three kids to three different schools in two different towns, with overlapping start times, and only ONE of them was late. A huge win for me, my ADHD, and the mounting attendance shame I endure at each of the three school front offices.

The commute time, during school, is around three hours a day when we have all three kids, with just about five hours in between unpaid Uber rides. That means I have five hours to answer all my emails, text messages, and phone calls; attend client meetings and doctor appointments; do the grocery shopping; tone photos; design albums; get to the post office to mail out 117 boxes; and MAYBE drop off the three giant donation bags that have been living comfortably in my trunk since the last time it snowed, 7.25 months ago. I am a forty-seven-year-old mom to an eight-year-old and bonus eight- and twelve-year-olds. All girls. That role alone is a full-time, seventy-five-hour-a-week job (time they are in our care, not sleeping, not at school, NOT in the summer). On top of that I am self-employed as a photographer, mentor, and keynote speaker. This requires, on average, at least sixty hours a week of my attention. According to Old Ass Mom Survival Math, there are 168 hours in a week. Between the kids and my career, that leaves me with roughly 4.7142 hours a night to sleep. If no one needs thirty-one glasses of water, we've successfully been spared all nightmare-induced insomnia, and no masked strangers have scaled thirty feet up our house, without a ladder, to stare at one of the children with emerald glowing eyes and a pink boa, convincing one of us they need a donut to make him go away, I can get a whole 4.7142 hours of sleep a night.

I am the furthest version of perfect when it comes to motherhood. Furthermore, I am just barely surviving some days doing life in general that has nothing to do with my family. I have all these wants, desires, dreams, and goals for how to better show up, and still I feel like I'm failing. I cannot recall whether I moved the laundry from the washer to the dryer before leaving the house this afternoon, which would make it the fourth time I'll have to run that load again to remove any evidence of my continuous house-chore incompetence. One of the things I fear most is not knowing how long the wet, now dry, laundry has been neglected and having to wear it because I reached the negative-clean-underwear phase of the week. I mean, that's not my fear; my fear is realizing I am wearing wet, now dry, dirty laundry by the waft I smell running through the store. You know this smell. It's the combination of wet dog and kombucha, otherwise known as Rich Hippies Caught in a Rain Storm, *all huddled together under the awning in front of Whole Foods*. (Raquita, I can hear you cackling.) The worst thing for me is running into someone I know while smelling so awful and trying to negotiate how far away I need to stand to not be caught. And, if I am being completely honest, there is a 99% chance that despite looking them in the eyes, shaking hands, and saying a stranger's name three times, the next unexpected moment I run into them I'll rely on their initiation to introduce themselves to whomever I'm with so that no one will ever know my deep, dark secret. And that isn't even in the same hemisphere as what happened last week, when out running errands this exact thing happened. A familiar-looking human smiled, shook my hand, and said, "Hi, Kirsten! It's so good to see you! Is this your daughter with you? What's her name again?" And I just stood there . . . for a longer-than-comfortable amount of time it should take to introduce your eight-year-old, the only human who exists because I exist.

The only living thing that has been physically surrounded by my internal organs, face pressed between the walls of my birth canal. The only person who navigates life in constant knowing of this deep, dark secret. "Hi, my name is Byrdie, what's yours?" I had to rely on my own daughter to introduce herself because I could not remember HER name.

The irony is:
I can tell you my childhood phone number, backwards, forwards, and in word form. Ya know, the word it makes when you look on the dial pad?

I still remember, almost three decades later, to send my first boyfriend a HAPPY BIRTHDAY message on November 22. Every year. Without fail.

And if you handed me a Nintendo controller with *Contra*'s START page on the TV, I'd instinctually press up, up, down, down, left, right, left, right, B, A, B, A, select, select, start.

As we get older, as more life is experienced, our entire system becomes tired. I truly believe it's nature's way of reminding us to breathe. To rest. To reset. Unfortunately, we have single-handedly created a world where we now feel it's impossible to do that because that would present as imperfection. Defeat. Failure. Many of the memories we hold closest to us, that bring us the most comfort and joy, are the ones before we became "grown-ups." Why? Because we loved ourselves more, forgave ourselves, leaned into the messiness of "growing up." We also gave ourselves permission to be PRESENT, to feel everything all at once without worrying about how much time it was taking away from being productive. We just allowed ourselves to . . . be.

While the intention of this book has always been to give the global community of parents an opportunity to be seen, honored, and celebrated, this process has revealed something much more personal. At the end of the day, I created a book I, Kirsten Lewis, needed. Kirsten, the little girl who never felt understood or valued just for being her. The little girl who never fit in because she was the "weird kid with divorced parents," was the black sheep of her own family, and was "excused for" because she was a "dancer and artist." The little girl who fought superhard to hide the fact that her mom worked three jobs just to pay the mortgage, stood in the "red line" to get free lunch and wasn't allowed to have friends over for dinner because we just couldn't afford it. The little girl who questioned God at a very young age, was the only Jewish kid in her neighborhood, and realized very early on that the world was not built to protect and empower everyone.

The most prolific, productive part of this creative process came at the very end, when I had been struggling the most. Financial stress, divorce, blended families, death, perimenopause . . . just one at a time could take out a two-ton steel ox statue. I've been attempting to manage it all at the same time. If you can visualize a bear-maced clown after a pitcher of margaritas, attempting to juggle eight flaming bowling pins while balancing on a frozen golf tee? That's me, only in a straitjacket. There have been moments when I have questioned my sanity, my career, my own life, and all of it very alone, terrified of what someone may think if they could listen to the ever-running one-sided dialogue in my head. I have survived because of all who have come before me and will continue on after me. In making my final edits I found tremendous comfort in reconnecting with every parent and child in this book, reflecting on all the beautiful ways in which I have grown through spending time in their lives. It is through their imperfections, humility, vulnerability, honesty, and transparency that I am able to continue leaning into the perfection of complete and utter imperfection.

And so, finally, the gift I needed to give to myself first, I can FINALLY give to all of you.

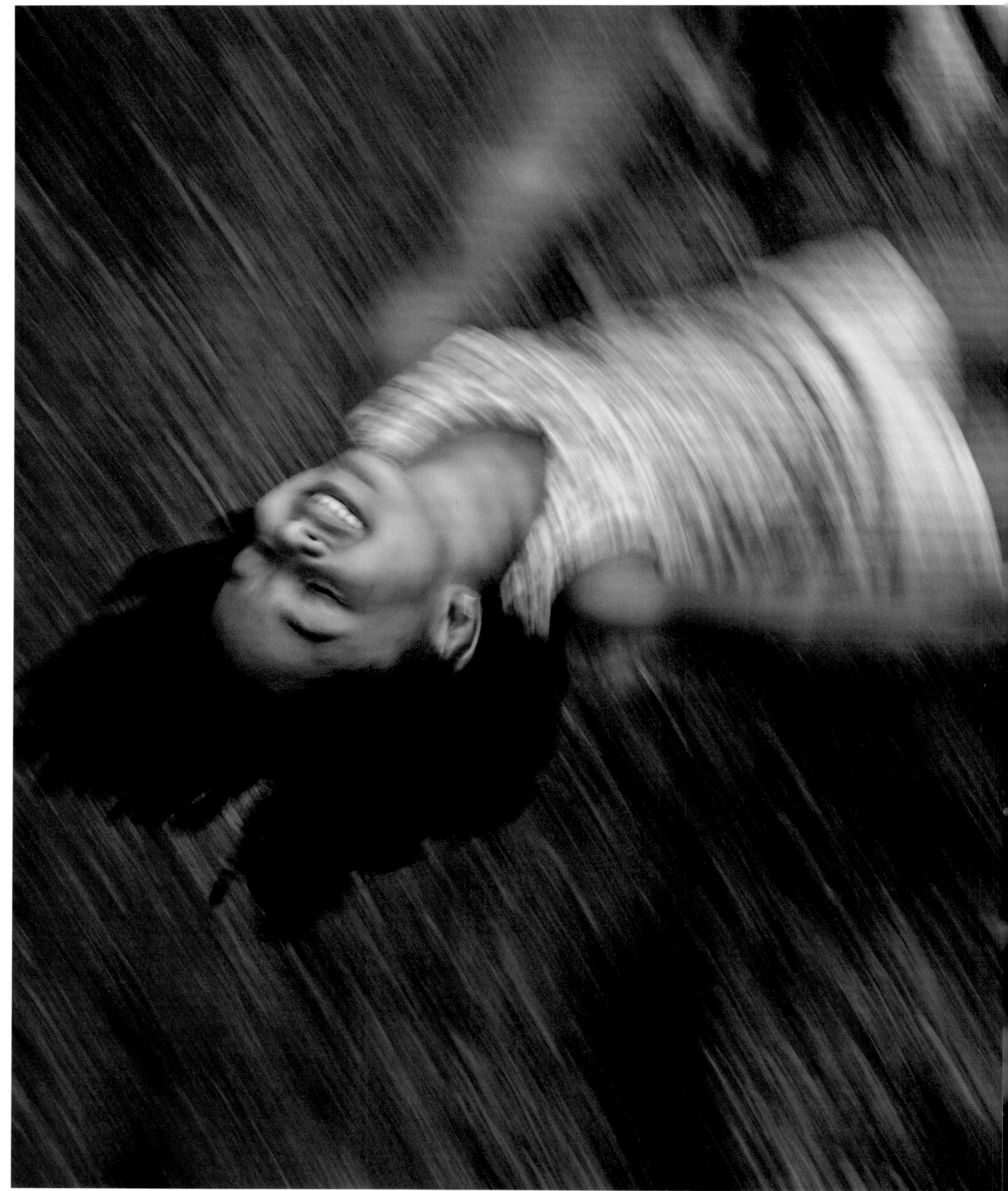

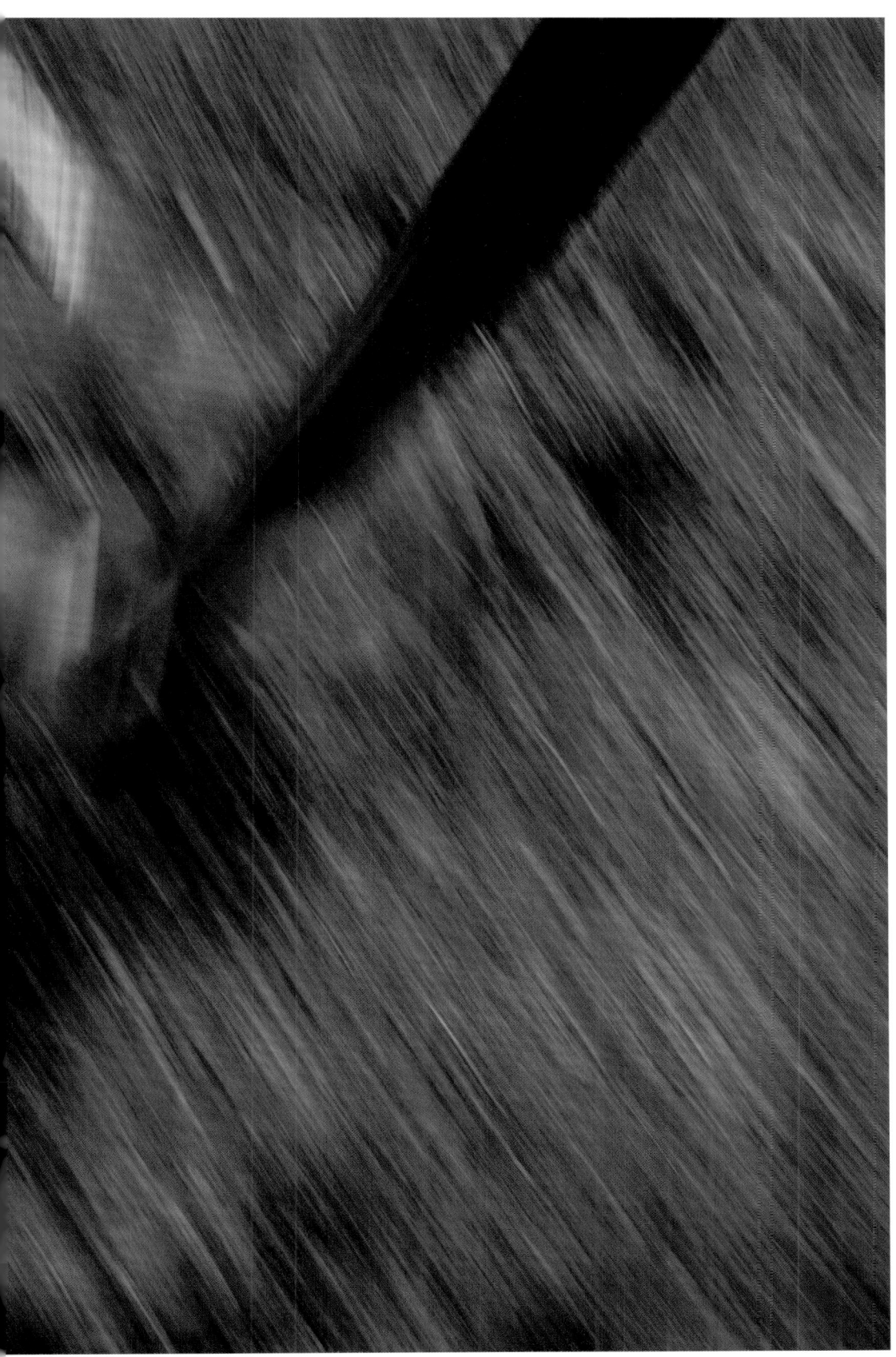

You can't feel the
world under your feet
with your shoes on.
—Byrdie Mae, age five

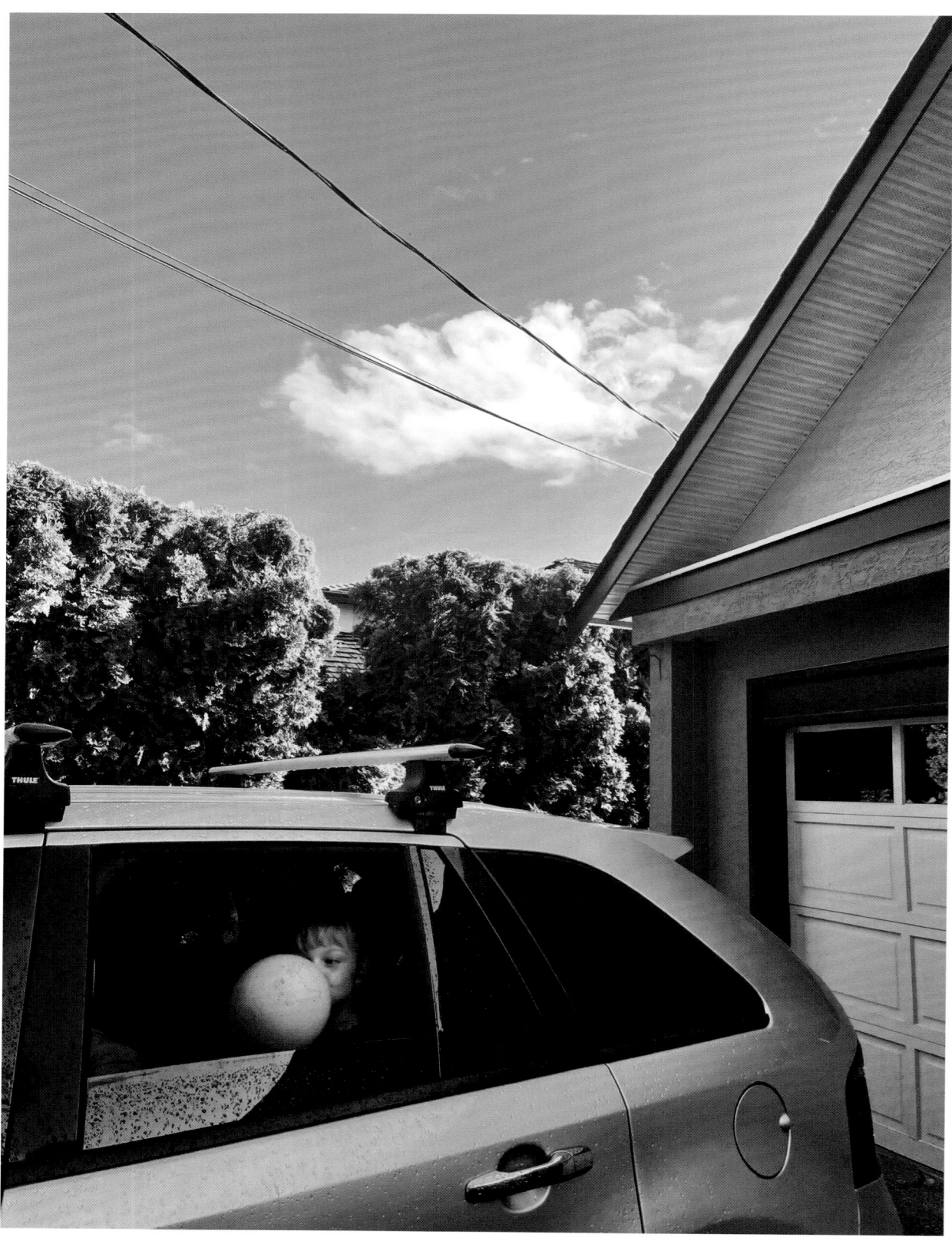

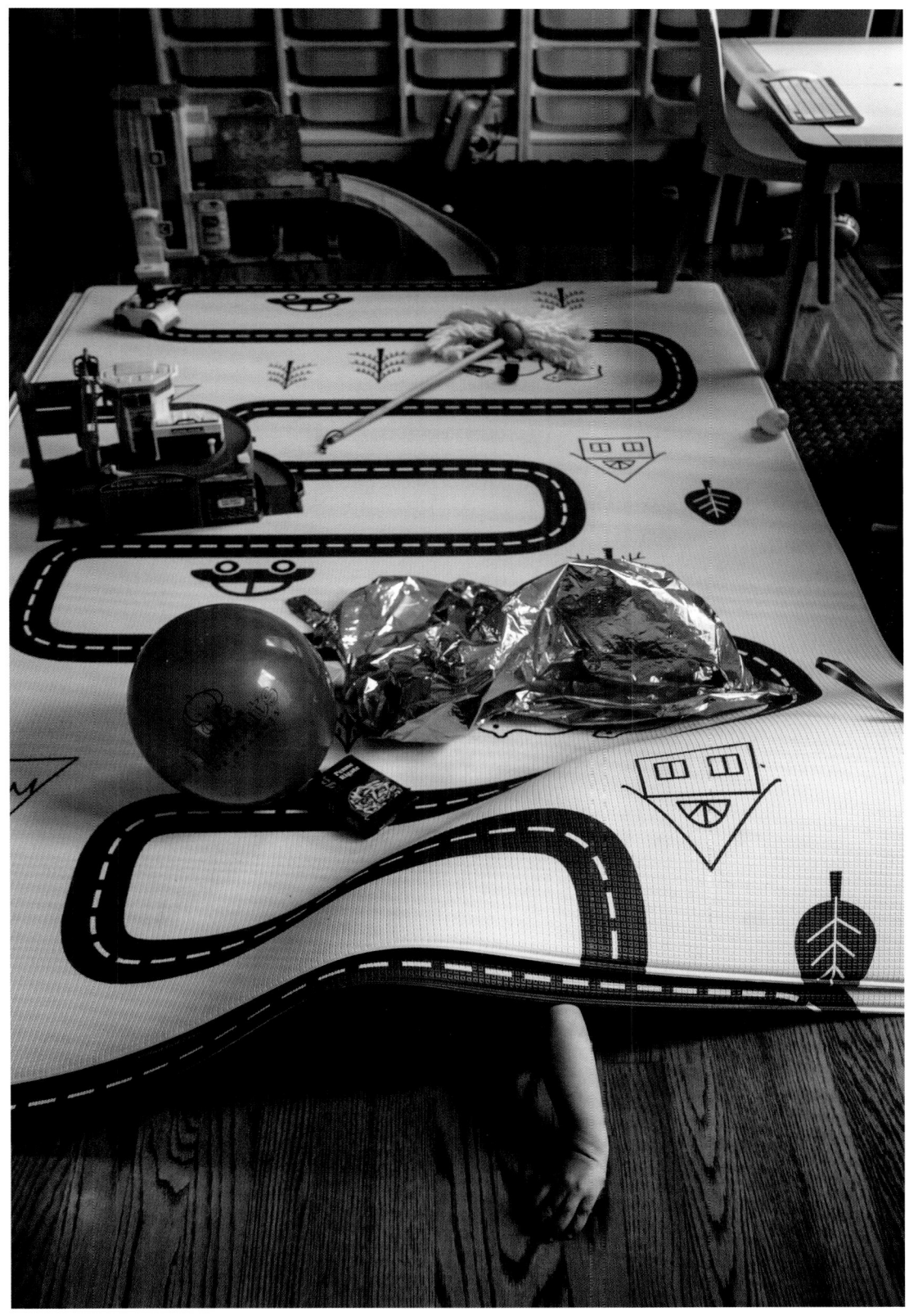

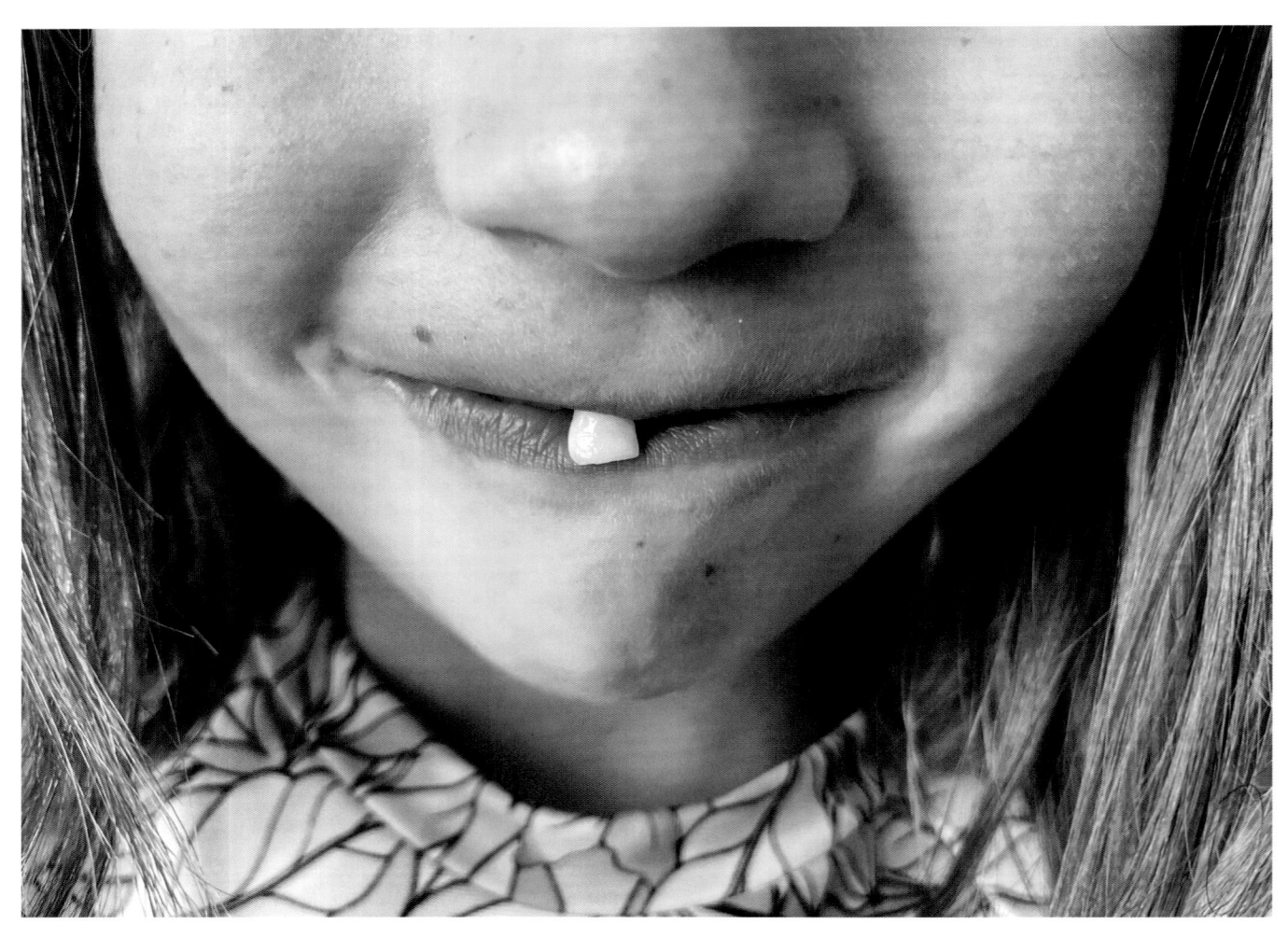

Did you ever think about the fact that our nipples are older than our teeth?
—Tim, age eight

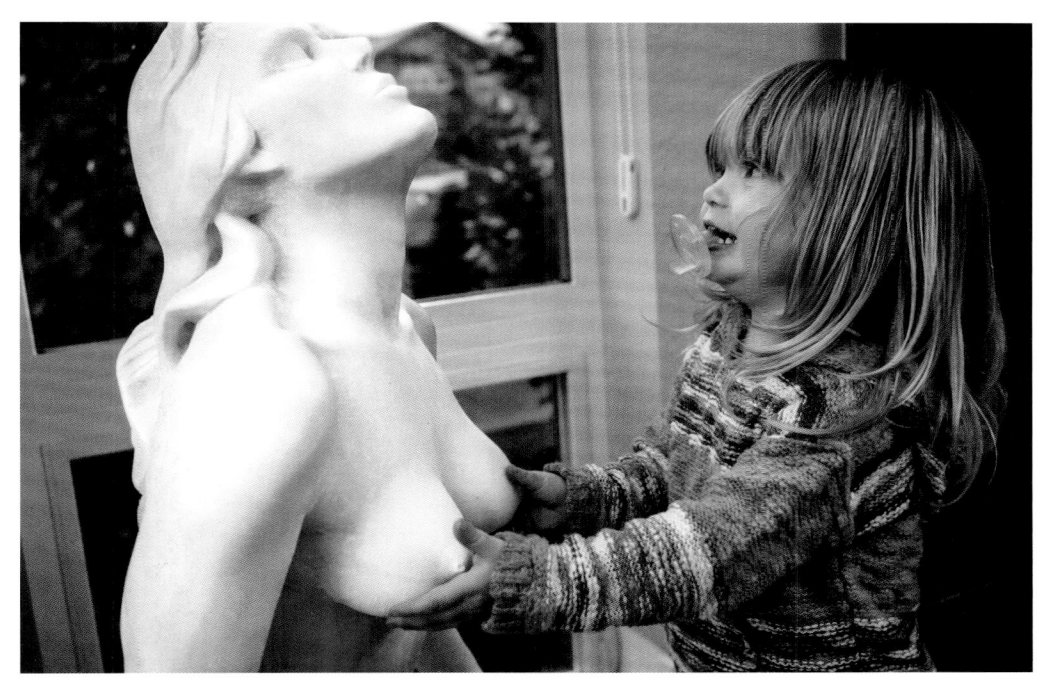

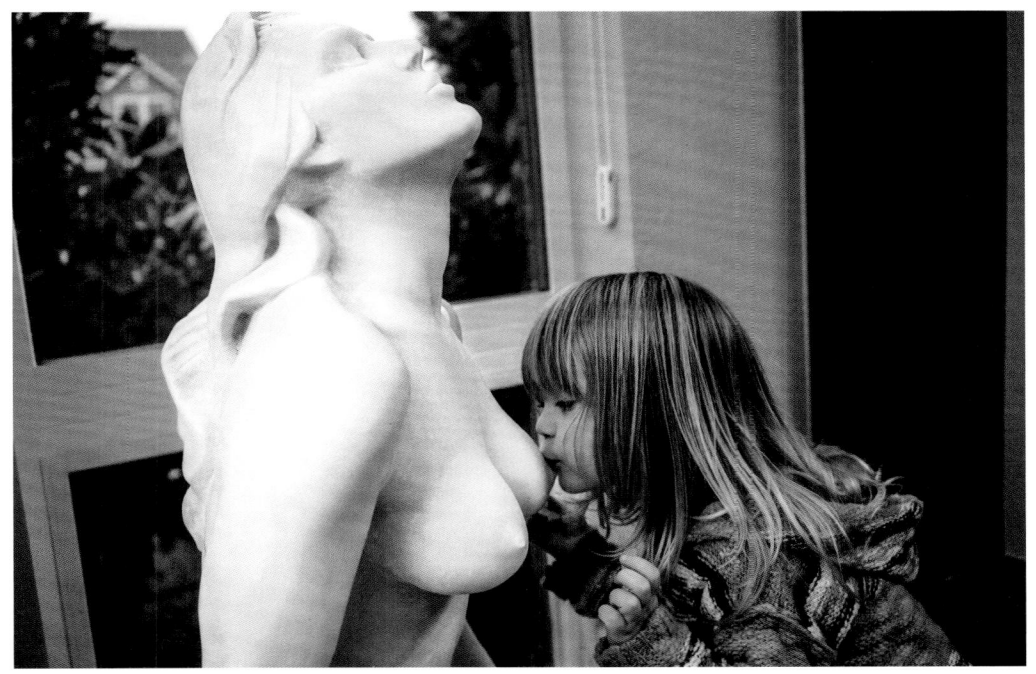

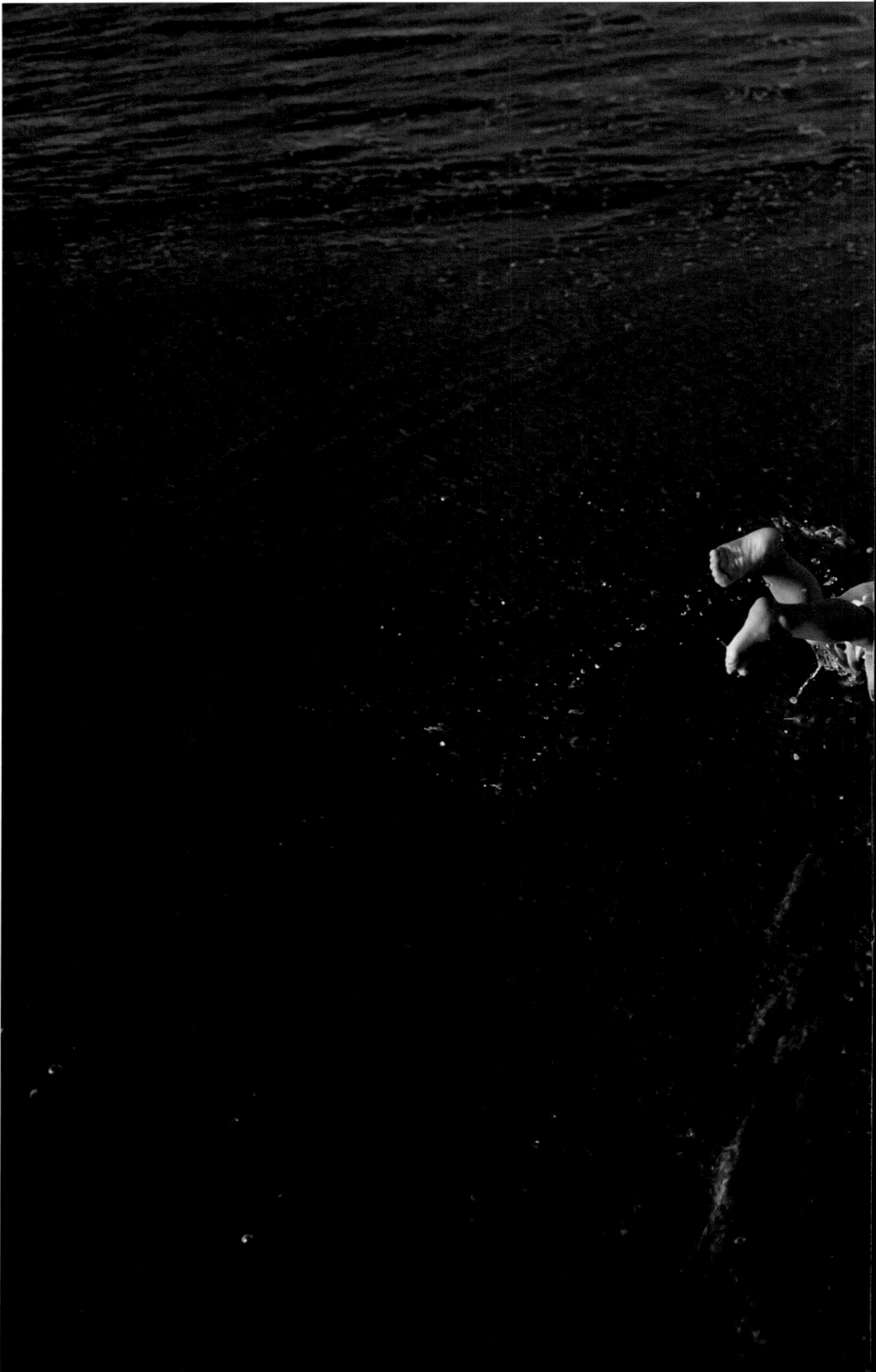

If I was never born, you
guys would never have
any fun at all.
—Brynn, age six

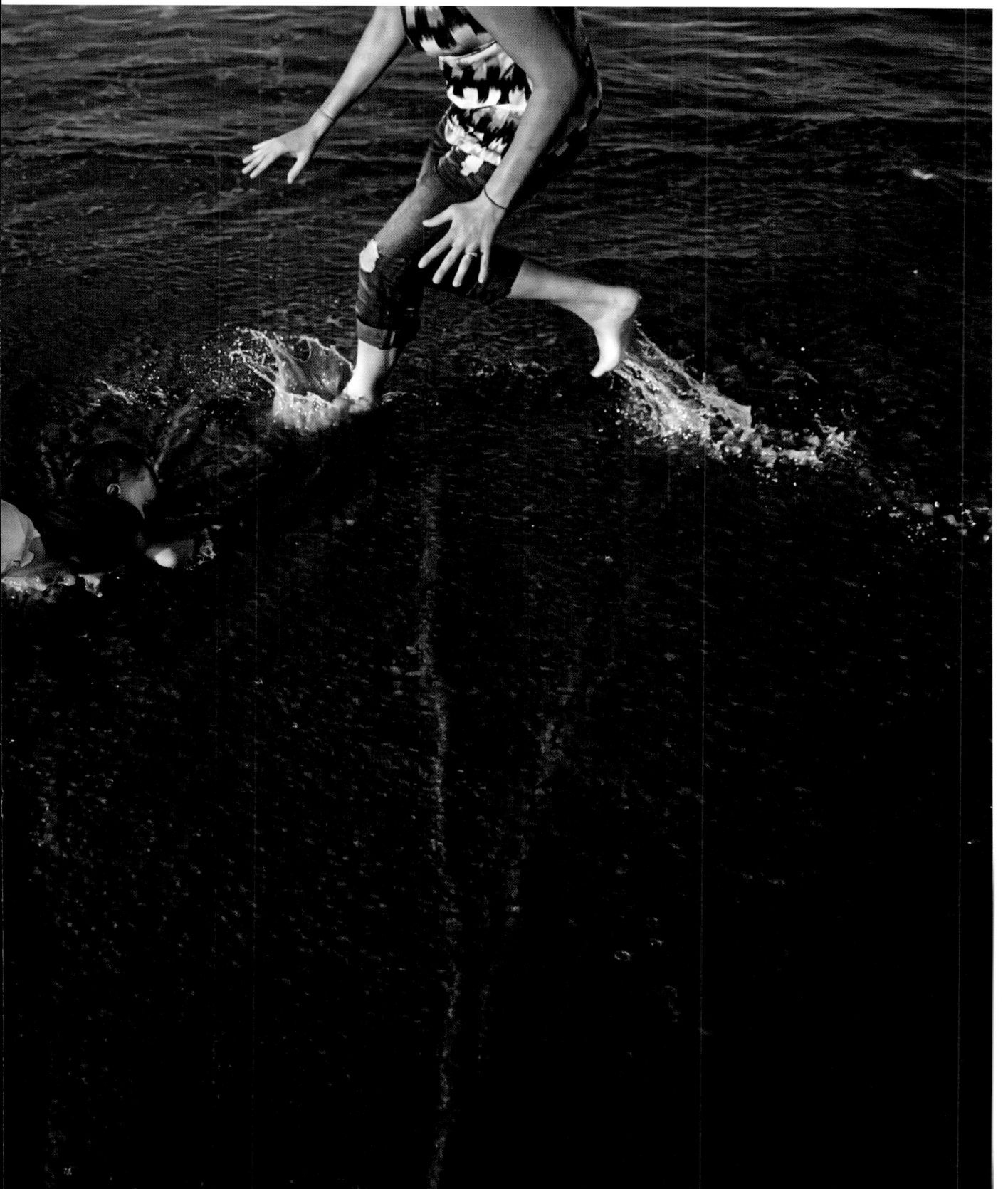

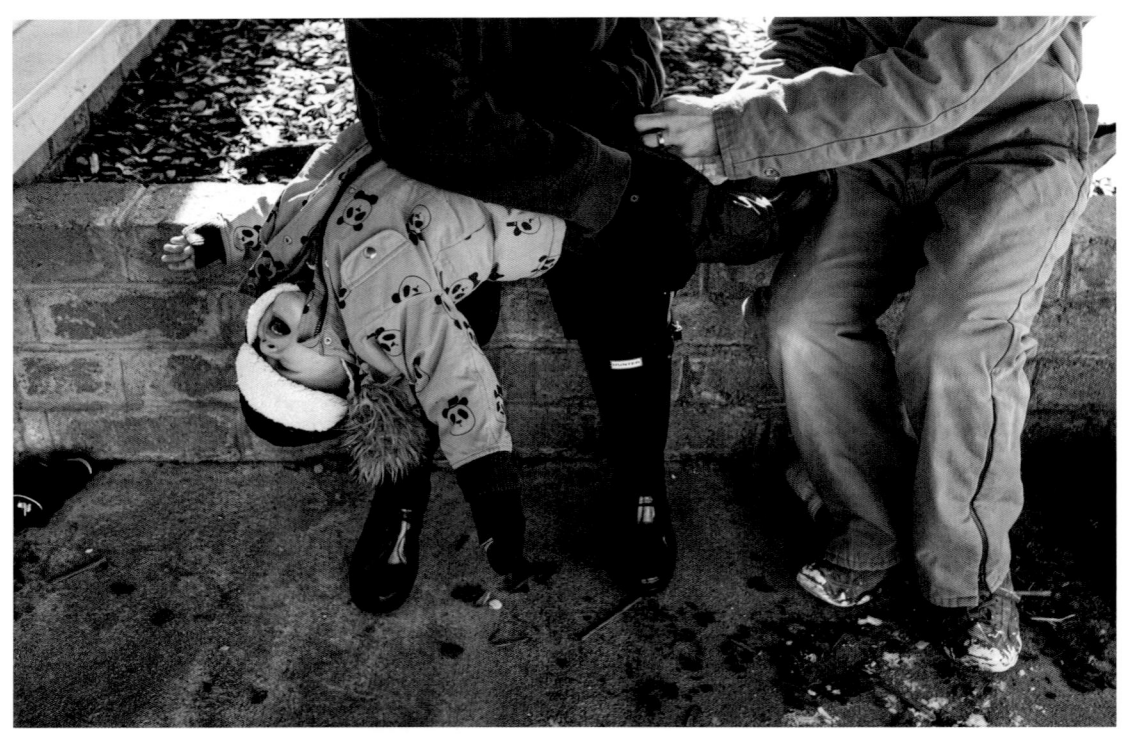

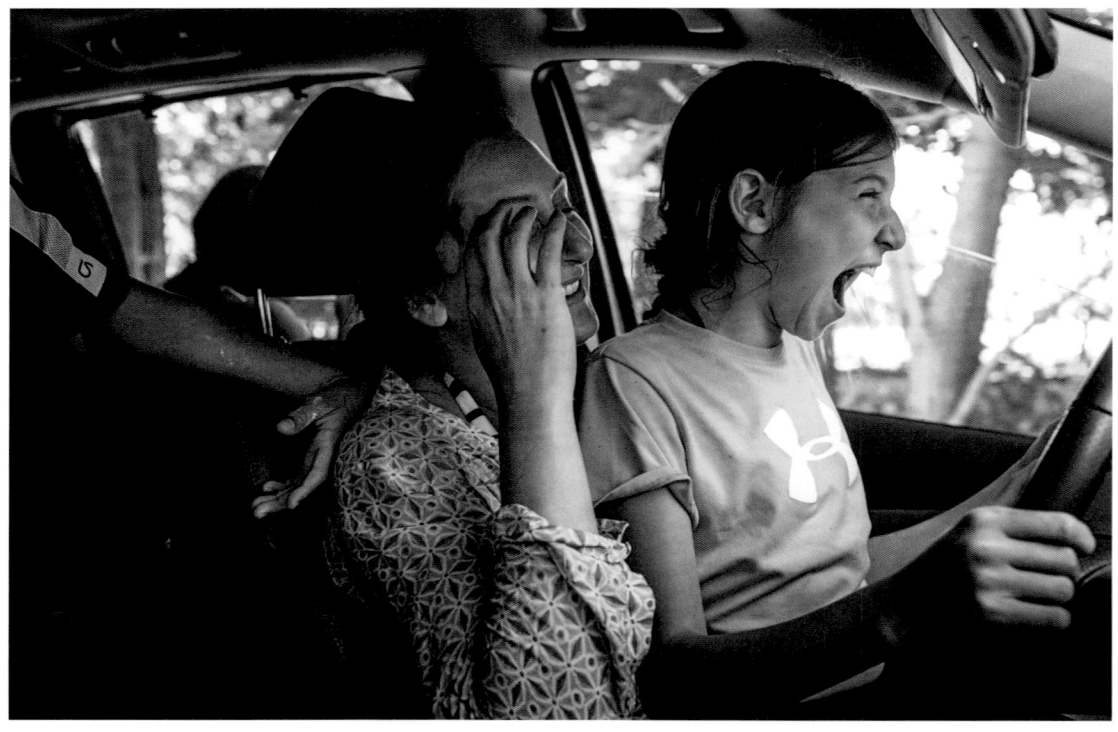

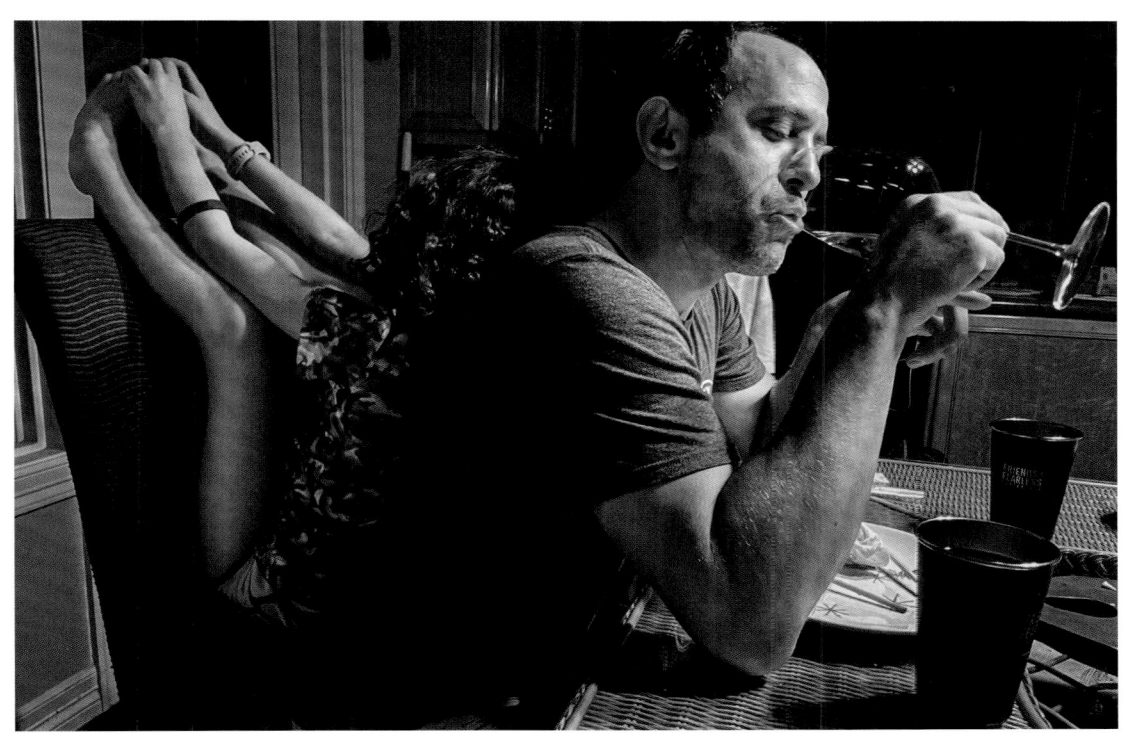

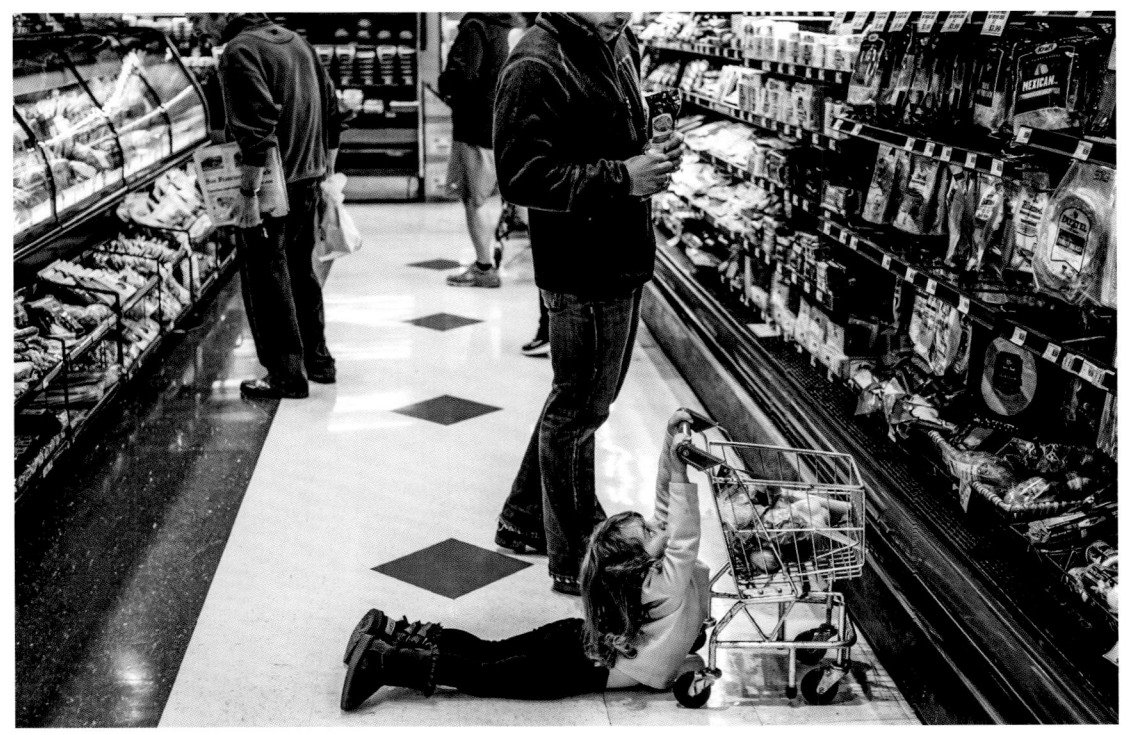

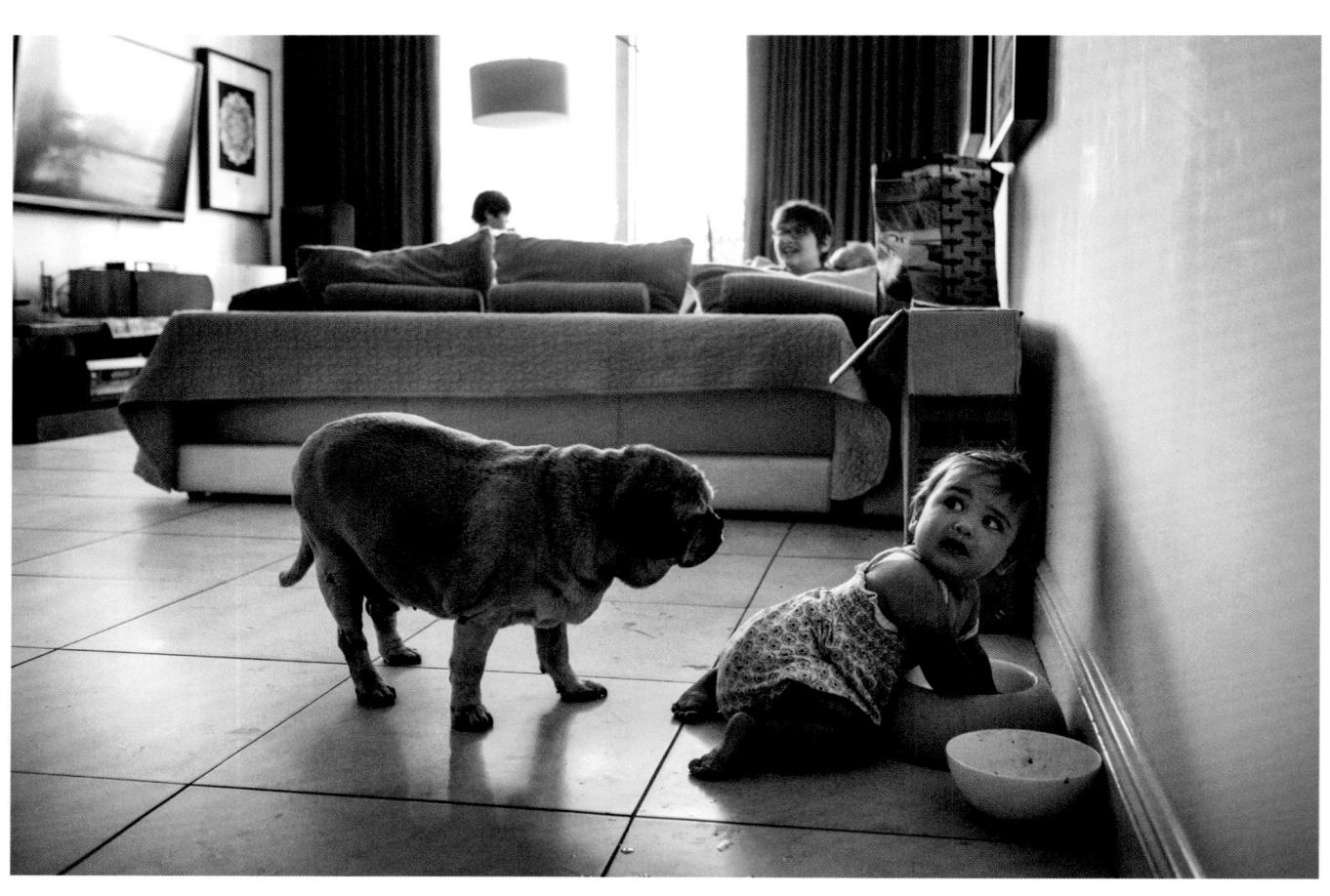

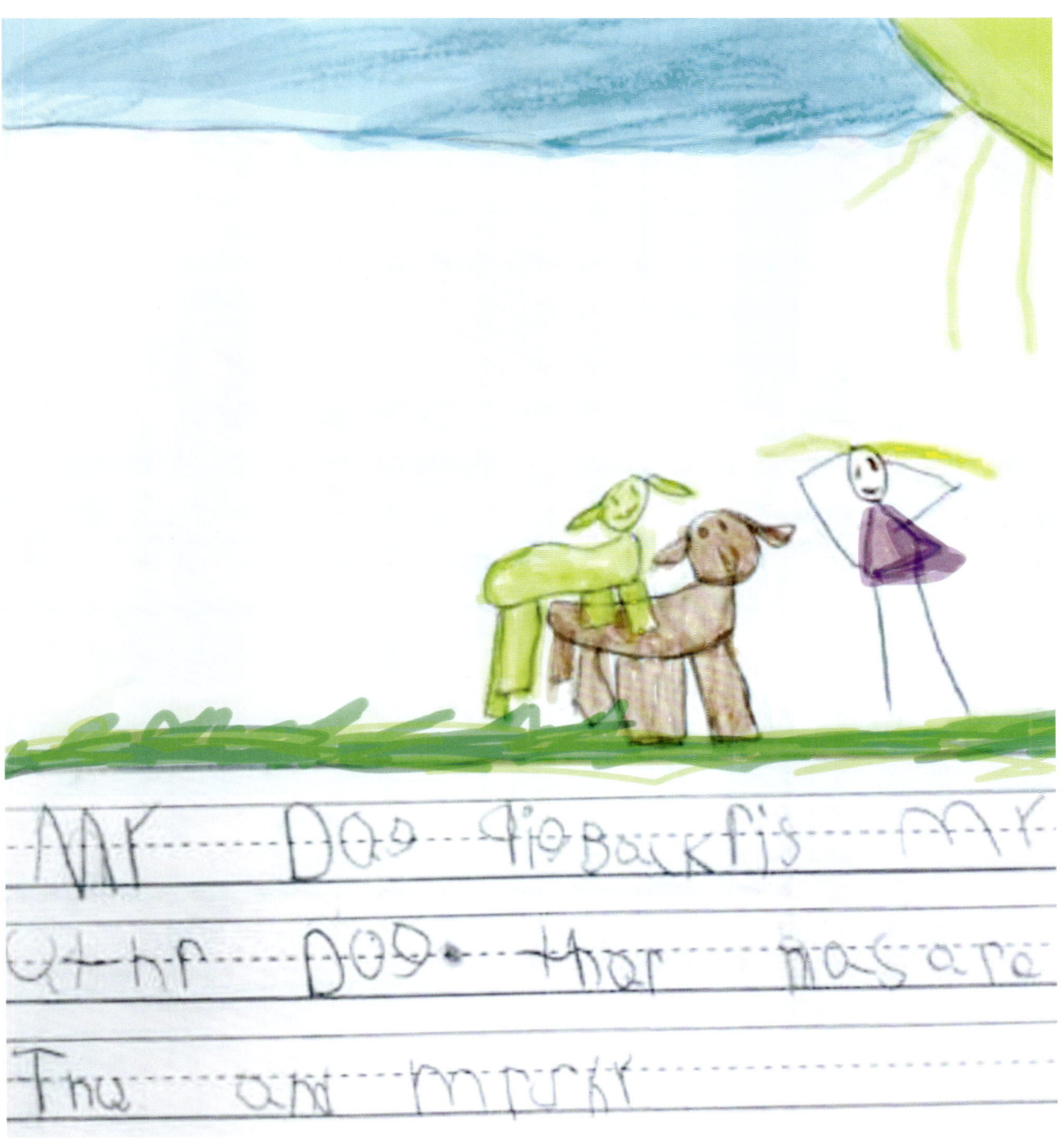

MR DOO flOBackfis MR
Qthr DOO thor nasare
Tnα aN mrrkr

My dog piggyback rides my other dog. Their names are Tuna and Marshy.

Enjoy every moment . . . time is fleeting . . . remember you were a kid once. Do what you think is right and know that even when you think they are too young to notice or not paying attention, that what you do and how you act matters.

But most of all, hang on, have fun, enjoy the ride!

—Henry L. Berman

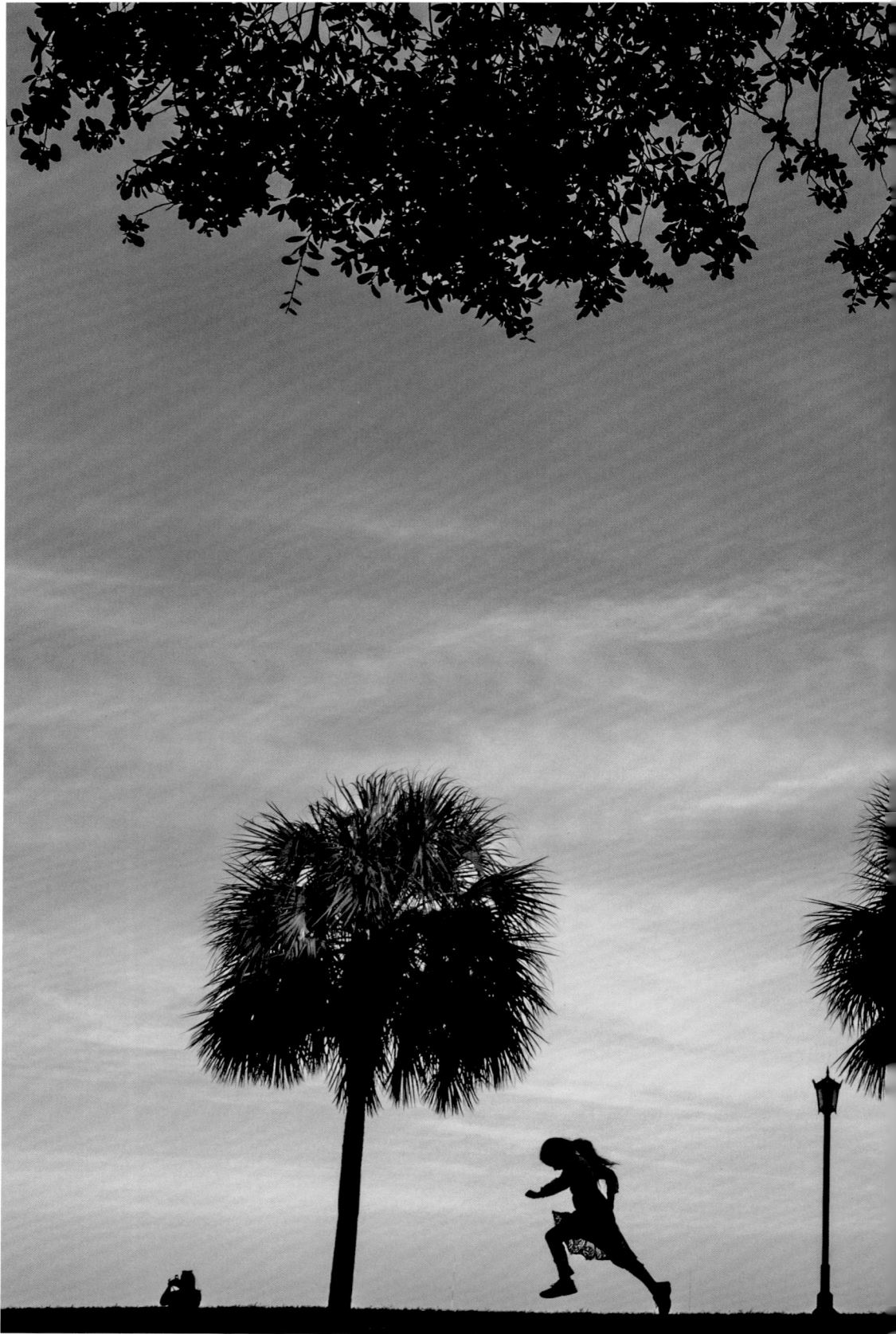

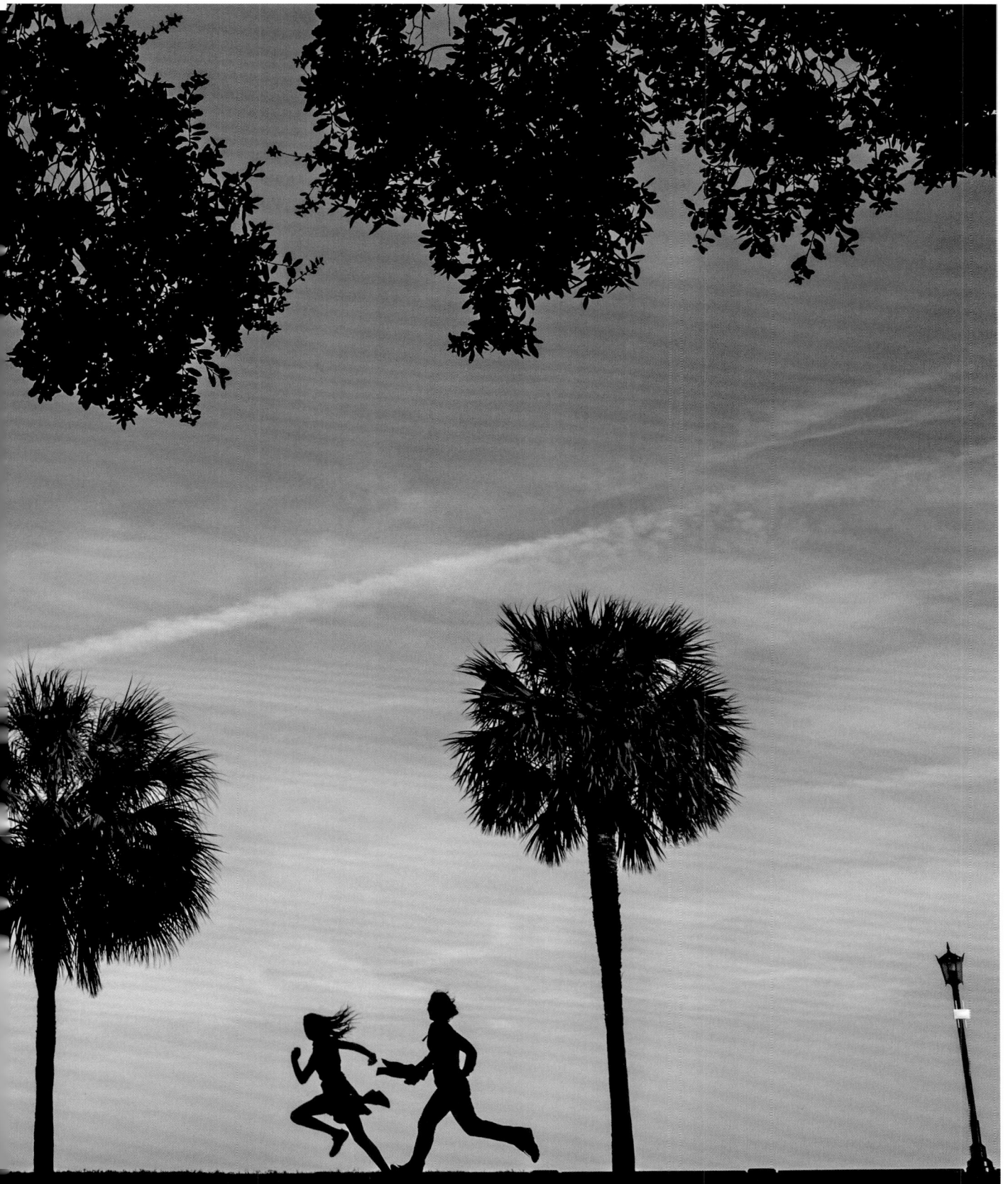

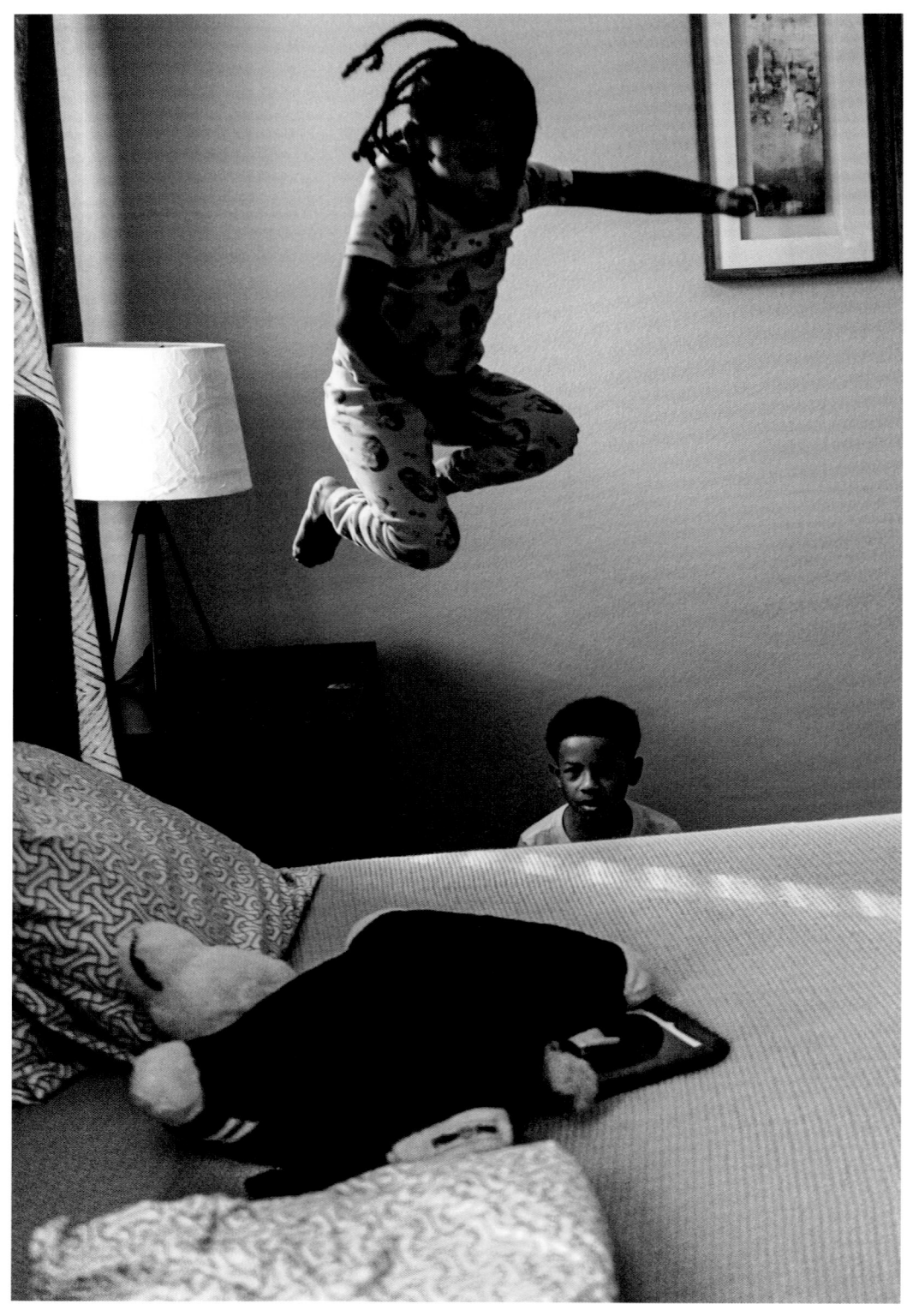

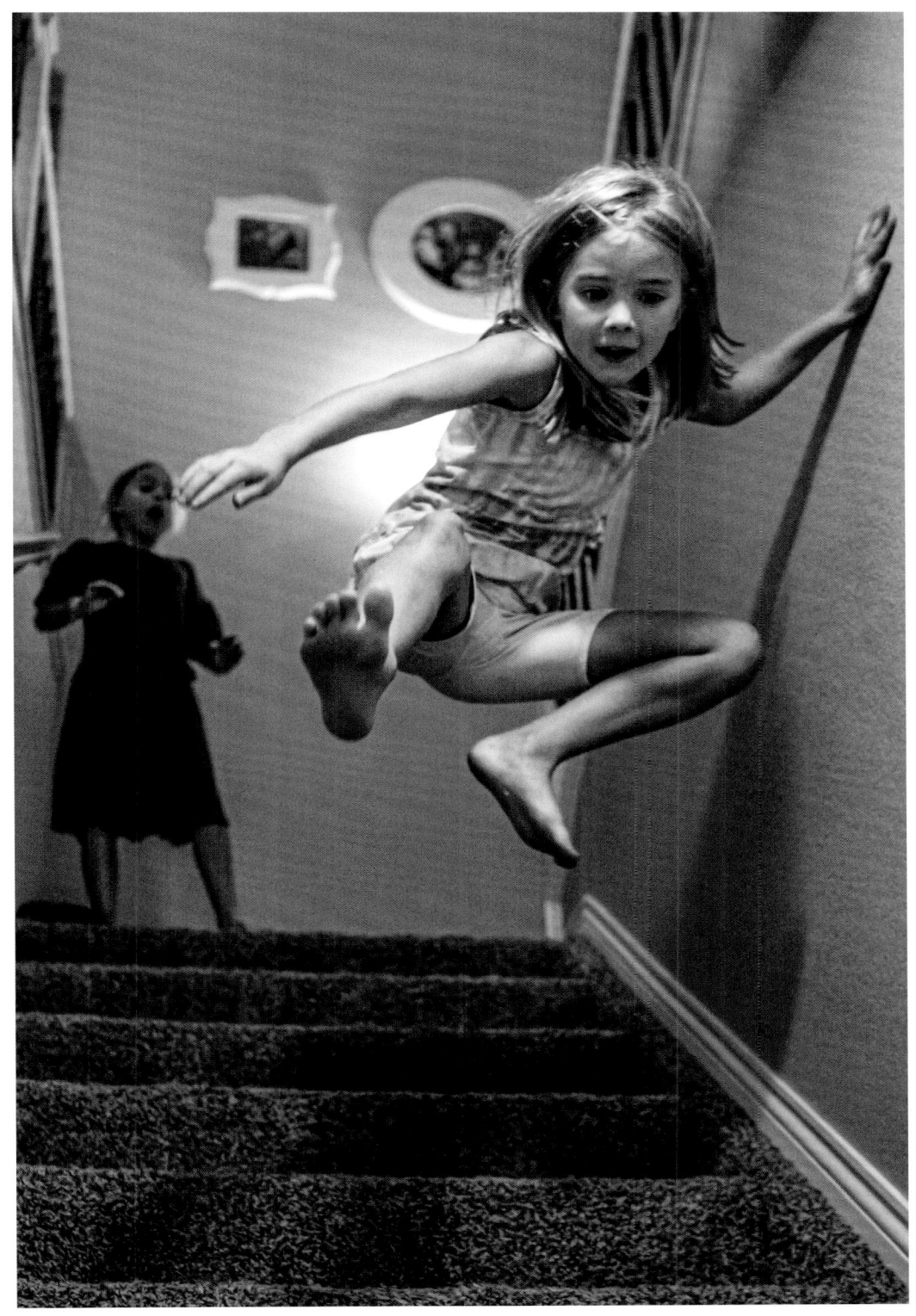

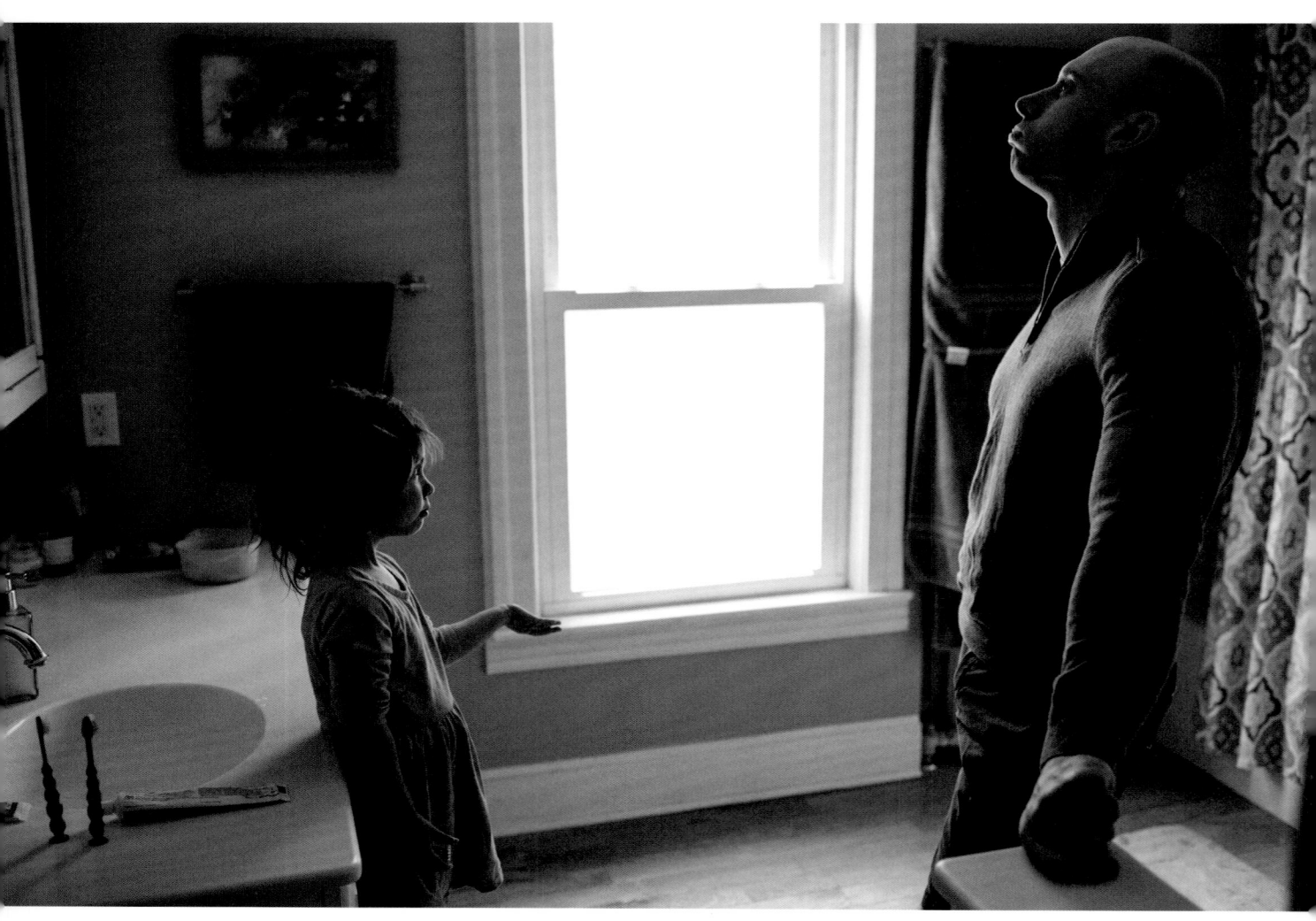

Patience takes patience.

—Byrdie Mae, age four

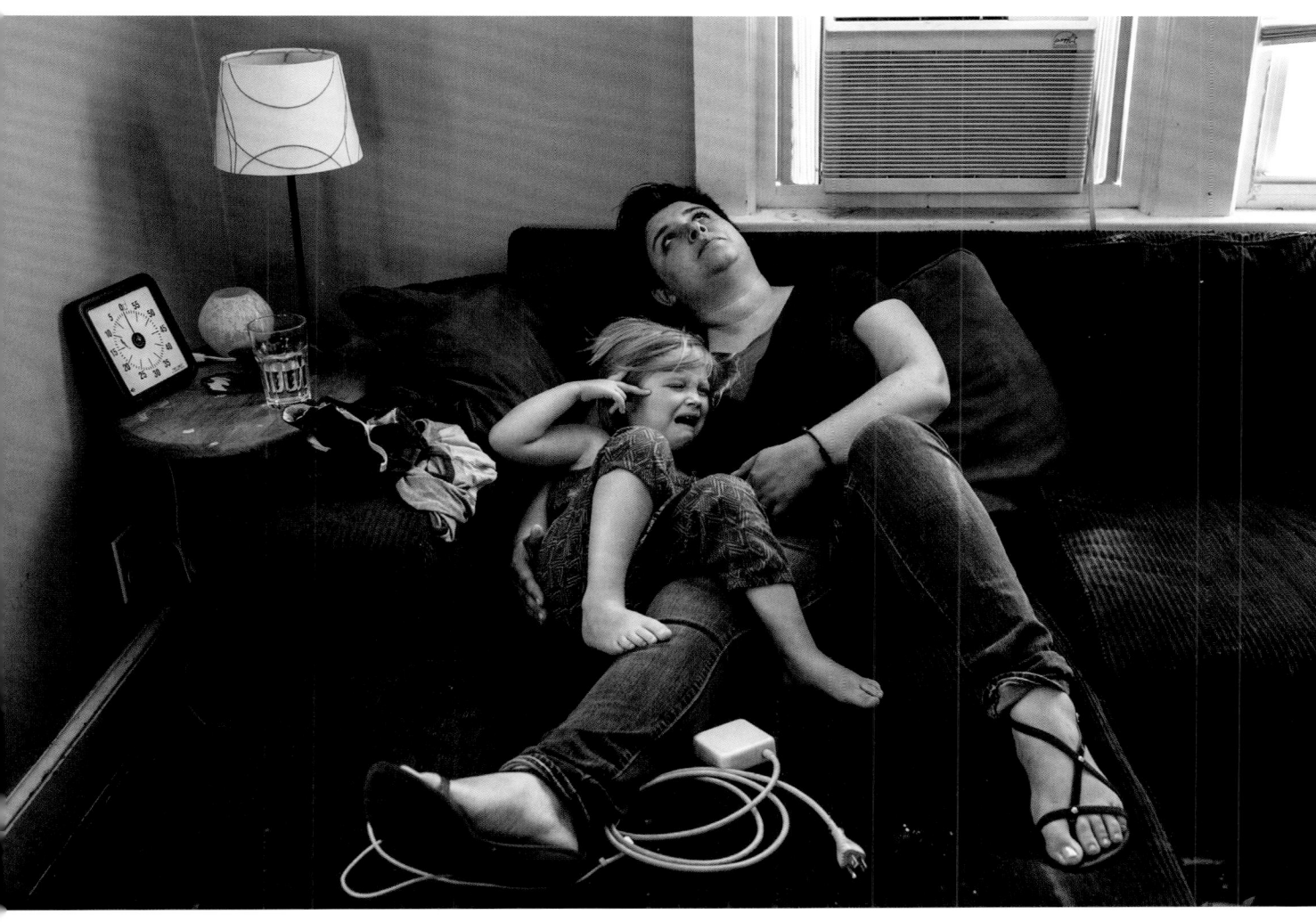

The key to parenting is consistency … and wine.
—Andrew Marton

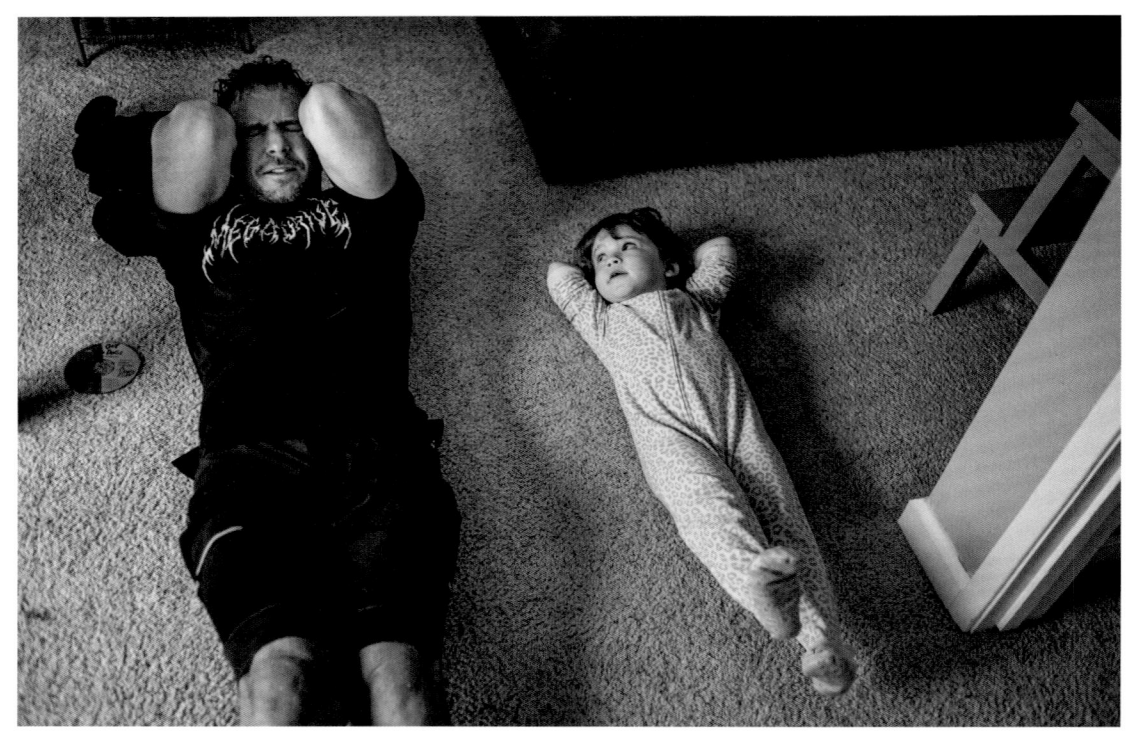

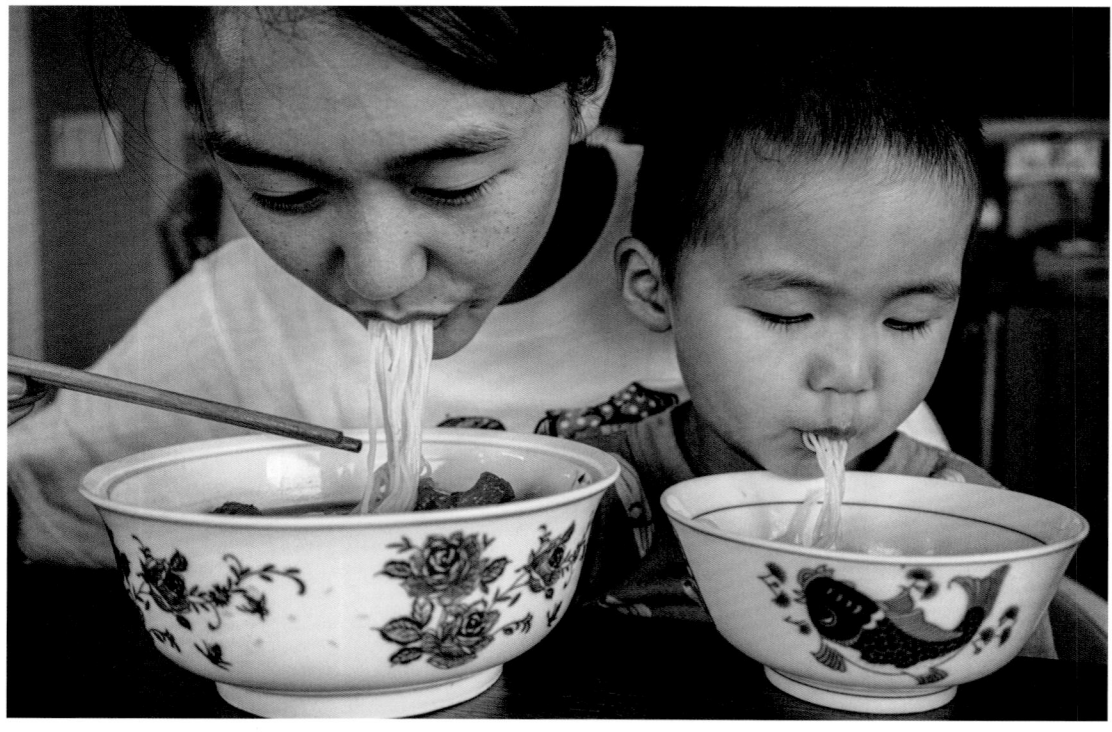

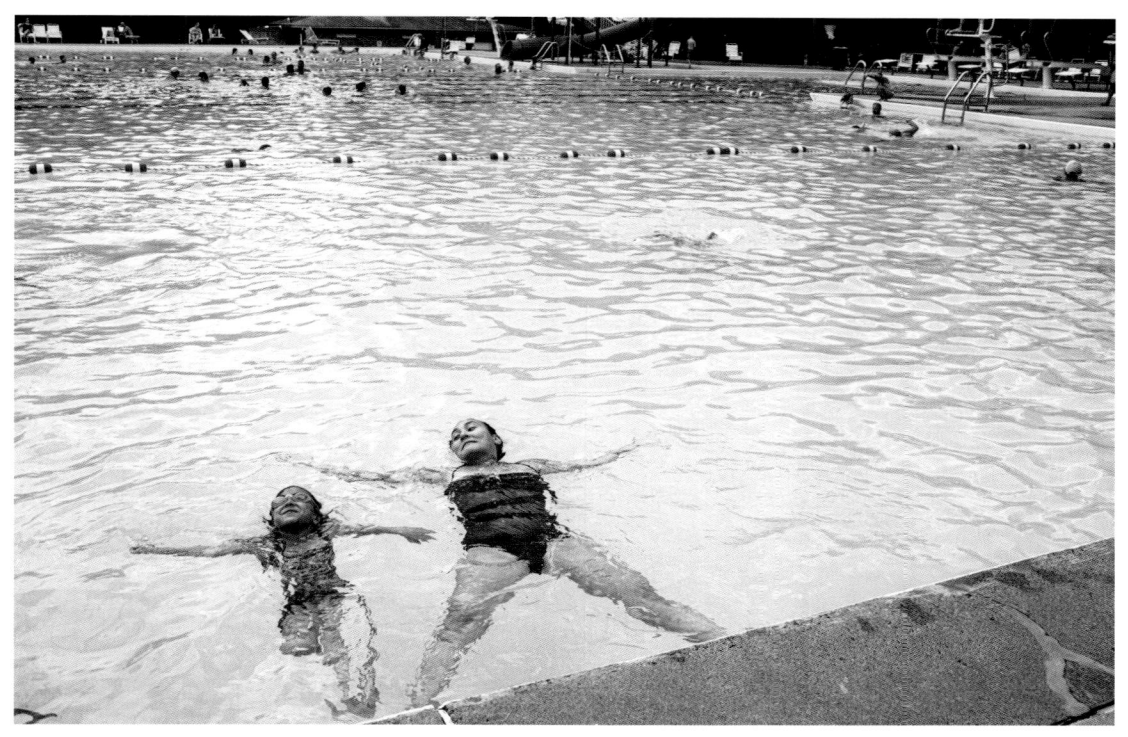

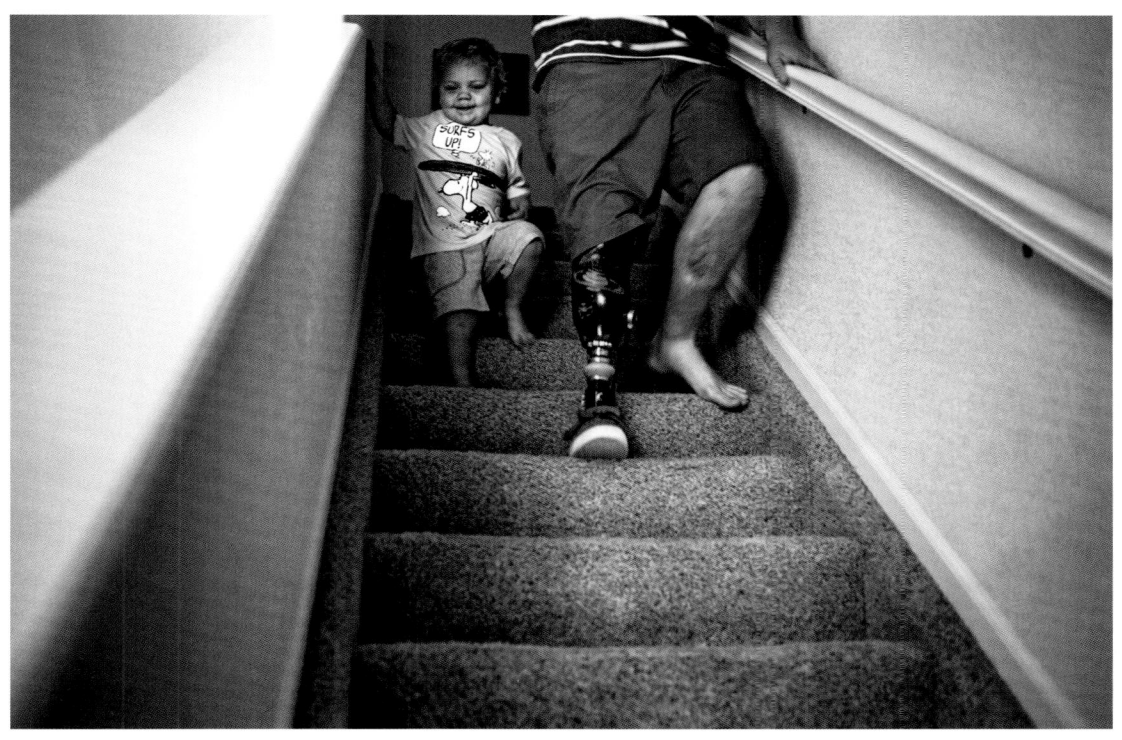

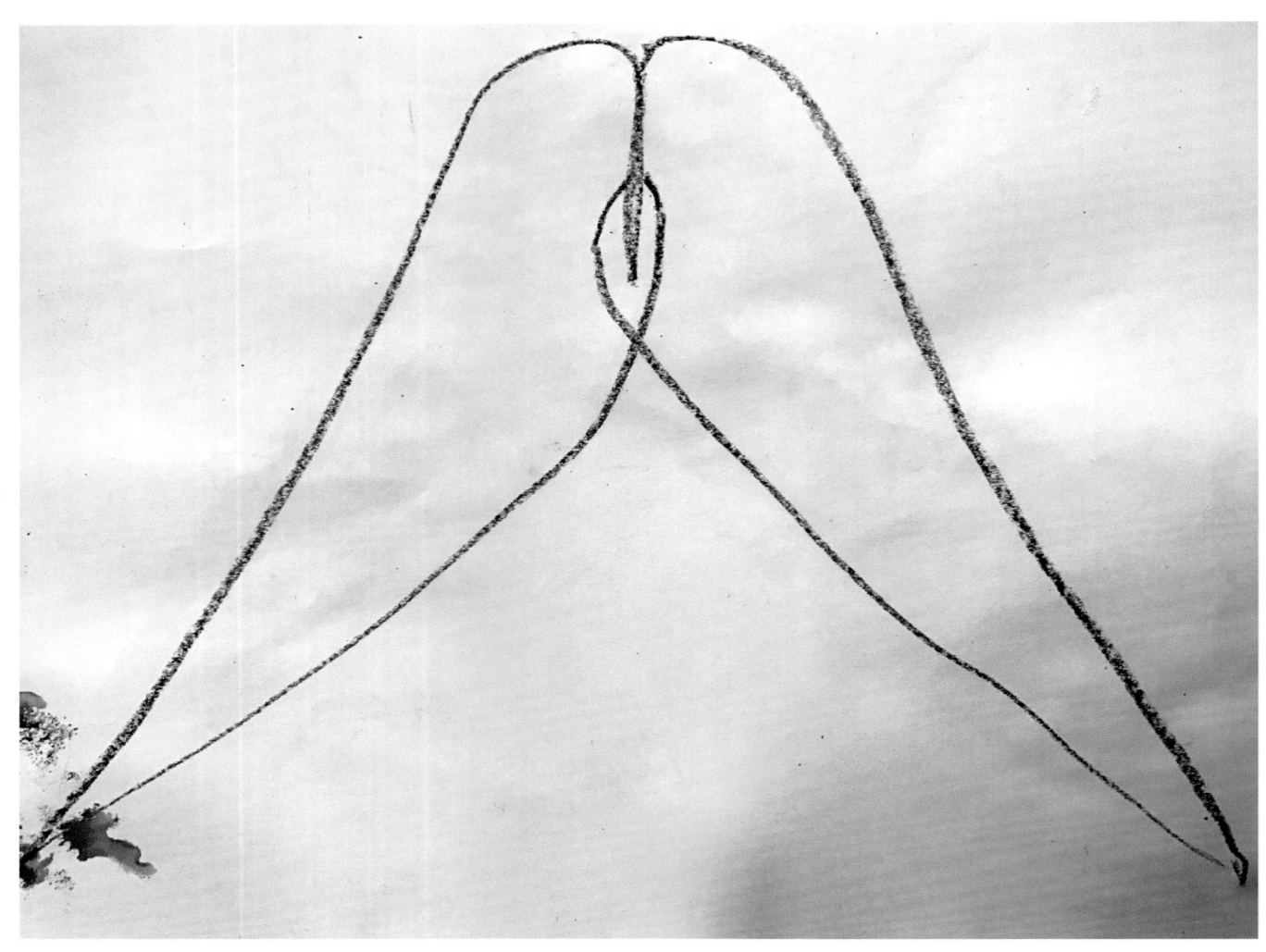

Flowers —Lucy, age six

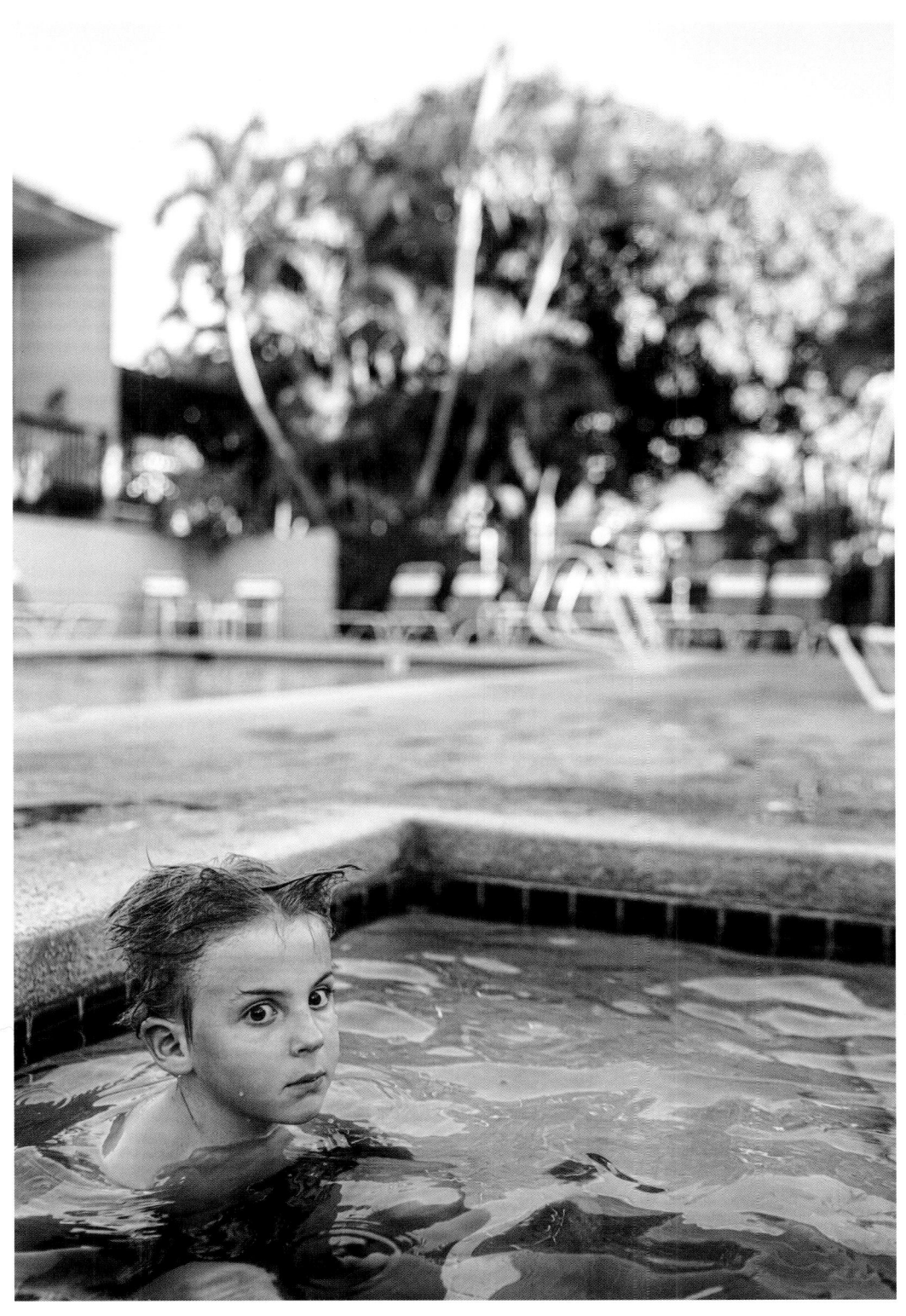

No offense, I love
Dad more.
—Byrdie Mae, age six

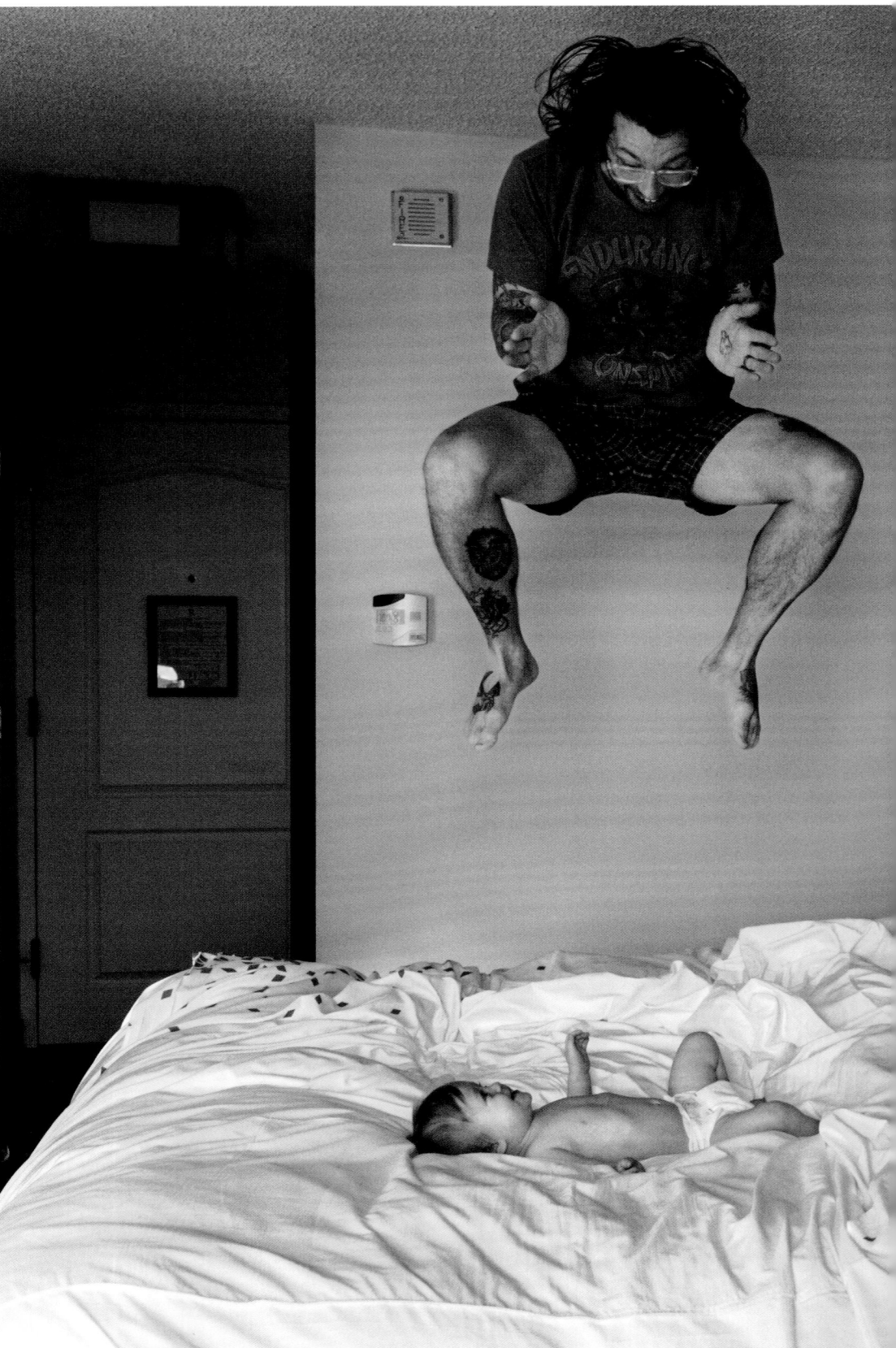

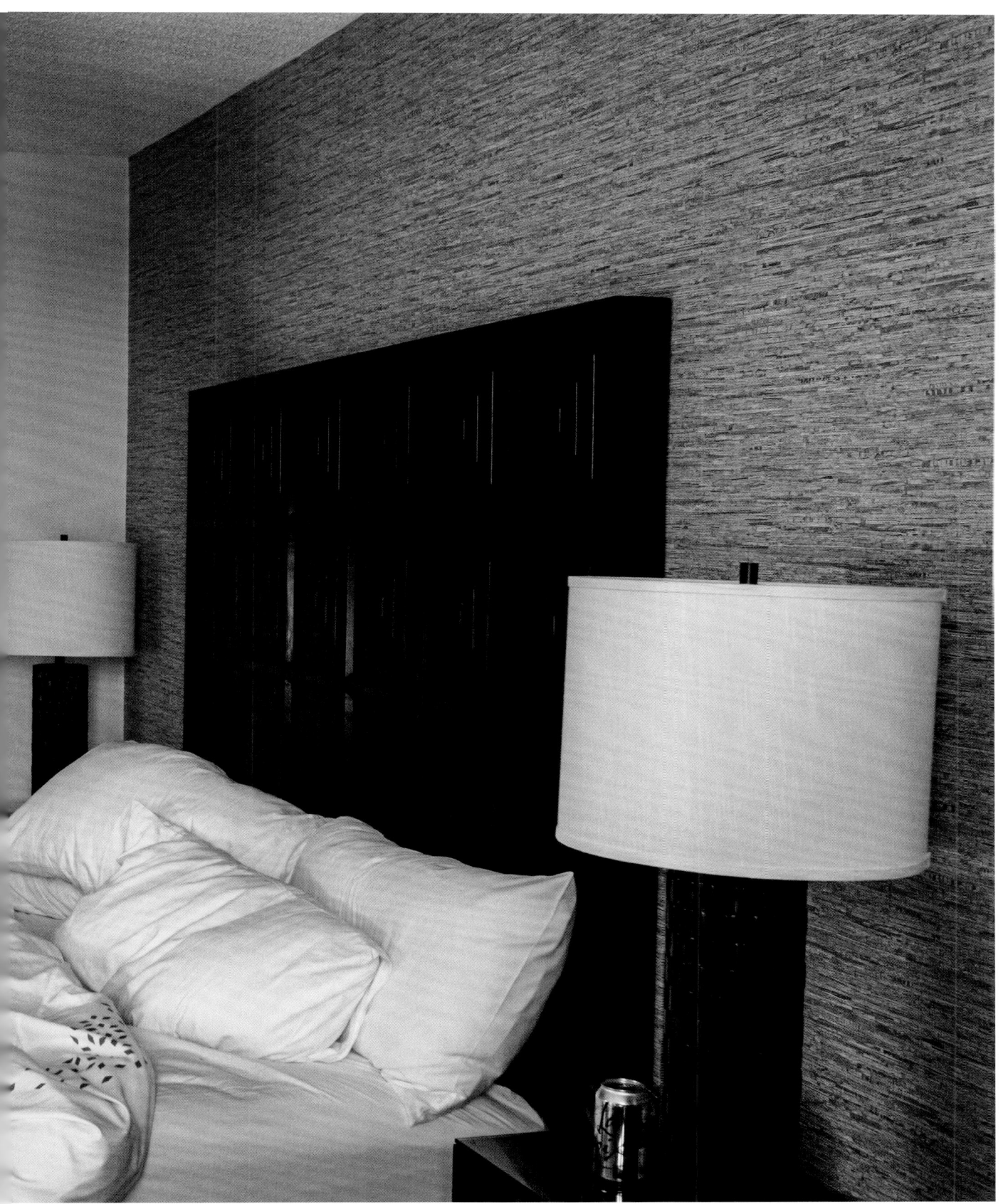

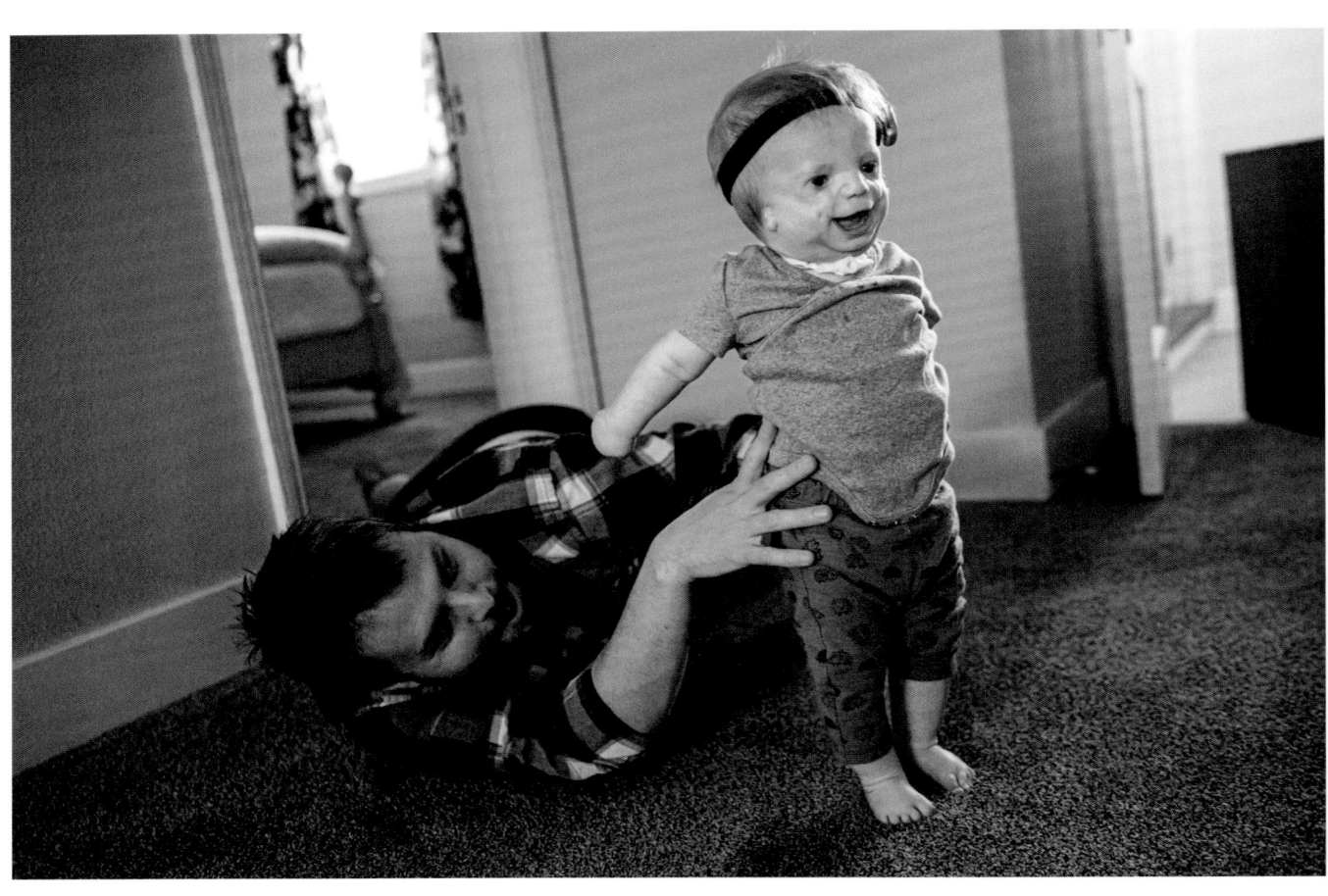

When a child learns to walk and falls down fifty times, they never think to themselves, "Maybe this isn't for me."

—Unknown

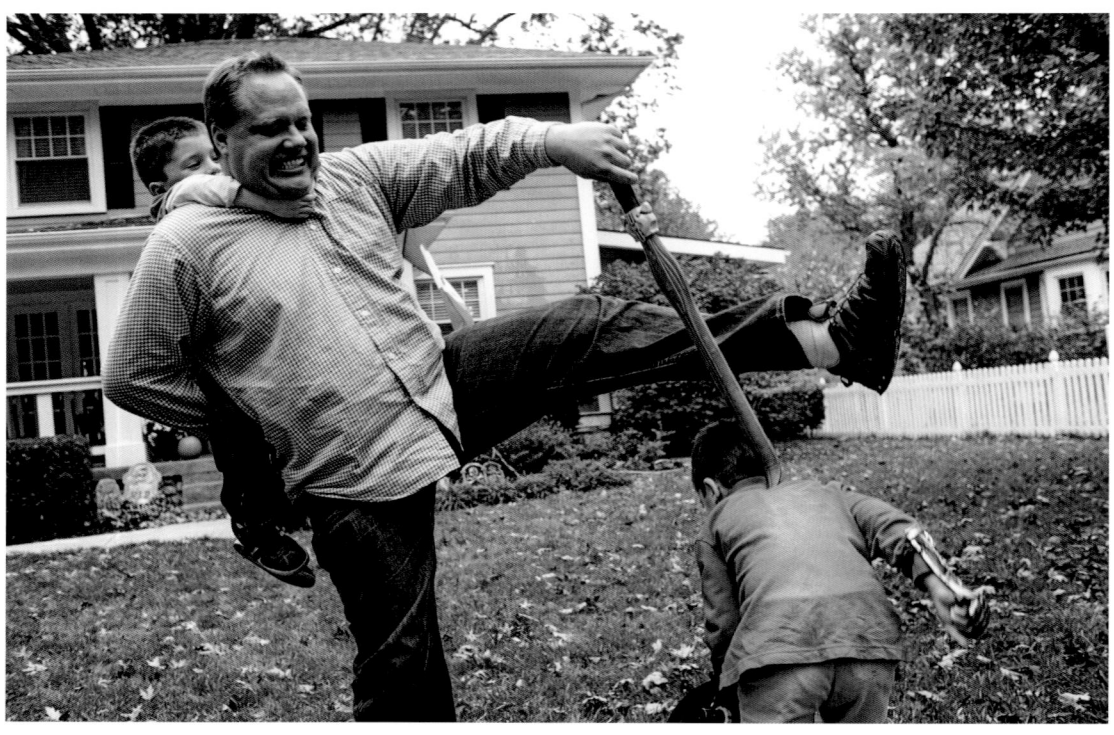

I'm always looking back on how my father raised me as a single parent and the yawning gap I always felt between us, and my desire to be as close as possible with my own children . . .

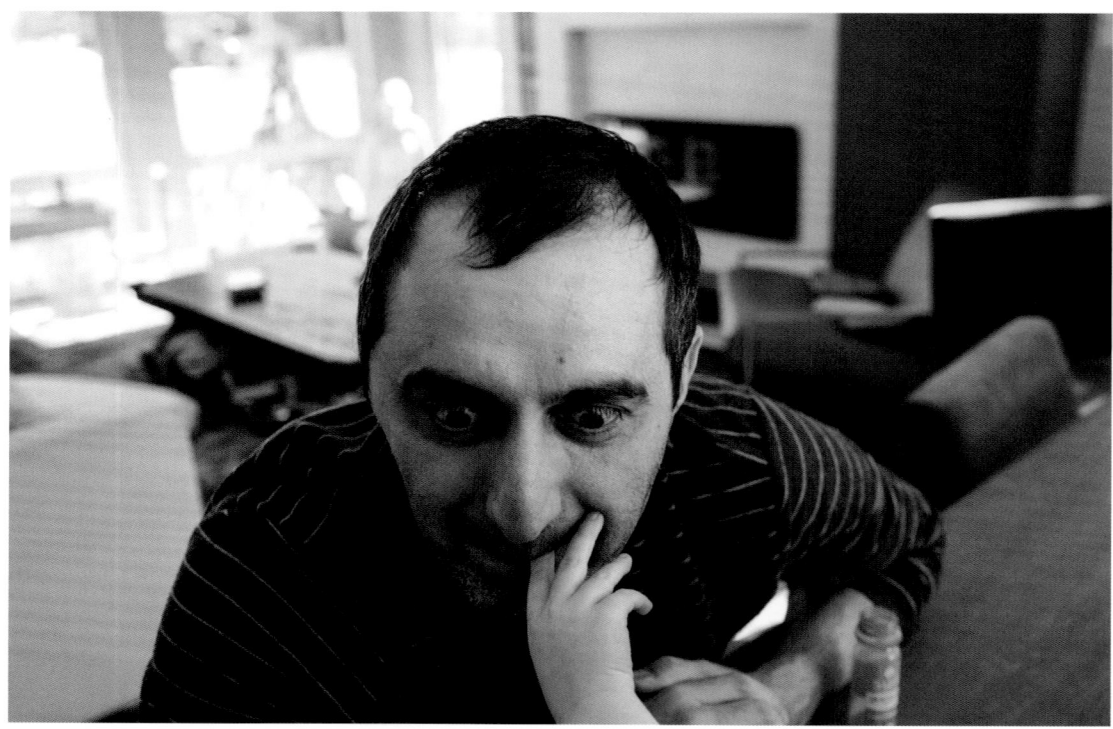

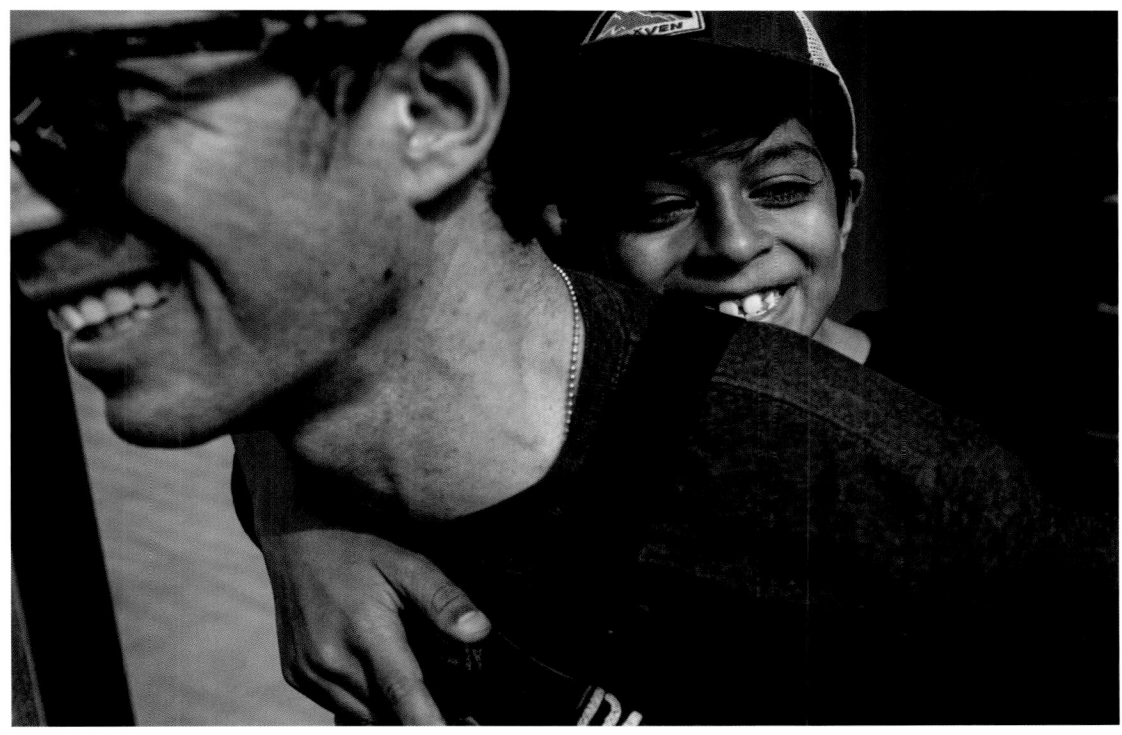

I guess the biggest thing is to lead with kindness, humor, and playfulness. That an angry word lasts far longer in ears than the mouth. That meals shared should always be a time of joy and celebration. —Jerry Henderson

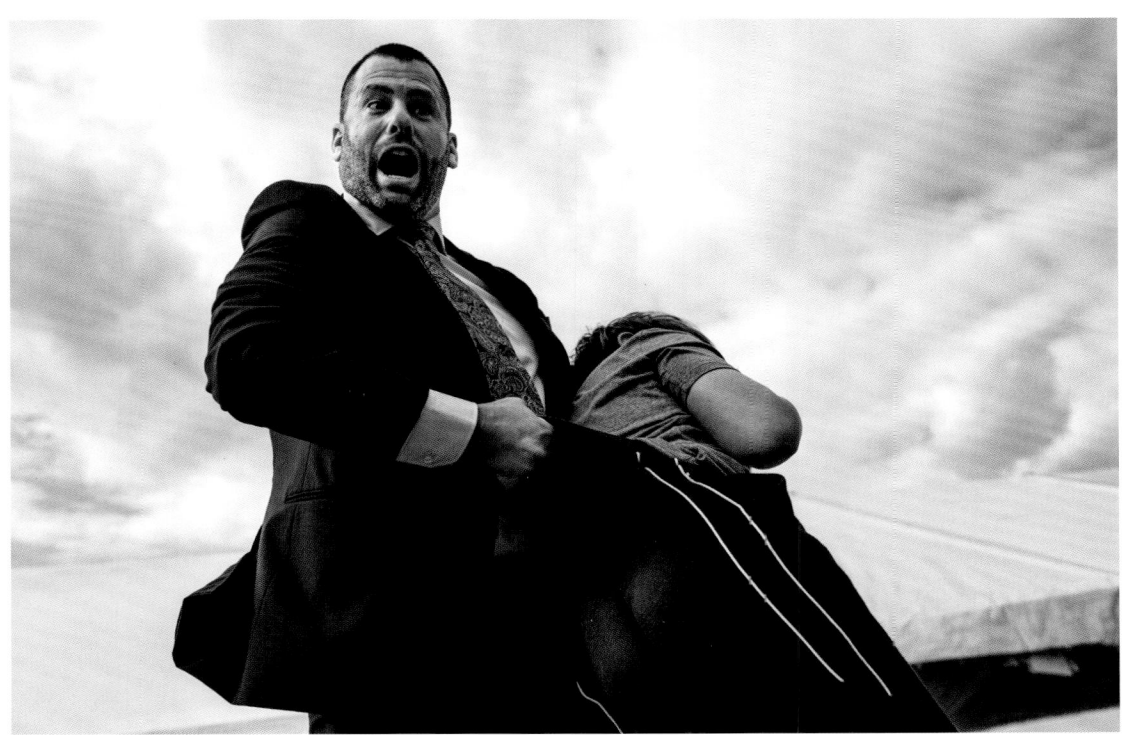

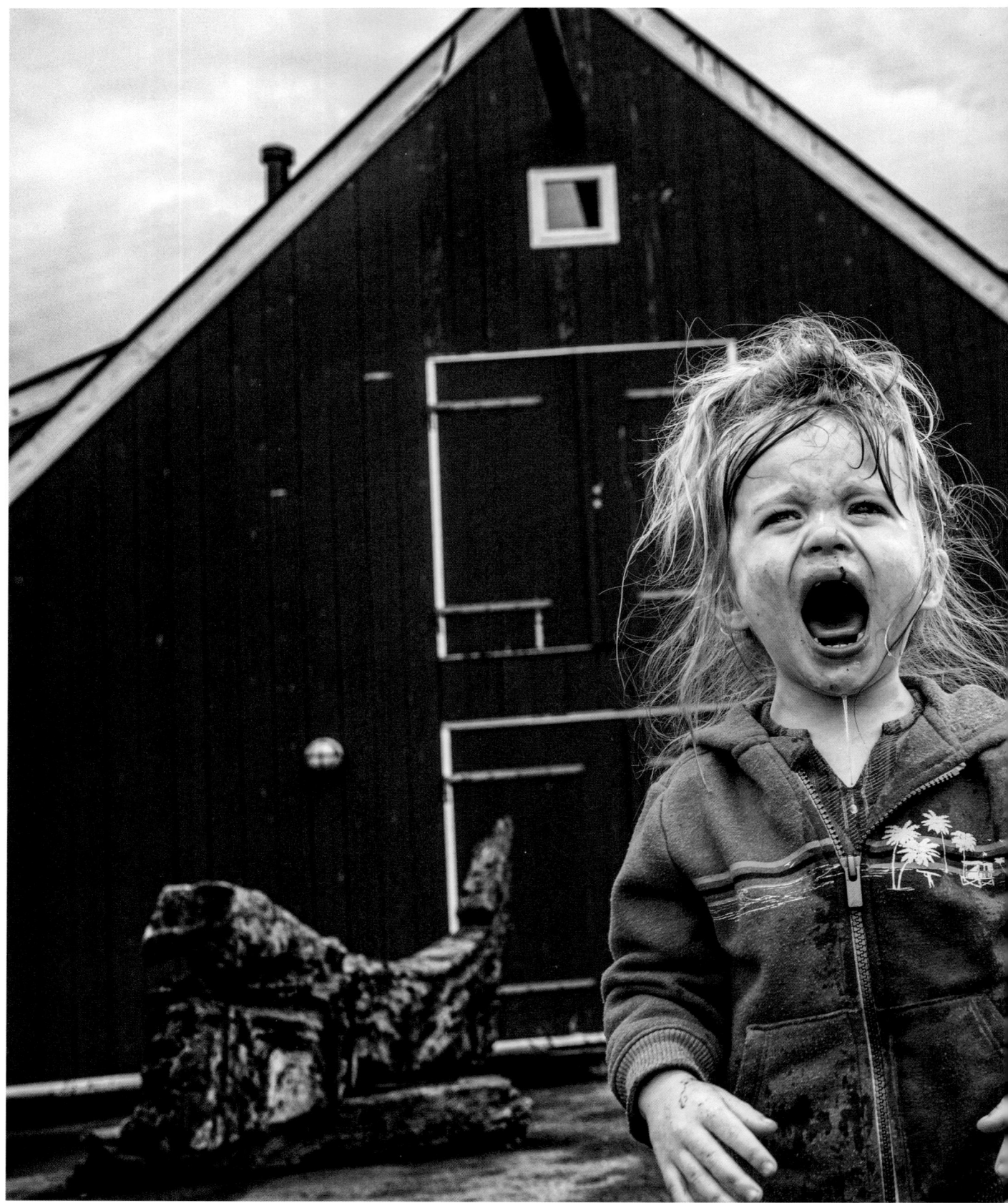

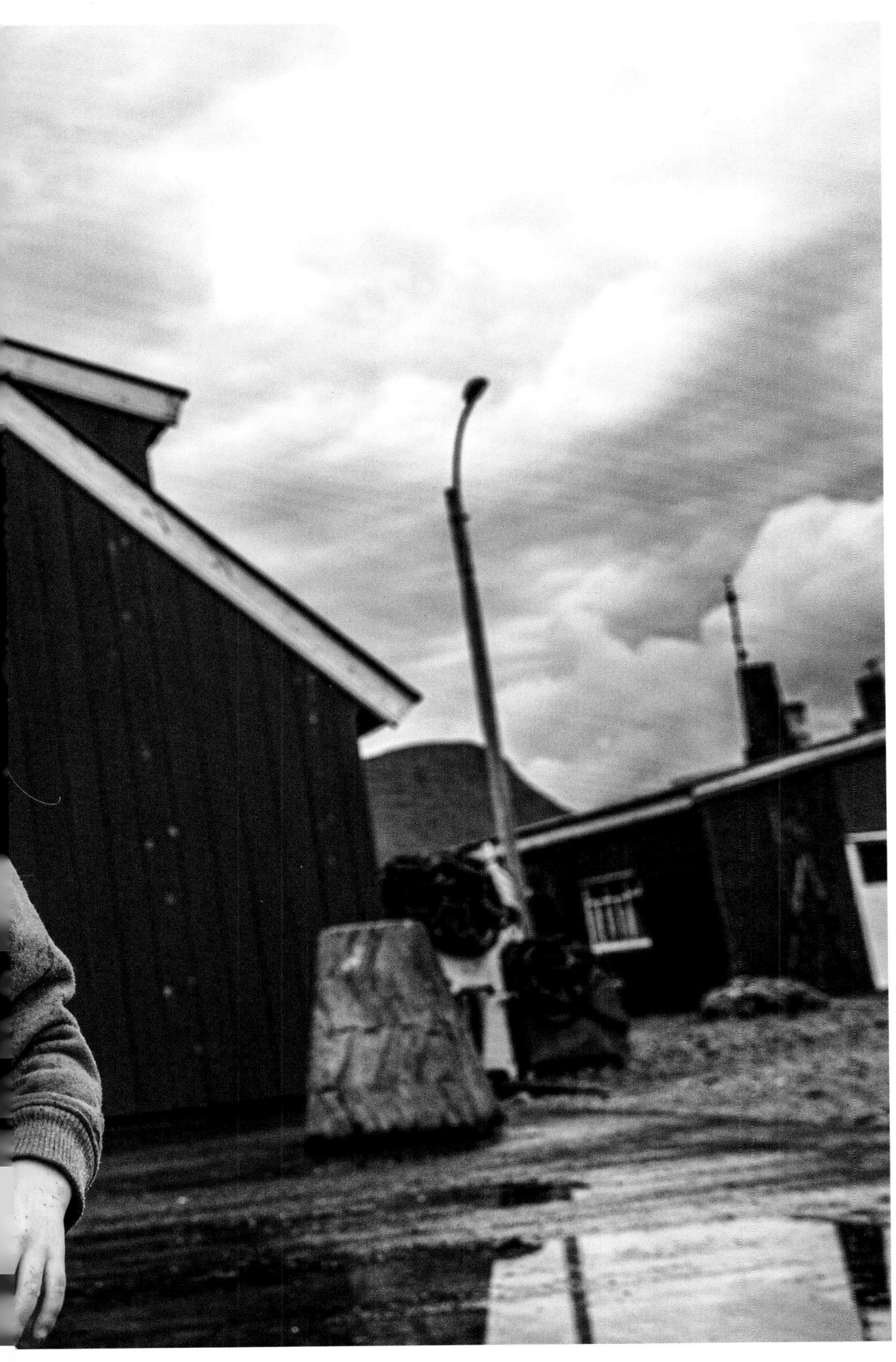

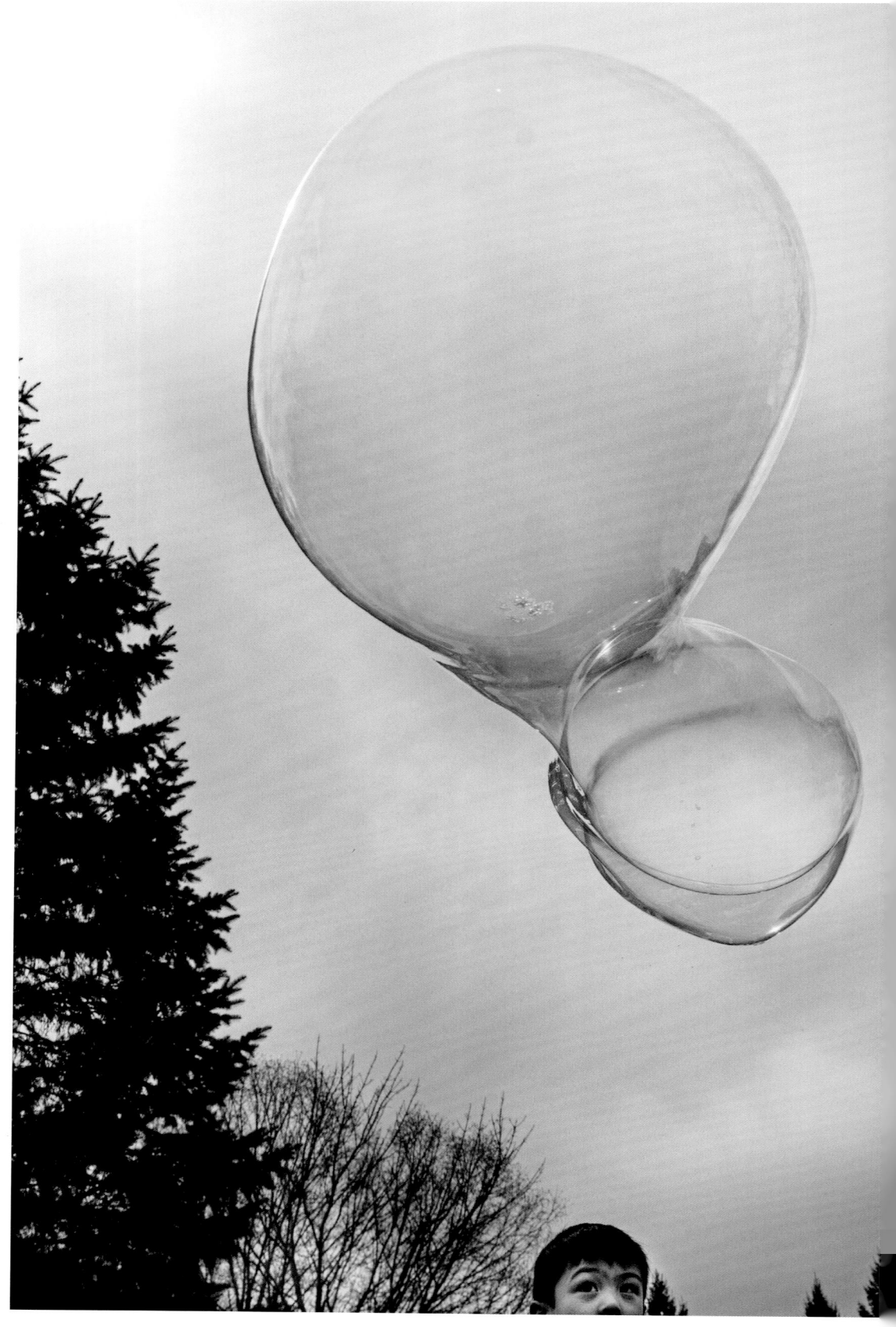

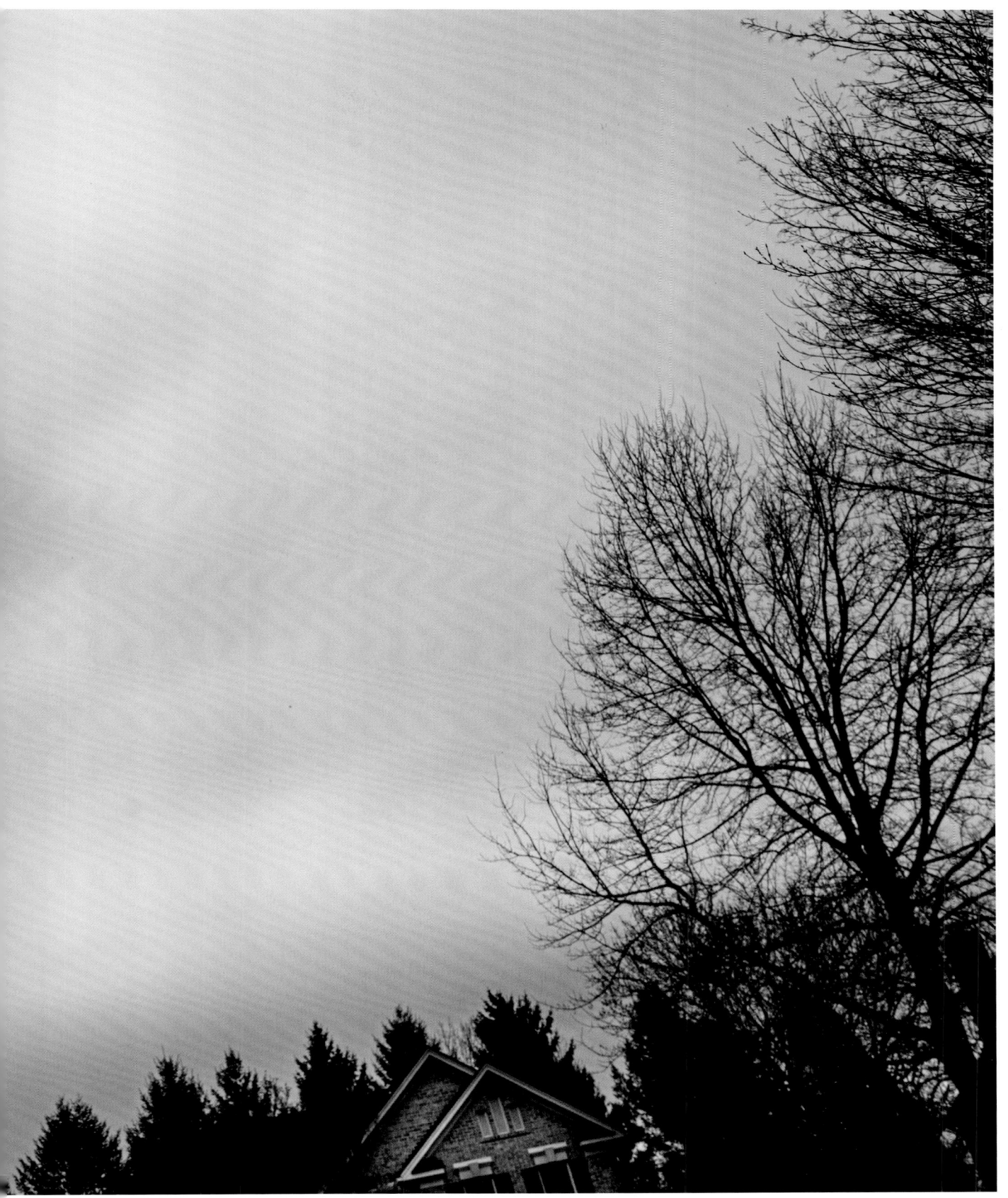

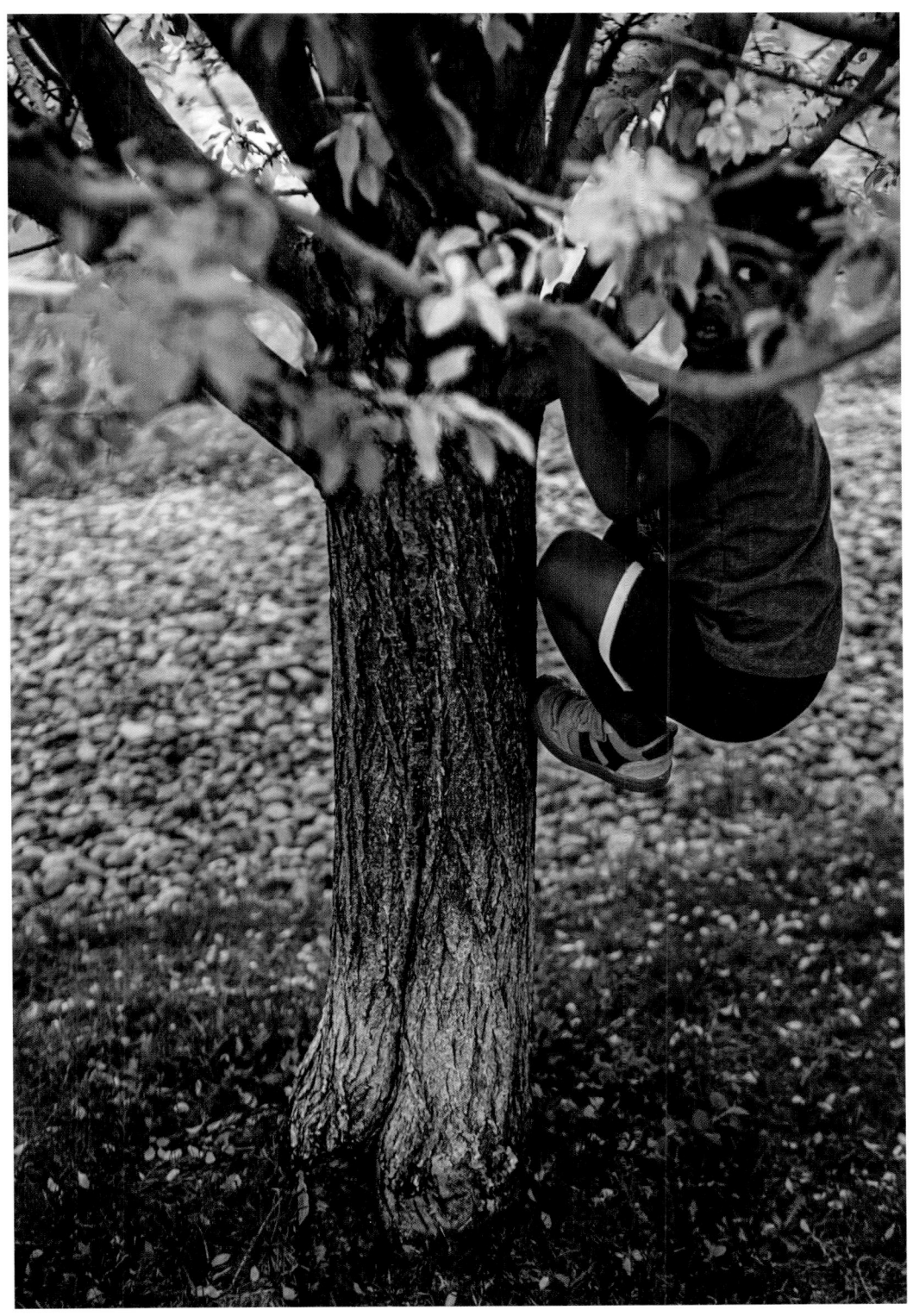

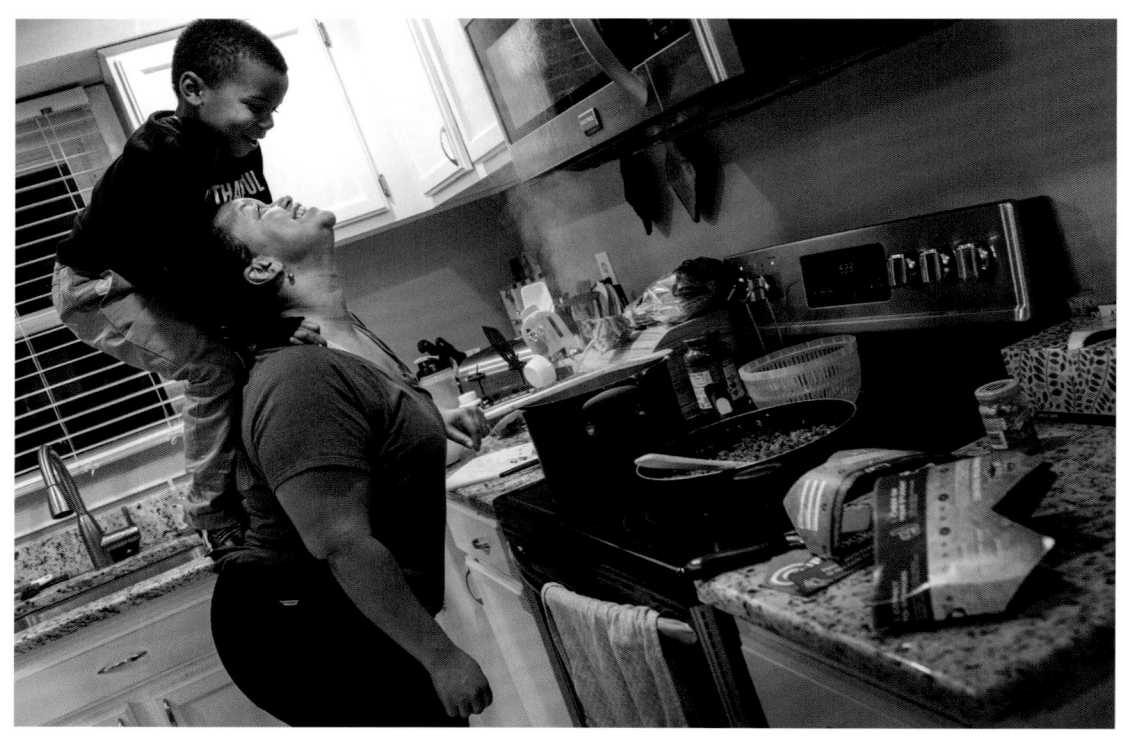

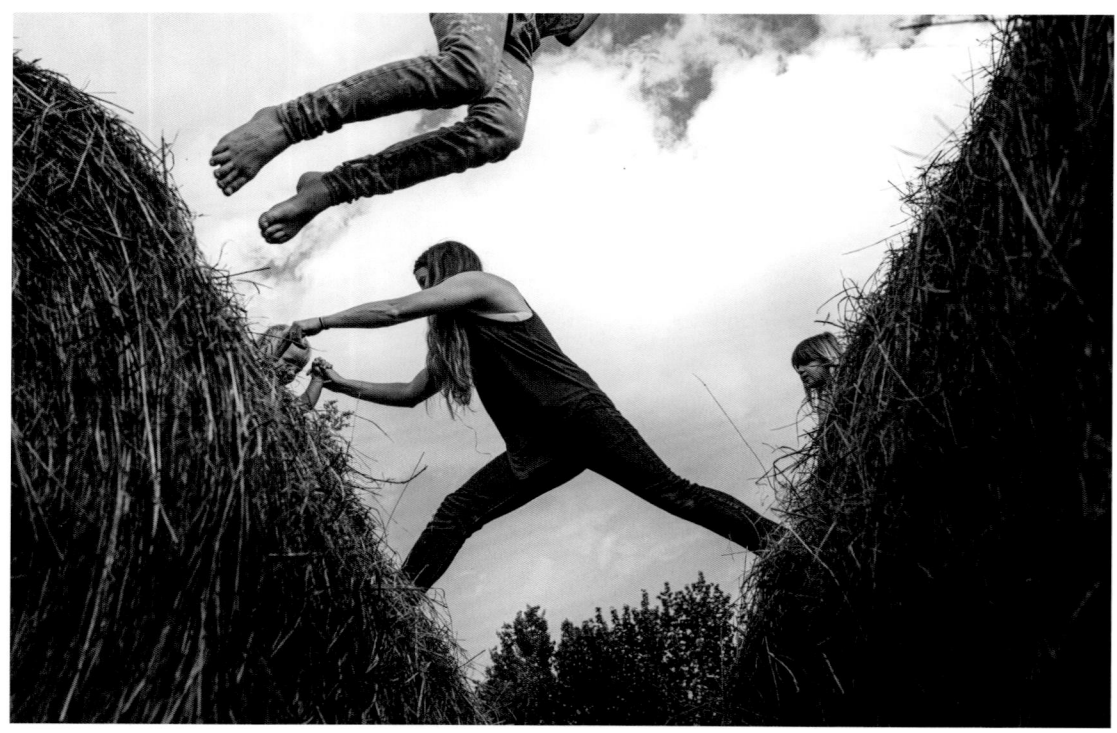

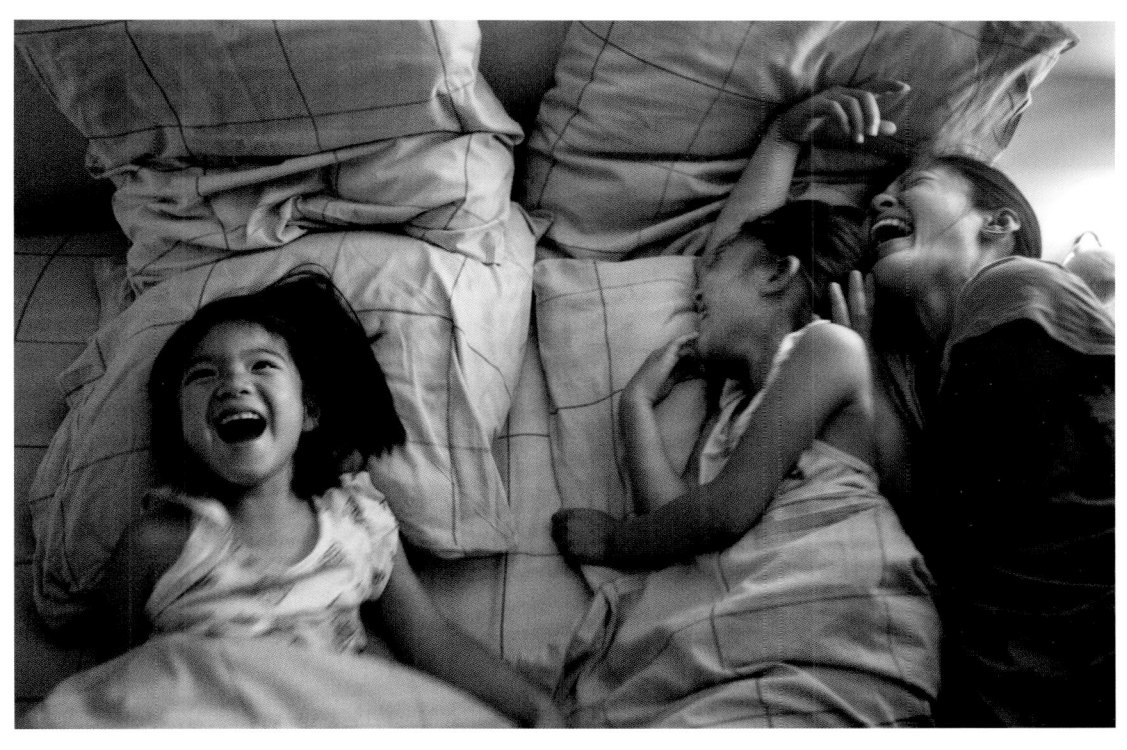

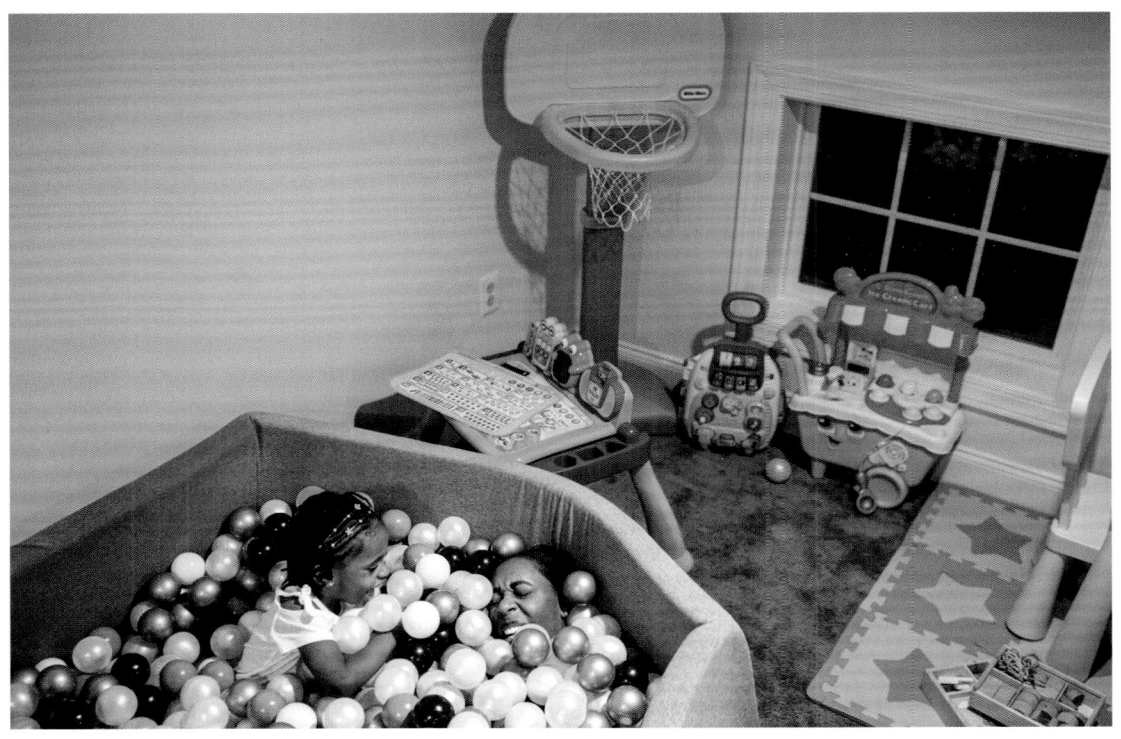

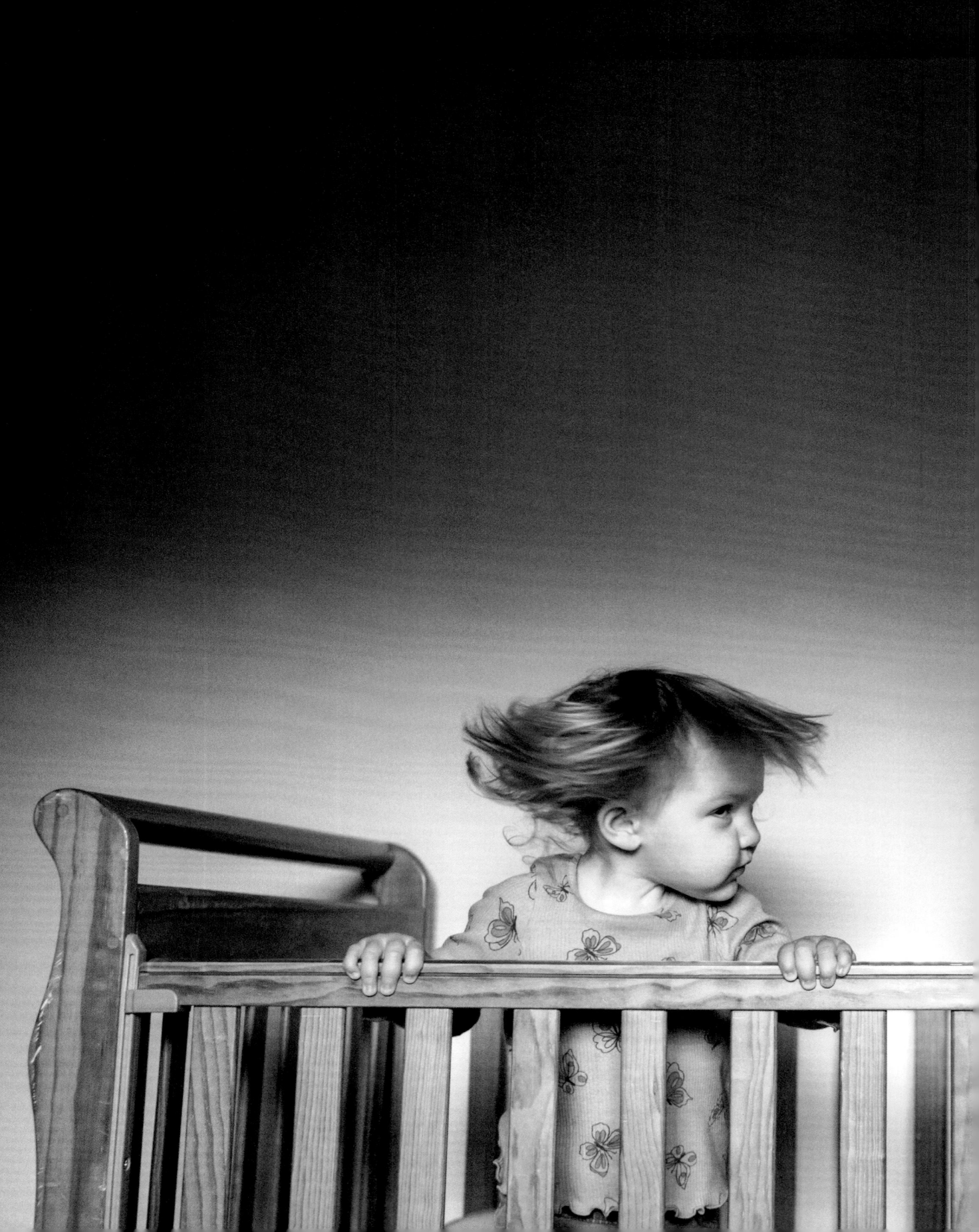

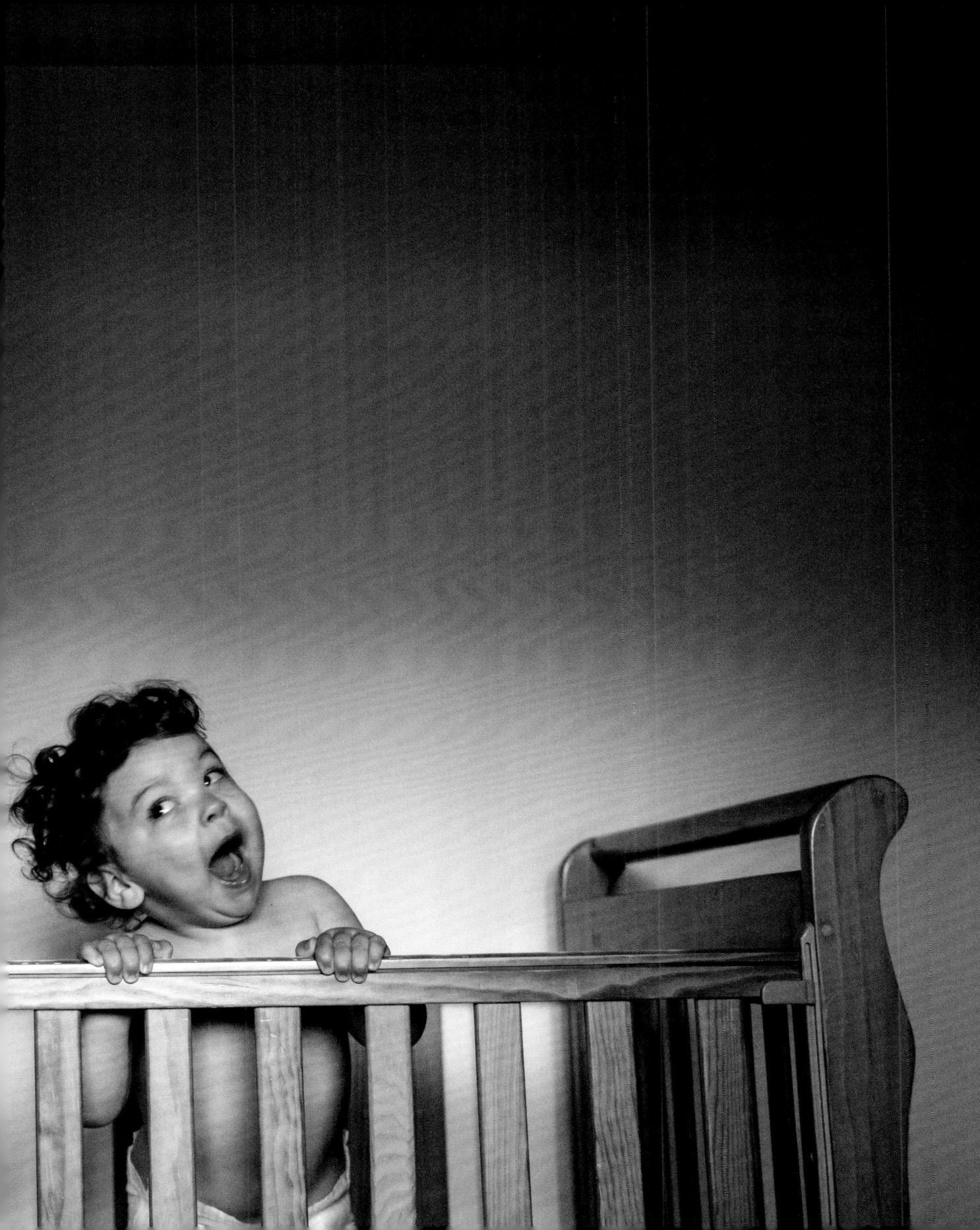

From the diary of a perpetually confused mom:

I am literally a shell of the evolved member of *Homo sapiens* I used to be. I have zero clue why I go into rooms. Like, at all. Almost every time, I must go back to the room I started in, retrace my steps back and forth, stand and stare blankly into the nothingness hoping my memory will decide to reactivate. A dramatic plant in the far corner will catch my attention, begging me to use my plant app to diagnose what is wrong with it. This will lead me to the kitchen to get water to hydrate the almost deceased fern. This will remind me that I forgot to resend the password to the Rose family, so I go down to my office, sit down, and notice one of the mean girls from high school has sent me a friend request on Facebook, which then triggers my memory of the time they legit LAUGHED at my outfit the first day of high school as I walked past them to find a seat in homeroom. I then remember that the Broadway *Mean Girls* tour is coming to Denver in two months and the kids asked me to find tickets. I proceed to spend the following thirty-seven minutes attempting to find the best seats that do not cost an entire semester's tuition to community college, only to realize I will be out of town the entirety of the tour. This revelation makes me sad, and I begin spinning, feeling completely overwhelmed to realize that I cannot continue living with this schedule any longer. I tell myself that I need to find a way to work less, and a lot of that has to do with terrible time management and distraction and the fact that I am a horrible business owner. And then it hits me! I remember why I was in the TV room: to take my Adderall.

The Perfect Paper air plane.

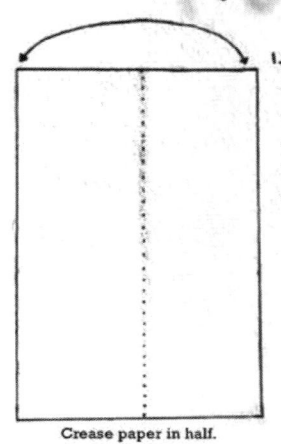

Crease paper in half.

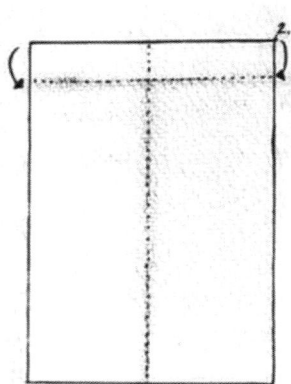

Crease paper 2 inches
from the top.

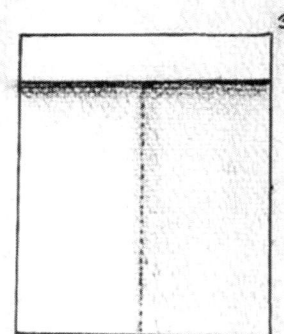

Fold paper along top crease
and flip over.

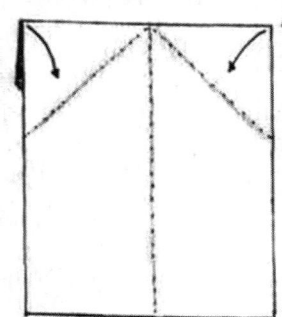

Fold corners in to meet
center crease.

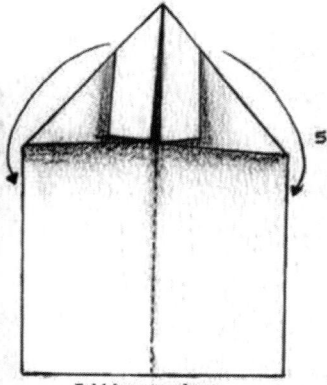

Fold from top down.

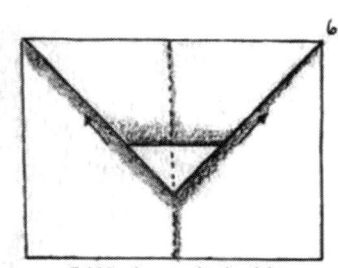

Fold back up so the tip of the
triangle meets the top edge.

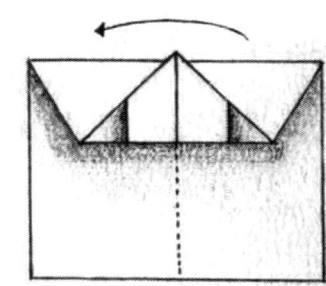

Flip over.

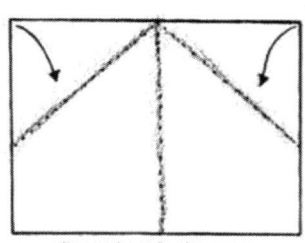

Crease from the corners to
meet in the center.

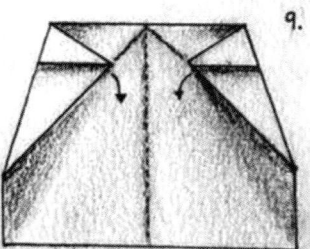

Fold from top corners twice, once
so corner edges meet the crease
and then again to meet along
center crease.

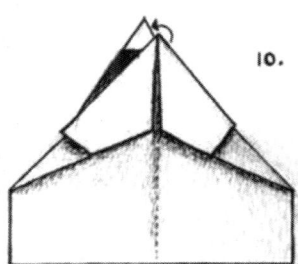

Tuck top tip into the back fold.

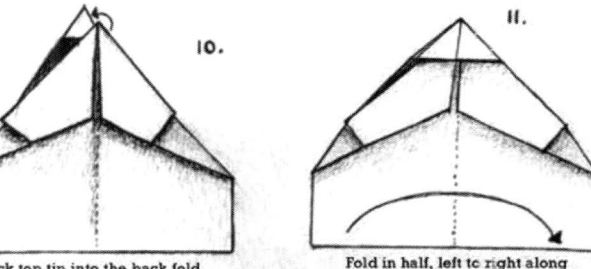

Fold in half, left to right along
center crease.

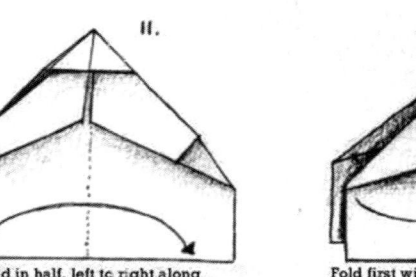

Fold first wing to meet the
center edge.

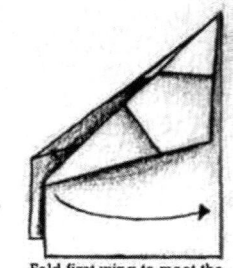

Fold the second wing.

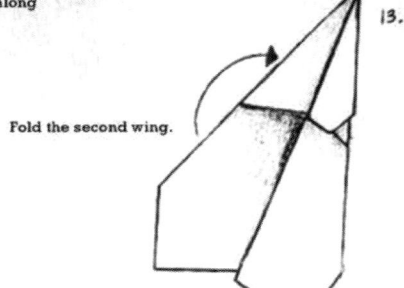

Have fun flying.

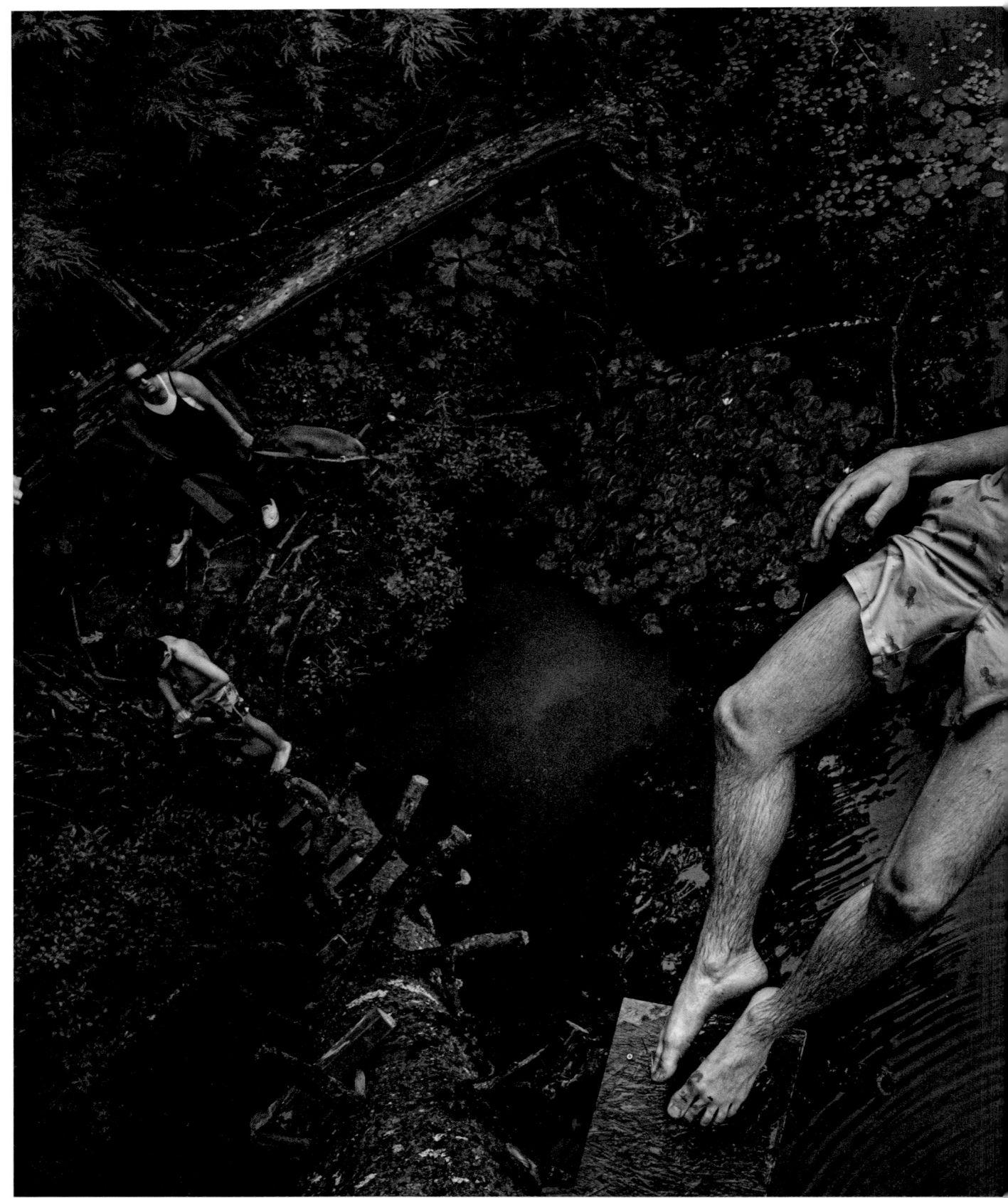

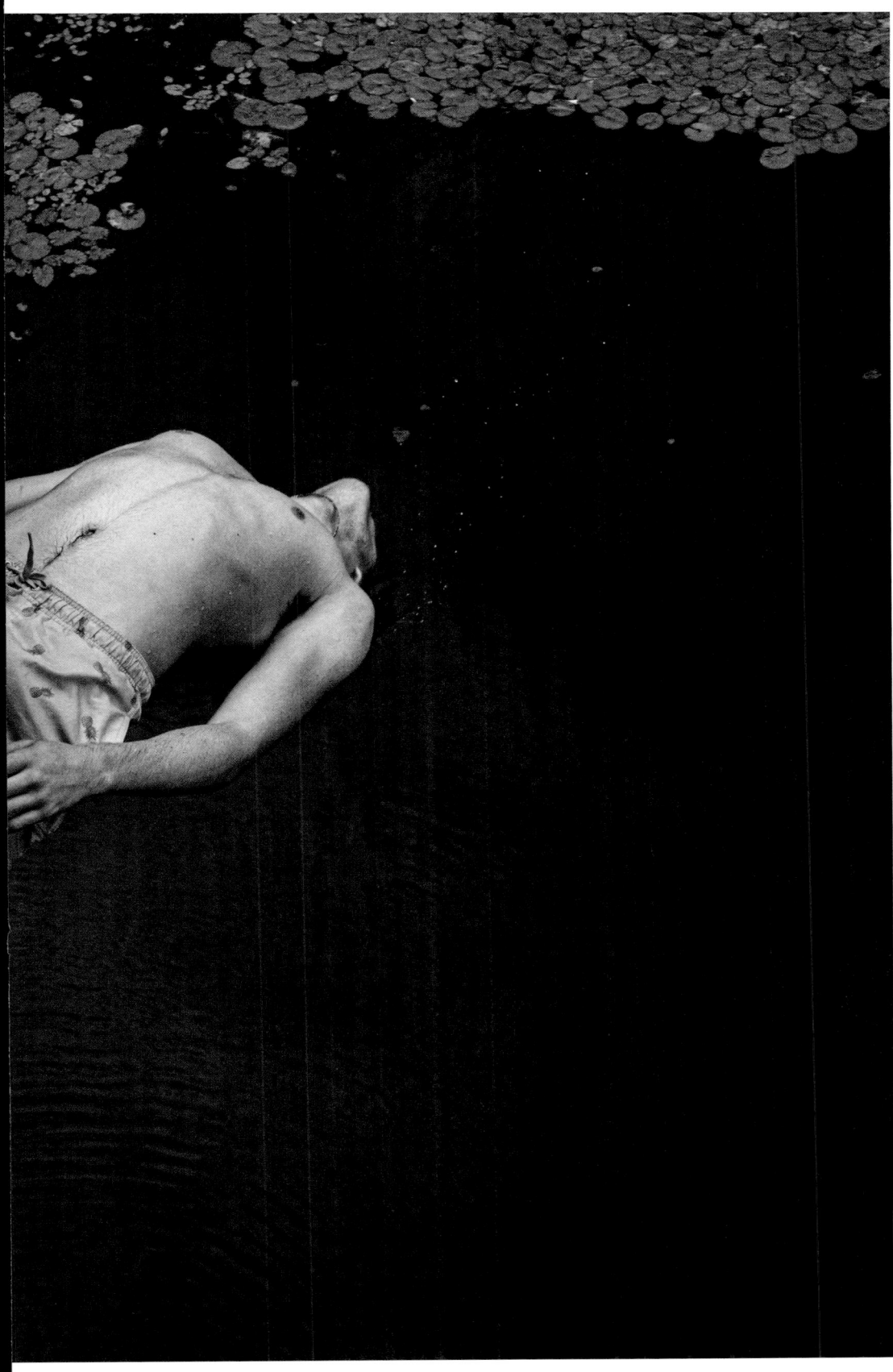

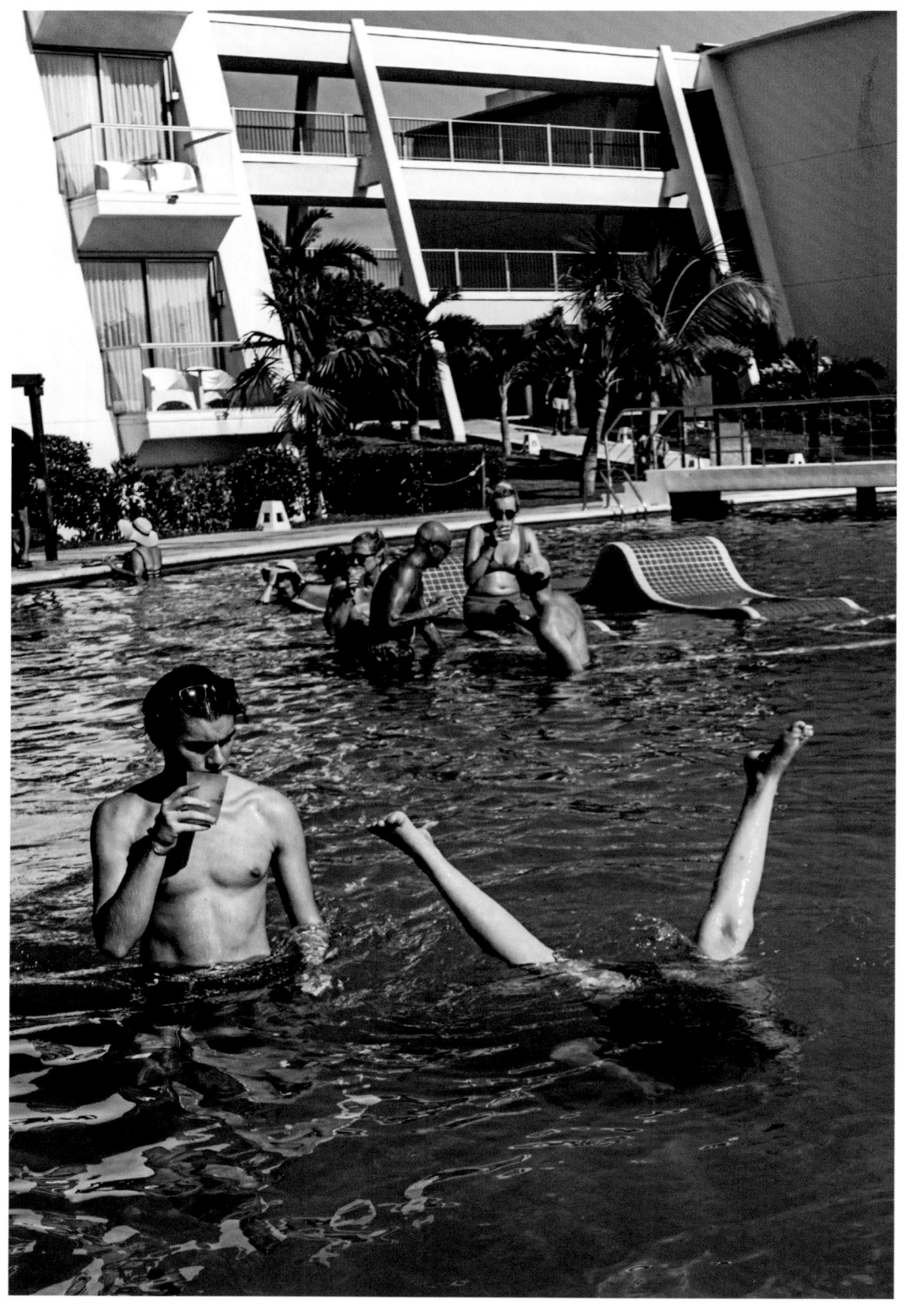

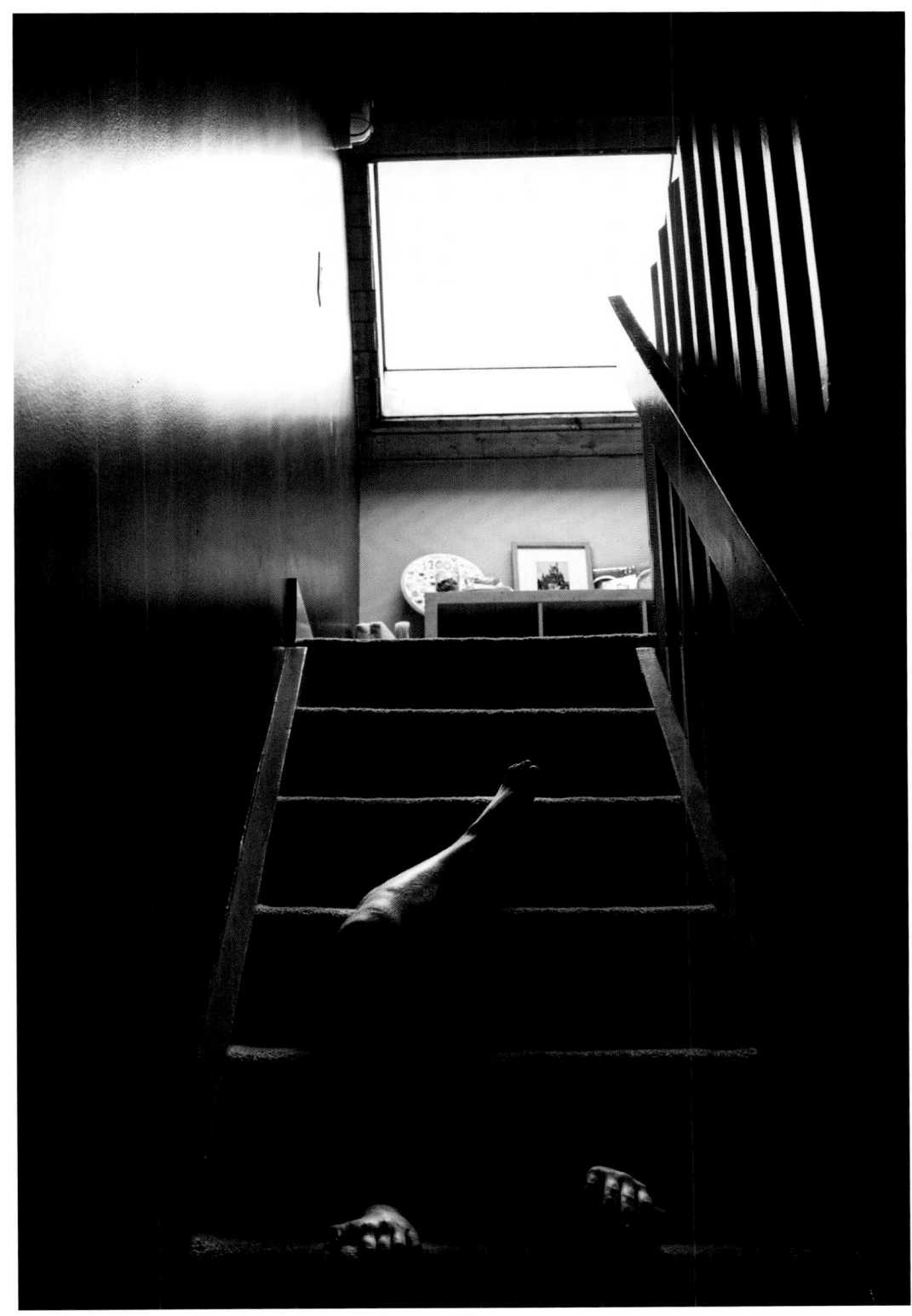

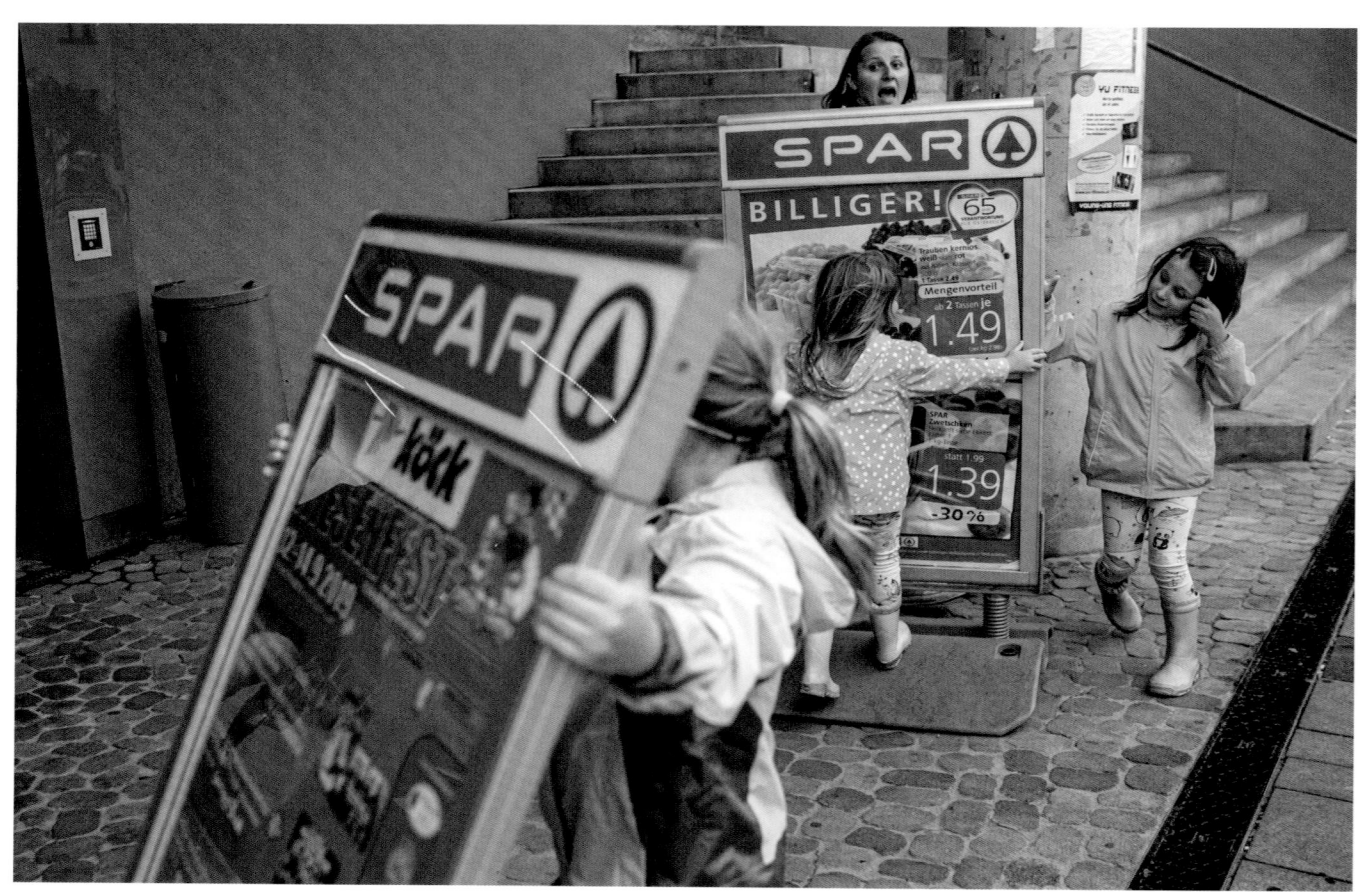

Older moms, never tell a woman with younger children, say, two years old and five, in the checkout line at the grocery to "enjoy these days" because kids get harder as they get older, particularly if the two-year-old has managed to . . .

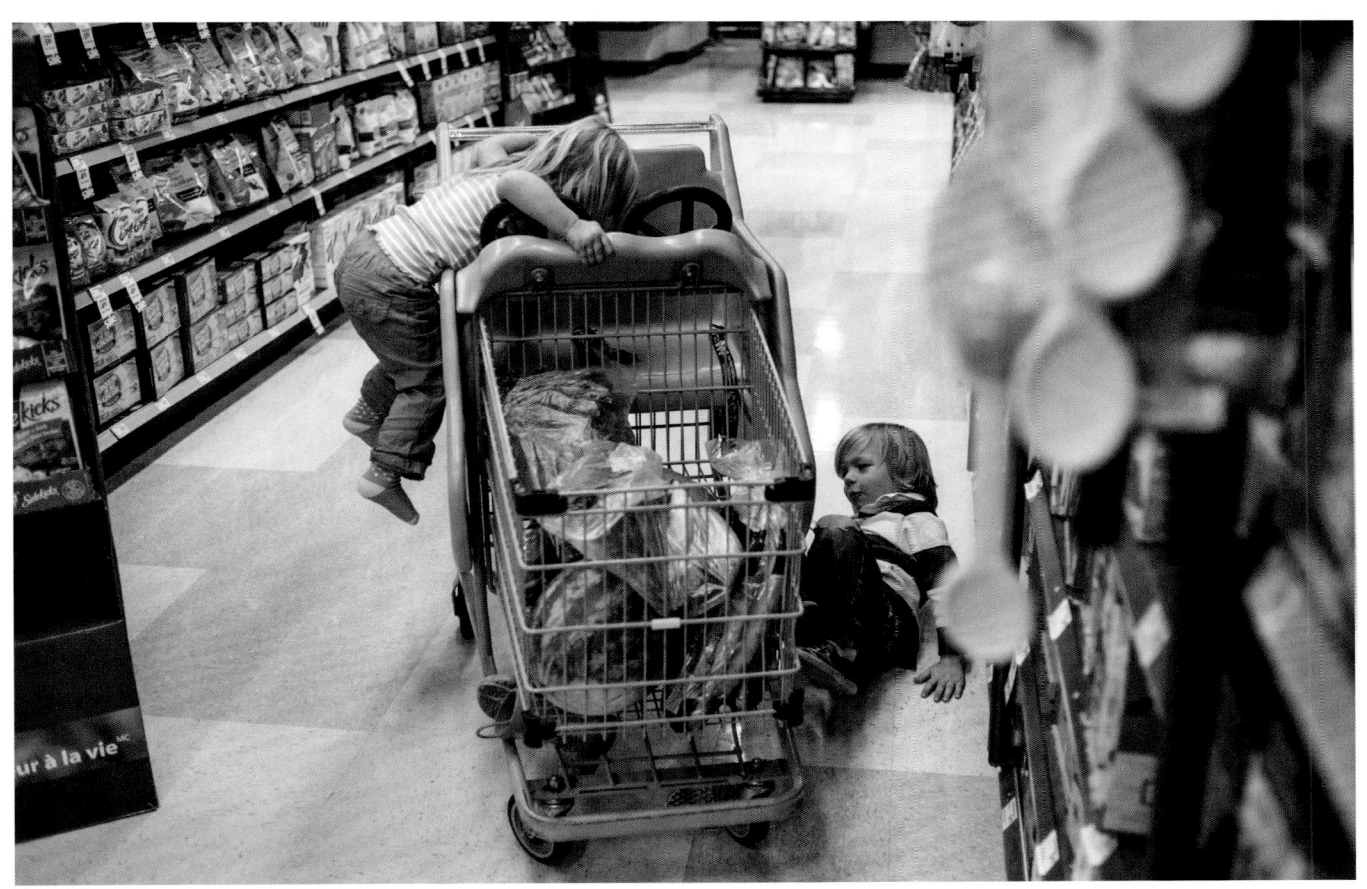

escape the cart and is scaling the cash register and the five-year-old is beating the hell out of the lottery ticket machine to "see if money comes out," because THAT SHIT IS NOT HELPFUL. — Sarah Meader Holbrook

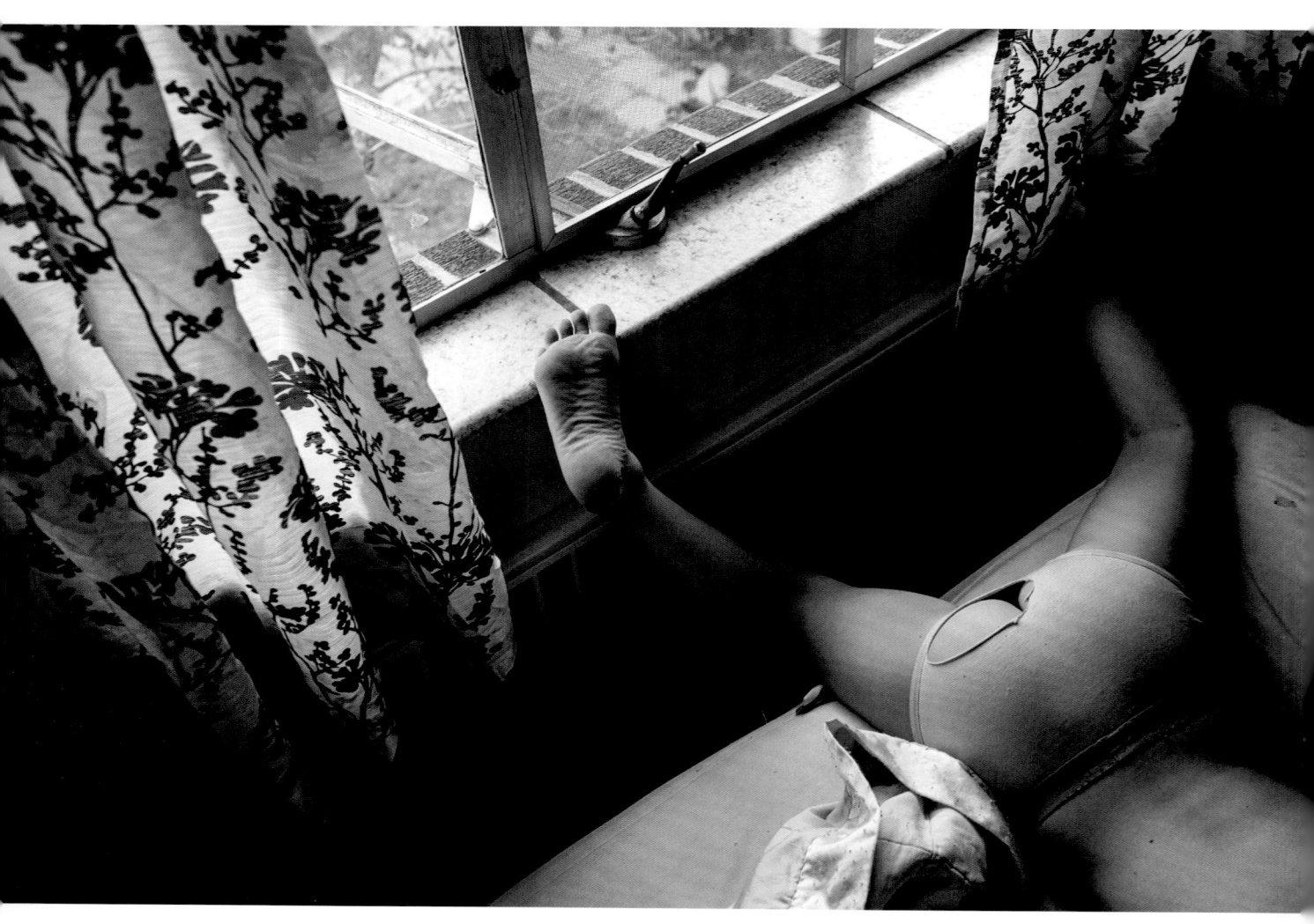

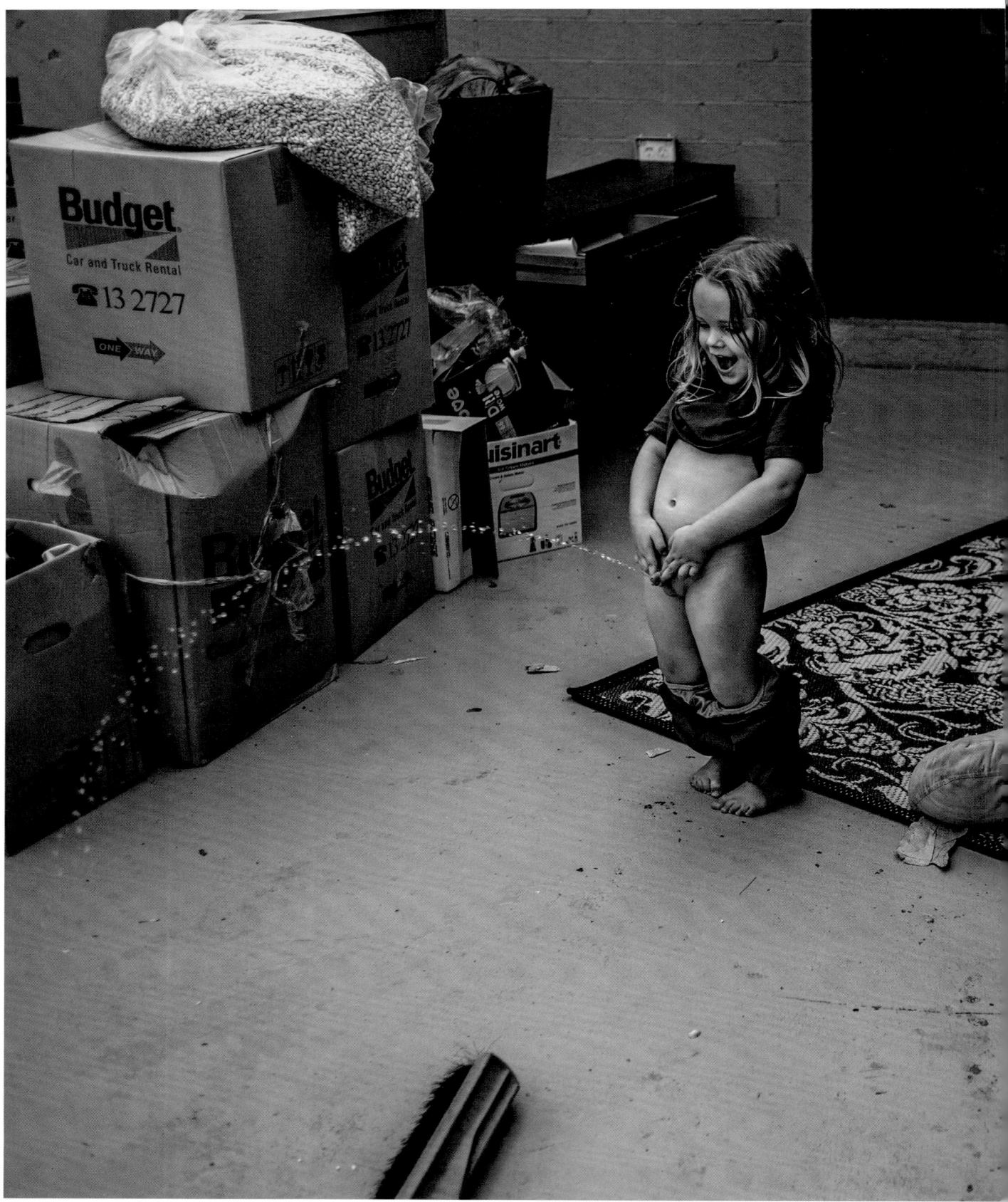

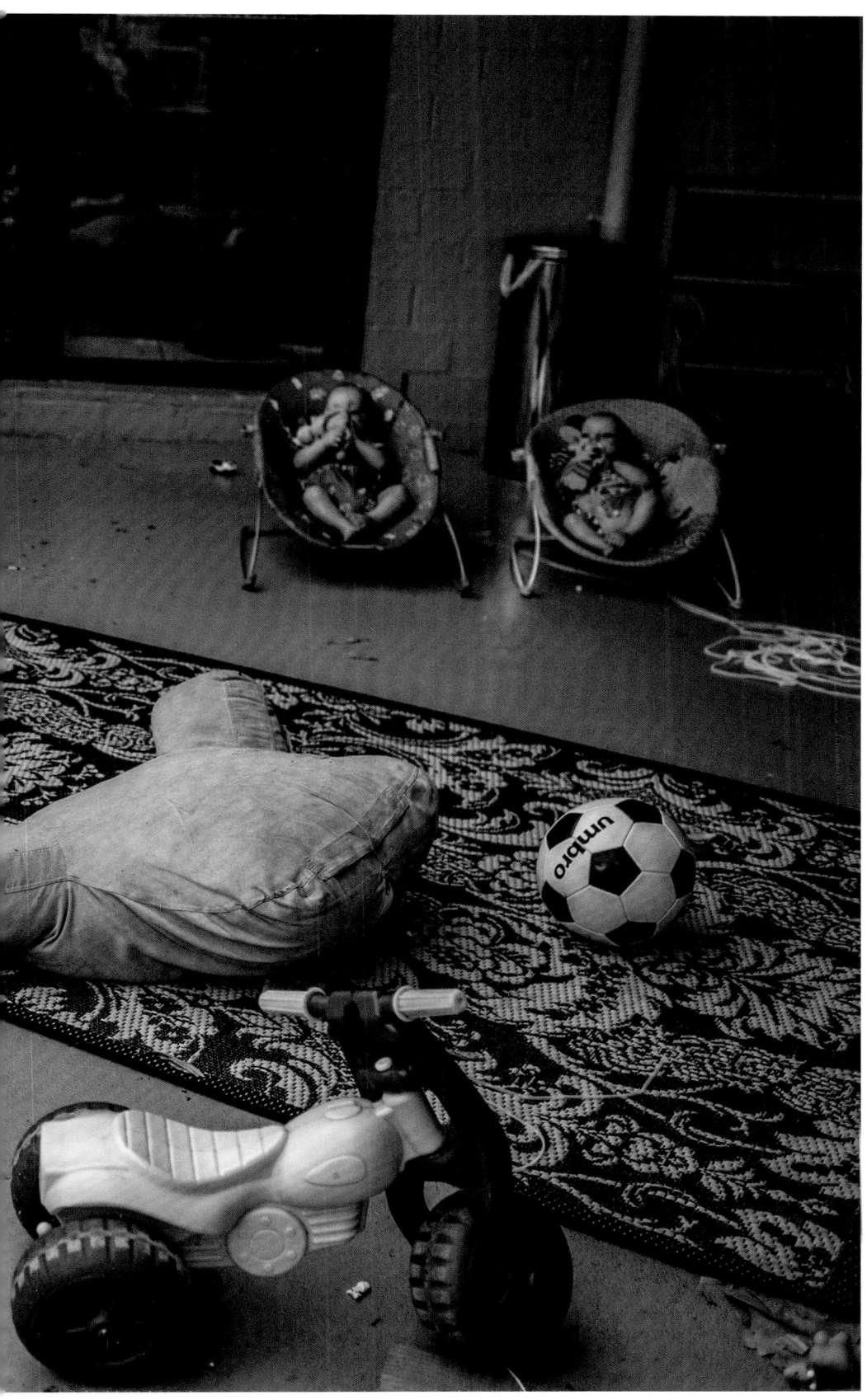

HOME REMEDY FOR URINE STAINS

1. Absorb said urine with the brand-new paper towel roll you had to open because someone left an empty one on the counter.

2. Rinse with some sink water and the T-shirt your kid threw on the floor three weeks ago and still refuses to pick up.

3. Grab that old bottle of hairspray you haven't used in 1,027 days. Rinse with water. Fill with one cup distilled white vinegar, one cup of water, and two teaspoons of baking soda (the soggy one shoved in the very back of your fridge).

4. Spray on the pee spot. Wait. Then spray again because you got distracted making four different meals for dinner and it dried up. Soak up with yet another new roll of paper towel.

5. If the smell remains, just go ahead and grab a Sharpie and pair of hedge trimmers. Trace around the pee and then cut out that piece of carpet. Place a large plant on top; no one will notice.

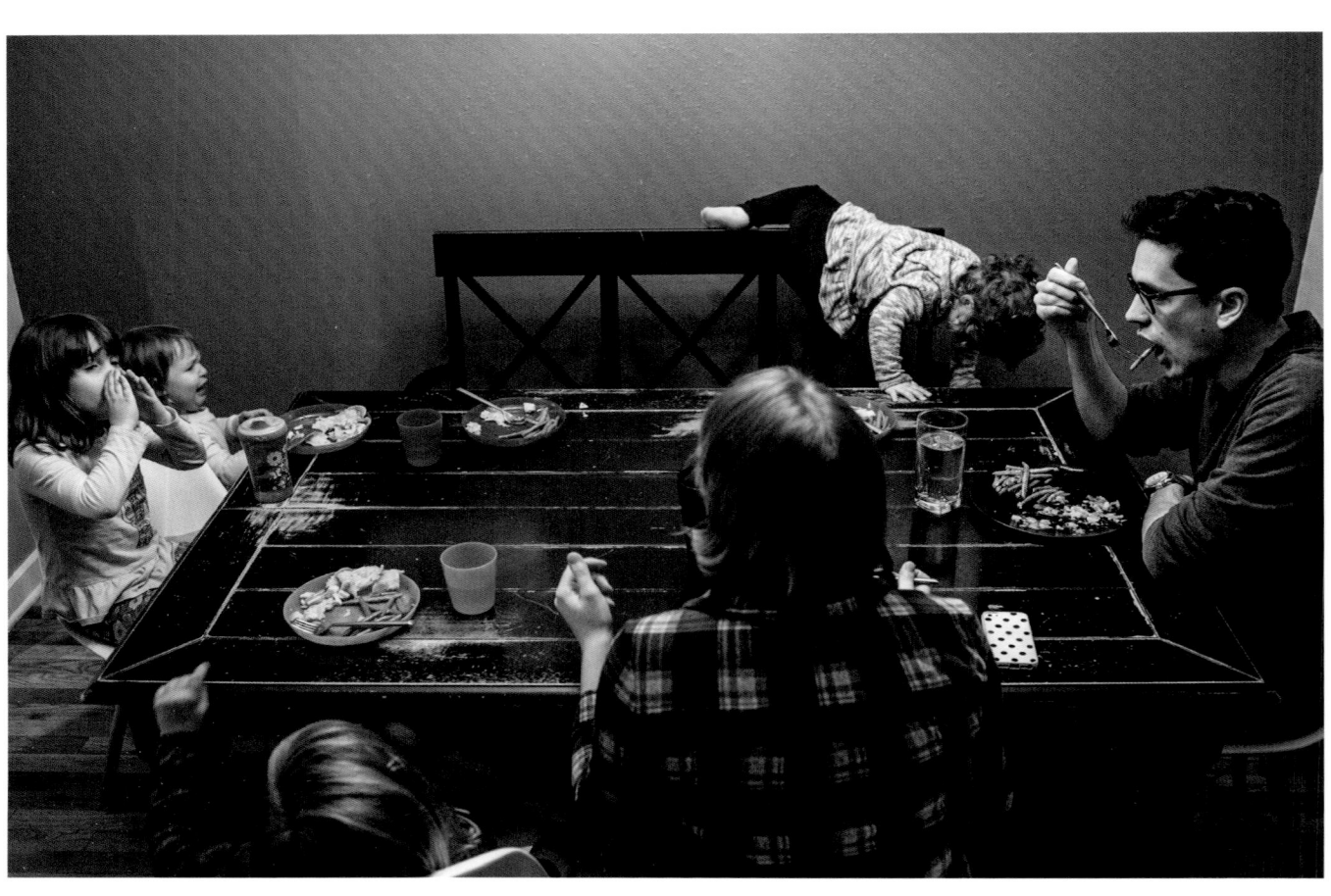

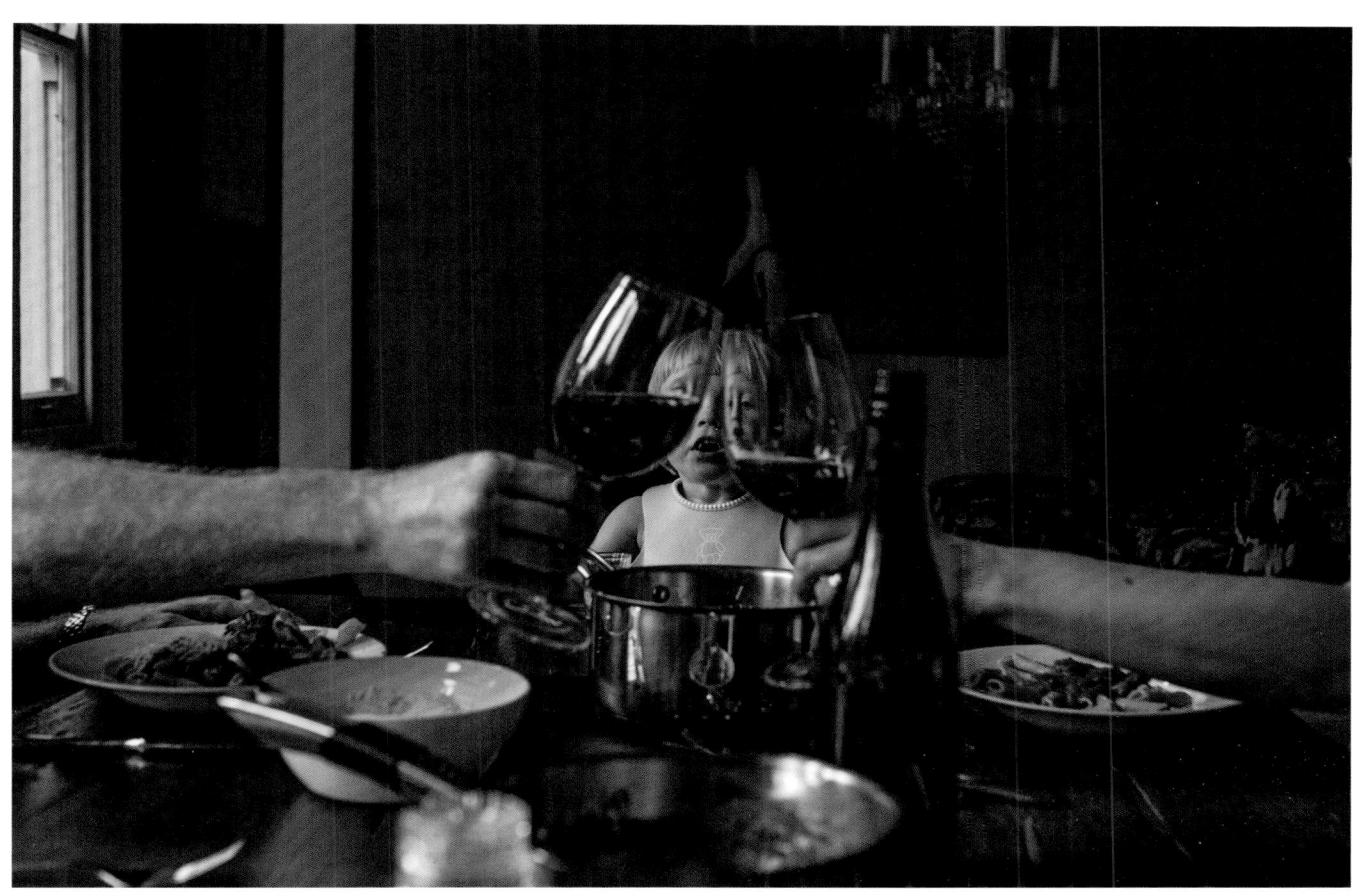

Every meal doesn't have to make sense. If your kid eats, it's a win. No one is coming to dinner
to grade you. Fed is best at any age.

—Sarah Smith

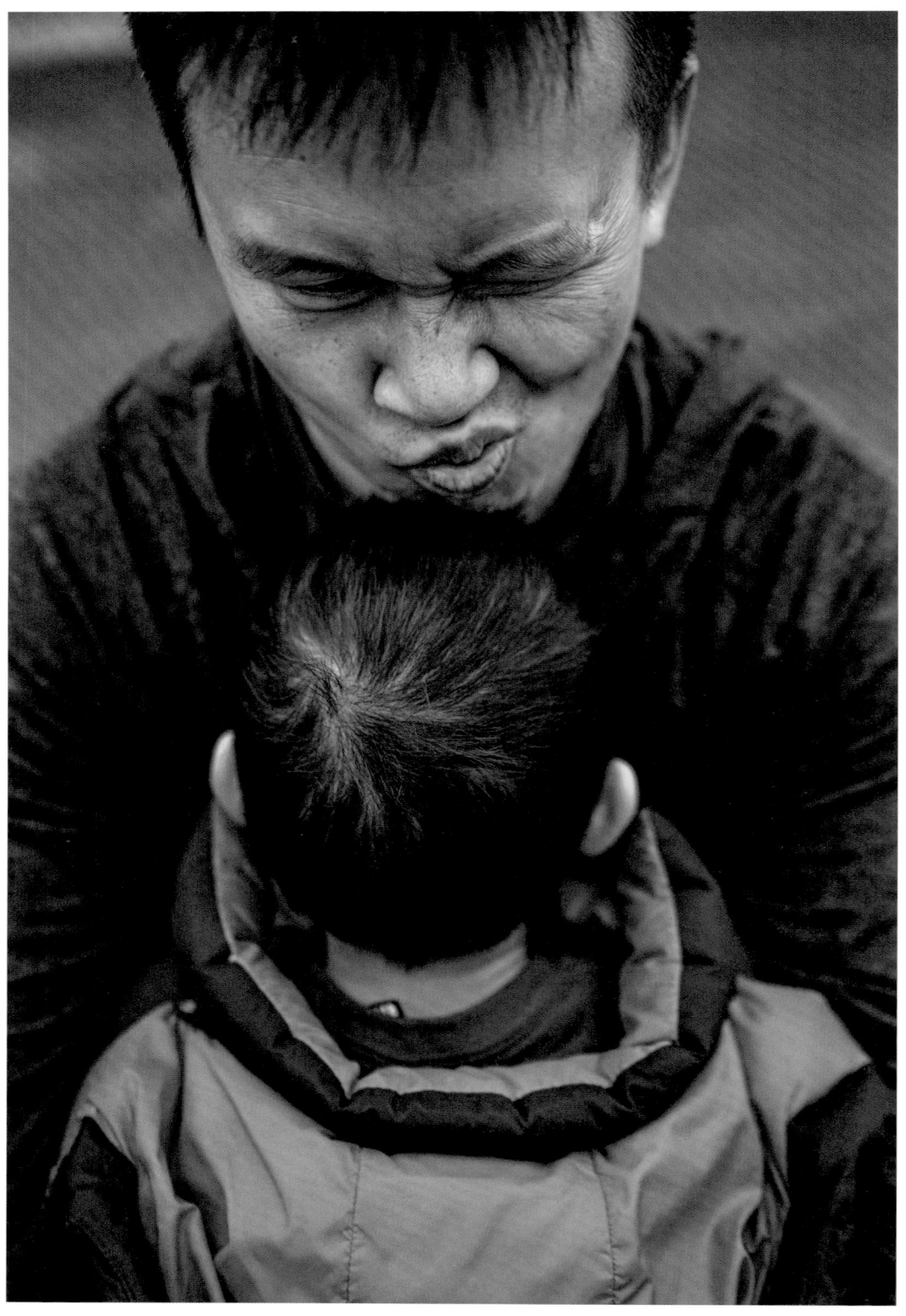

Dear Sleep Deprived,

We know. You can't remember what you are trying to find no matter how hard you look. Sometimes you hide in the pantry crying until you forget why you are crying and get hungry, so you shove a handful of stale Goldfish in your mouth hole. You've been known to binge-watch episodes of *Gossip Girl* at midnight and worry that the thirteen coffees in a day might be starting to become a problem but seem to be the only glue between you and survival. When was the last time you showered? Oh, you can't remember? Welcome; you are in good company. And don't worry; that unrecognizable version of you staring you down above the bathroom sink will eventually start to become familiar. I want to share just a bit of retrospective wisdom from a veteran "operating at less than 17% at all times" mom to remind you, you are definitely NOT alone. In fact, you are doing amazingly.

Check all your expectations at the door. Your kid is going to be who your kid is going to be, and you'd best be prepared to meet them where they are at and love them where they are. Giving your kids boundaries, love, and stability is all they really need.

Parenting is a total mindfuck. One moment you are so over everything and want to walk away from it all and the next moment you are cradling your five-year-old because he's allowing you, and you're so afraid this will be the last time. Not all moments will be great. And that's OK. Give yourself grace when it's hard. and enjoy the hell out of everything else.

Listen to your gut feeling. Yes, getting advice from others is good, but at the end of the day that child is yours and you have that instinct that was given to you for a reason. Anytime someone asks me for advice about their kids, I always ask back, "What does your Mommy instinct tell you?" Chances are their instincts are right.

I can wholeheartedly say, walking the tight rope of raising a young mind while trying to keep one's own shit together is best done in community.

You are the stopping point for unhealthy relationships. Do not ask your children to tolerate behavior that hurts them, even for family.

The hardest part of being a parent is the work you need to do on yourself. Reflecting on your own childhood. What parts of that do you want to (or not want to) embrace your child with? What do you want them to be like? Learning as parents to let go of the little things, that nothing will be perfect and that's OK. We have an incredible responsibility to raise responsible, caring, and compassionate human beings.

You have to give yourself grace and remember that we are all humans going through these things for the first time.

This is going to make you grow and stretch more than you can possibly imagine. It will be the hardest and best thing you ever do. Hold on tight.

Sincerely,
A Long Line of Sleep-Deprived Moms Who Stand in Solidarity with You

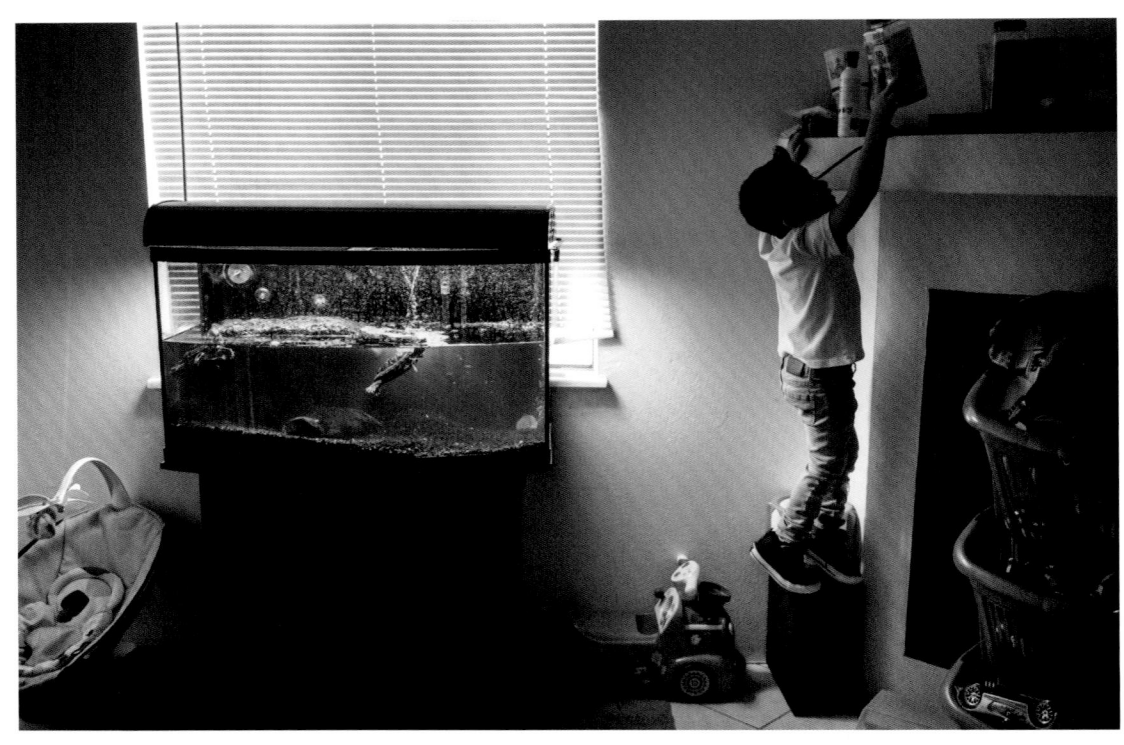

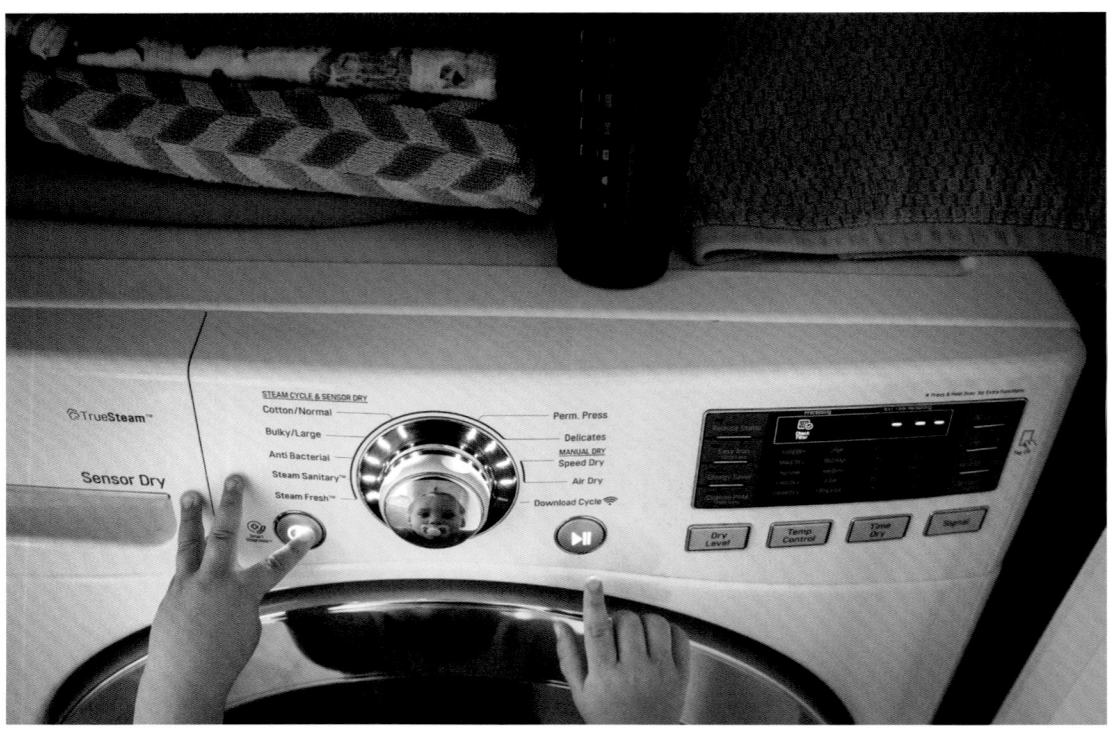

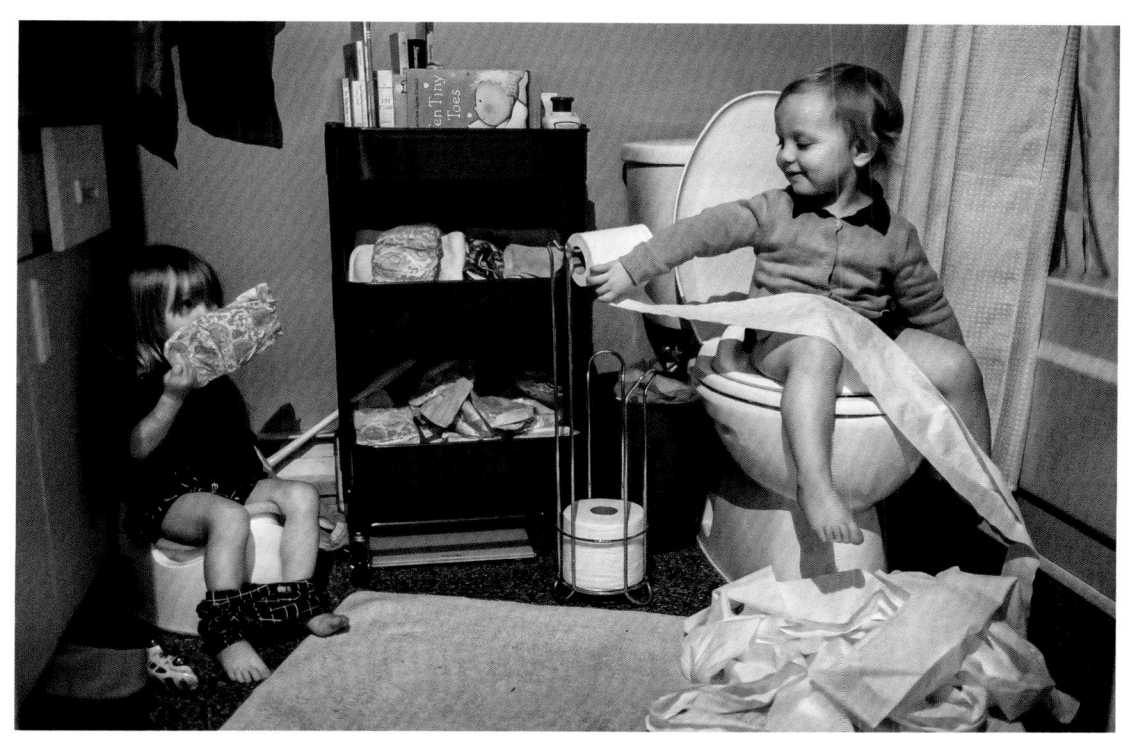

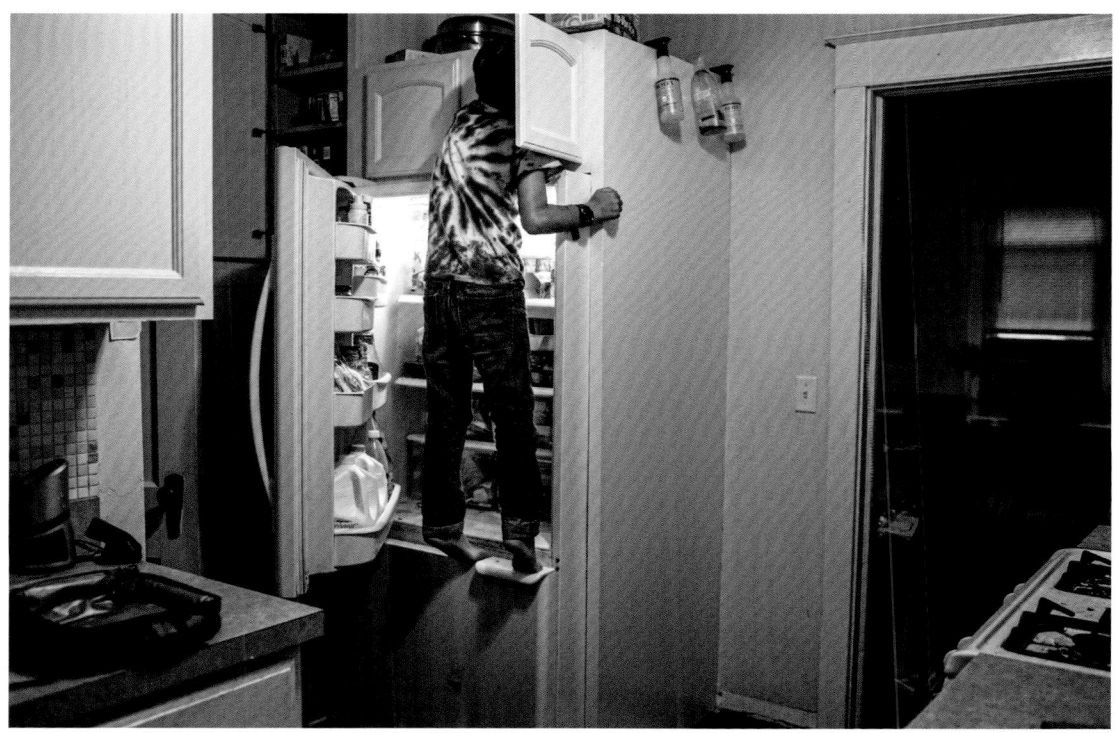

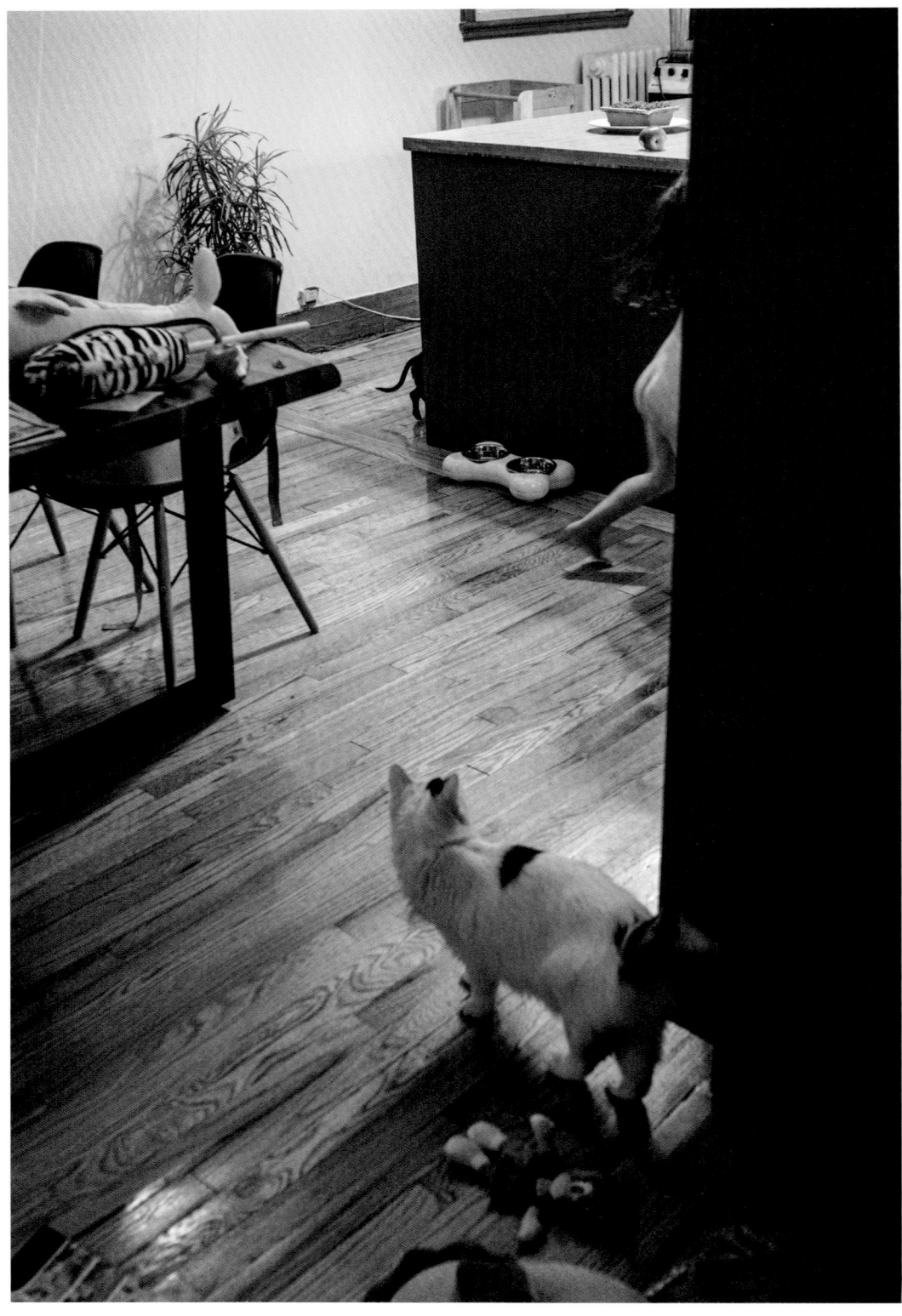

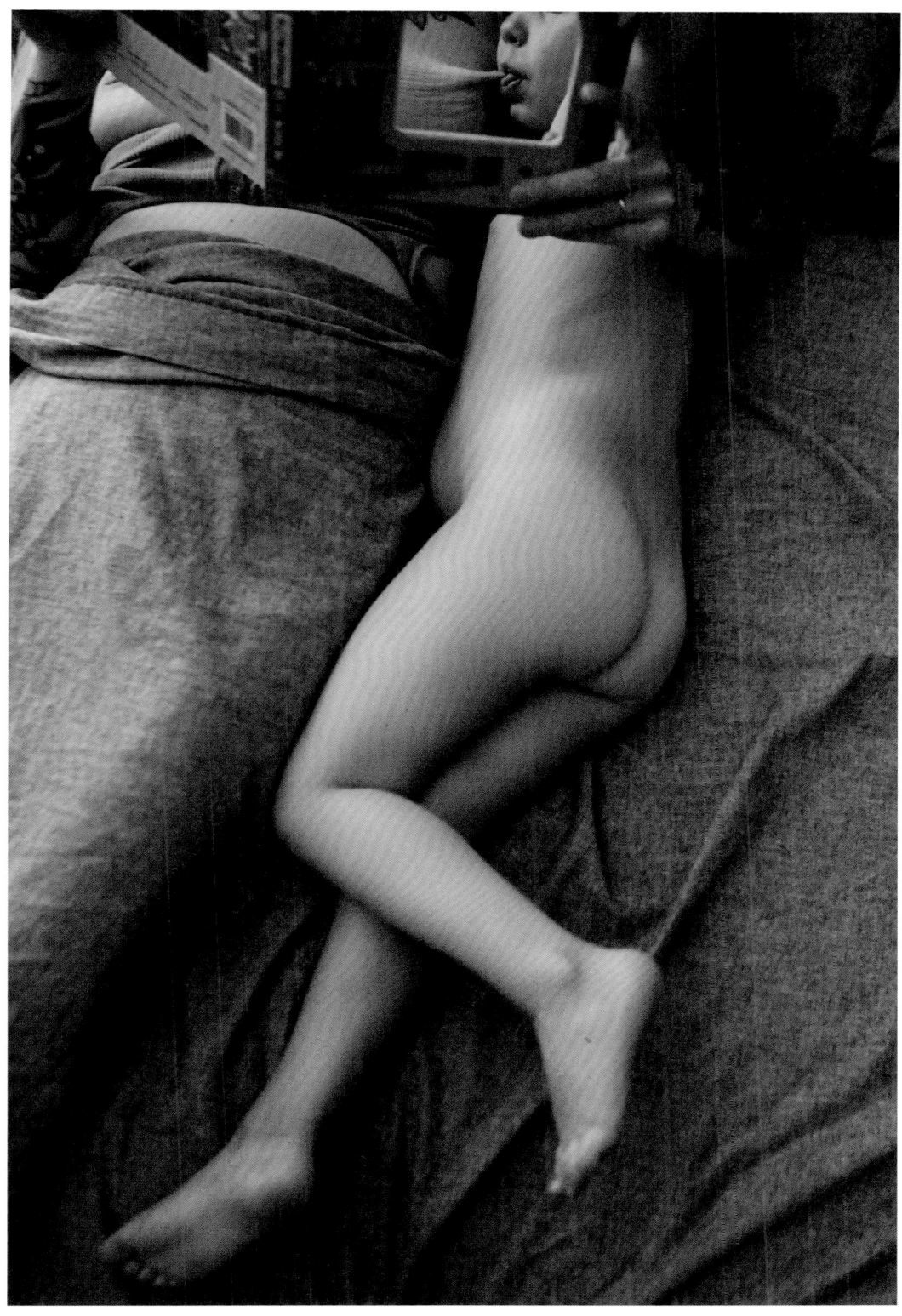

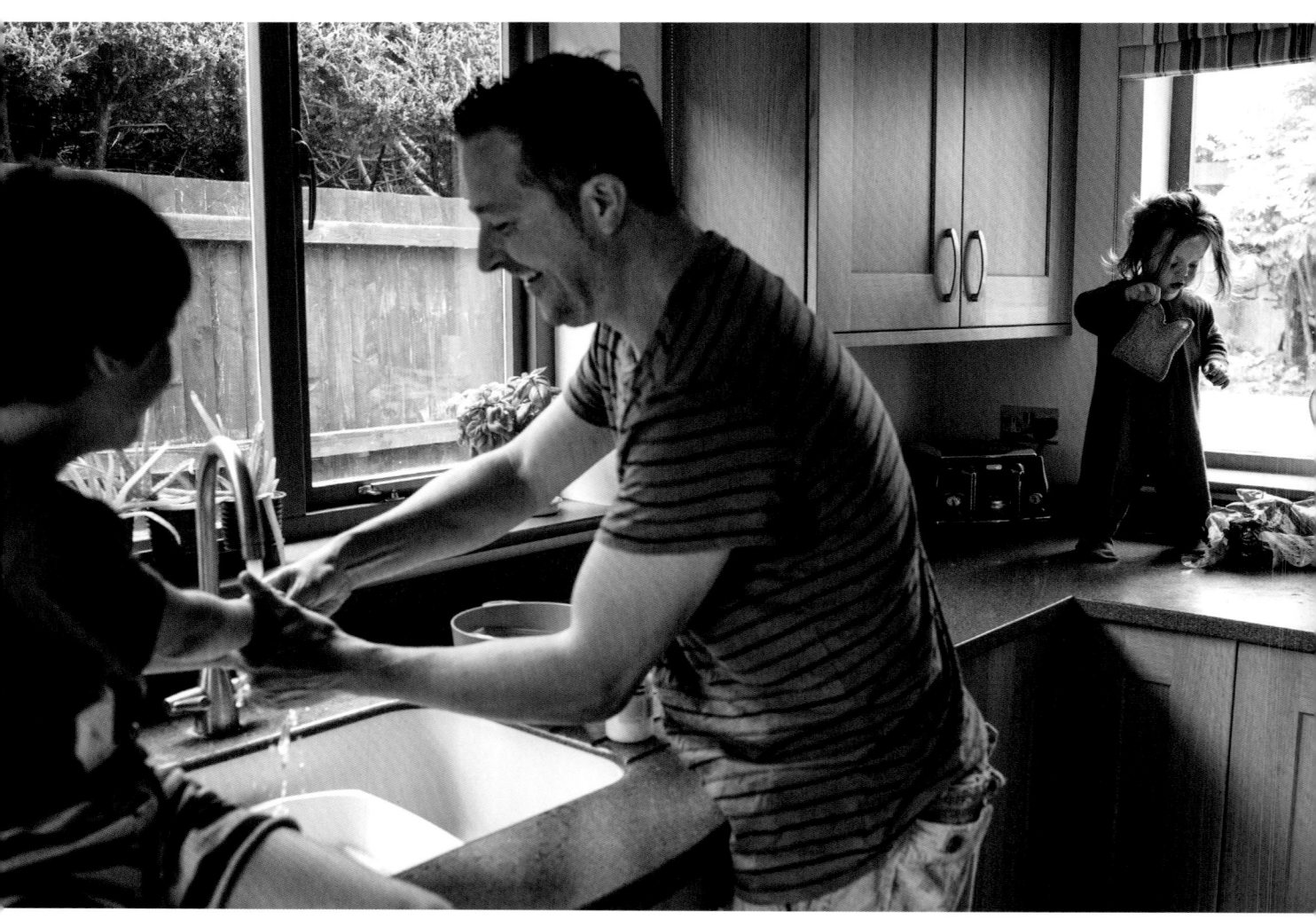

Show your kids that there are so many ways to learn things and let them guide the subjects.
—Lee Kamenitz

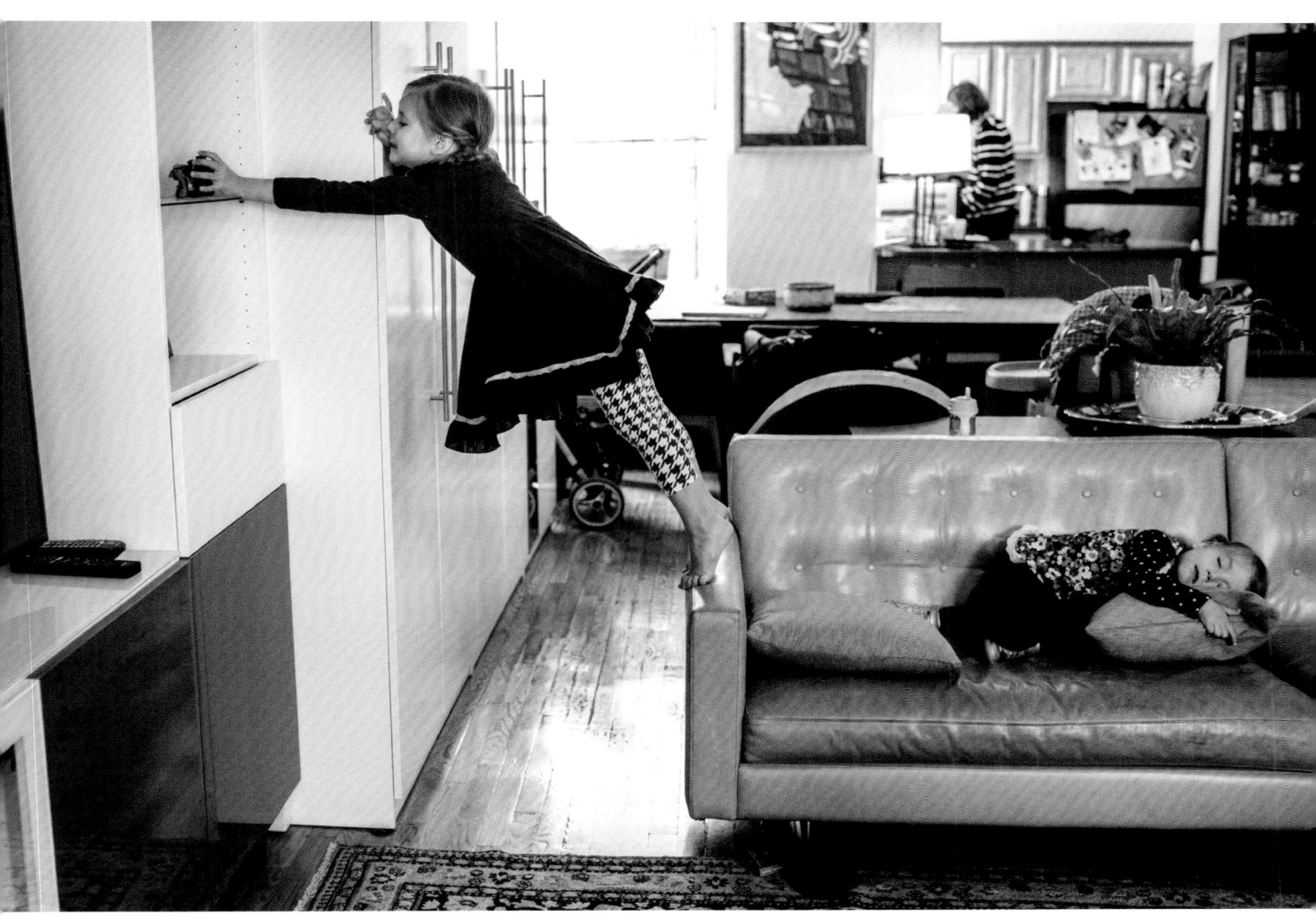

Take a step back; allow them to fail and learn.

—Nimrod Mankovski

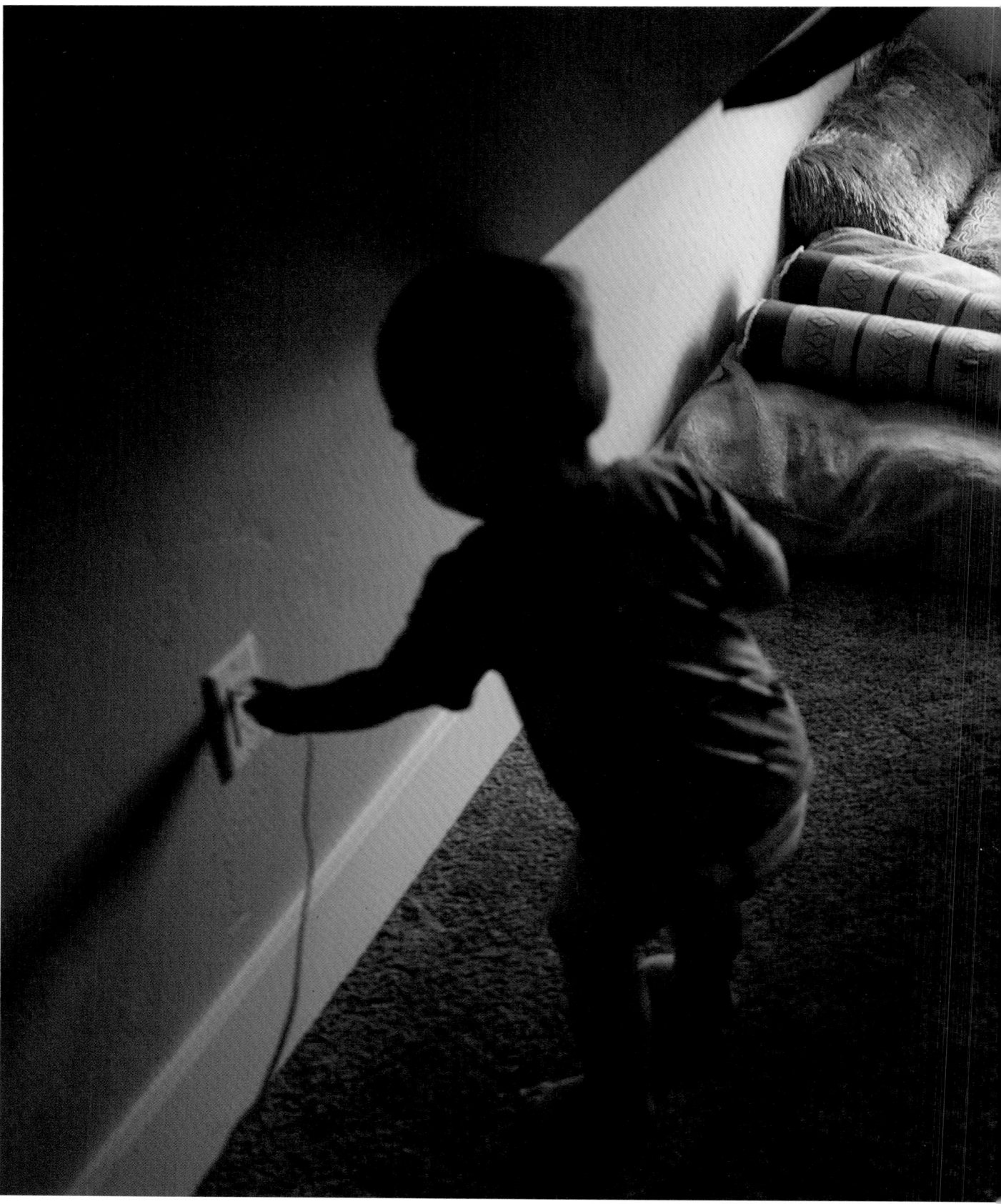

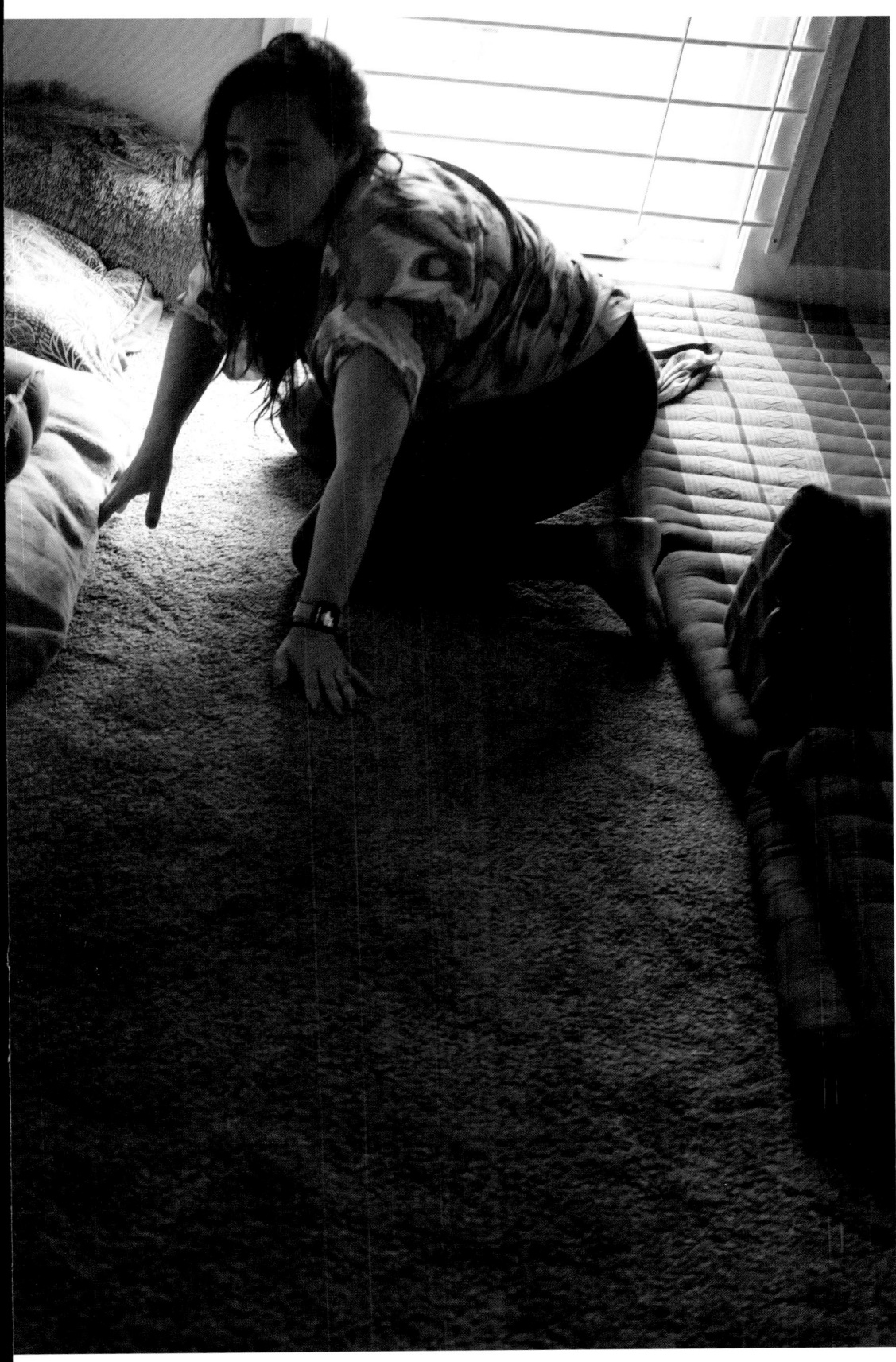

S is for Ssssshhh-
hhiiiit.

—Isaac, age three

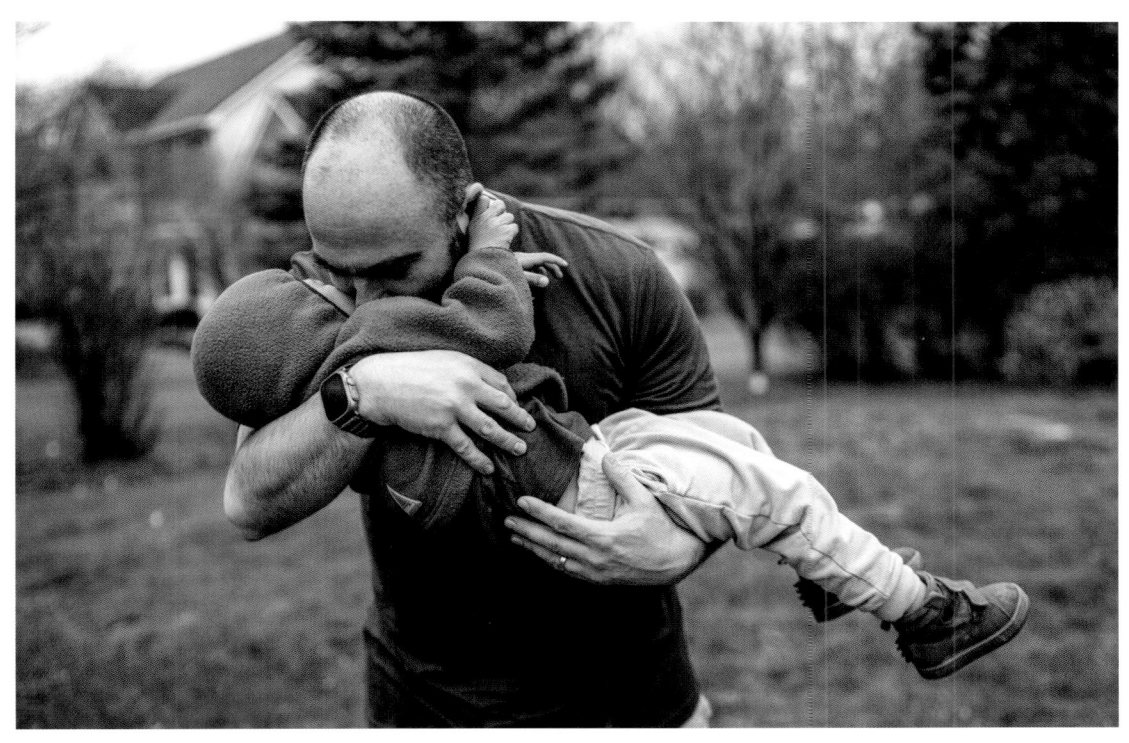

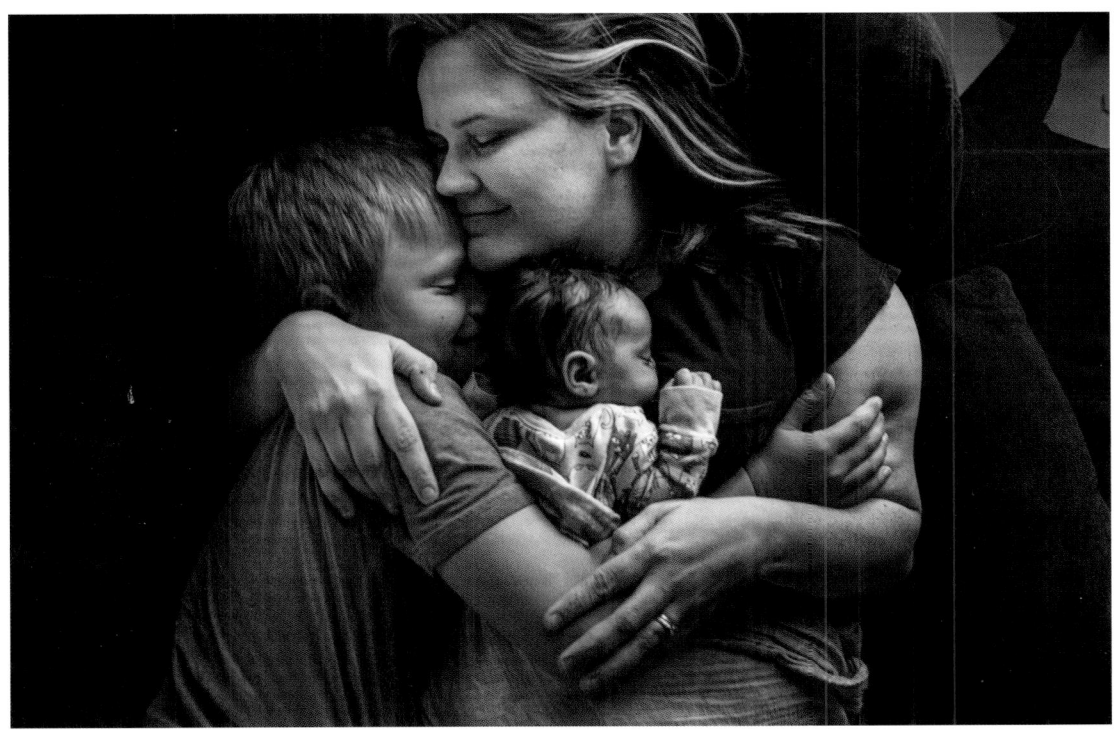

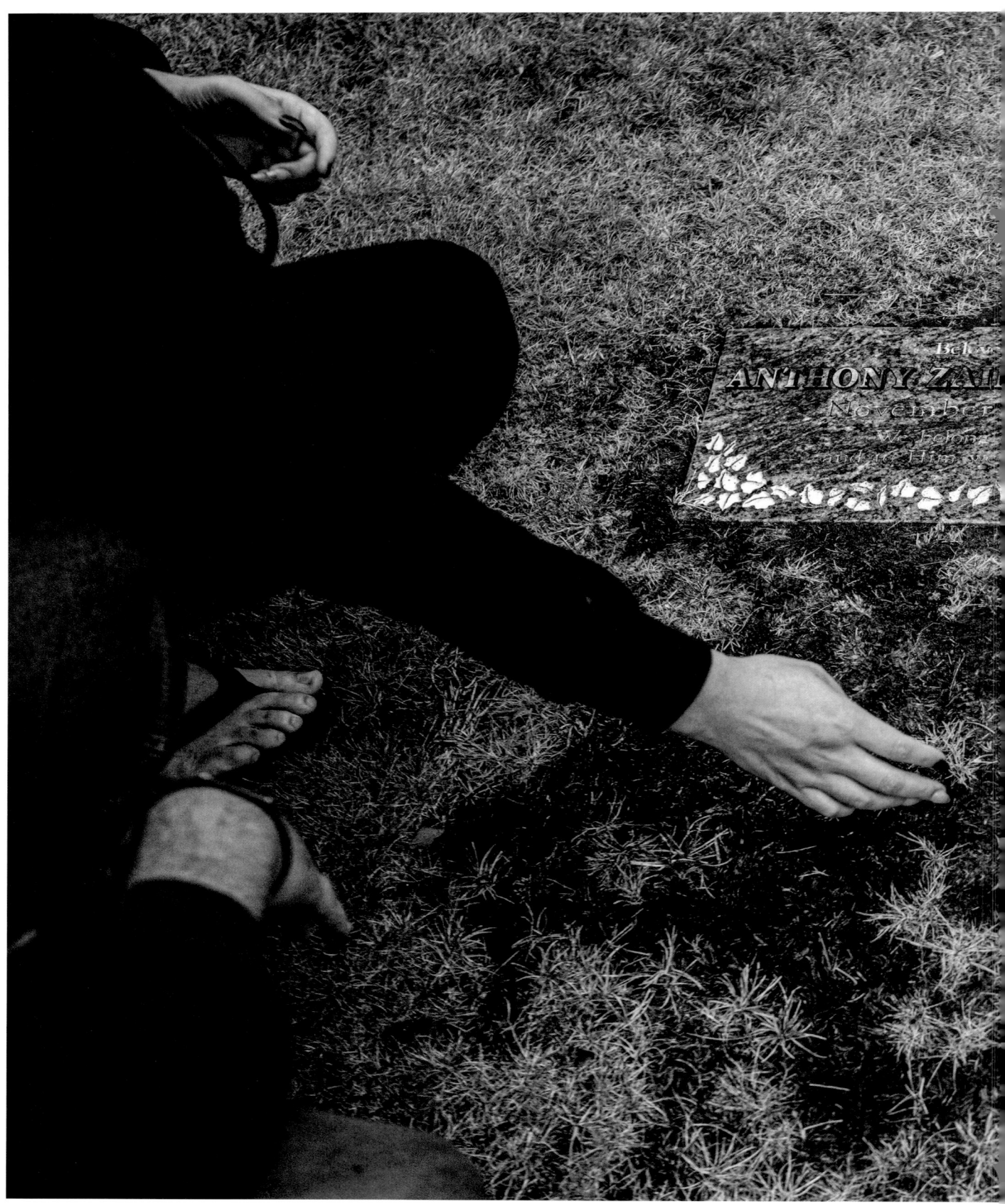

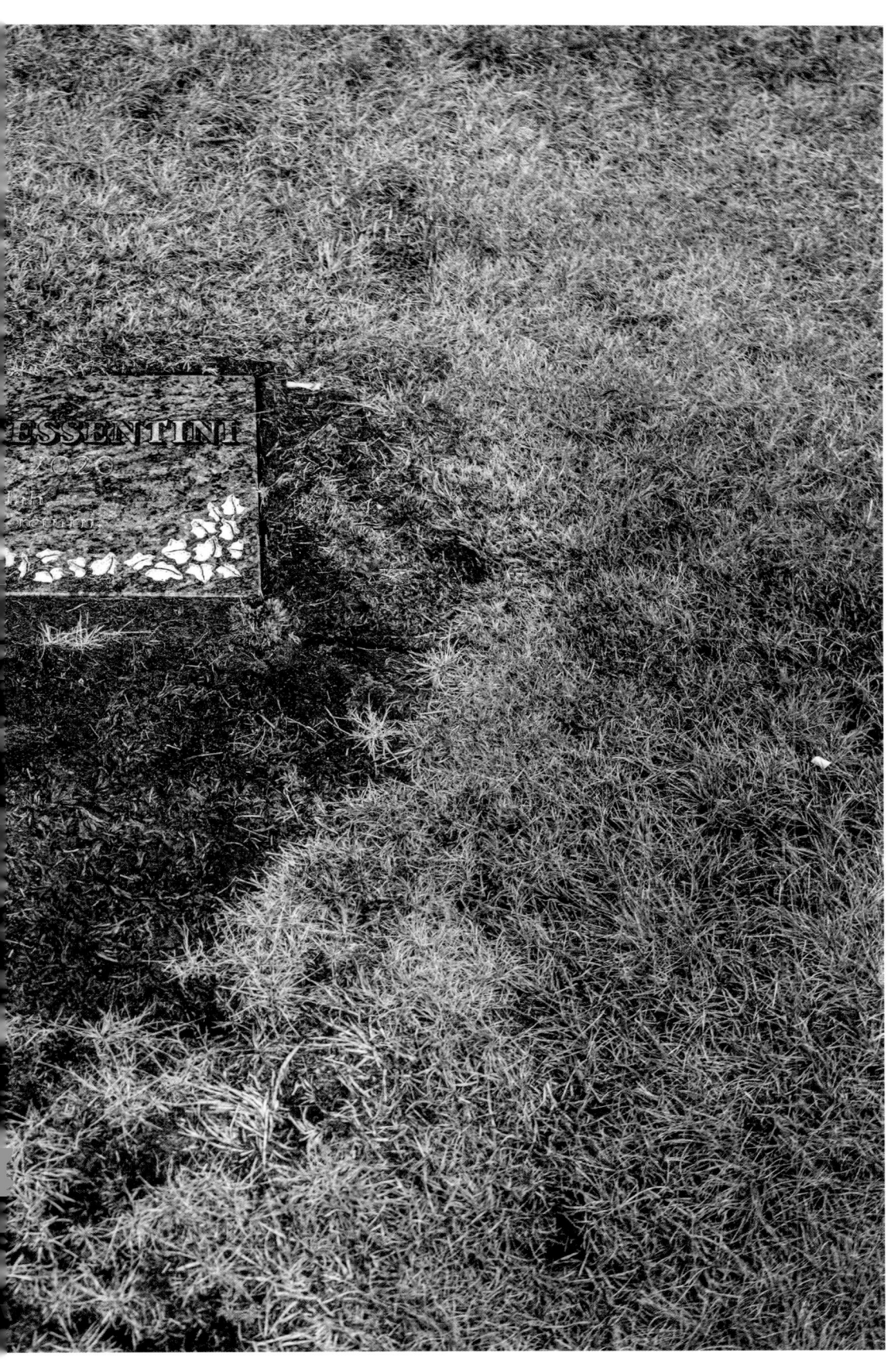

*Conversations with
a nine-year-old*

Flora: Do you think there
is life after we die?

Mom: I think so.

Flora: So we don't die
when we die?

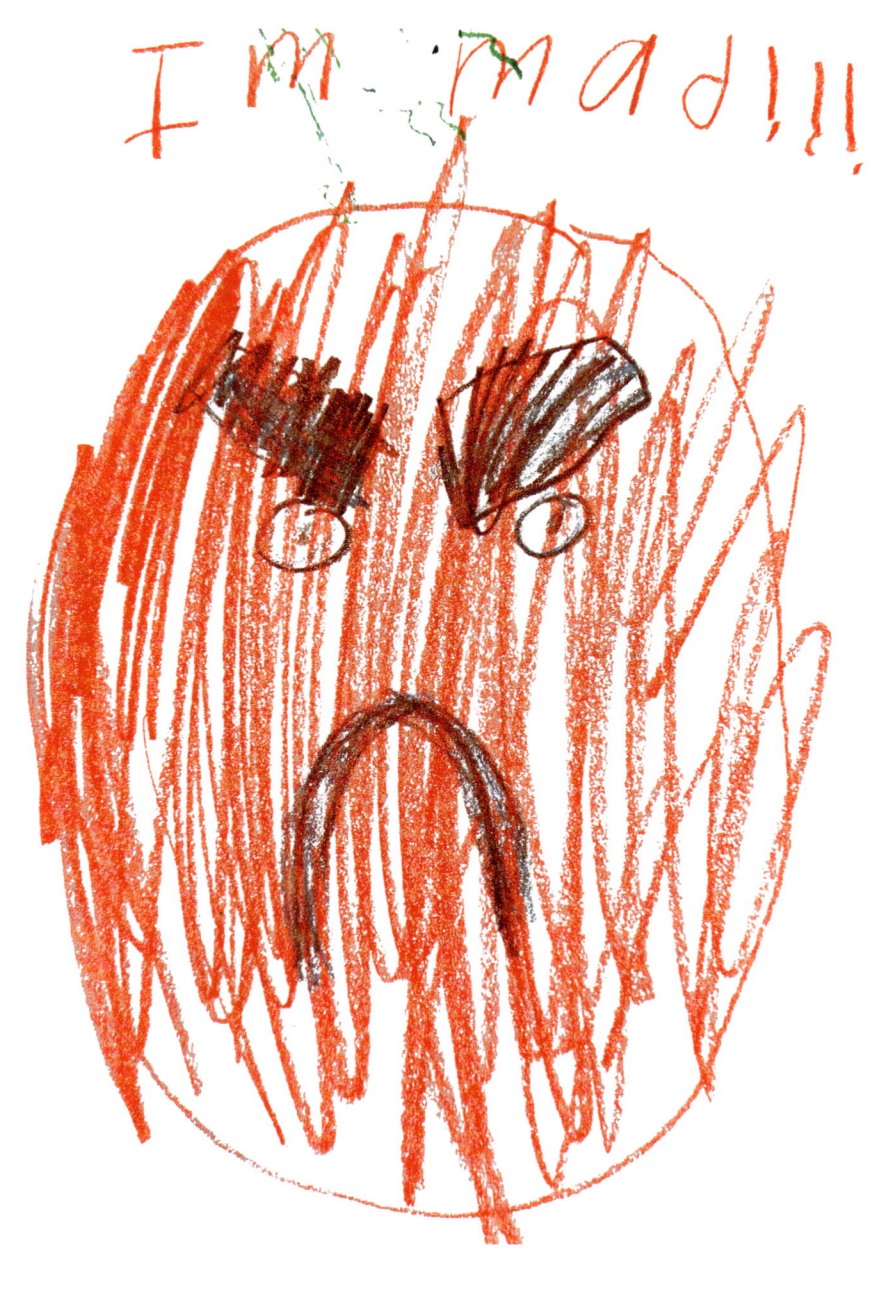

Mad
—Byrdie Mae, age seven

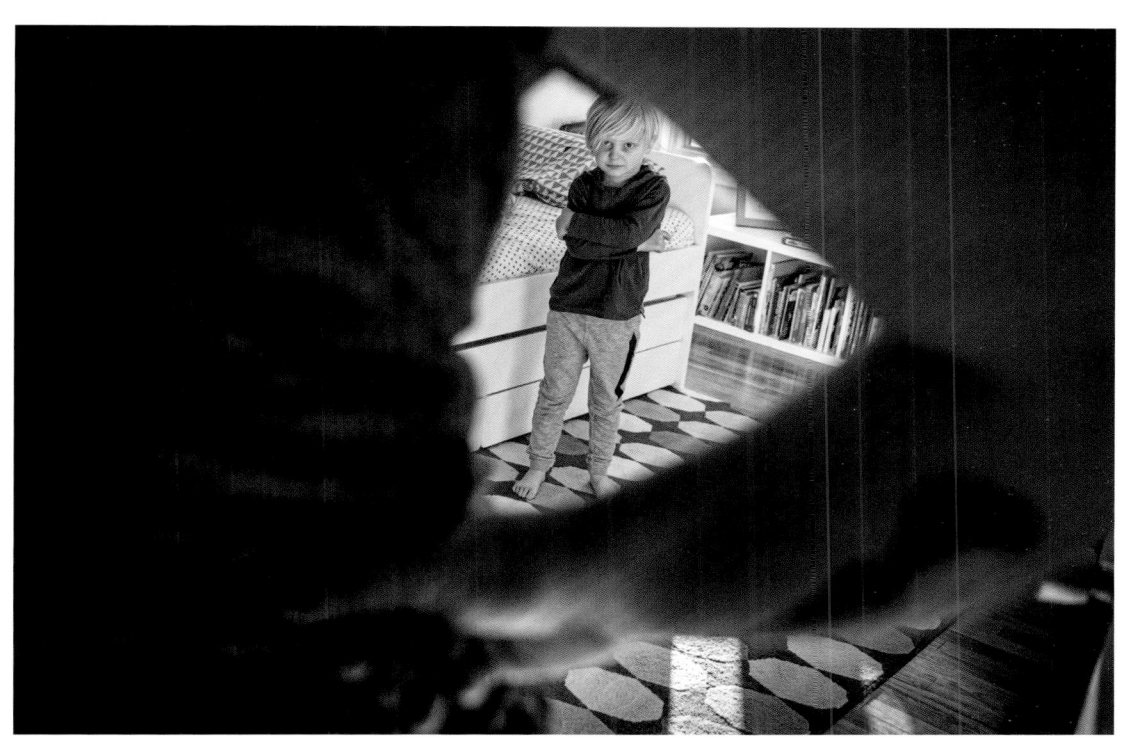

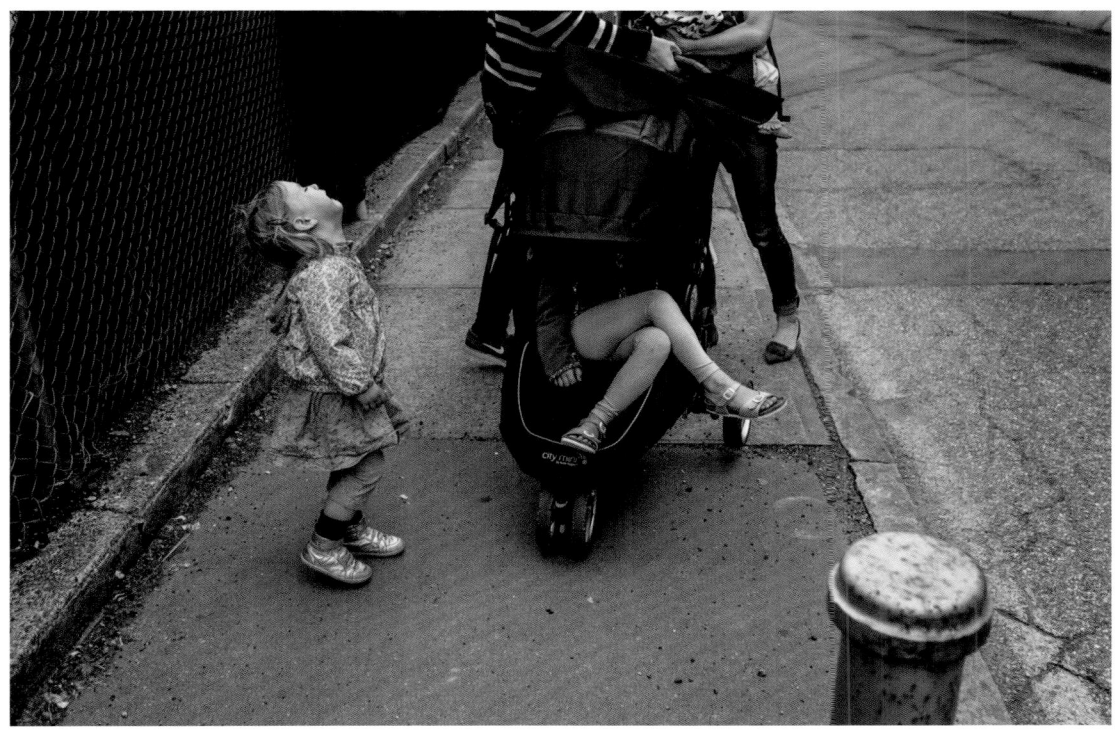

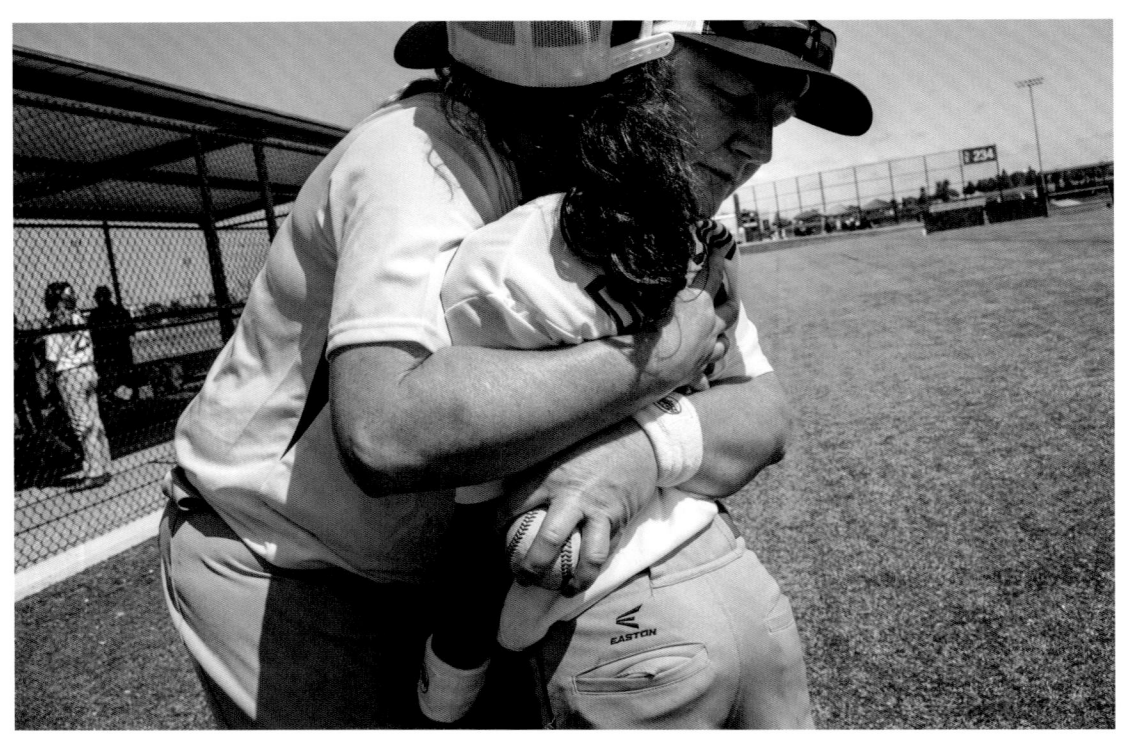

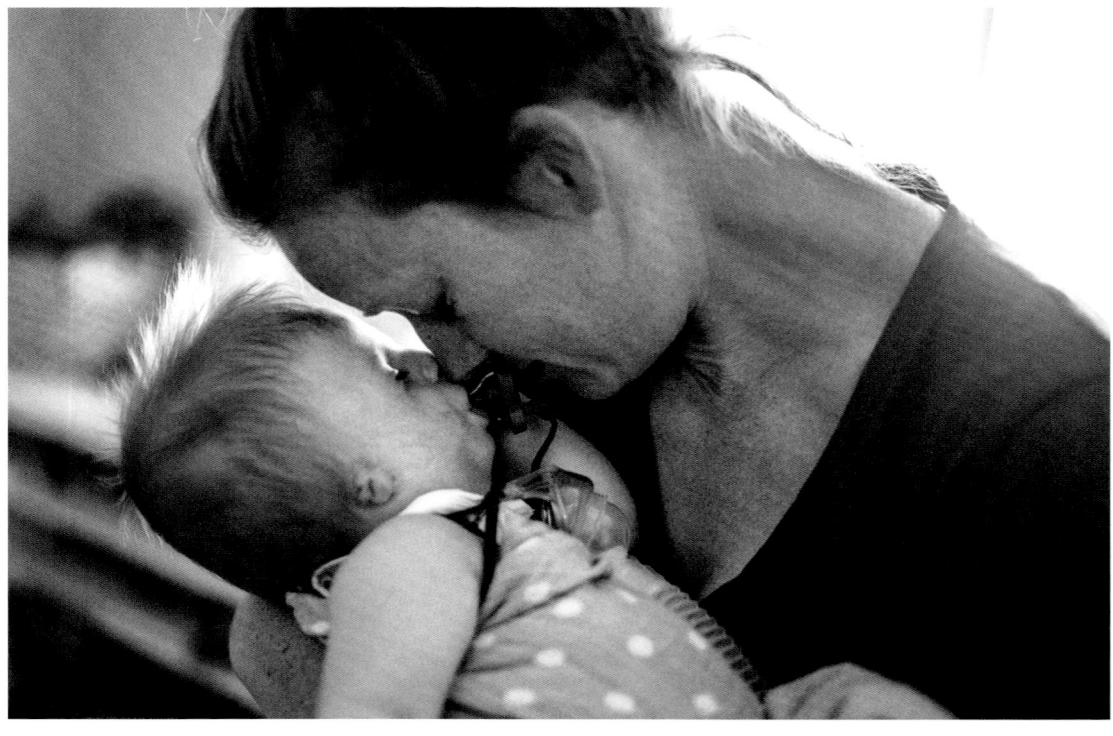

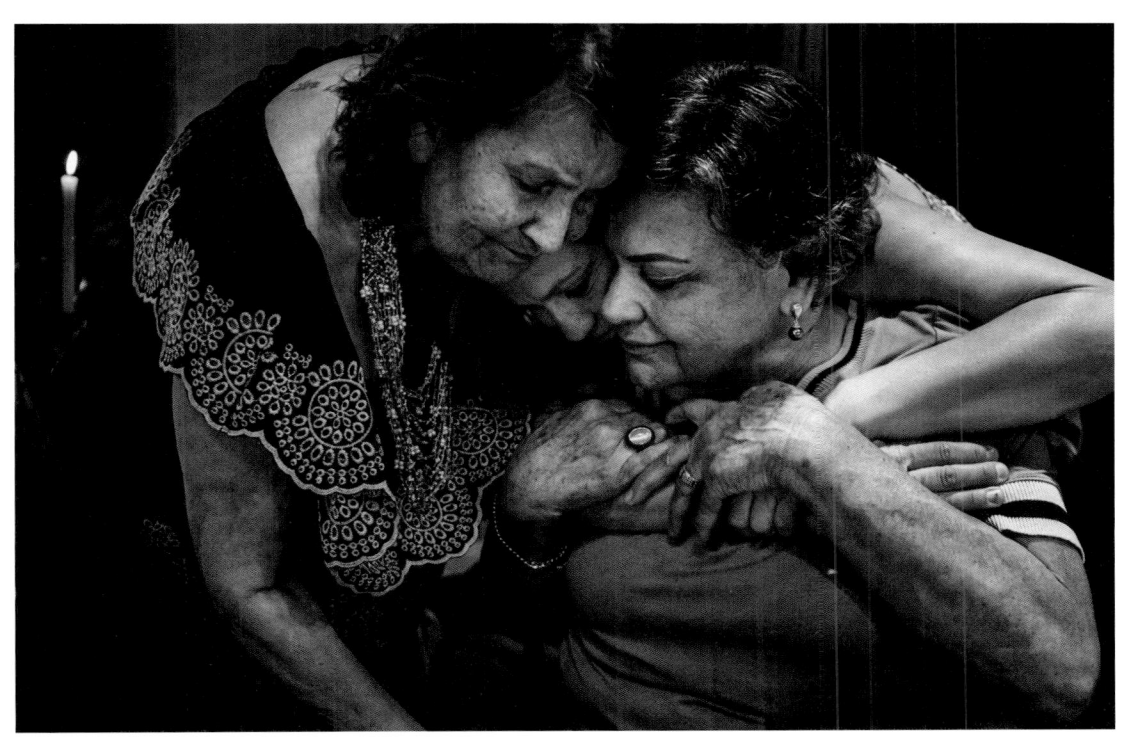

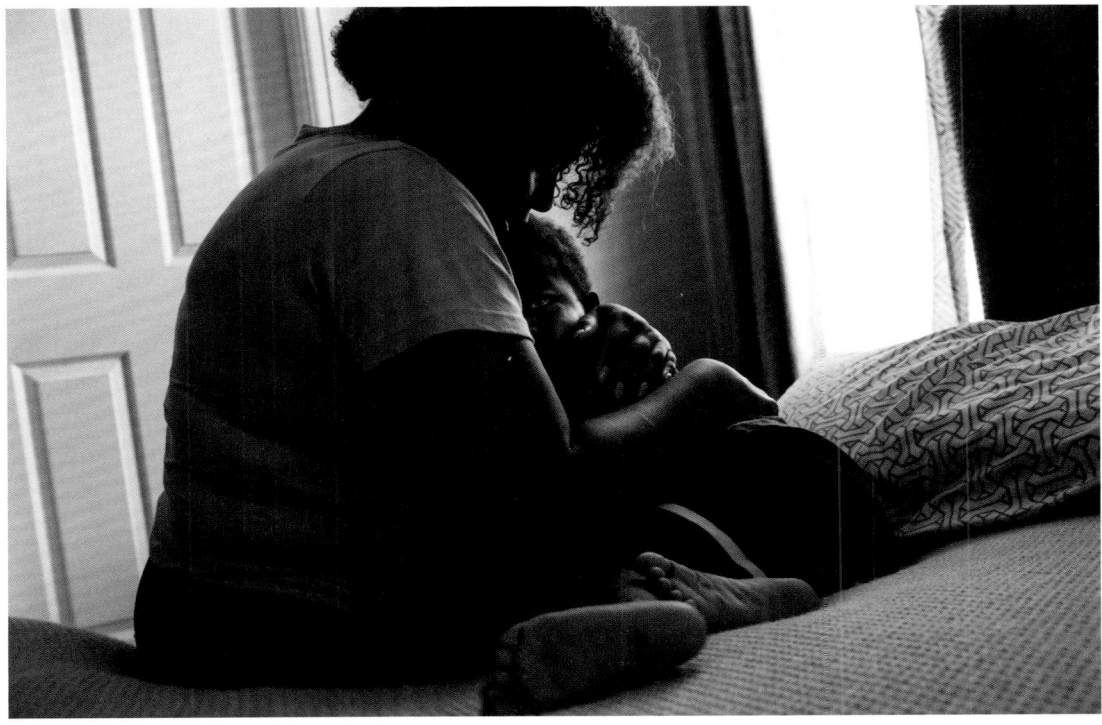

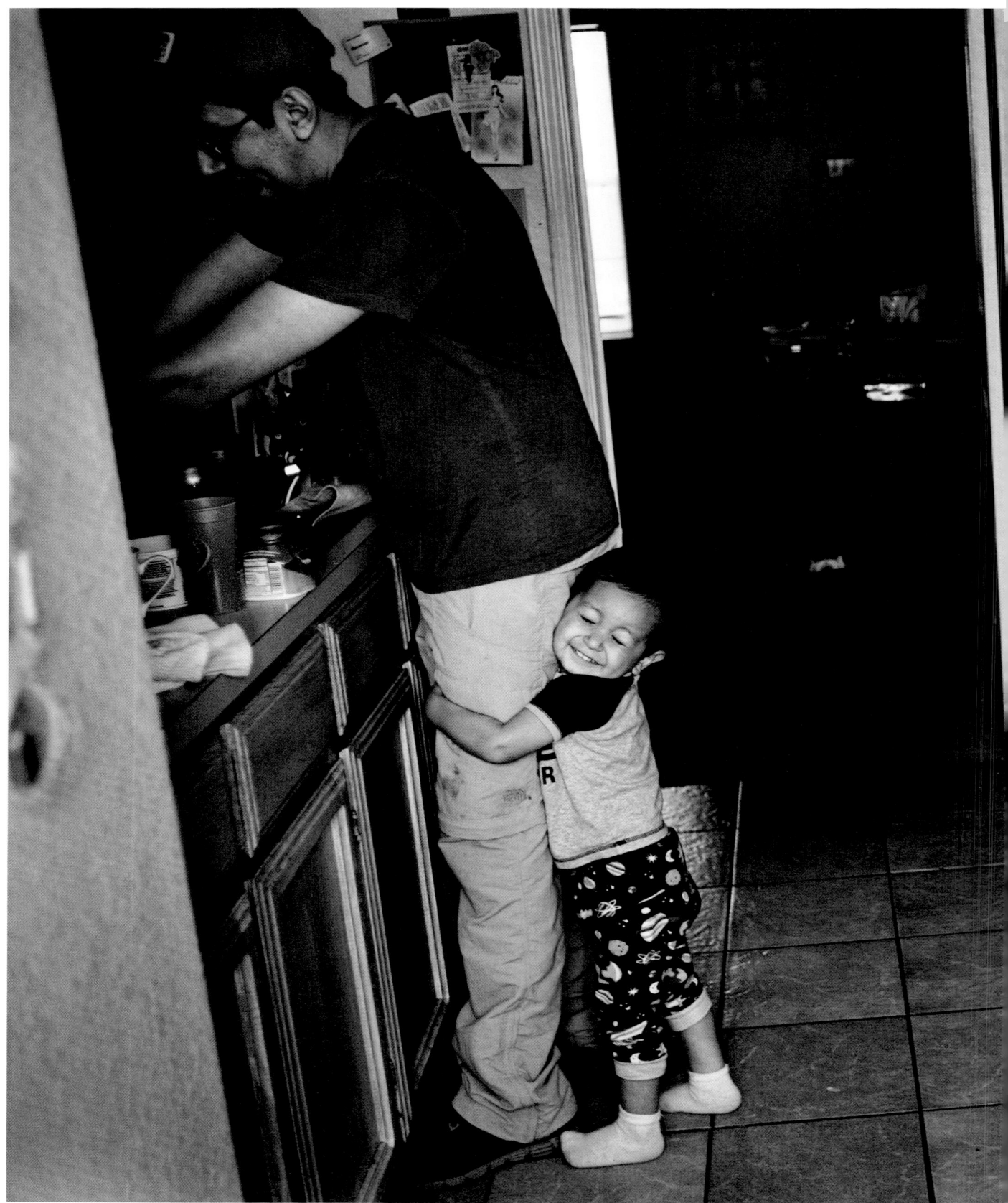

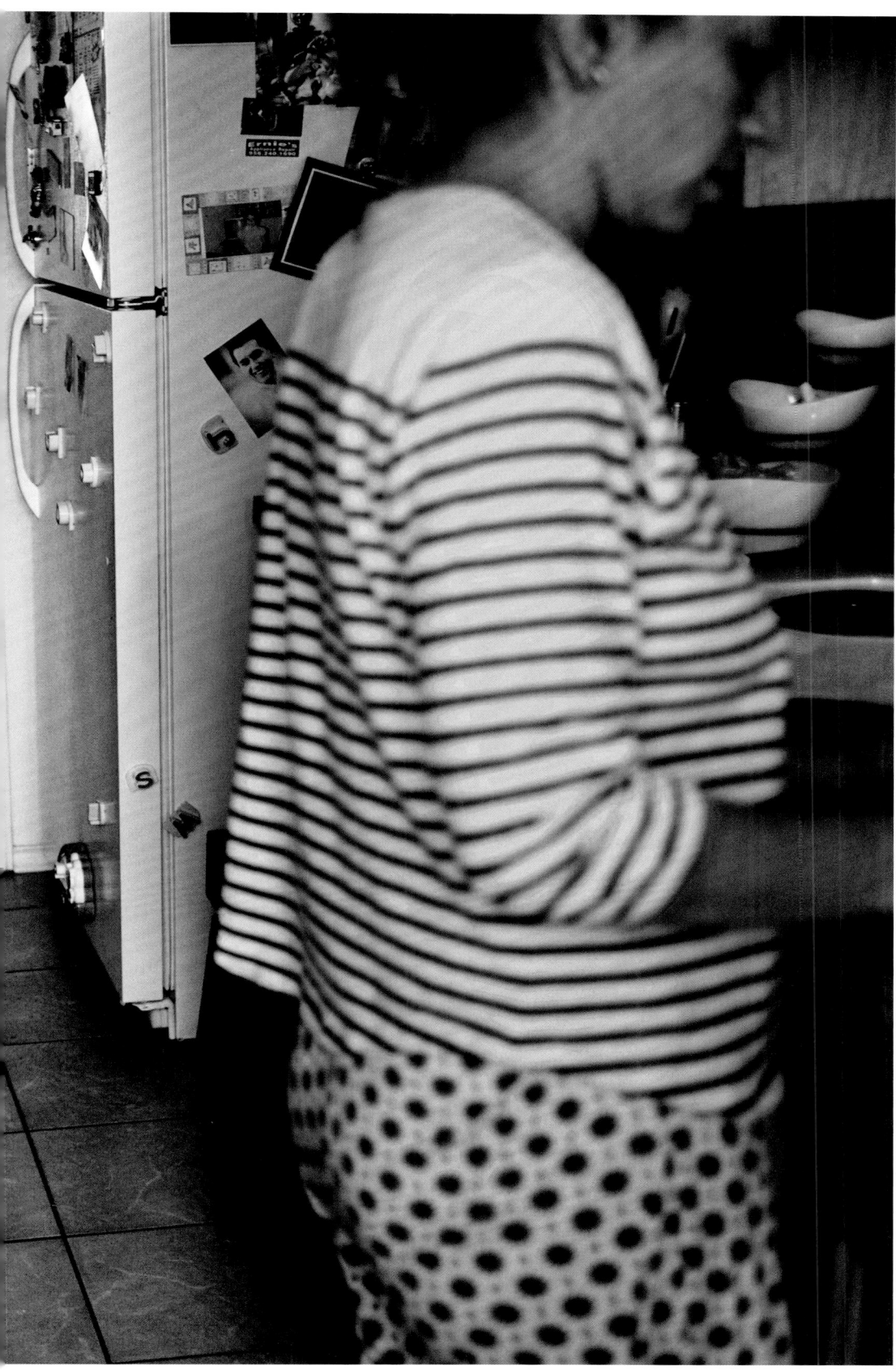

Fuck is a strong word, and you have to be careful with strong words.

But it's okay to say it when you're saying "I fucking love you."

—Oliver, age seven

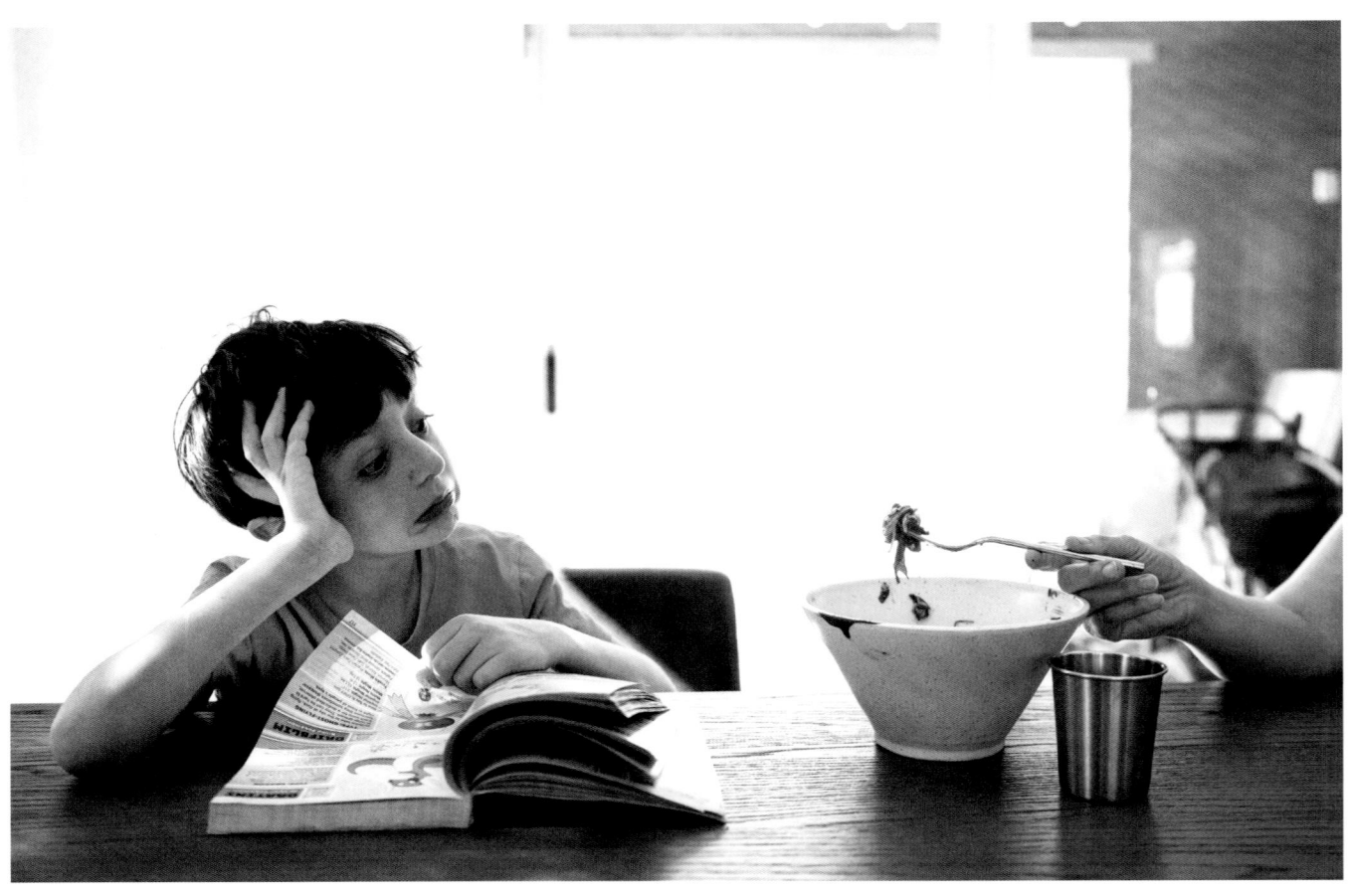

Parenting is basically a never-ending cycle of doing dishes, laundry, plunging toilets, catching vomit in your hands, apologizing for being late, and ramming your pinky toe into wood furniture over and over again.

Until you are dead.

So why waste it on eating raw celery?

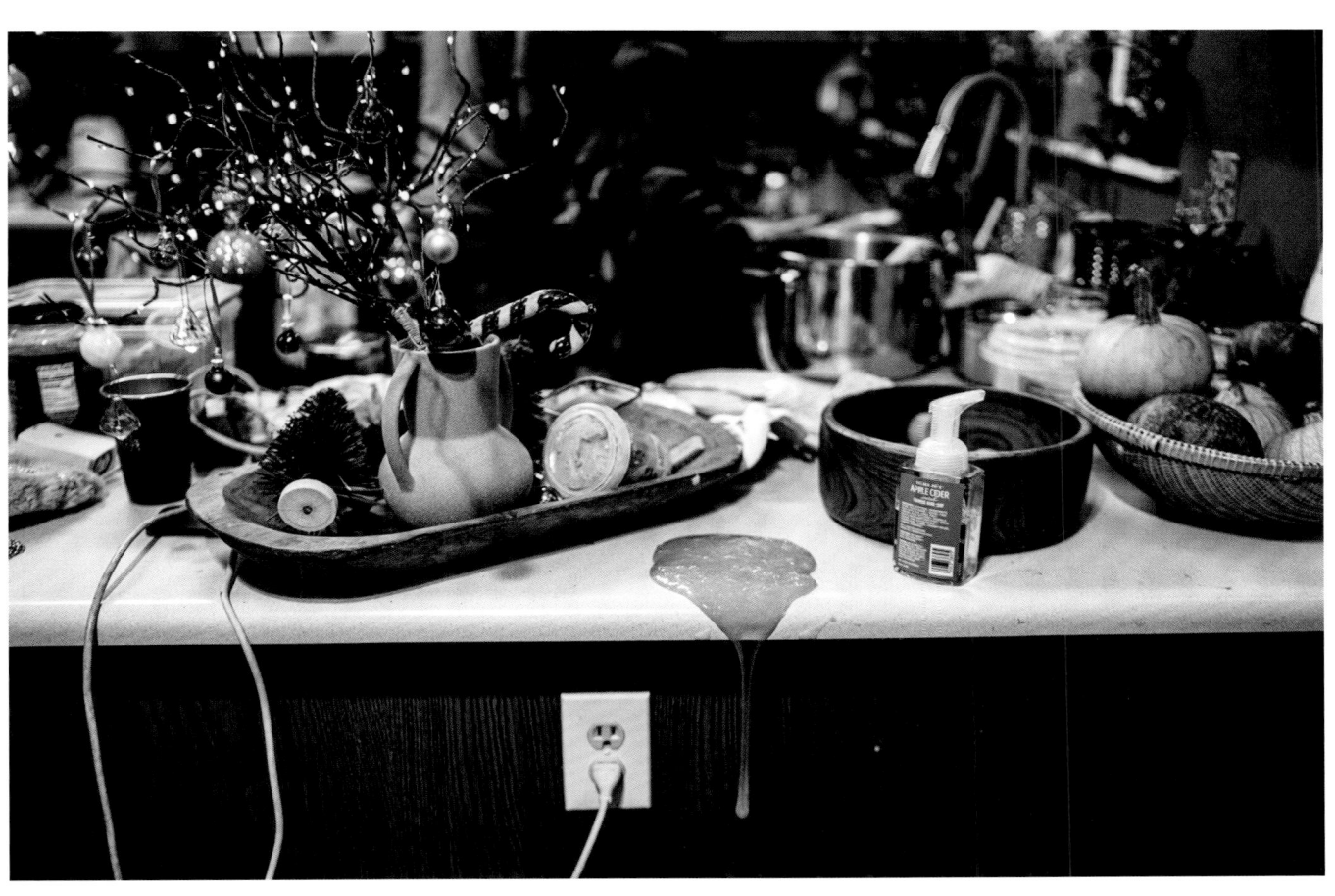

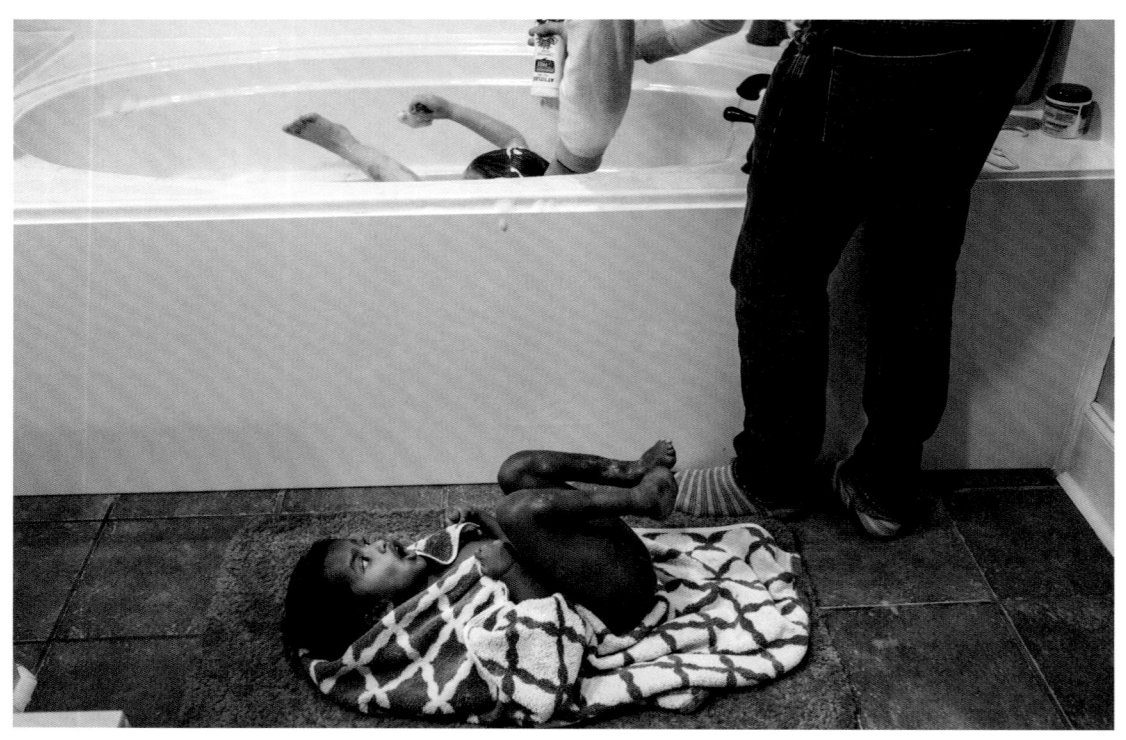

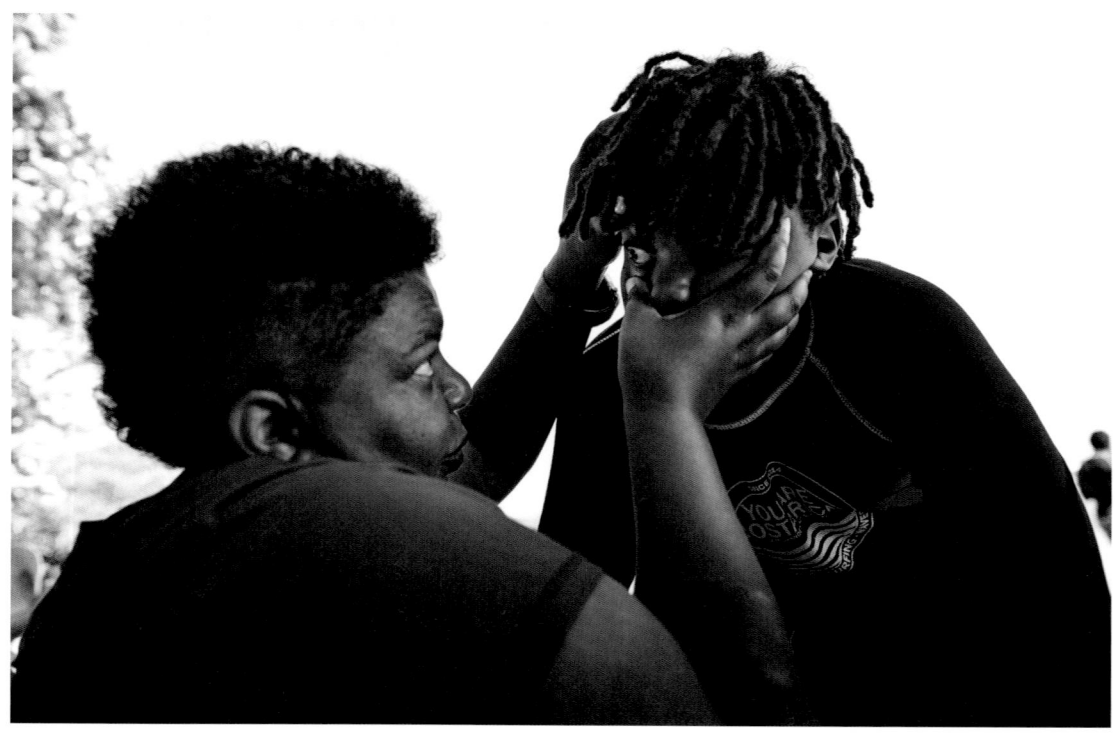

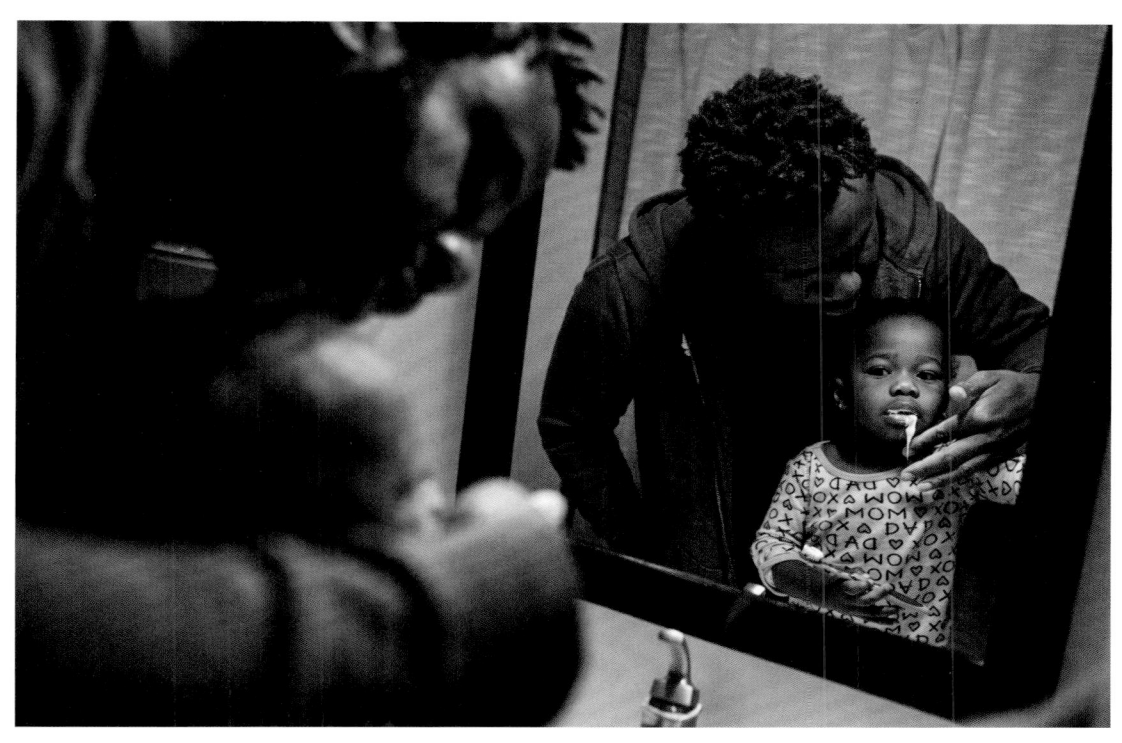

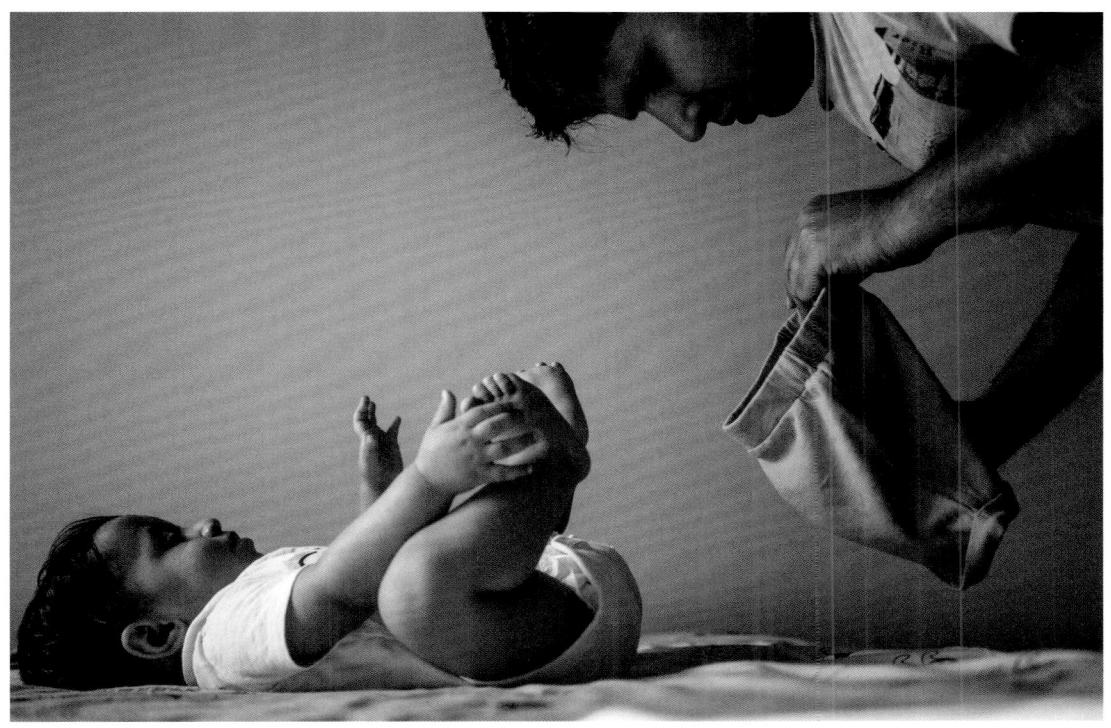

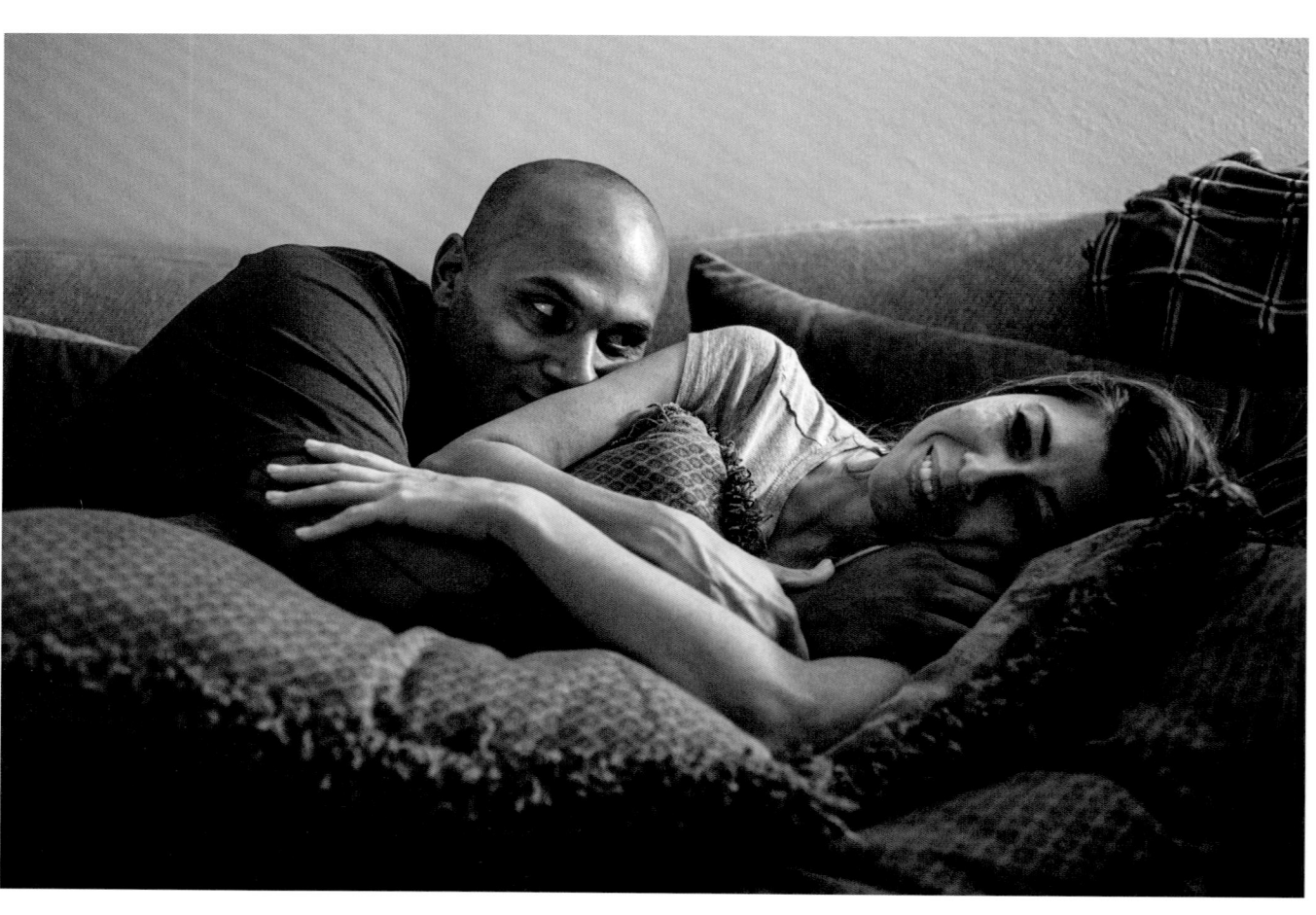

MODERN DAY FORTUNE TELLER

Prior to sending a pack of girls to deliver the most popular boy in 7th grade a hand written note requiring him to circle YES or NO, we'd consult our DIY paper oracle. The FORTUNE TELLER. Colors, numbers, places, random future predictions that sometimes included a secret message from Sloth and Chunk or getting a brand new Cabbage Patch kid from Caldors for Christmas. Before the invention of the Internet, hand held computer camera phones and virtual on-line worlds where anyone can be anybody, this nostalgic oragami toy filled in the gaps. In between sleep, school and kickball games in the dirt lot by the river, we would use fourtune tellers to engage with others.

It seems as though we are more disconnected than ever between technology, busy schedules and an over abundance of digital content. This is the *FORTUNE TELLER REINVENTED* . . . . .a kid made communication device to reconnect with other humans.

DIRECTIONS

1.

start with a square paper

fold the square in half diagonally from corner to corner. 'X' crease. unfold and repeat with the other corners. this creates an 'X' crease.

fold the corners to the center. with the paper flat, fold each corner inward so the points meet at the center of the 'X'.

turn the folded paper over so the flaps are face-down.

fold each of the new corners to the center point again.

create the finger pockets: fold the paper in half horizontally, press firmly, then unfold. repeat by folding it vertically and unfolding. these folds make it easier to manipulate later.

turn the paper over. slip your fingers under the flaps on the underside, creating pockets for your thumb and index fingers of both hands.

2. DECORATE

open each flap

write a fortune, action, or fun phrase inside.

on the outer triangular flaps, you can write numbers, colors, or symbols for selection.

3. QUESTIONS

Rather than fortunes, consider having questions that encourage entertaining, insightful, inspiring, vulnerable conversation!

EXAMPLES

What is the weirdest dream you've ever had?

If you could have any job, what would it be?

Who was your first best friend and why?

What makes you feel sad and what things do you do to make you feel better?

Where is your favorite place to go?

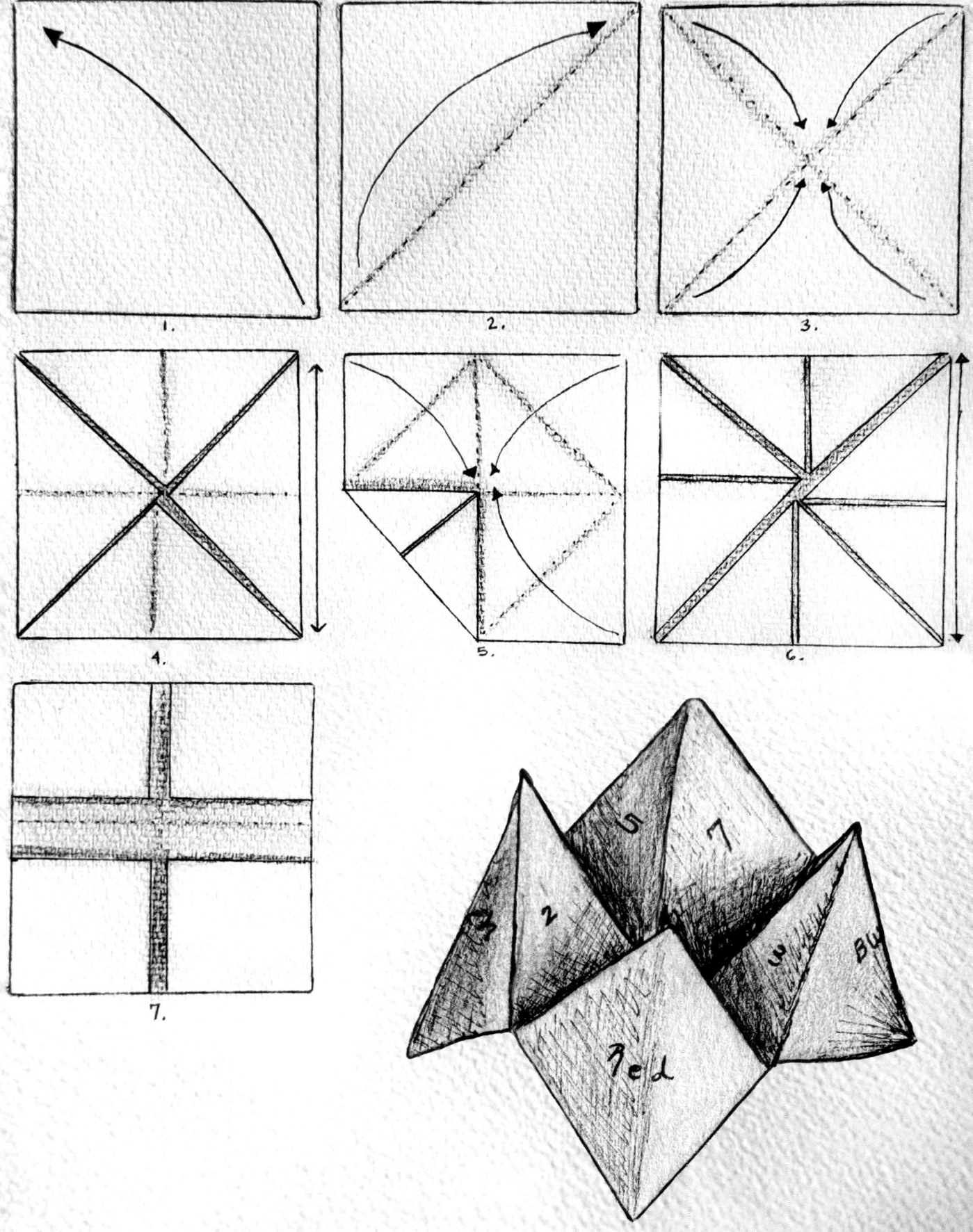

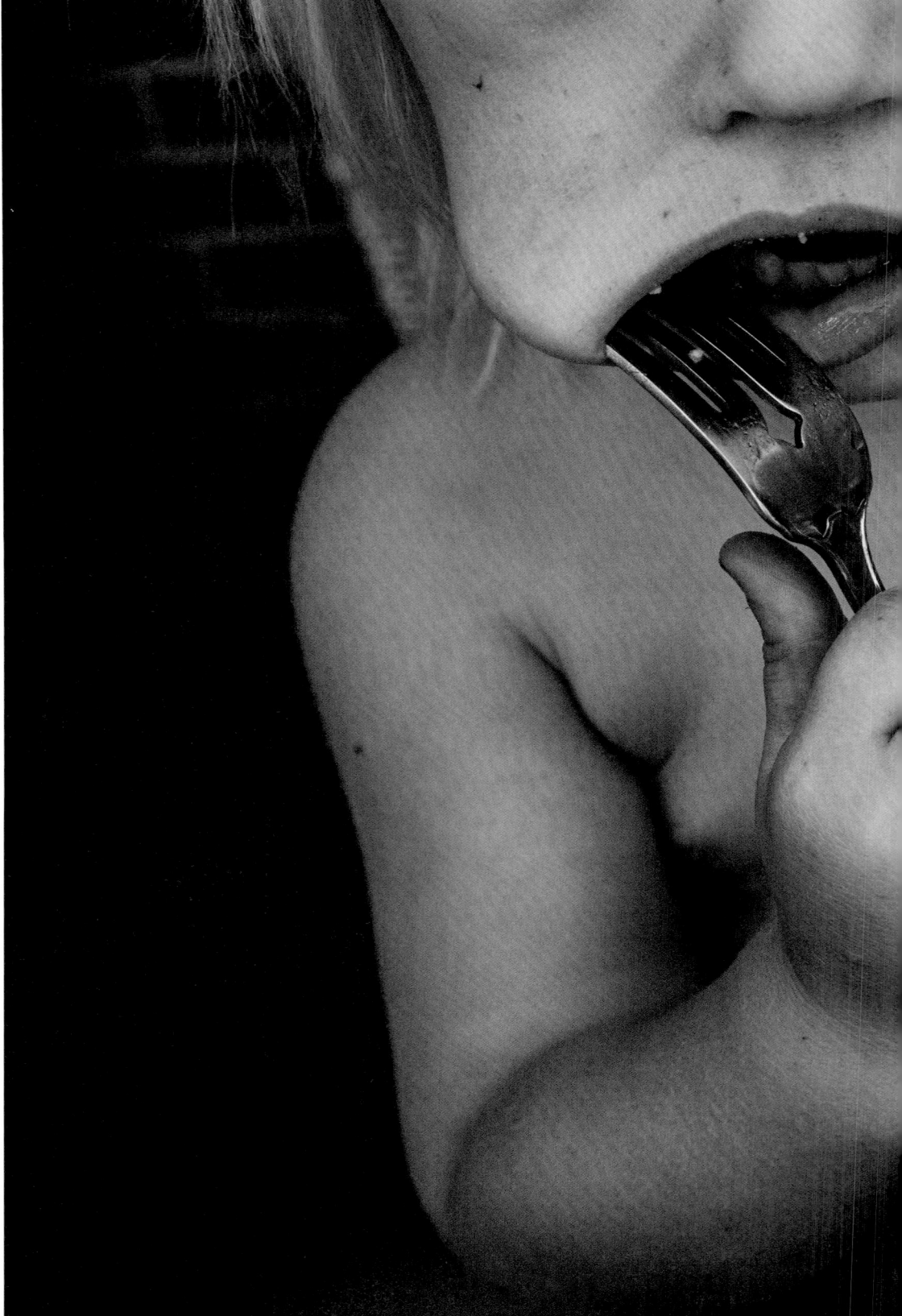

I hide peas in my
undies because you
never look there.
—Sarah, age three

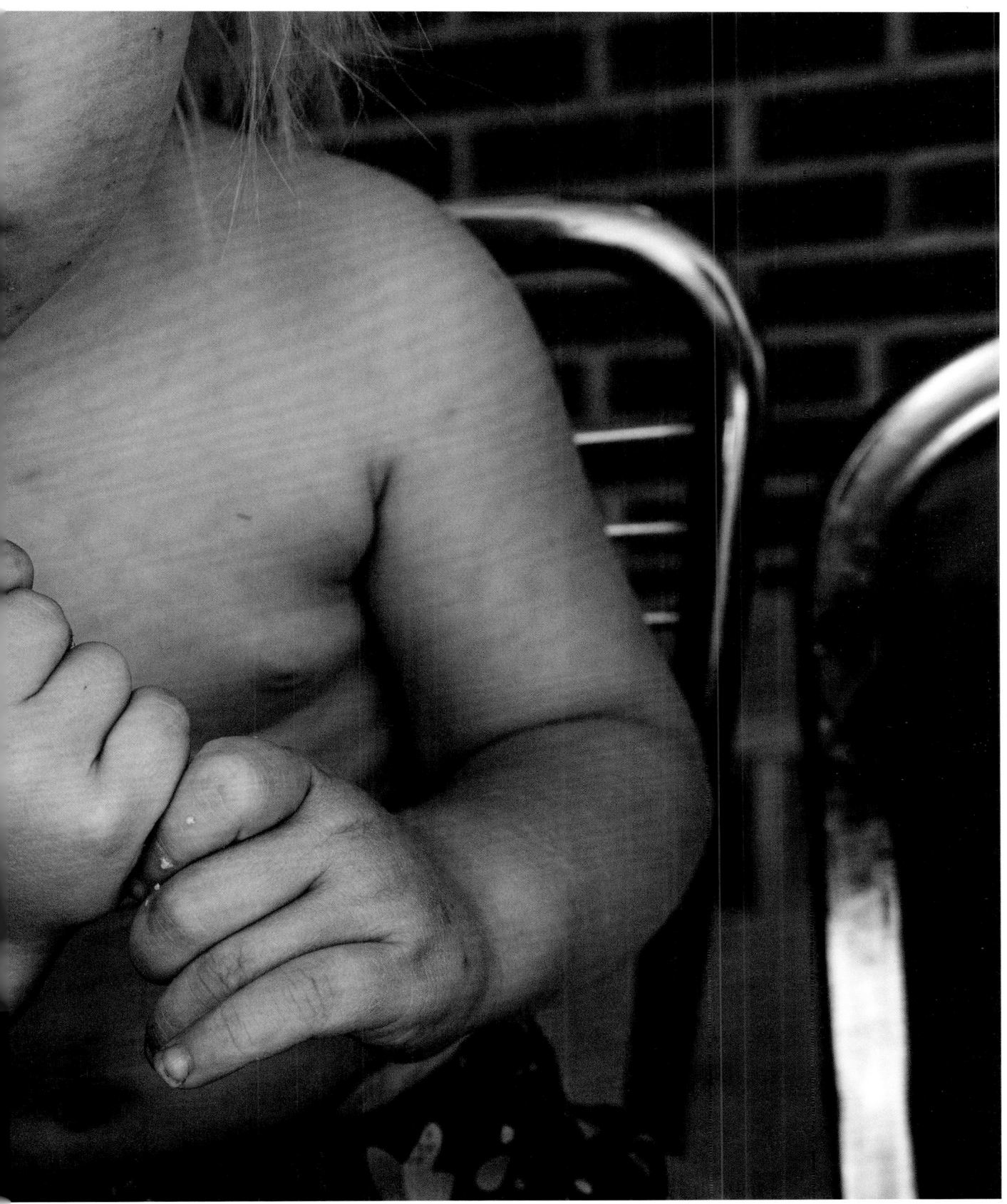

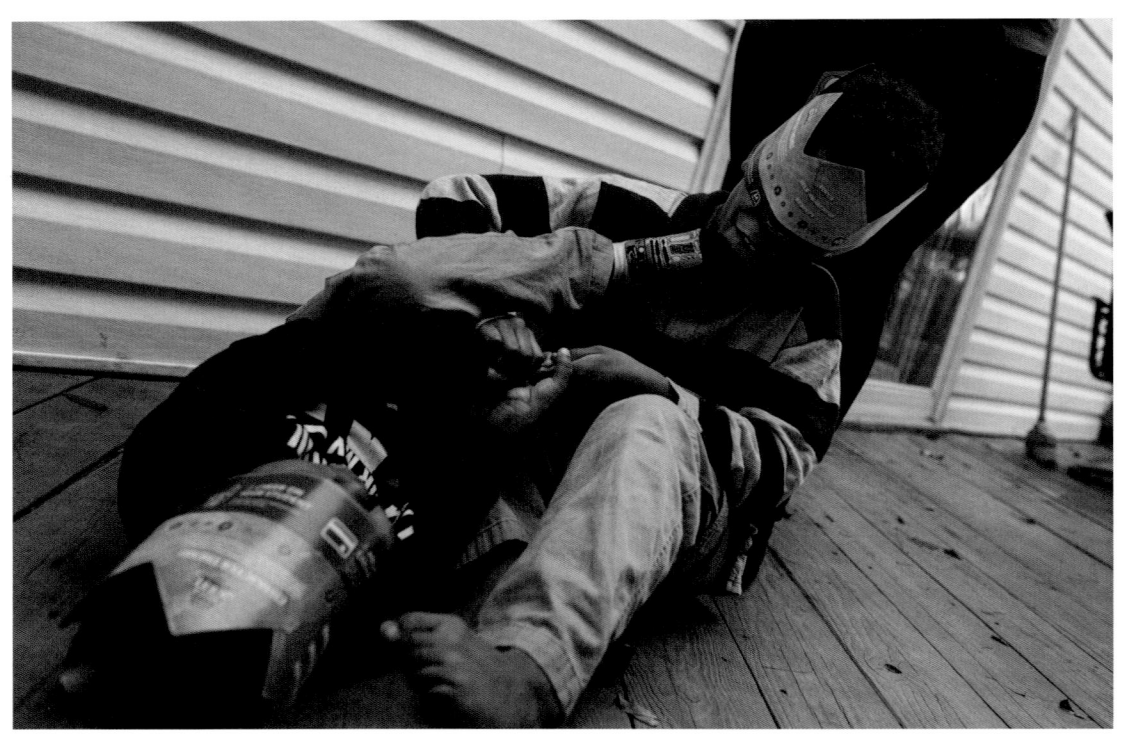

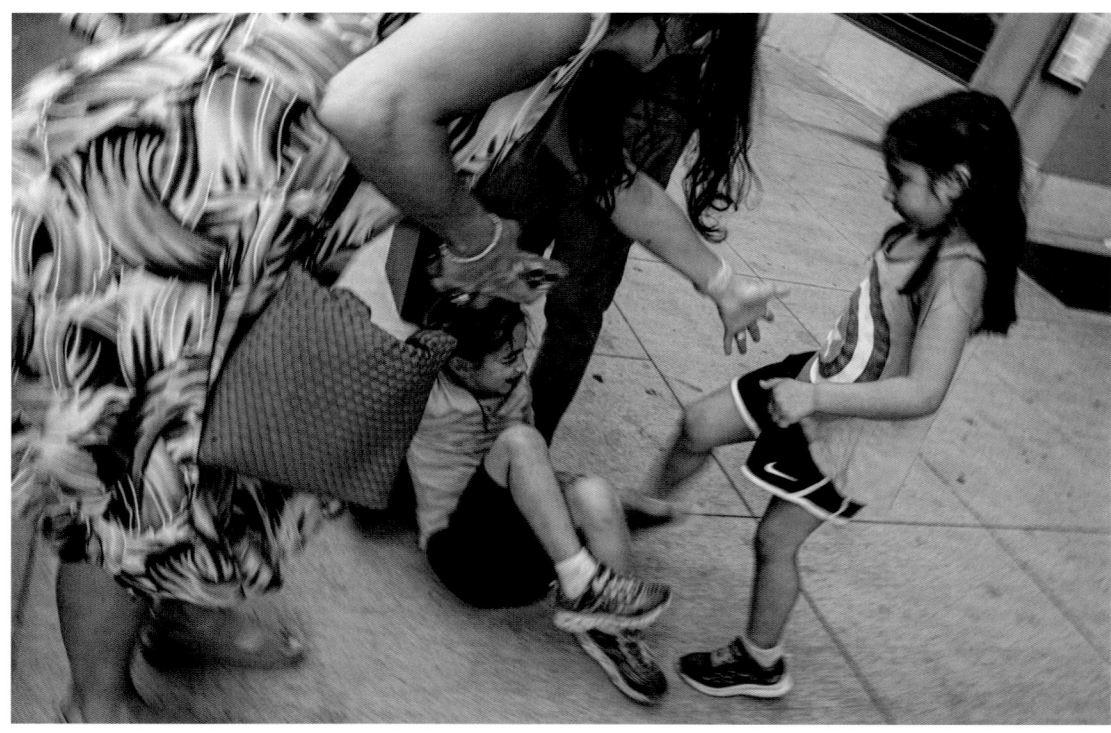

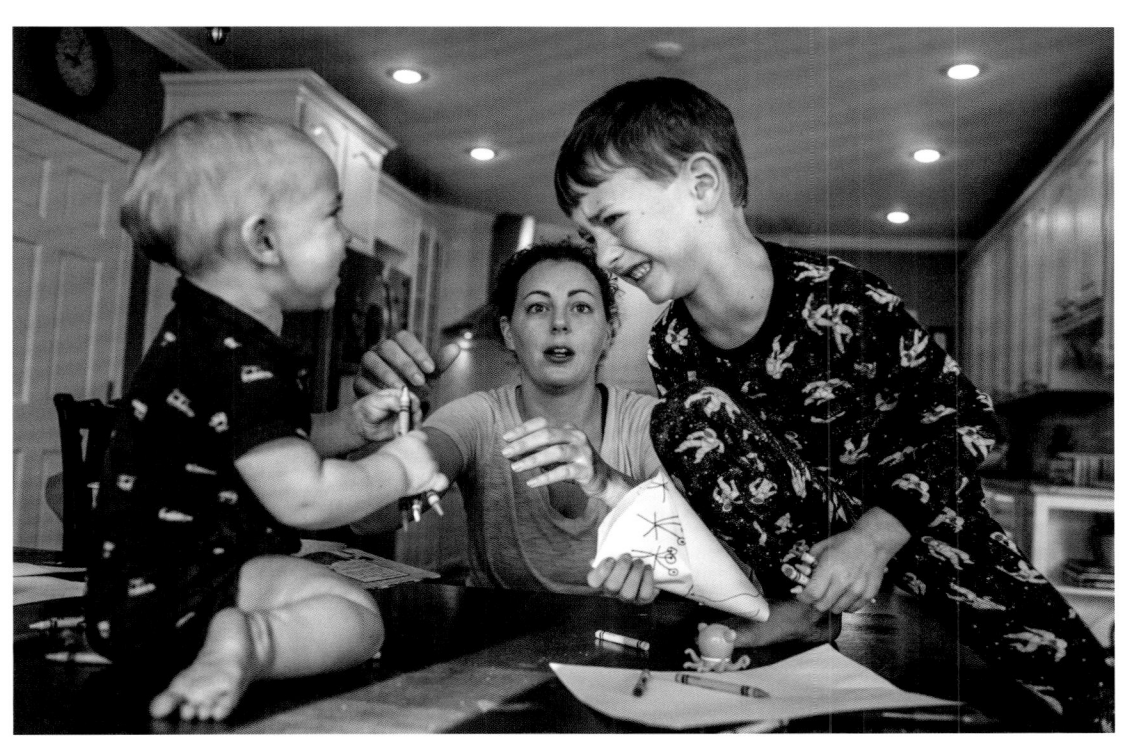

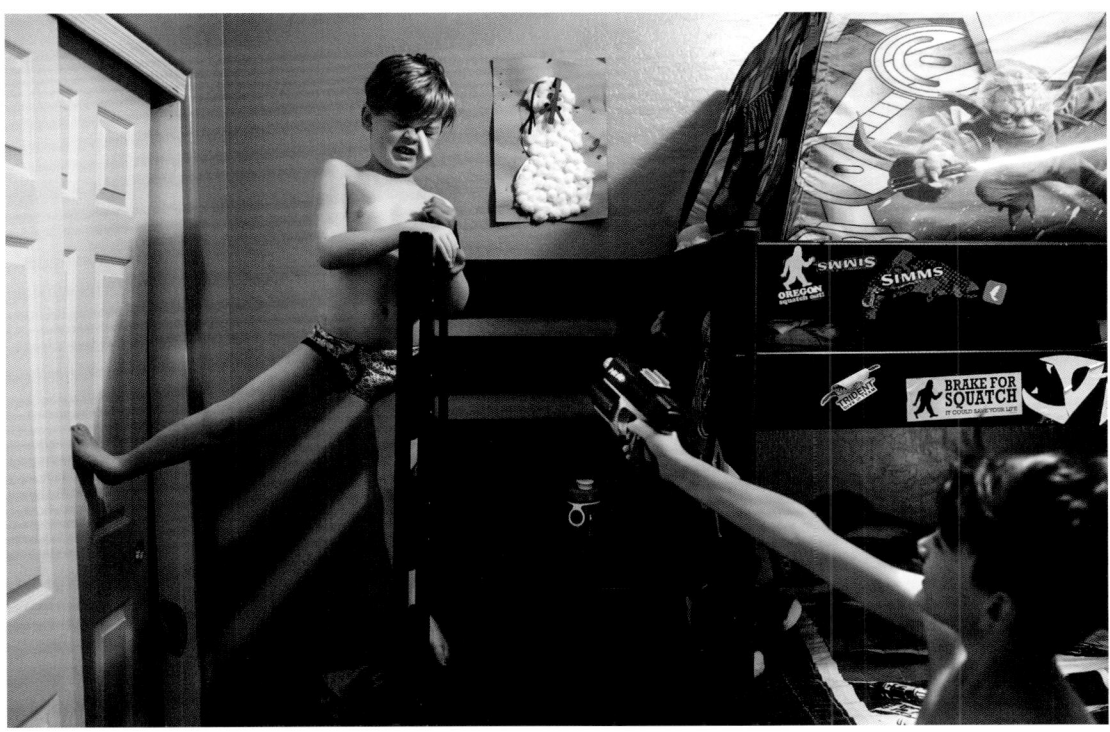

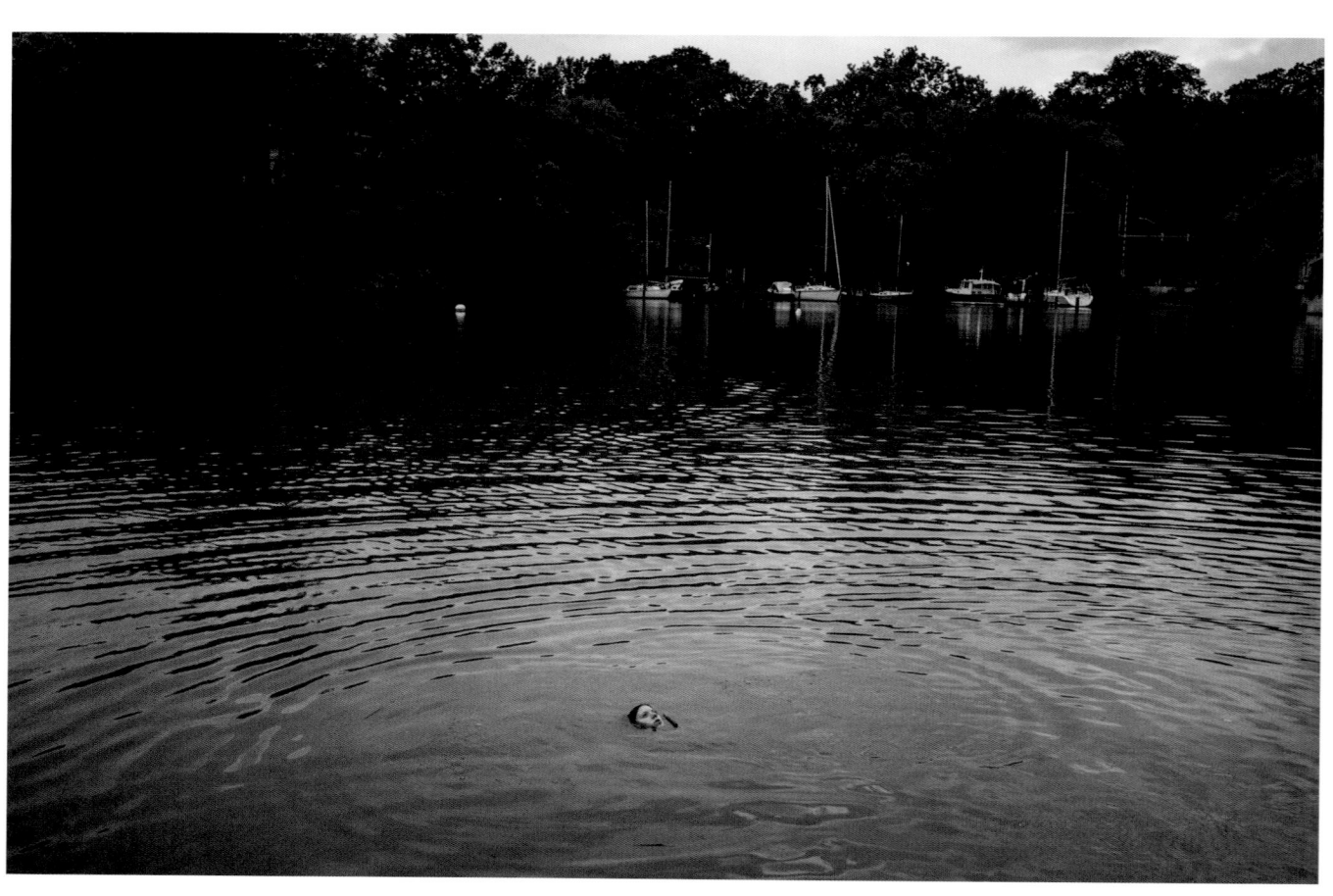

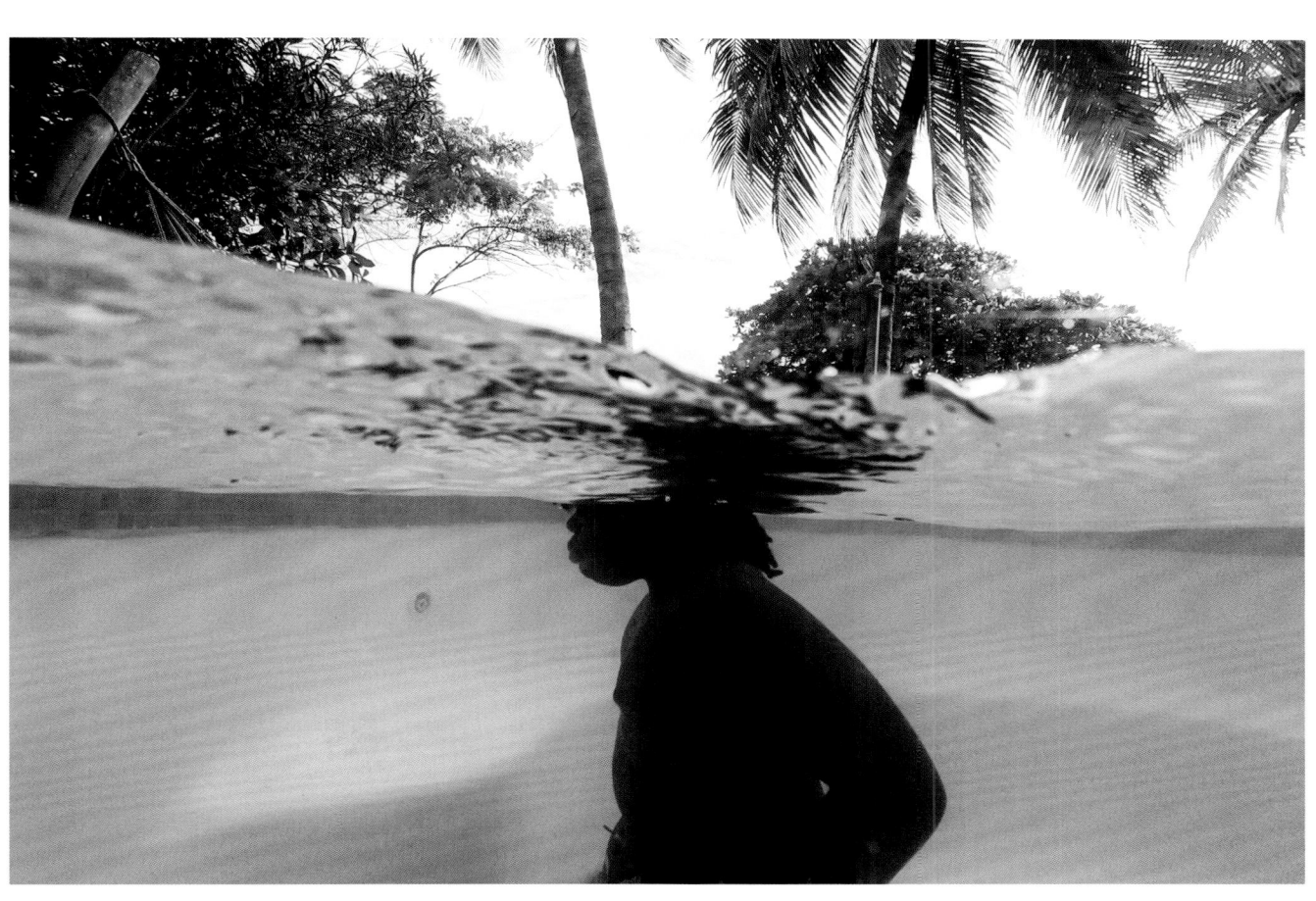

All humans experience what is referred to as childhood amnesia, where the brain is incapable of recalling episodic experiences. Photographs are a way to make up for the loss of these memories, preserving particular times in history.

While photographing this moment I, for the very first time in over twenty-five years, remembered the exact moment I watched my own father shave his face. I was fascinated that he could do so without ever cutting himself, followed quickly by intense fear: "Oh my God am I GOING TO GROW HAIR ON MY FACE TOO?" My father assured me that I would not, and now, at forty-seven years old I can confidently say my father is a big fat liar. You will, in fact, start growing hair on your face out of nowhere. And it will grow faster than any other hair on your body. You will go to bed one night with no hair and the next morning there will be three one-inch-long whiskers proudly thriving out of a brand-new mole on your chin.

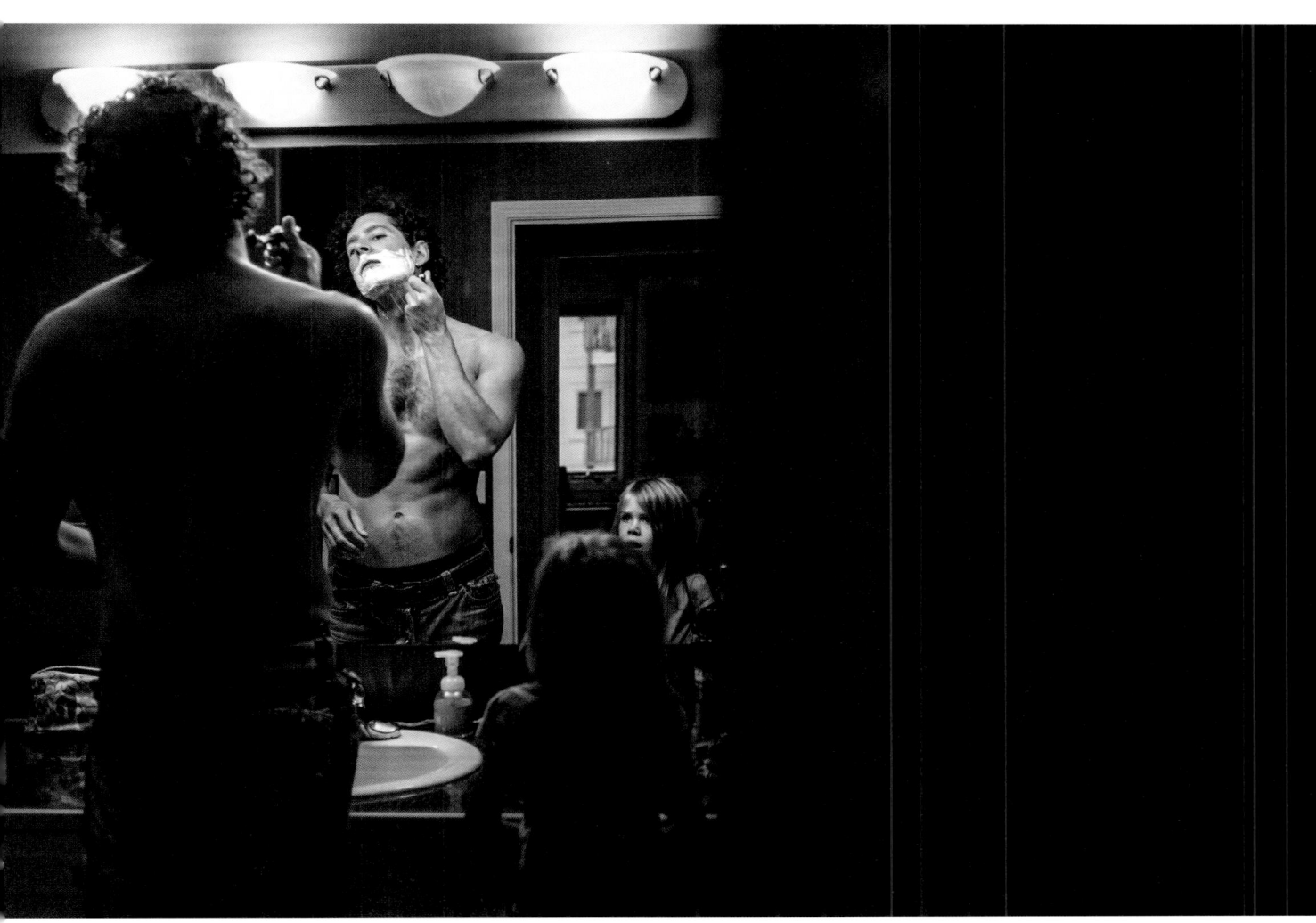

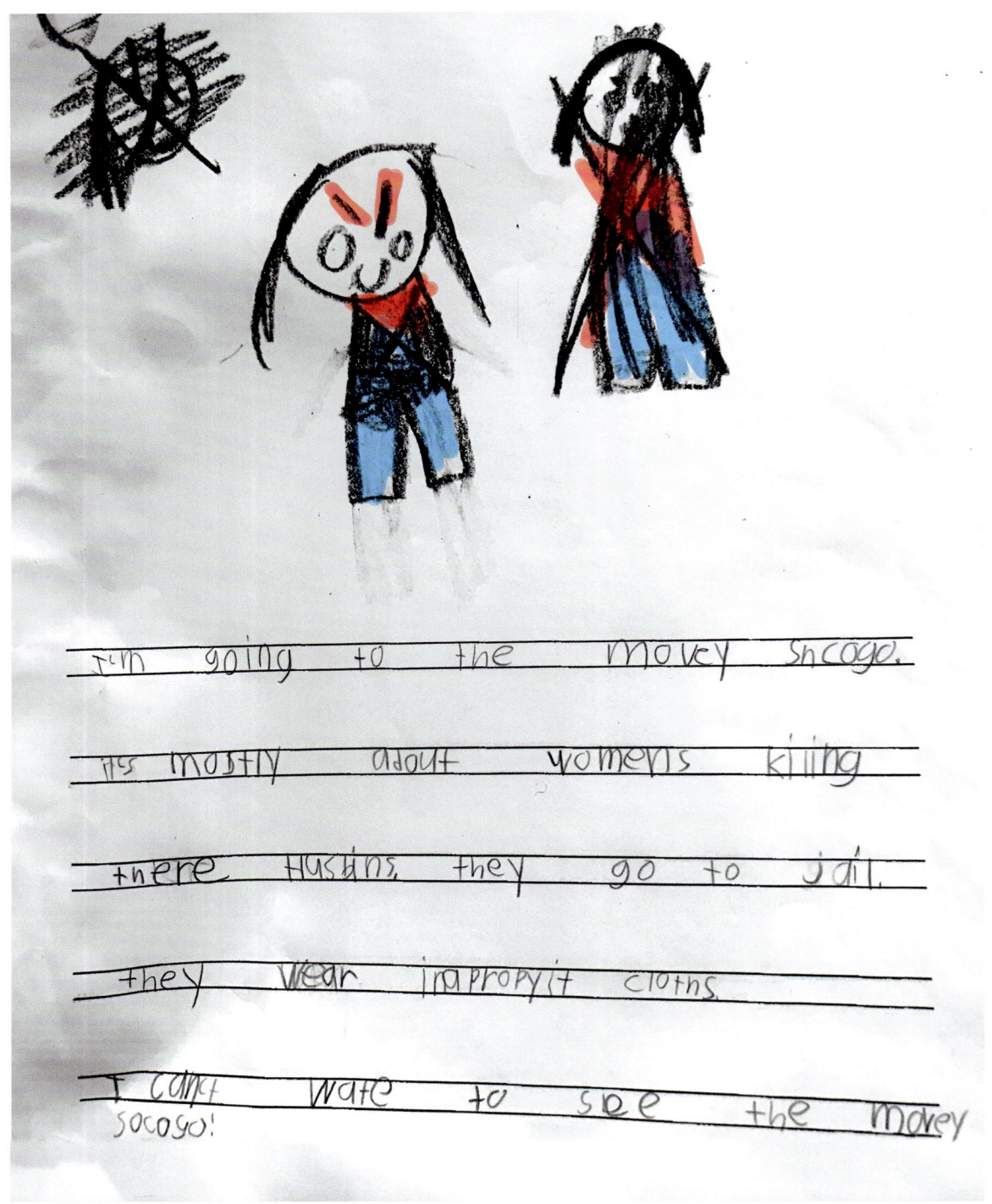

I'm going to the movie Shcogo.

Its mostly about womens kiling

there Husbns. they go to jail.

they wear inapropyit cloths.

I cant wate to see the movey socogo!

I'm going to the movie *Chicago*. It's mostly about women killing their husbands. They go to jail. They wear inappropriate clothes. I can't wait to see the movie *Chicago*.

—Lucy, age seven

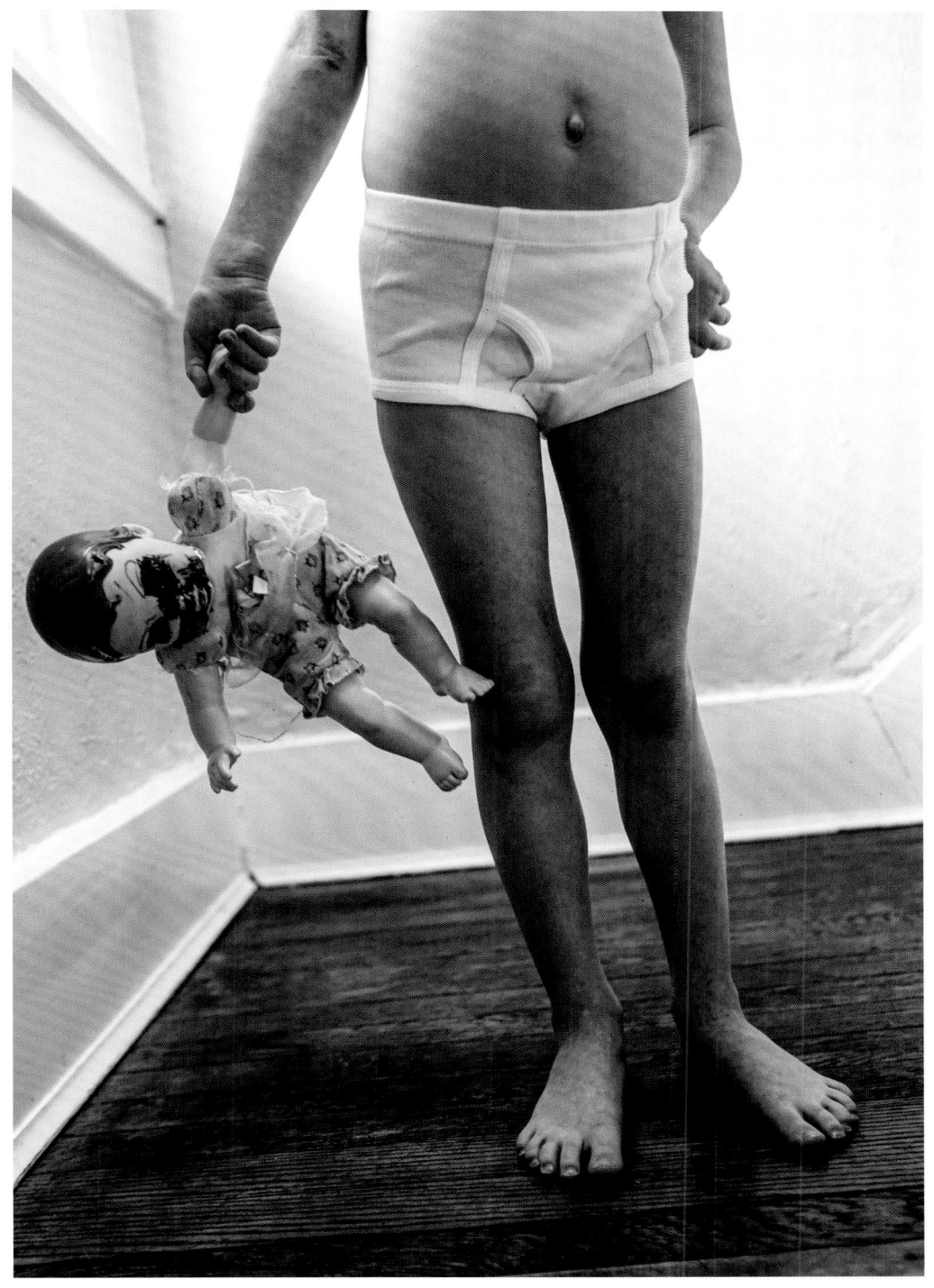

Conversations with a mom, a kindergarten teacher, and a five-year-old

Ruthie's teacher: I'm just calling to check in. Ruthie told a couple of her friends that you were in jail and I wanted to see if everything was OK.

Me: Definitely not in jail.

Ruthie: They wanted to have a playdate and I didn't feel like having friends over. It was the first thing I could think of.

—Kaysie Berry

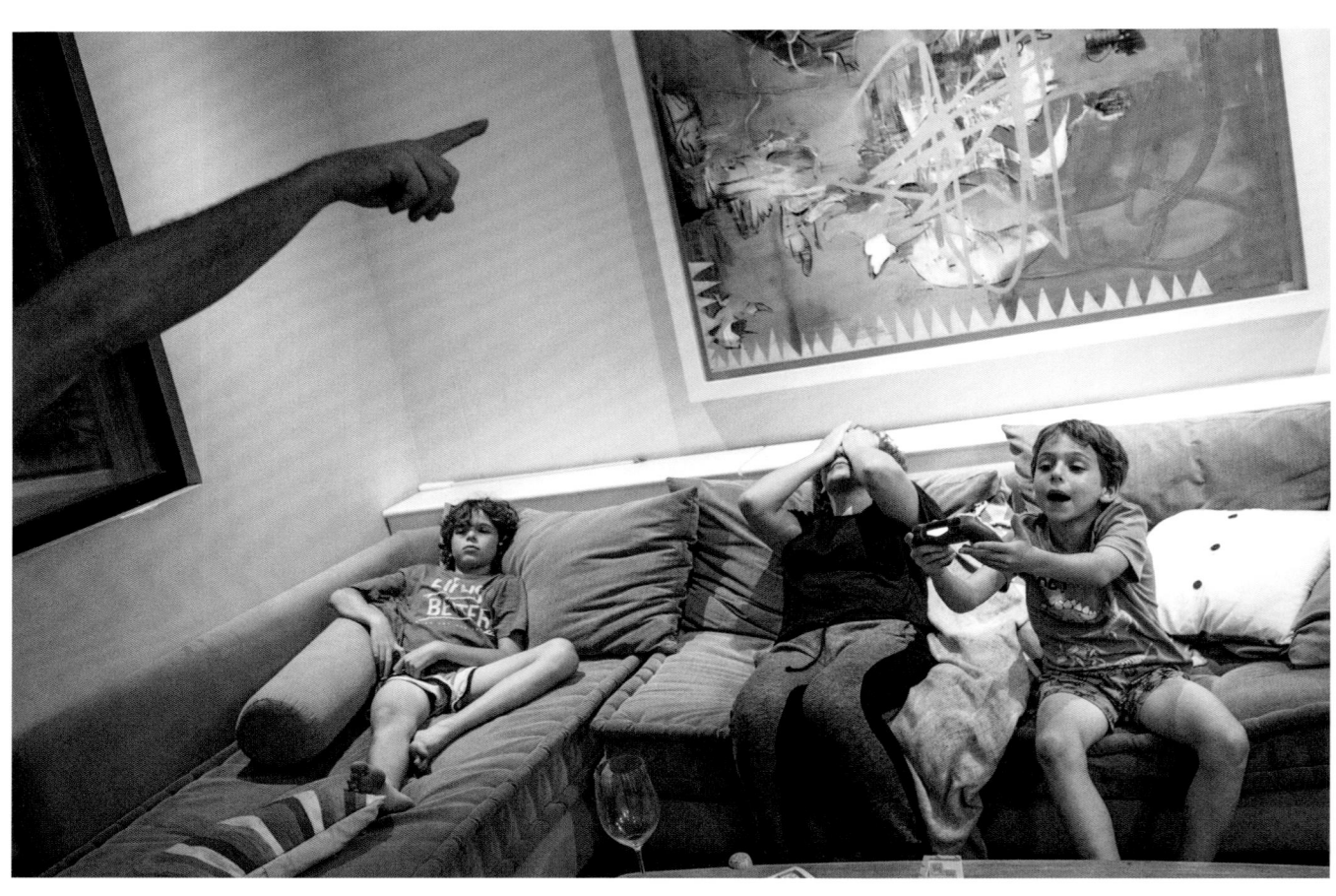

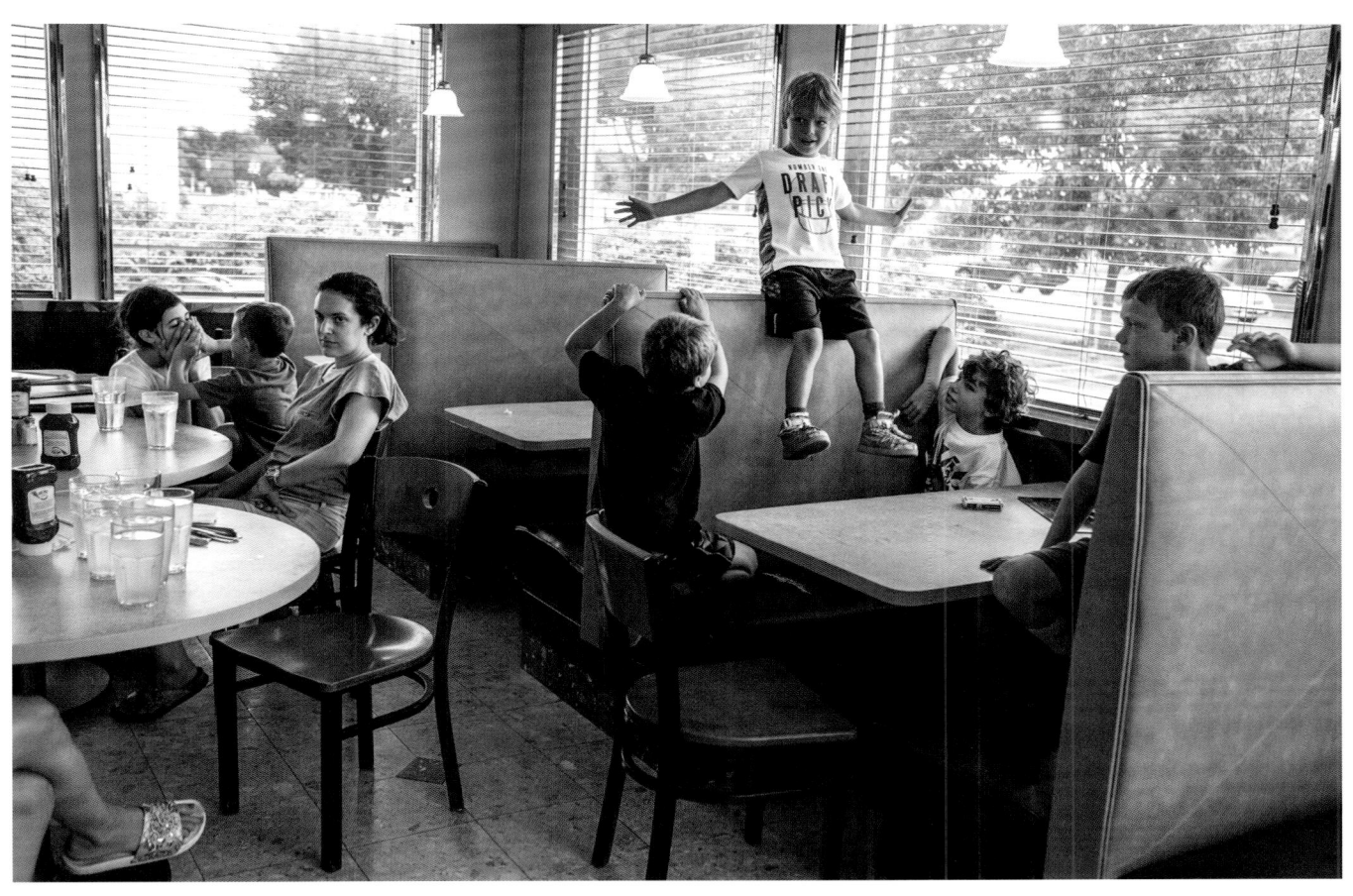

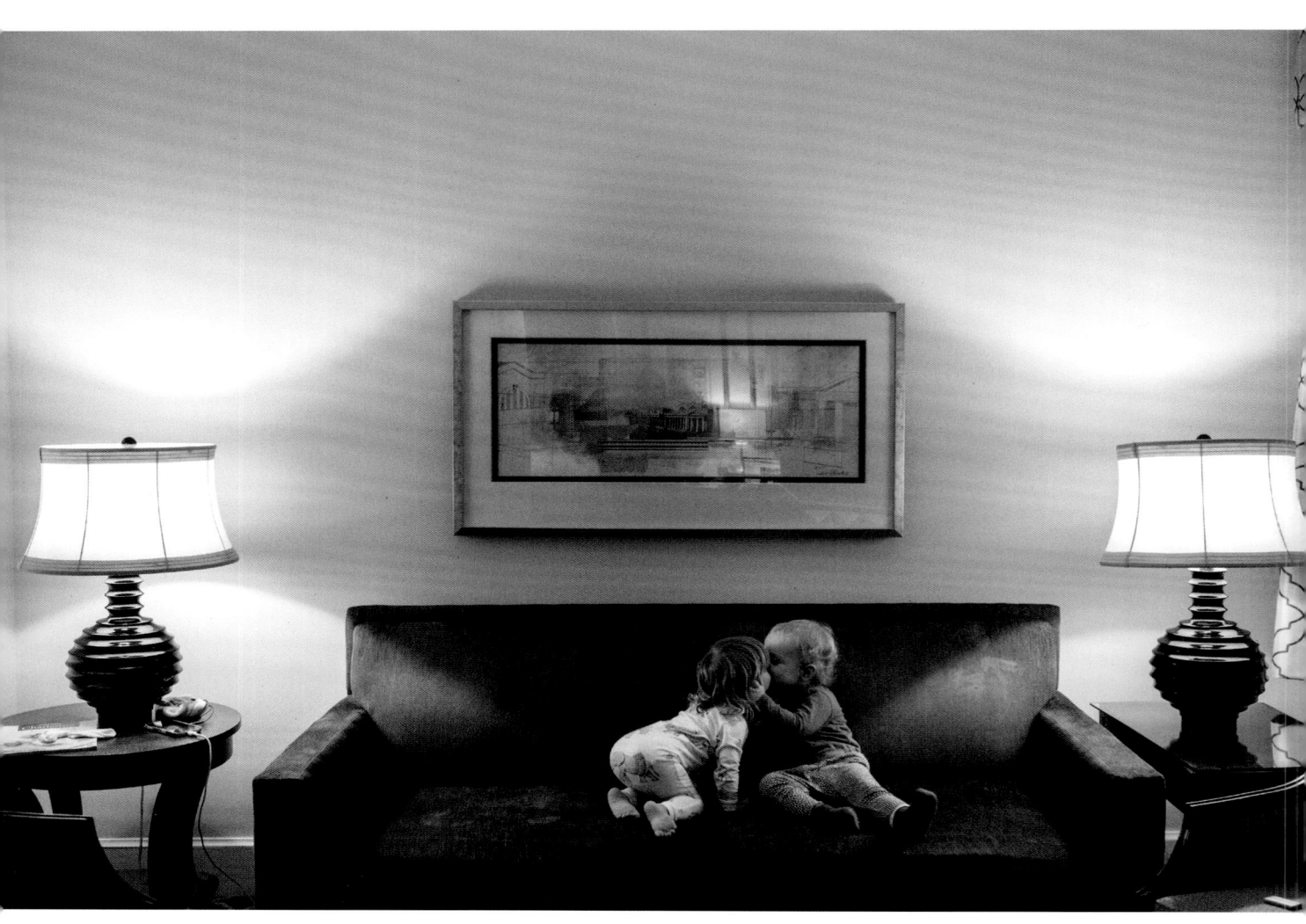

I'll open myself up to suitors at age twenty-five.
—Ainsley, age sixteen

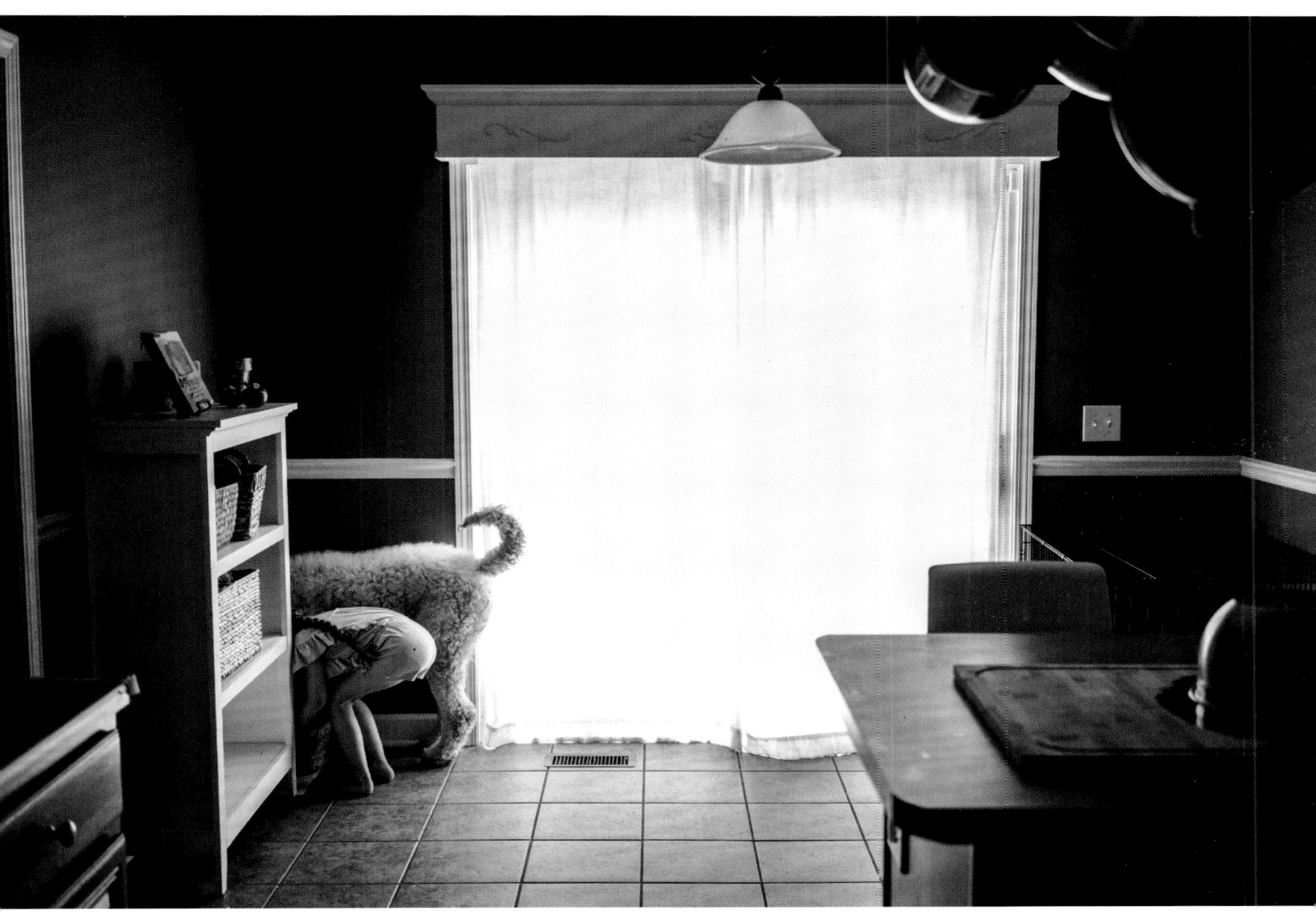

Without a face you're just an alien with nipples.
　—Olive, age six

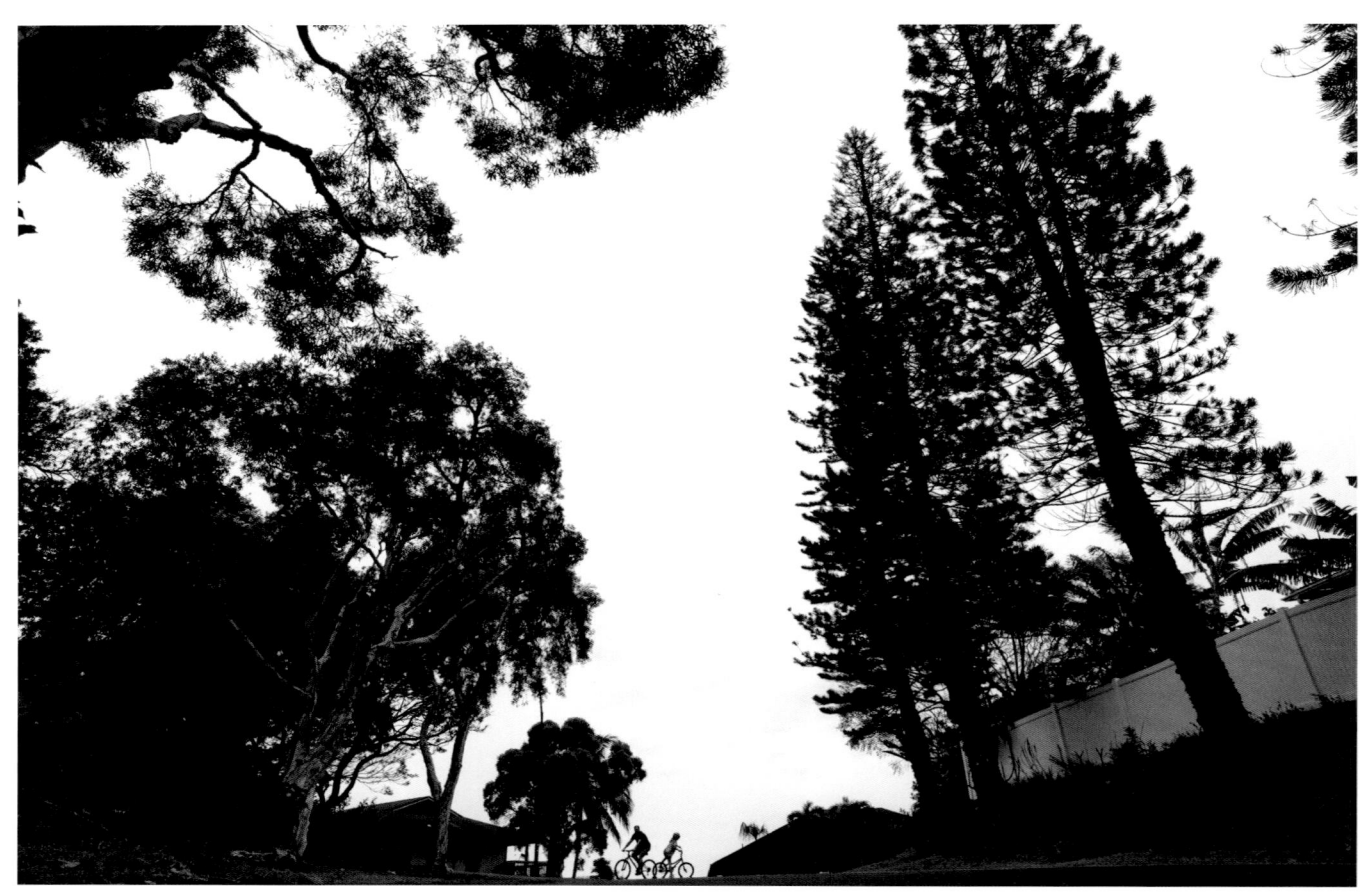

In my experience, men (including myself), whether by nurture or nature, tend toward being great at fixing things. However, emotion-based issues often can't be fixed by this problem-solving approach, and it's useful to stop and ask (sometimes out loud) whether an issue needs a solution, or whether you need to listen, validate, give a hug, or all of the above. I find this is great advice for all relationships.

—Robert Turek

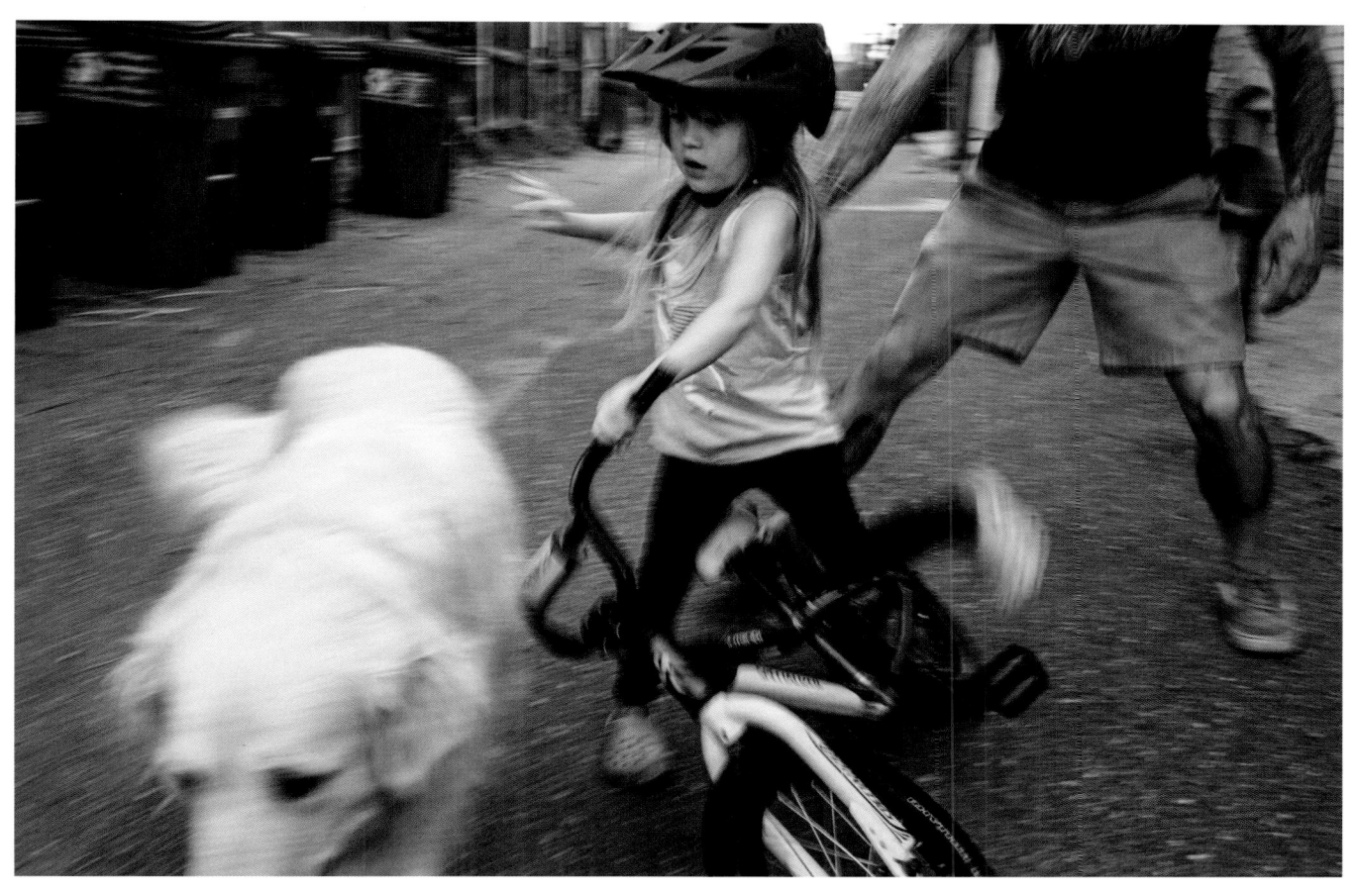

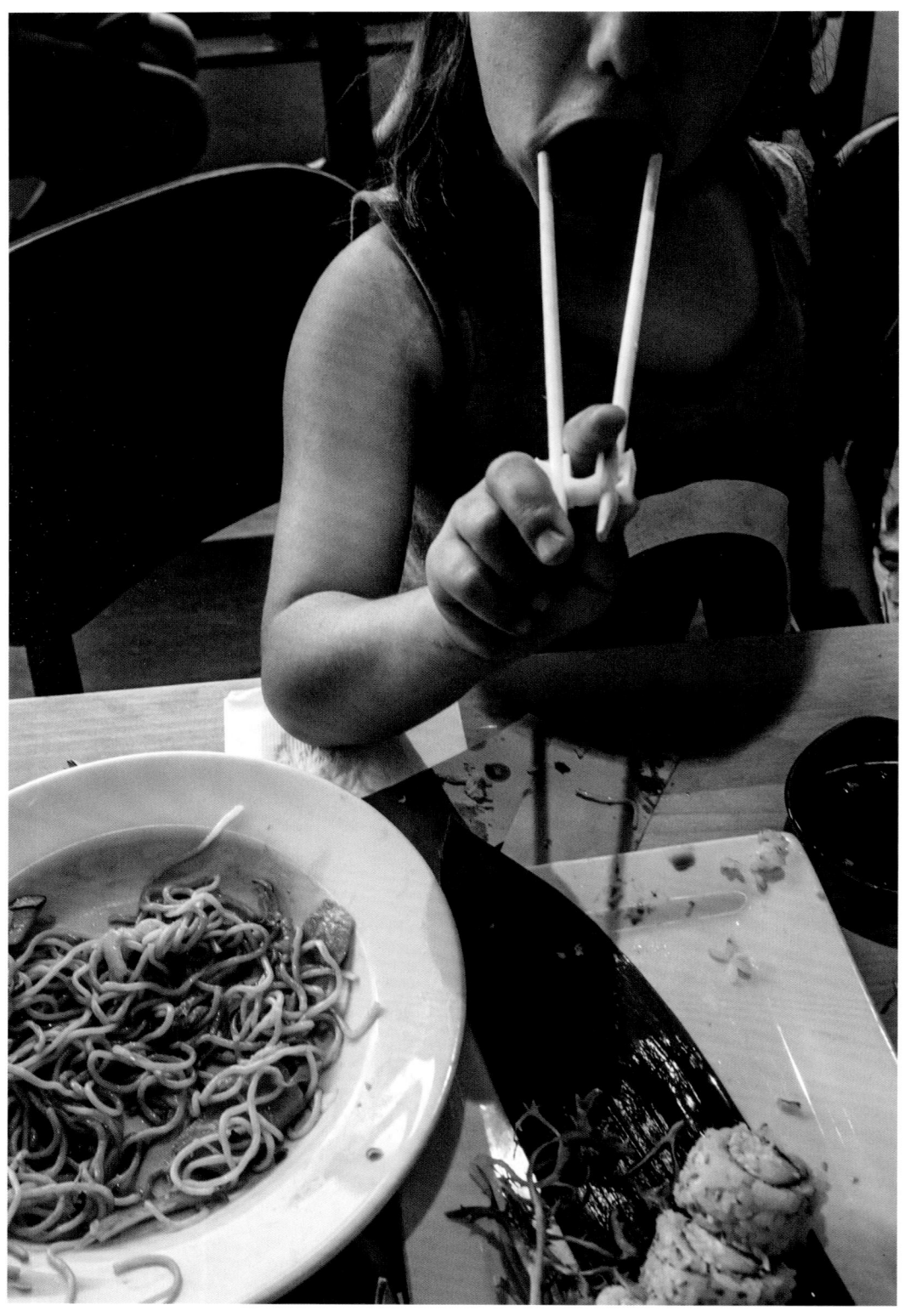

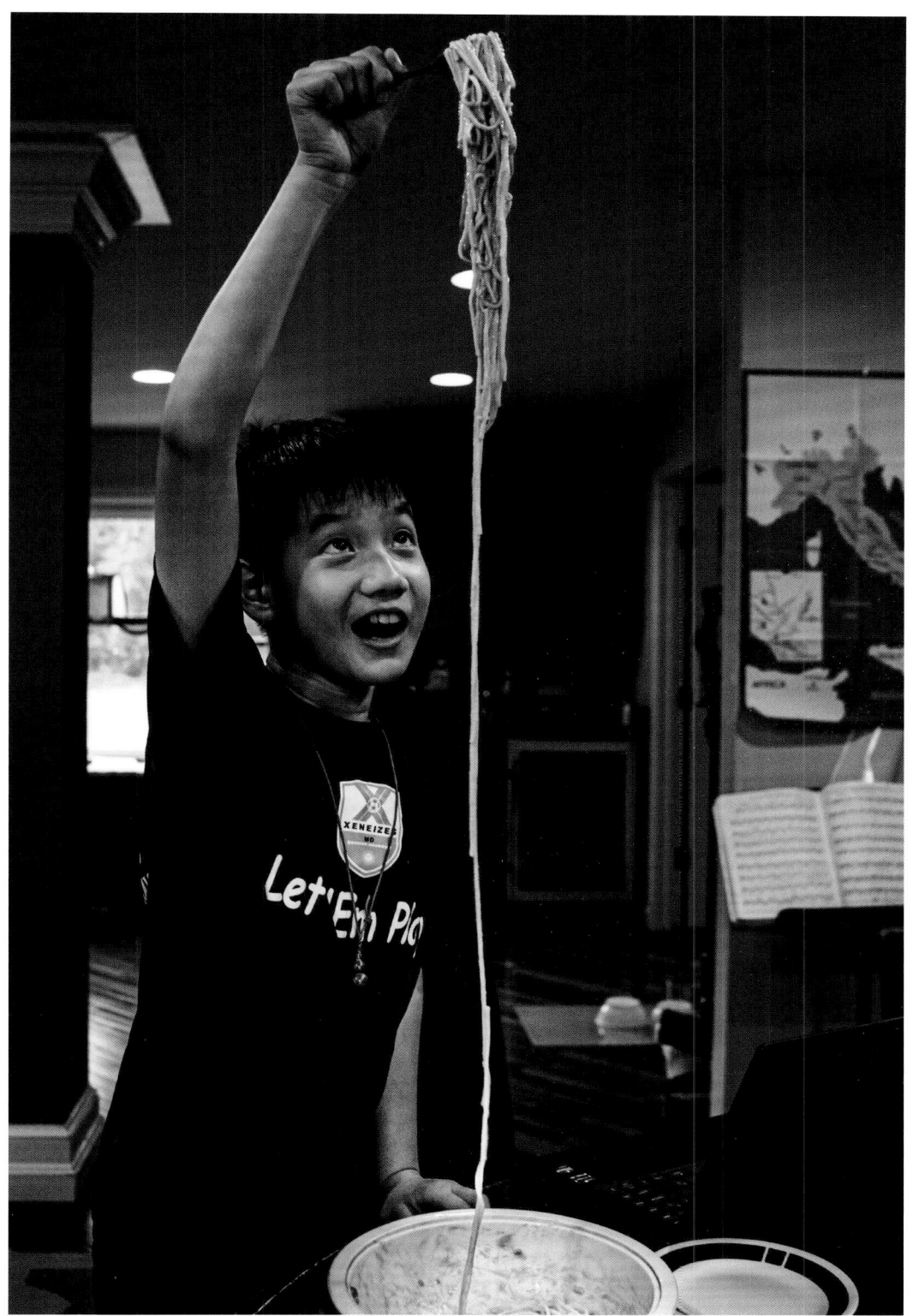

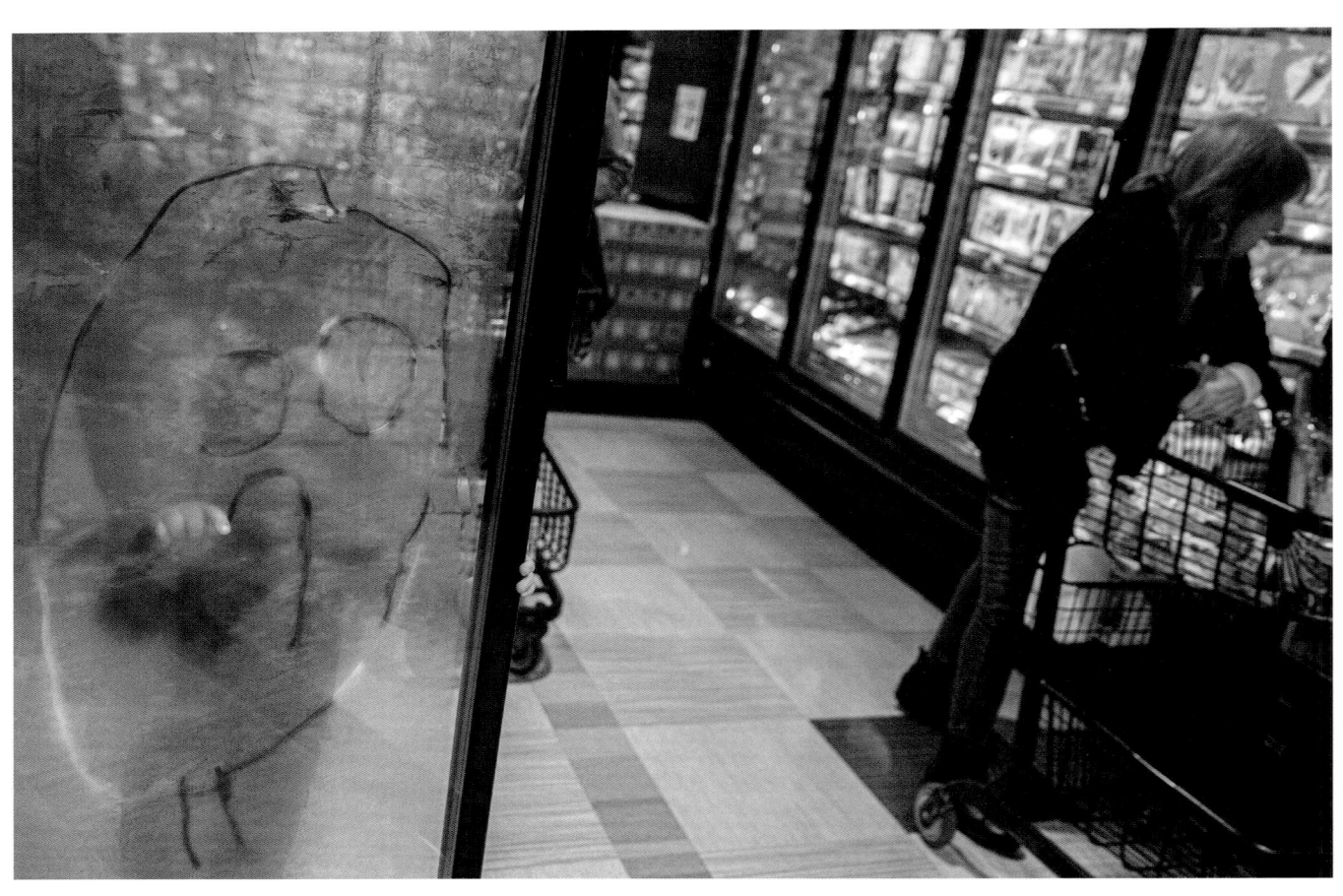

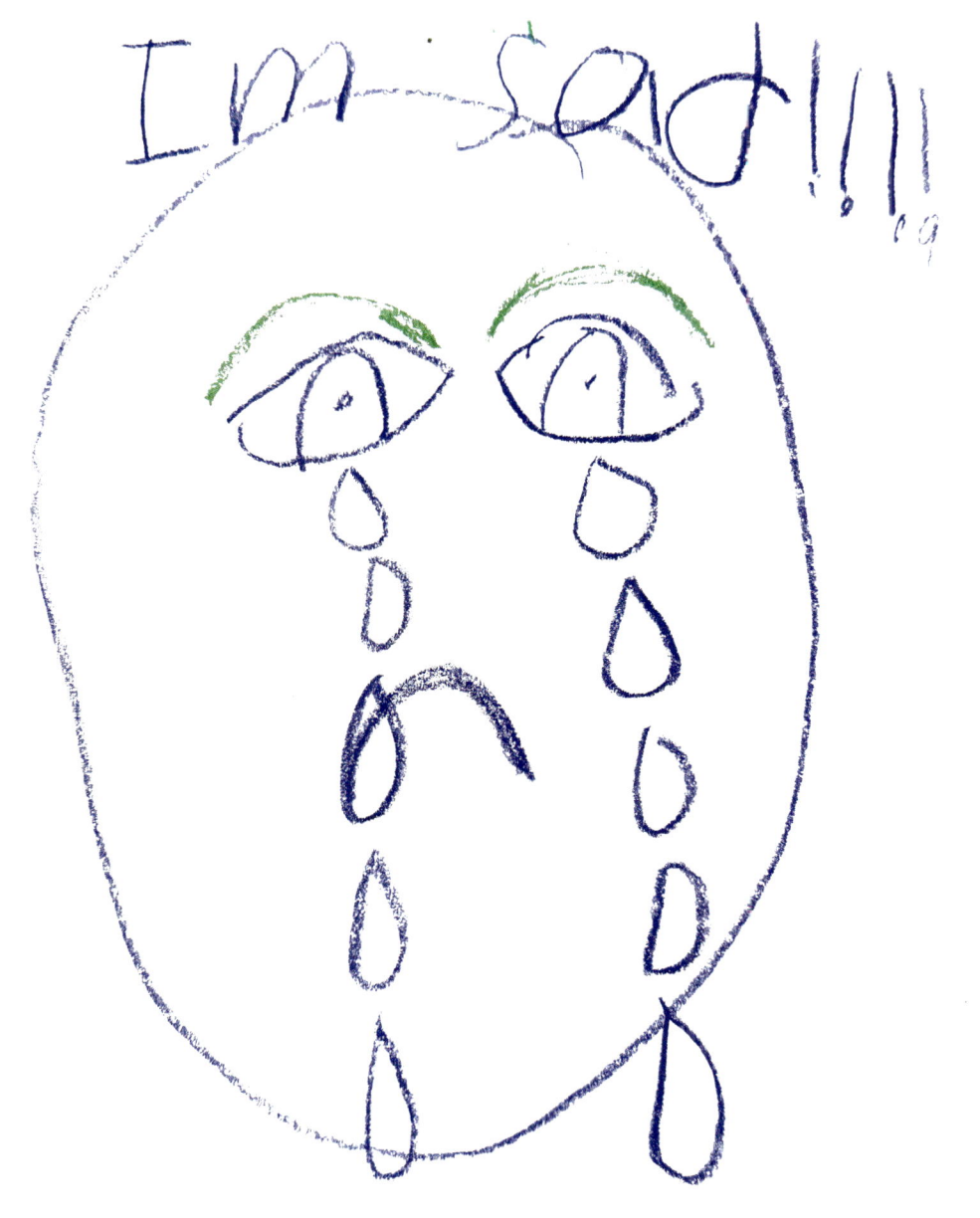

Sad

—Byrdie Mae, age seven

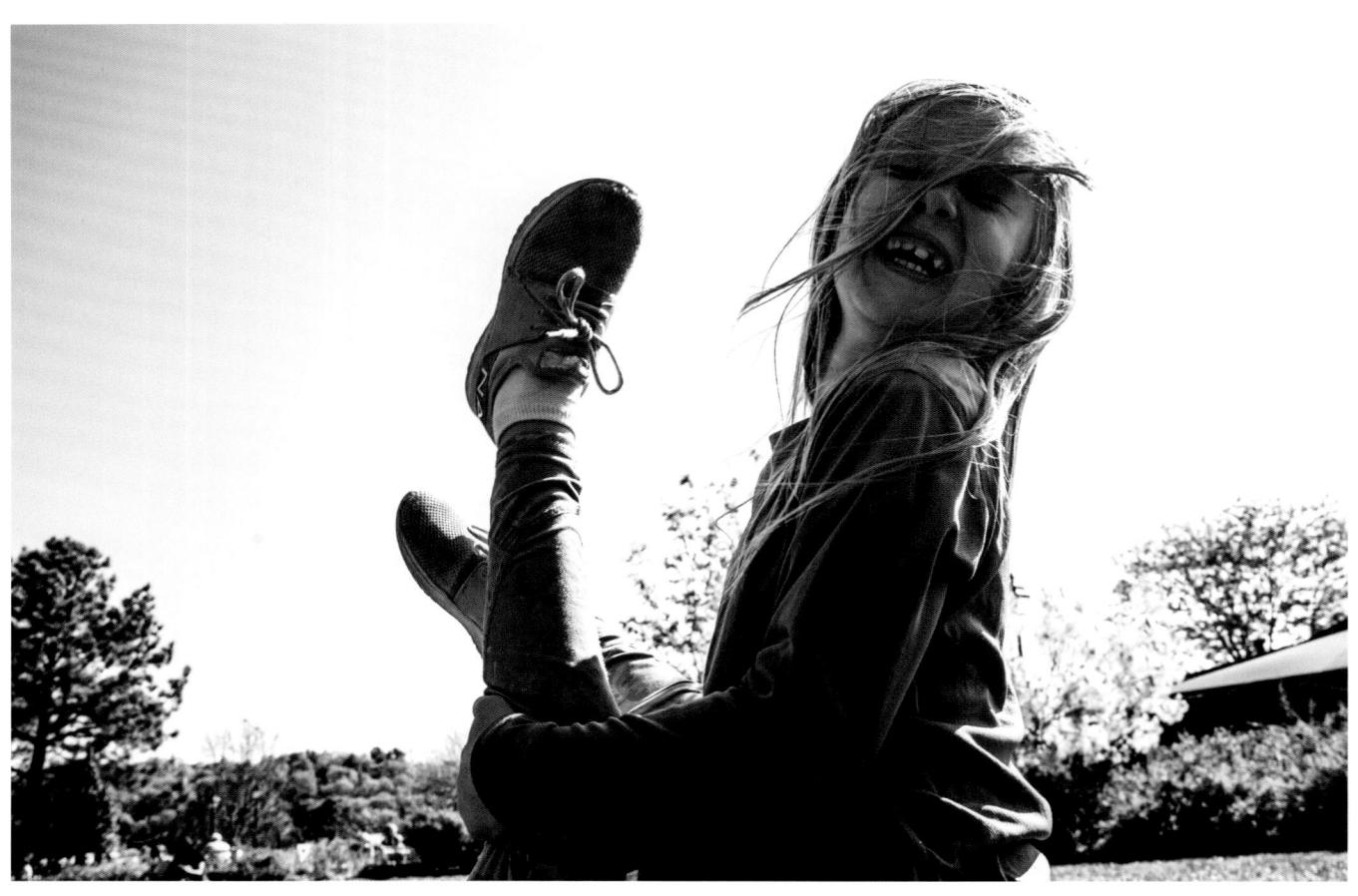

LETTER TO MABEL

A Ballad by Brett Magdovitz

I'm not the brightest or wisest man you'll ever meet.

I've spent my life searching for myself when I was just down the street.

But I've lived a lot of lives, many of which tell a good tale.

And I've learned some things I'm hoping might help you whenever you fail.

My darling, my Munchie, my sweet Mabel Joy.

You are the only messiah that you'll ever need.

My starling, my madcap, my most treasured joy.

Give it your best and embrace that it might make you bleed.

Don't be distracted by voices of doubt by decree.

Tune out the noises and tune in to your frequency.

Follow your bliss; only you can make yourself free.

Trust in your sources and choices intuitively.

My daughter, my delver, my conspiring little seed.

Never stop growing. Avoid too much knowing. Pay heed.

My child, be wild, . . . let your spirit take the lead.

Like water, keep flowing as your light keeps glowing. Let it breed.

Take good looks in the mirror and have some good laughs.

Reflections aren't static; they're not photographs.

Sing your songs. Right your wrongs.

Turn your conflicts into crafts.

And you'll be so far ahead of the game.

And you'll see yourself; authentic and humane.

And you'll free yourself of all the chattering mundane.

And all you have to do . . . is discover . . . over and over . . . what it means . . . to be you.

My rascal, my reacher, my brave Mabel Joy.

Searching for meaning will often yield loss before gain.

My sensitive teacher, my compassionate joy.

Sometimes when folks are mean, it's because they've been hurt and are in pain.

When you're lost, turn to nature; she's always just around the bend.

Or close your eyes and look inside yourself. You'll find she tends to blend.

Step into your fear; it's human. No need to pretend.

You will get broken . . . and brighter . . . each time you mend.

My flower, your power . . .

is your unique force to cultivate and aim.

Use it. And amuse it. Don't abuse it.

Light your fuse and fan your flame.

Take good care of your mind; speak it clear through your heart.

You'll need both to serve wisely when things fall apart.

Treat your body and soul as

the spacecraft for your art.

And don't forget just how quickly things can change.

And don't reject new people and ideas that may seem strange.

And don't expect each time you give you'll get a fair exchange.

And know that when you're blue . . . you'll recover . . . over and over . . . even if . . . it seems you're through.

My darling, my Munchie, my replete Mabel Joy

You are a steward of Gaia. Your life is your deed.

My starling, my madcap, my most pleasured joy.

Get some good rest and unbrace from the forces that impede.

My resilient, adaptable, beautifully flawed Mabel Joy.

Life's a fragile paradox; it owes you nought. That debt is guaranteed.

Be humble and gracious and respectfully tenacious Mabel Joy.

Surrender to your breath and let your branches and your roots extend to feed.

I've done my best to live these words. I've fallen short, and you may too.

Reset and proceed.

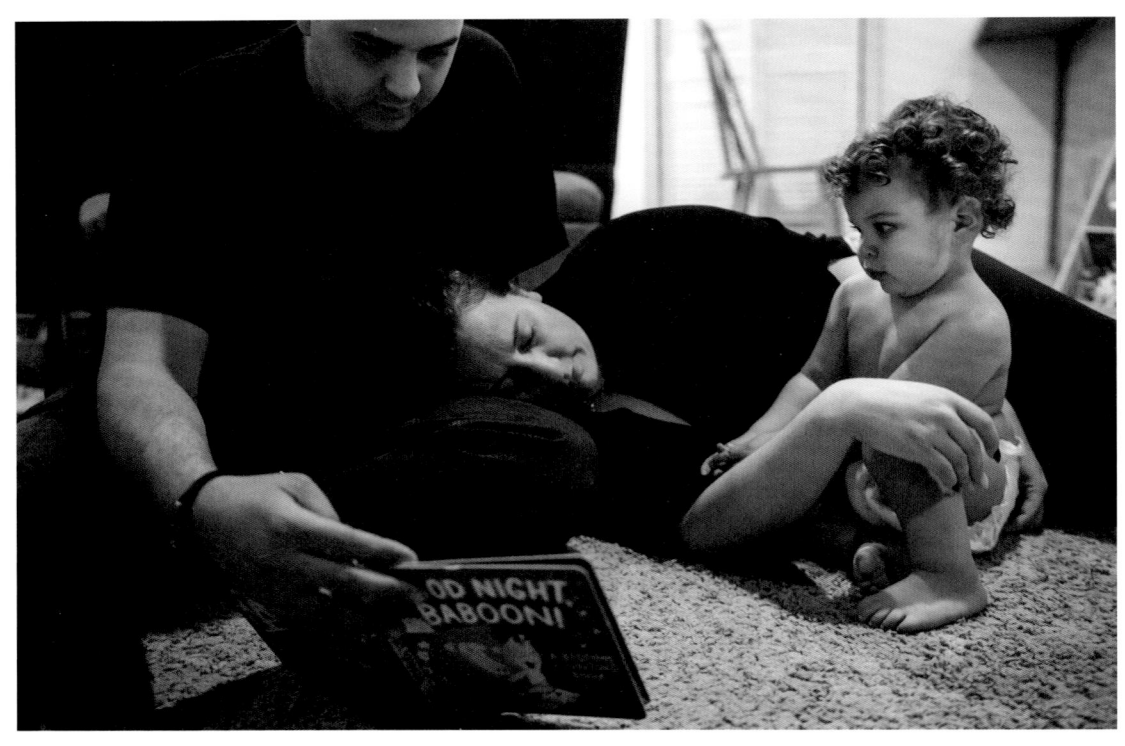

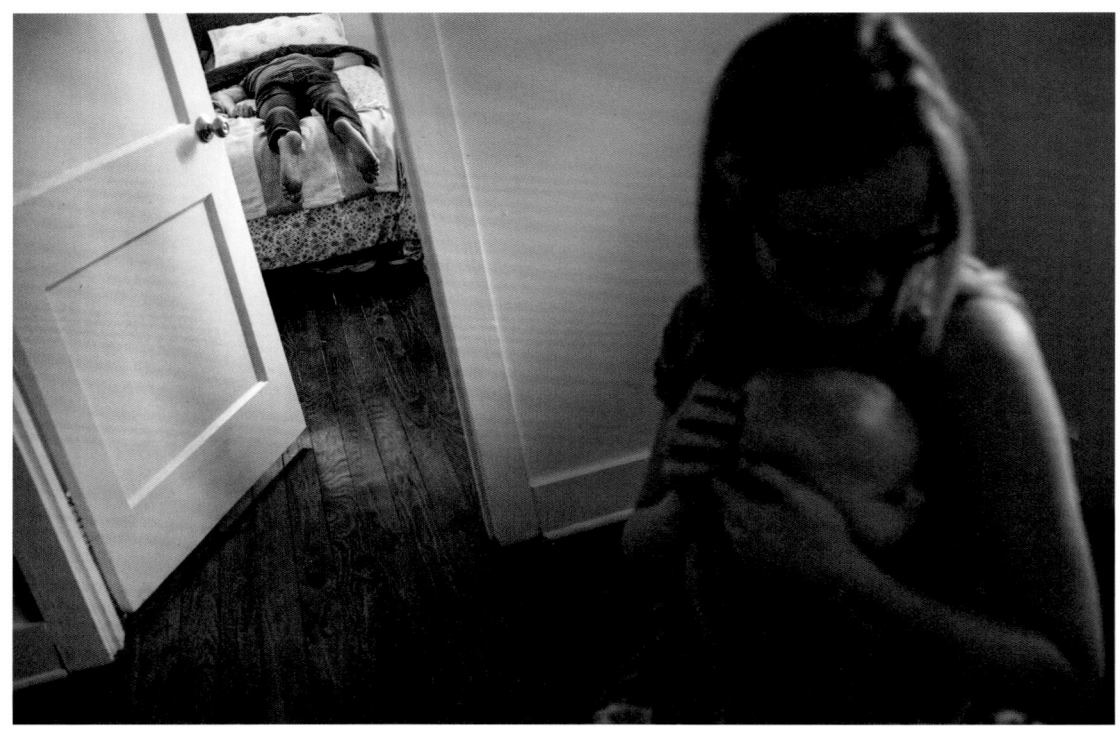

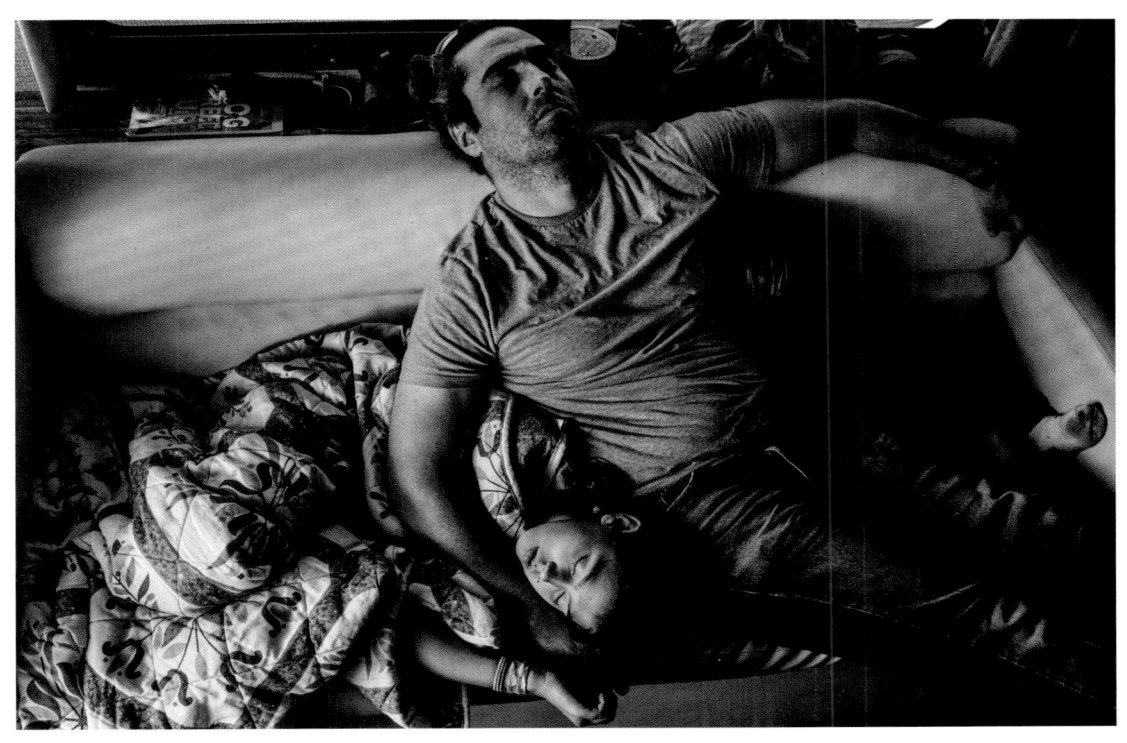

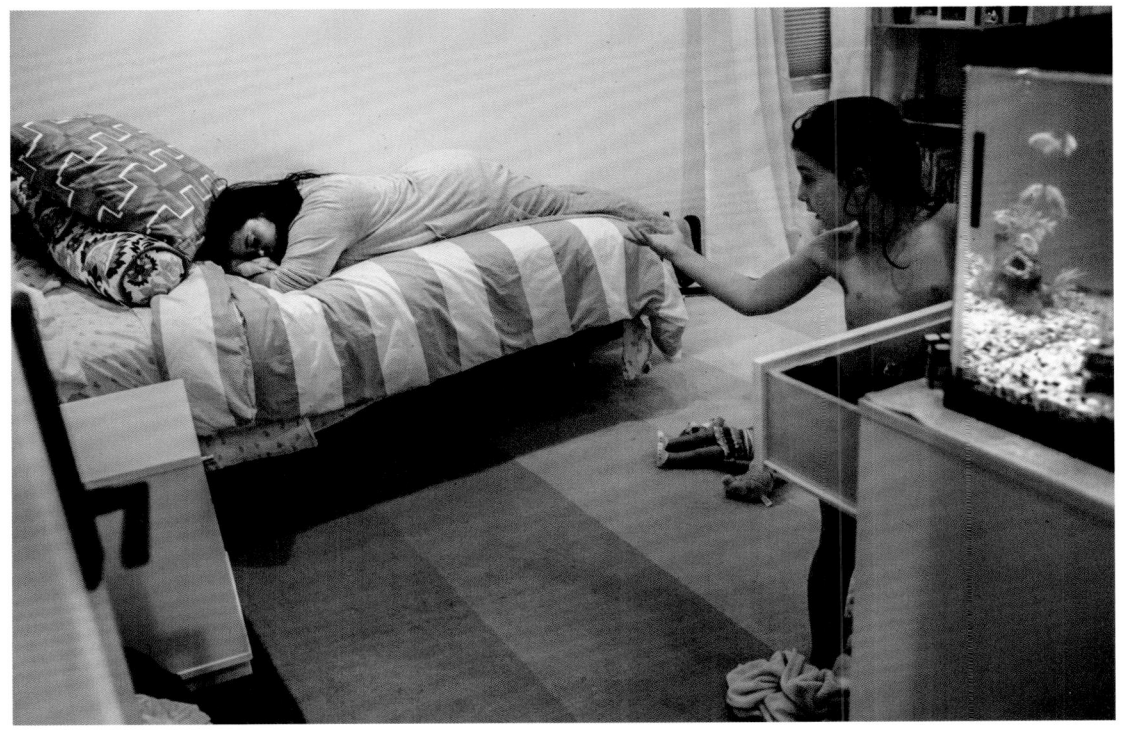

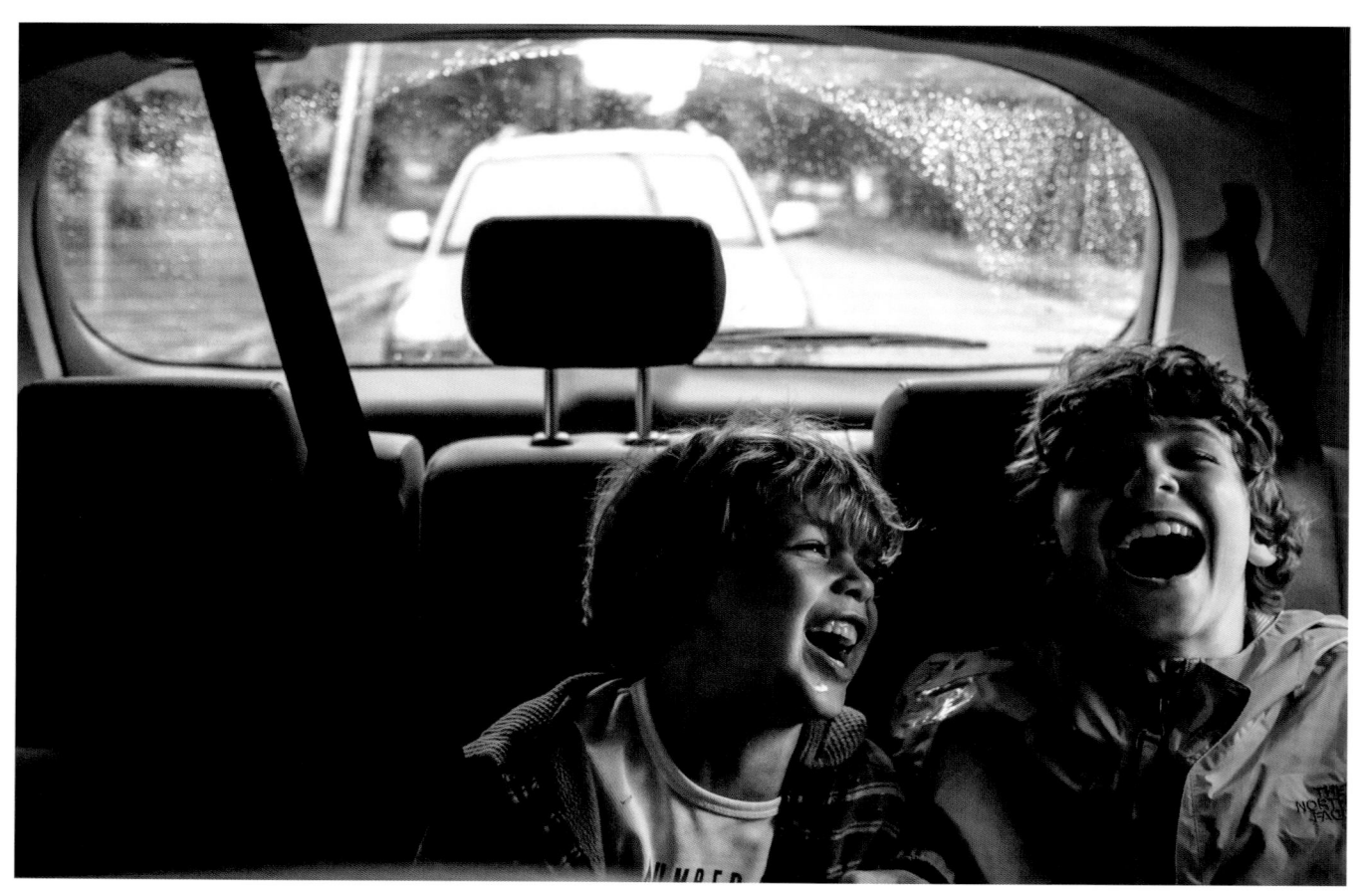

Conversations with a seven-year-old

Me: Can we please not use the word "balls" in front of Nana?! Not only do you not have them, but they are called testicles.

Juliana: Aren't those what octopuses have?

Me: No, those are tentacles.

Juliana: Whatever.

—Dawn Marazzo Ferragamo

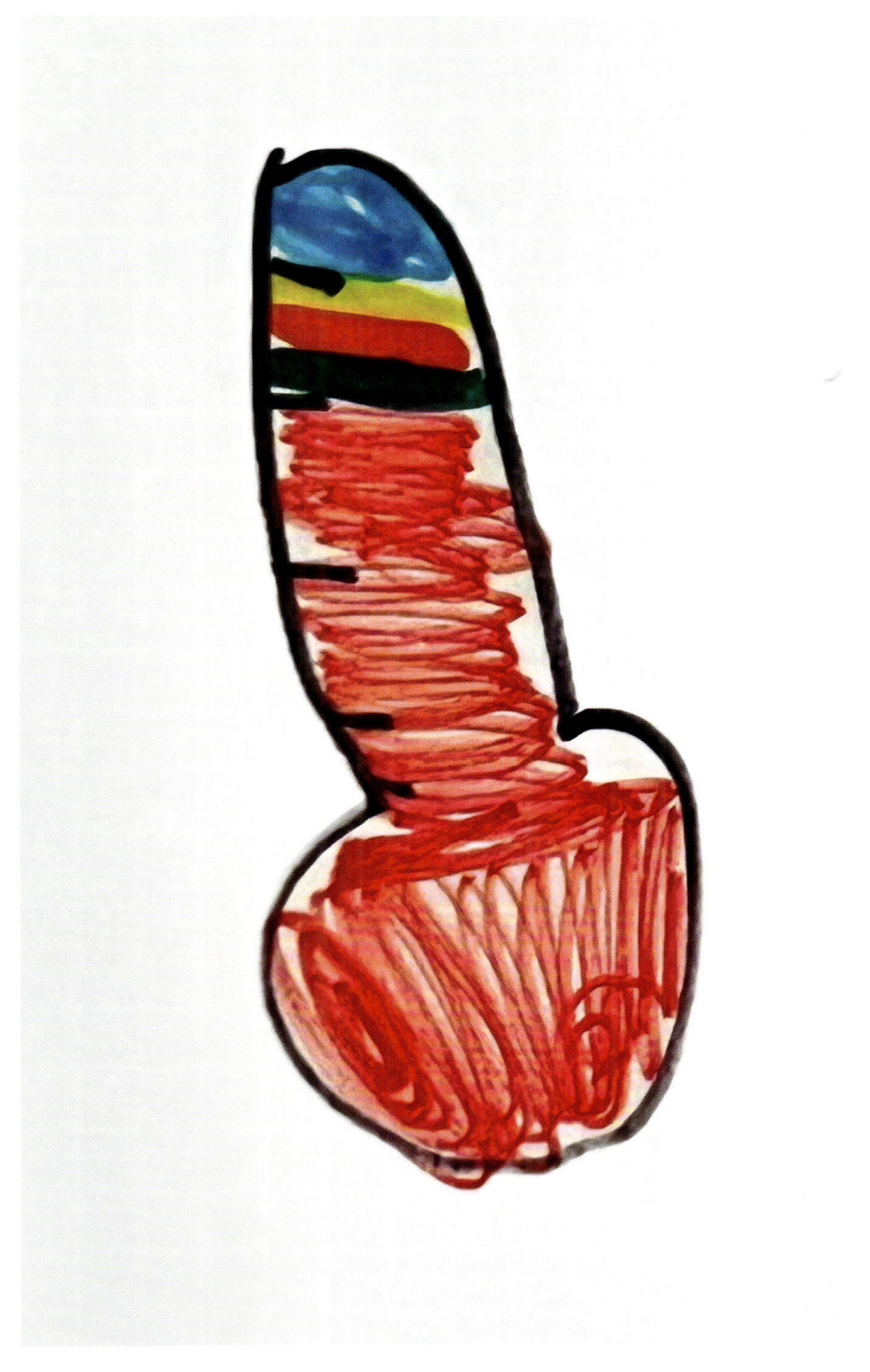

Thermometer —Nolan, age five-and-a-half

Feel free to contact me with any questions! —Nolan's Mom

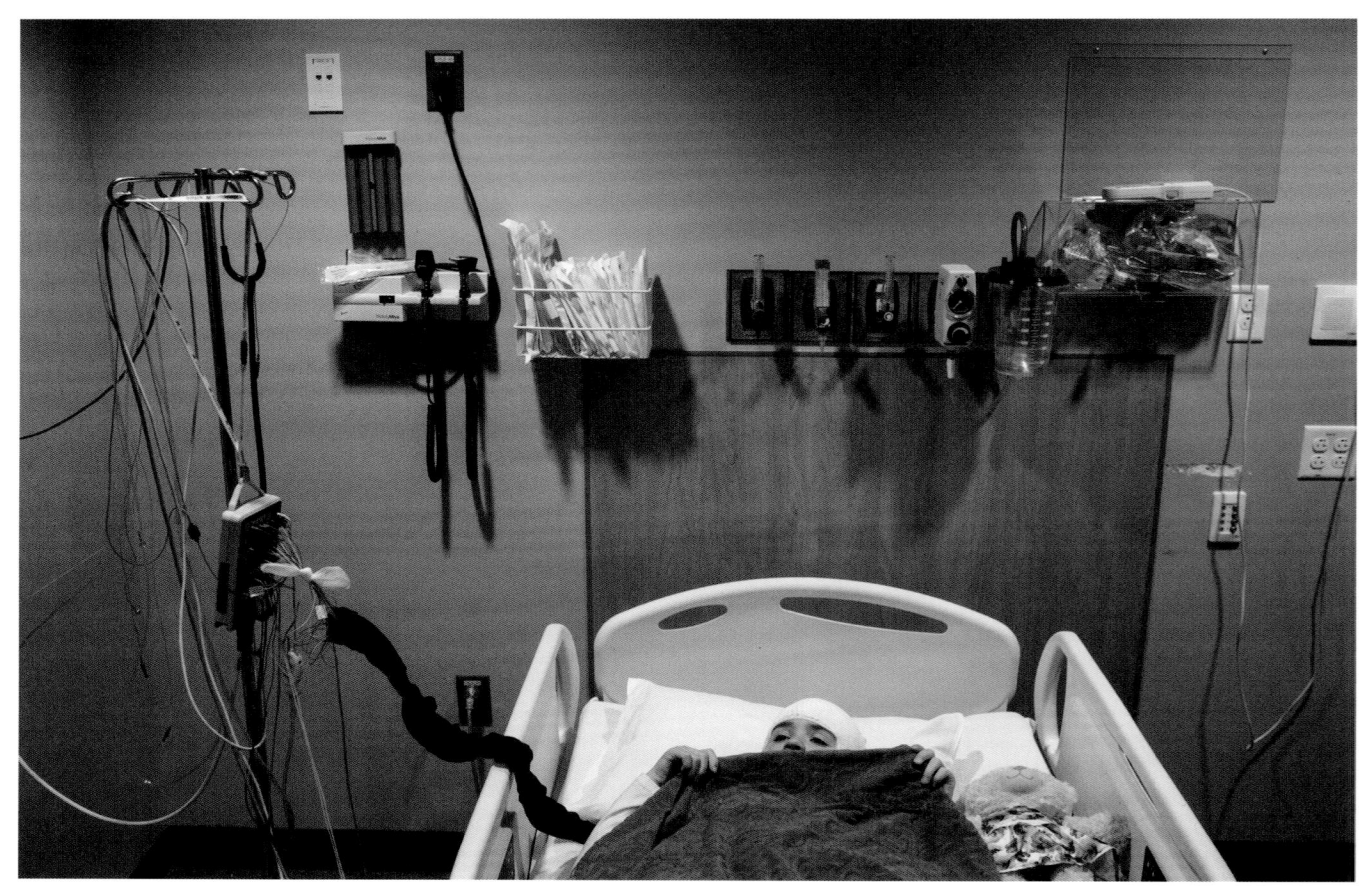

Everyone will tell you to enjoy your kids; they're only little for a little while. While you're at it, make sure you're embracing your whole family as an entire unit, taking nothing for granted. Tomorrow is never guaranteed, and everything can change in an instant. Those aren't just clichés . . . it's the truthiest truth that ever dared to truth.

—Erica Quinley

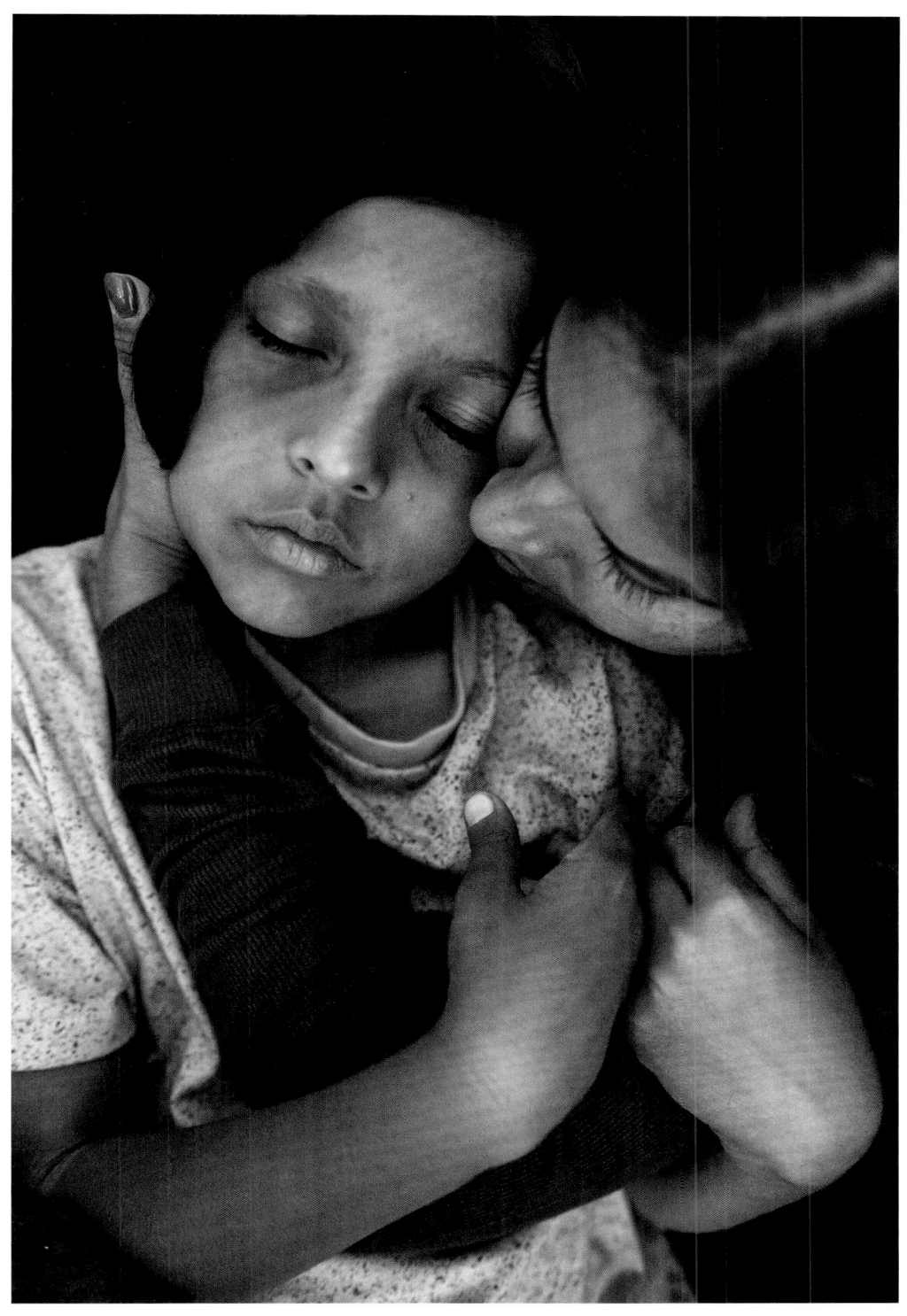

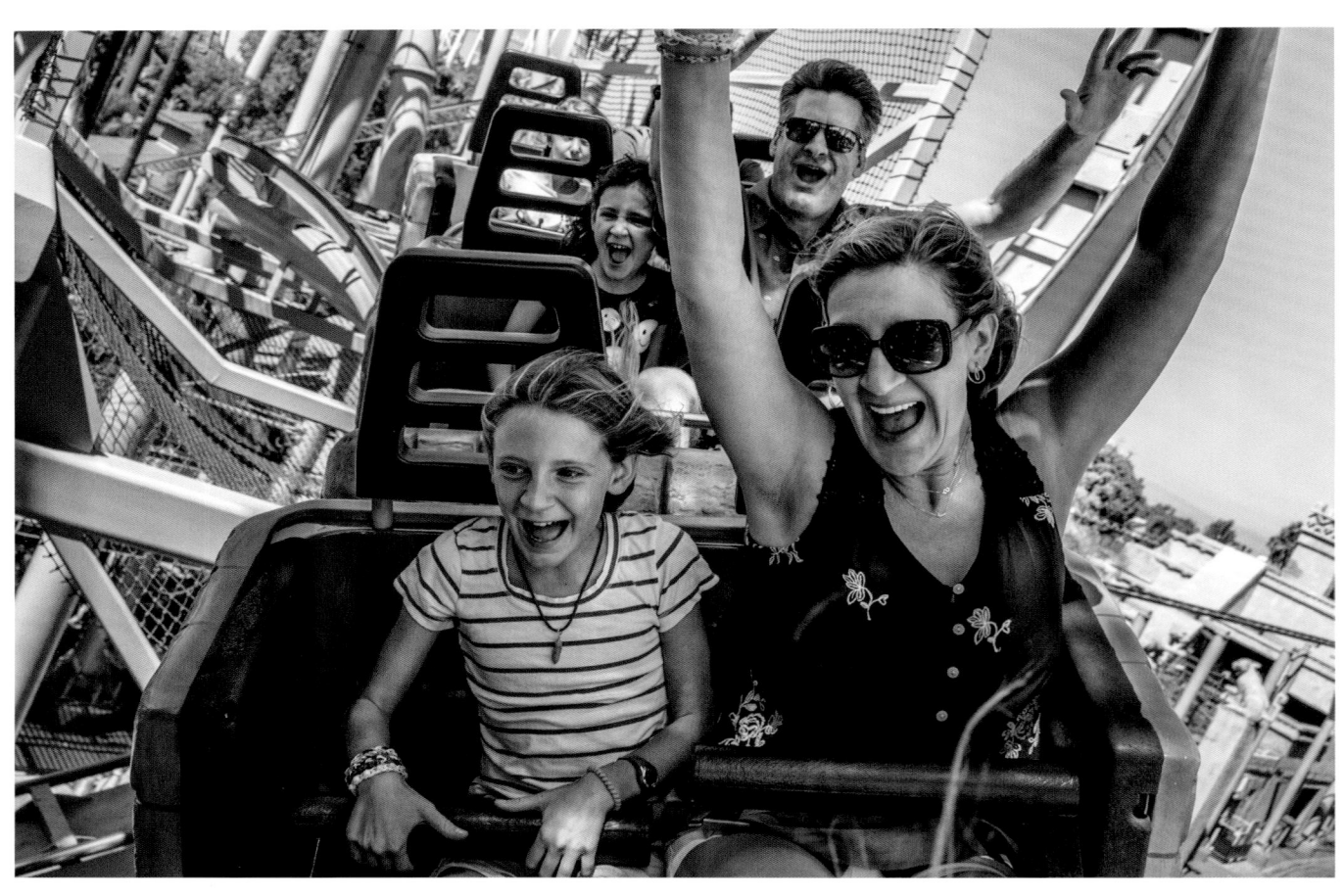

Enjoy the struggles as much as the joys. Neither will last forever.

—Lisa Slav

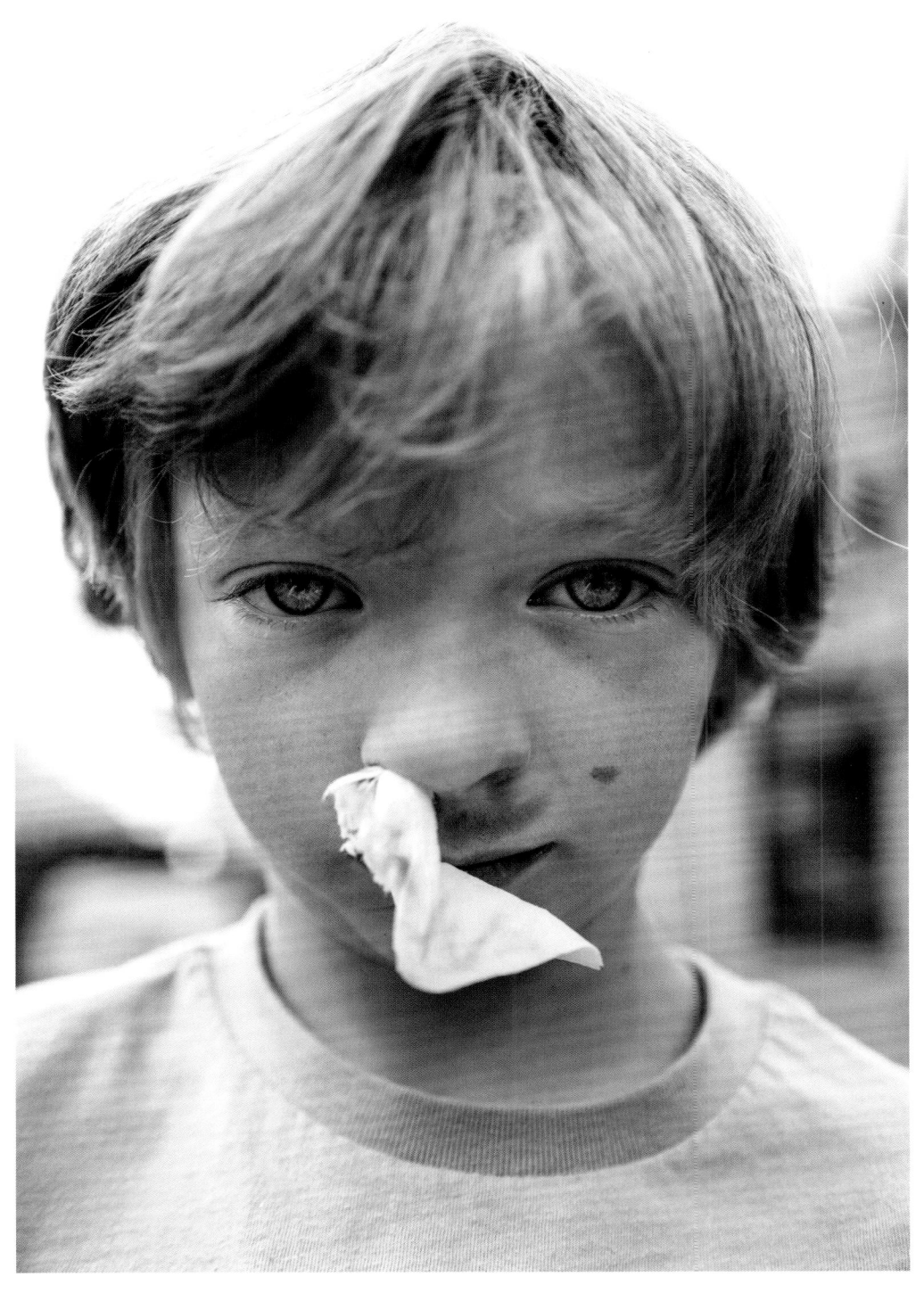

Mon, Mar 20, 12:51 PM

We lost the baby. Heart stopped beating two days ago. I'm sorry I didn't tell you about the ultrasound today. Amir didn't even go bc he assumed it was fine. I wish this was all a bad dream

Oh no!!!!!

I am so sorry.

I'm in shock.

I don't understand.

Everything was fine?

I'm leaving for Europe today or I would come over.

Wed, Mar 27, 9:31 AM

You're not gonna fucking believe this but our baby is OK!!!!! There is a heartbeat and she was wiggling around during the preOP ultrasound!!!!!

Wait what????!?!?!?

I can't believe this news!

I want to get up and dance in the middle of this conference.

Amir and Morgan Razi had tried for five years to get pregnant, and on their second attempt at IVF, they succeeded. At about nine weeks into the pregnancy, they went in for a routine ultrasound and the tech could not detect a heartbeat. A week later they went back to the doctor's office to have the miscarried fetus removed. But minutes before the procedure, the devastated Razis demanded a final ultrasound to confirm the loss of their daughter. Doctors and techs were shocked to discover not only a healthy heartbeat but a very active and healthy baby. Because of her parents' hope, love, and intuition Farrah's life was saved moments before a fatal procedure and is healthy and thriving today.

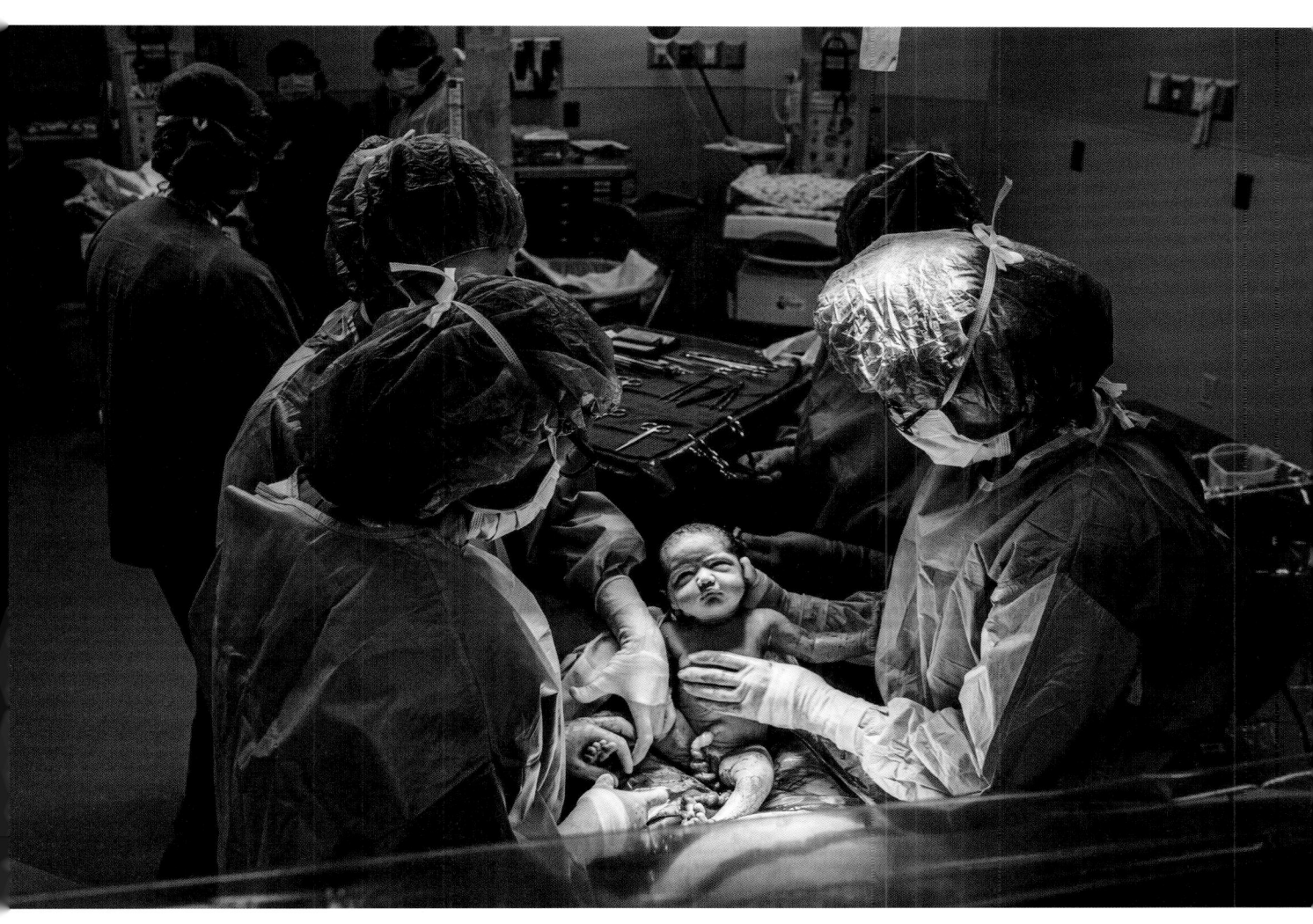

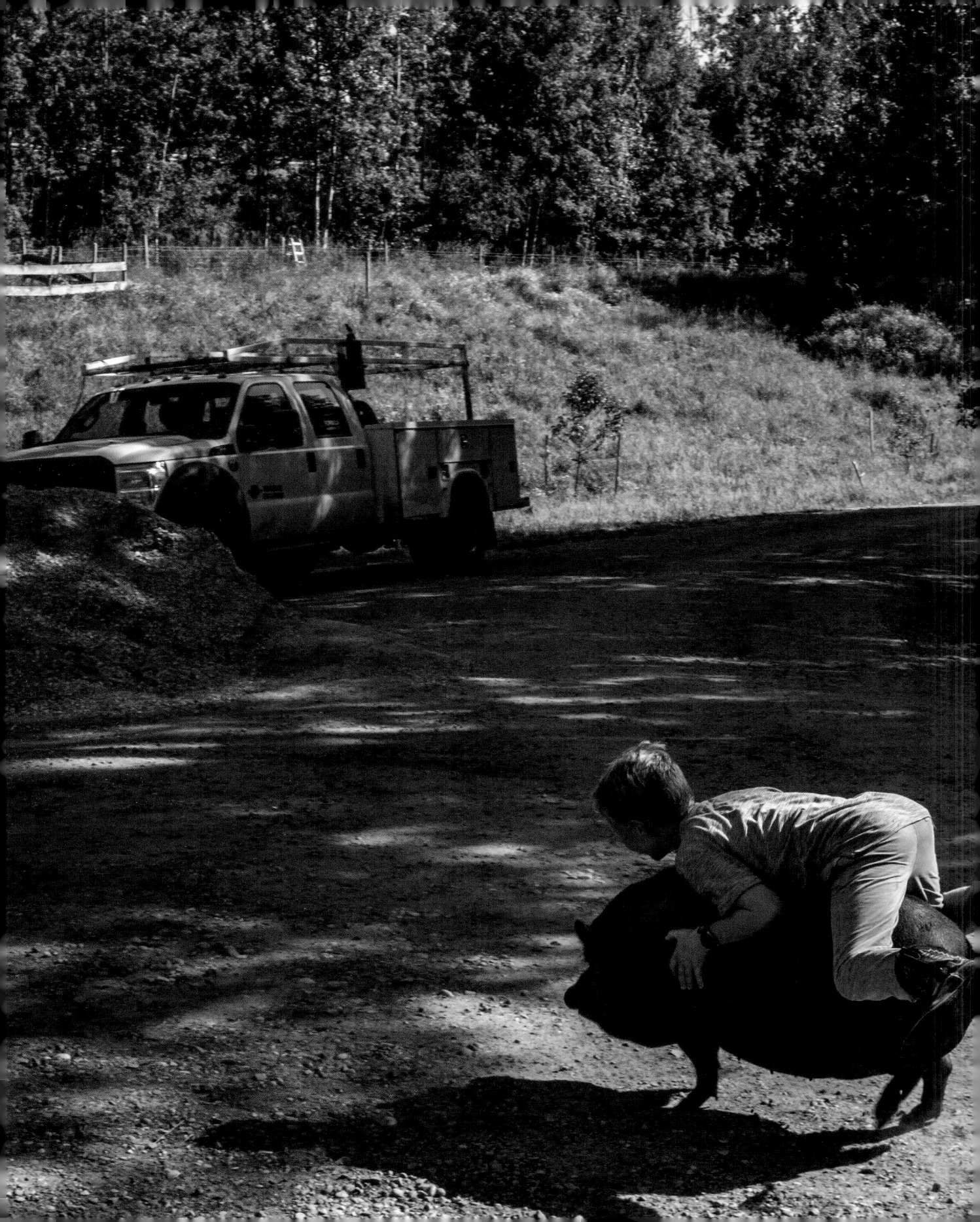

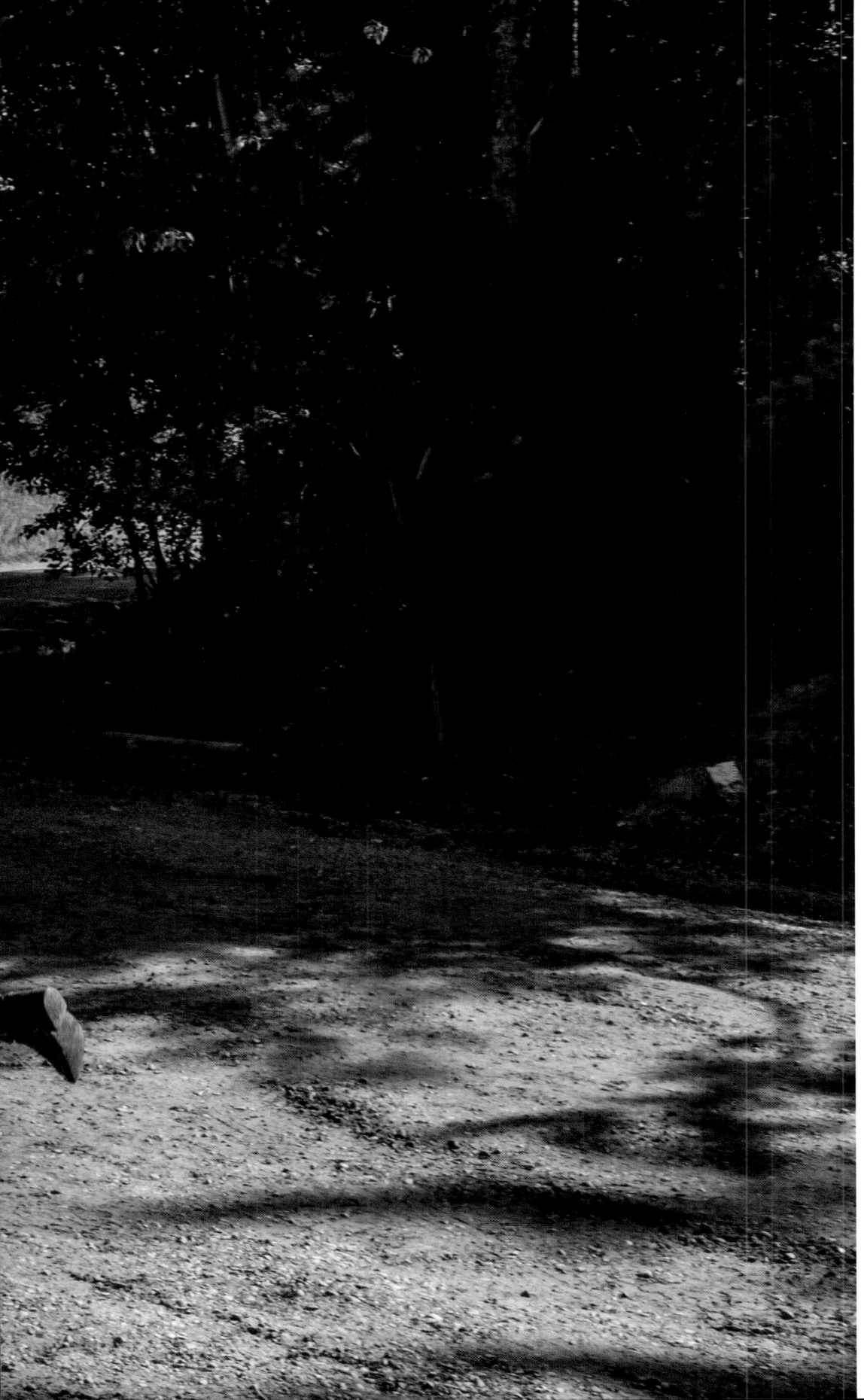

127

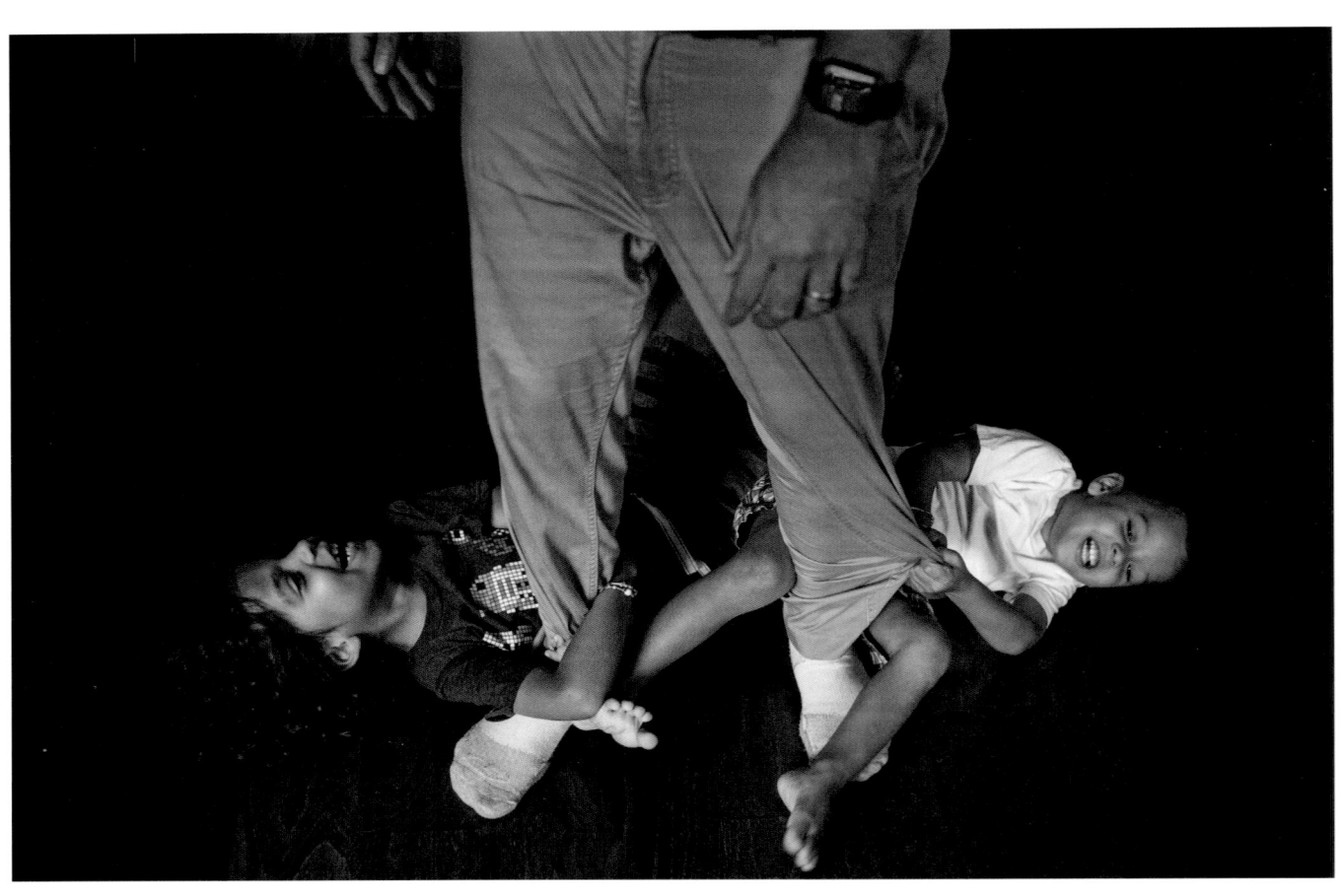

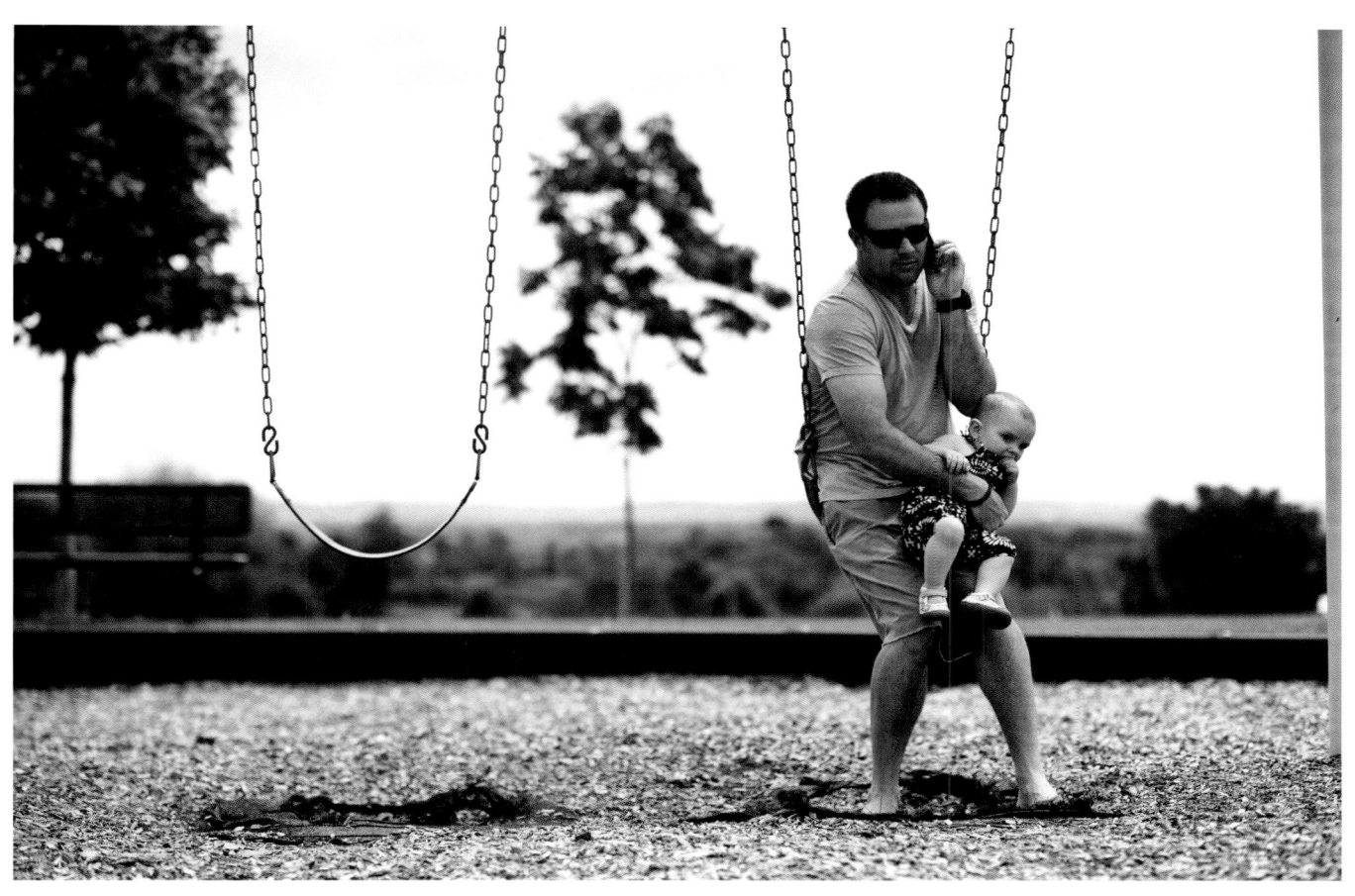

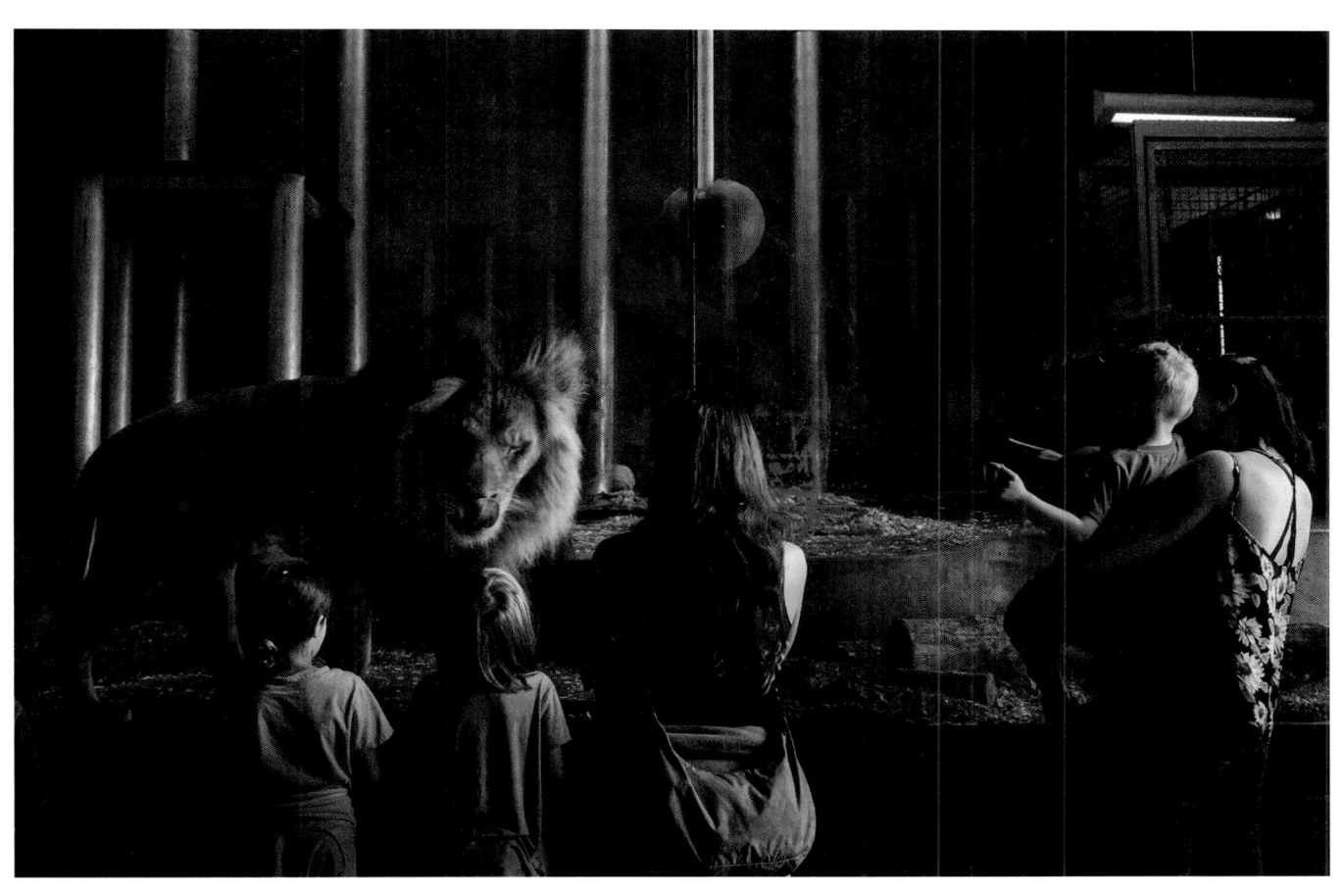

MOM FACT:

Vaseline does not come off a cat easily.

— Miria Morgan

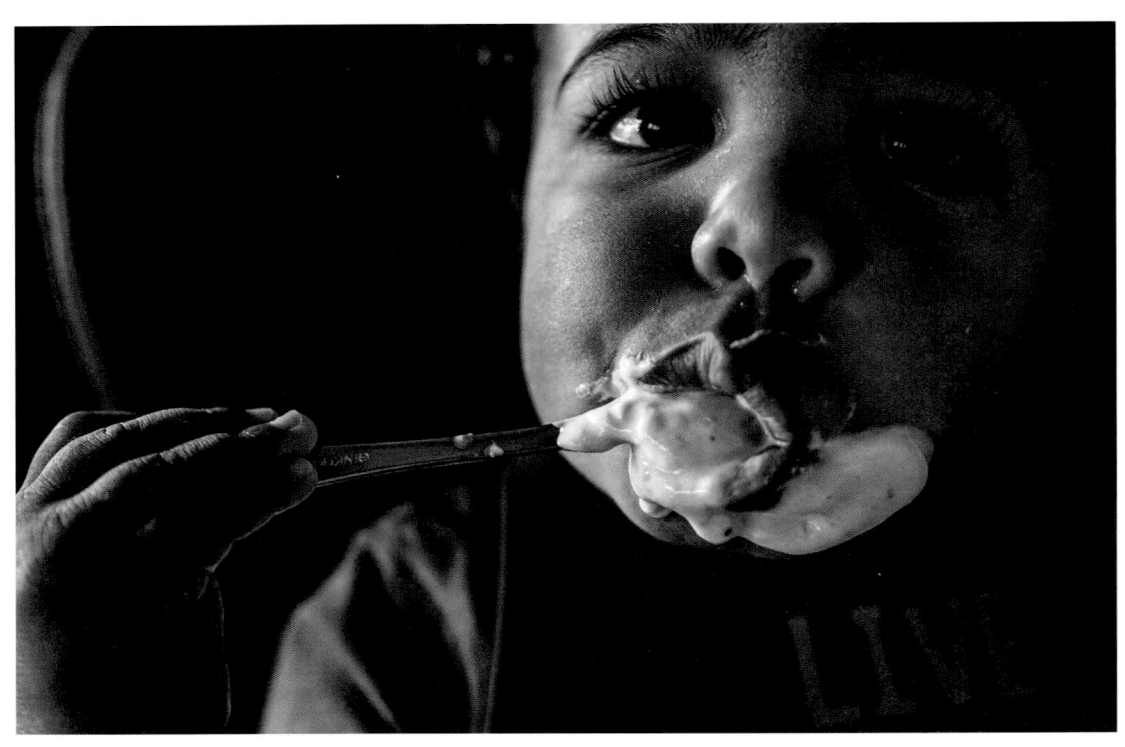

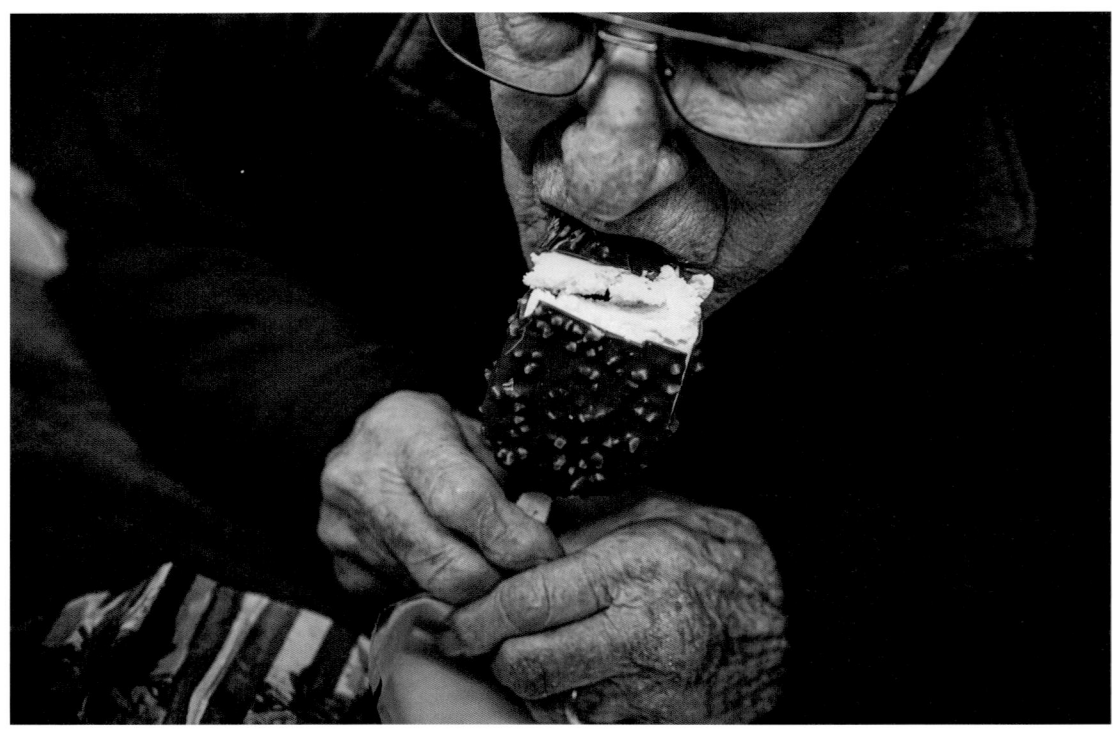

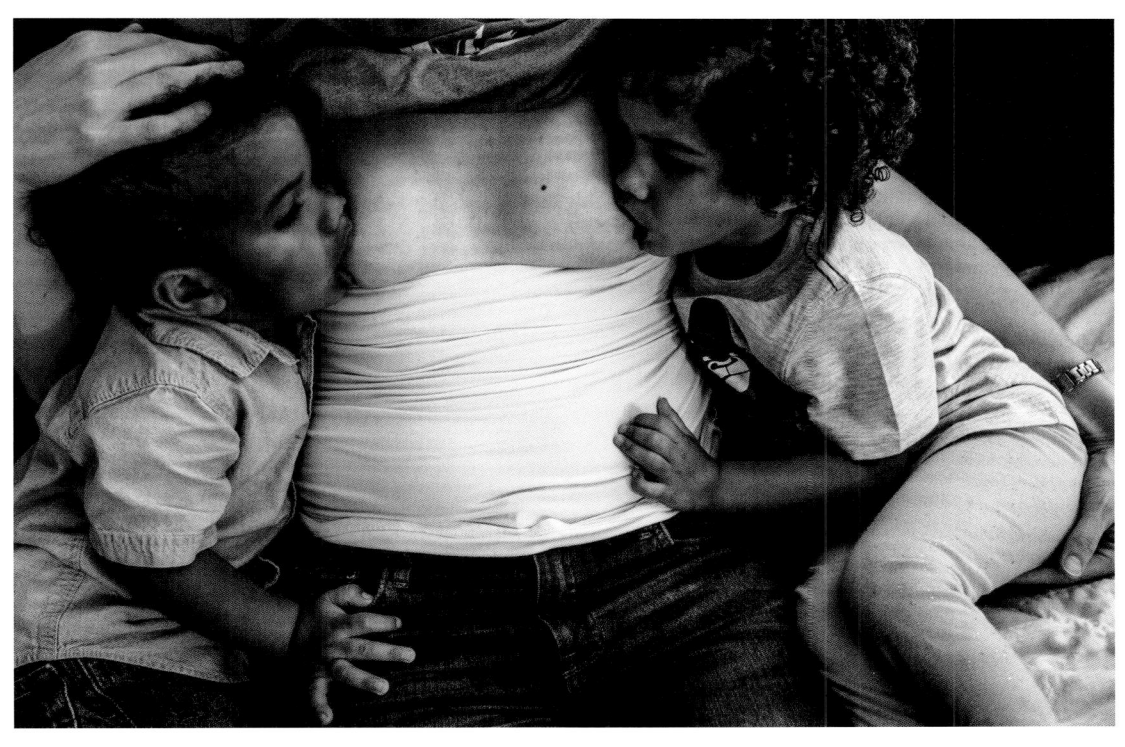

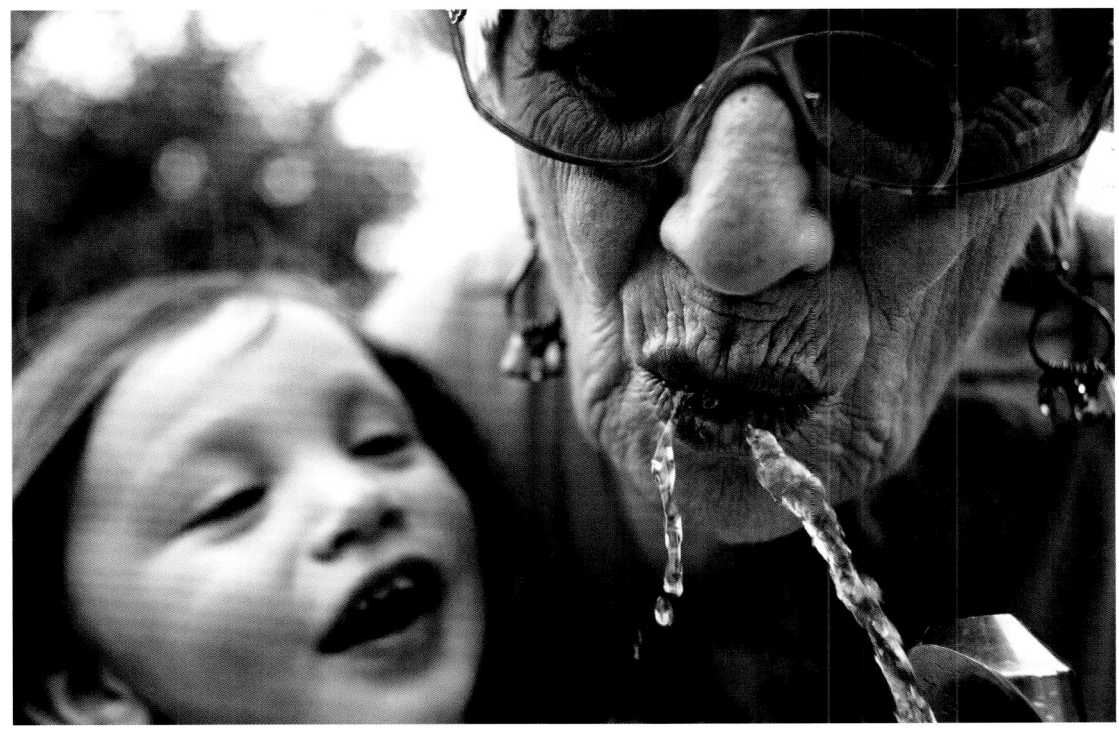

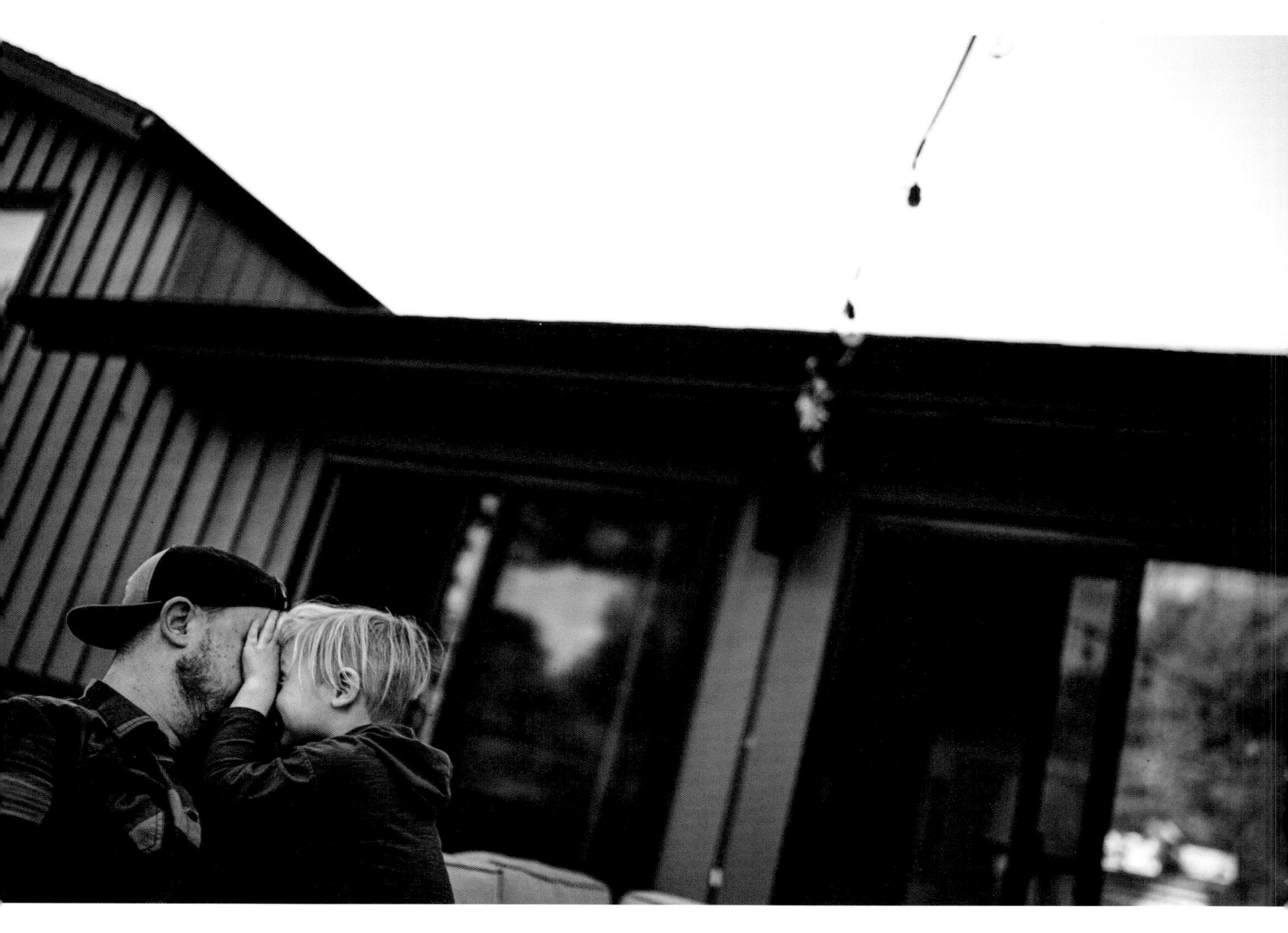

the

parent

I am

is

someone

I

am terrified

people

will

judge

As

terrible

so   I

just

cry

alone

in

the

dark.

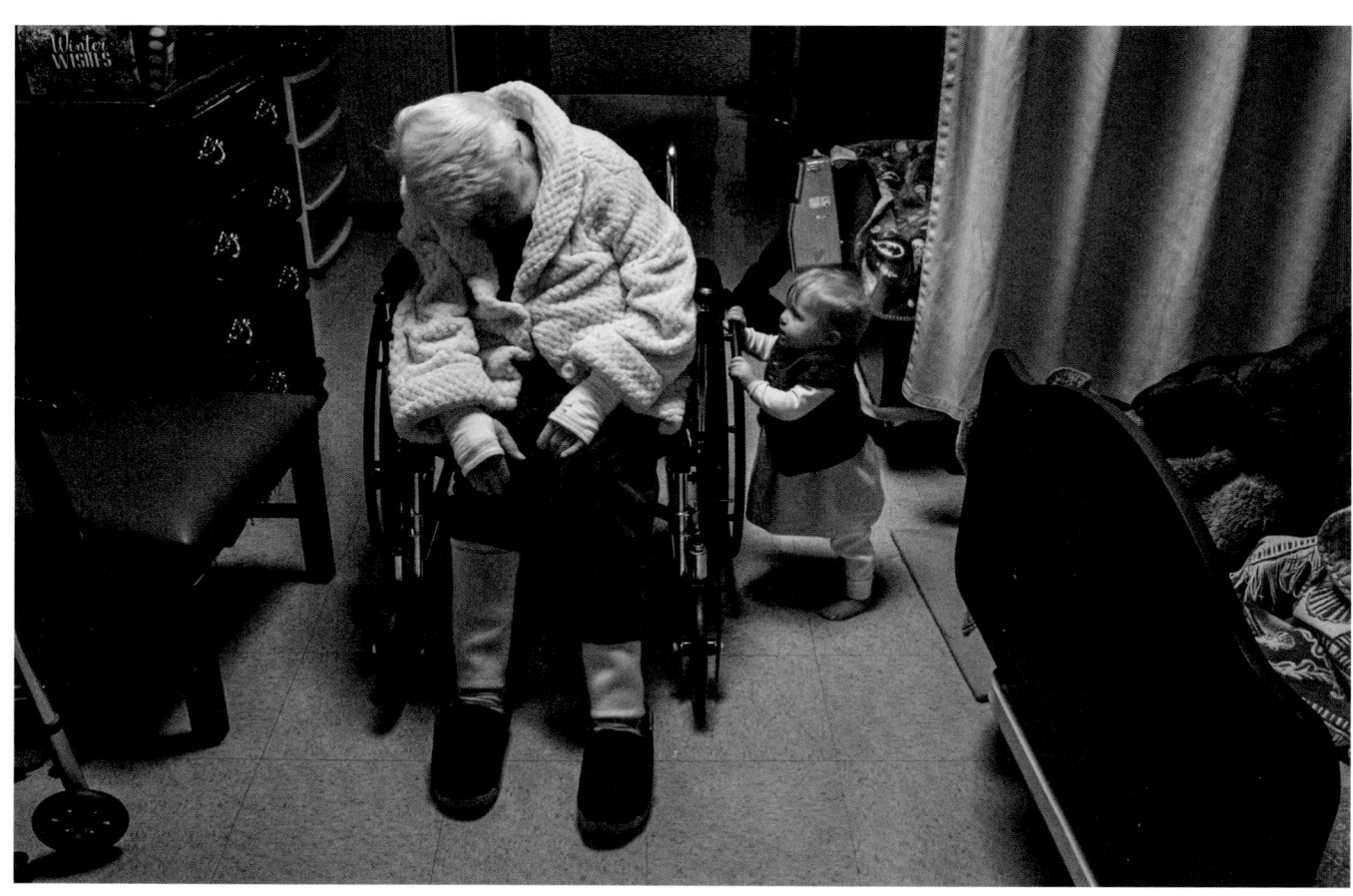

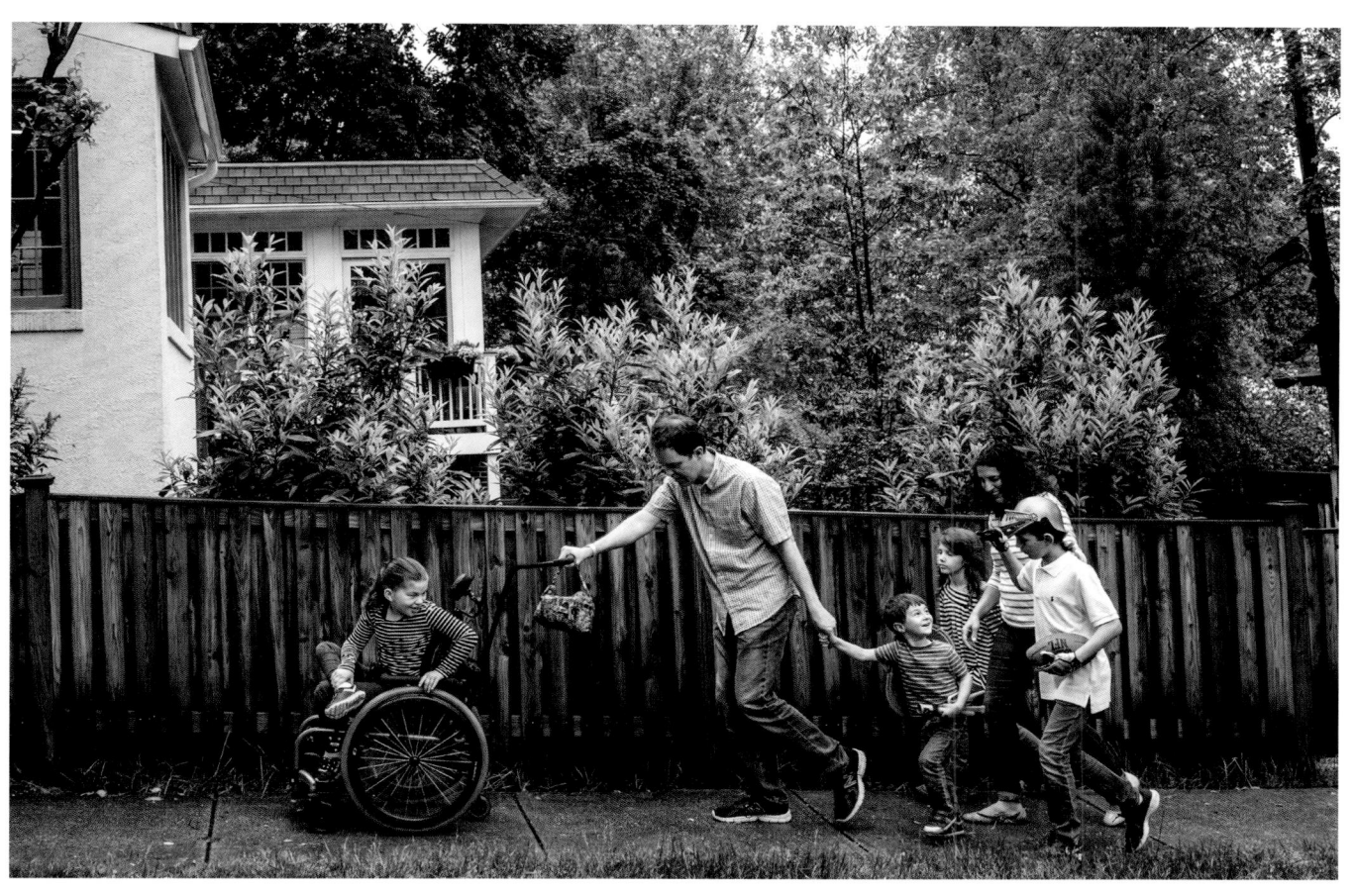

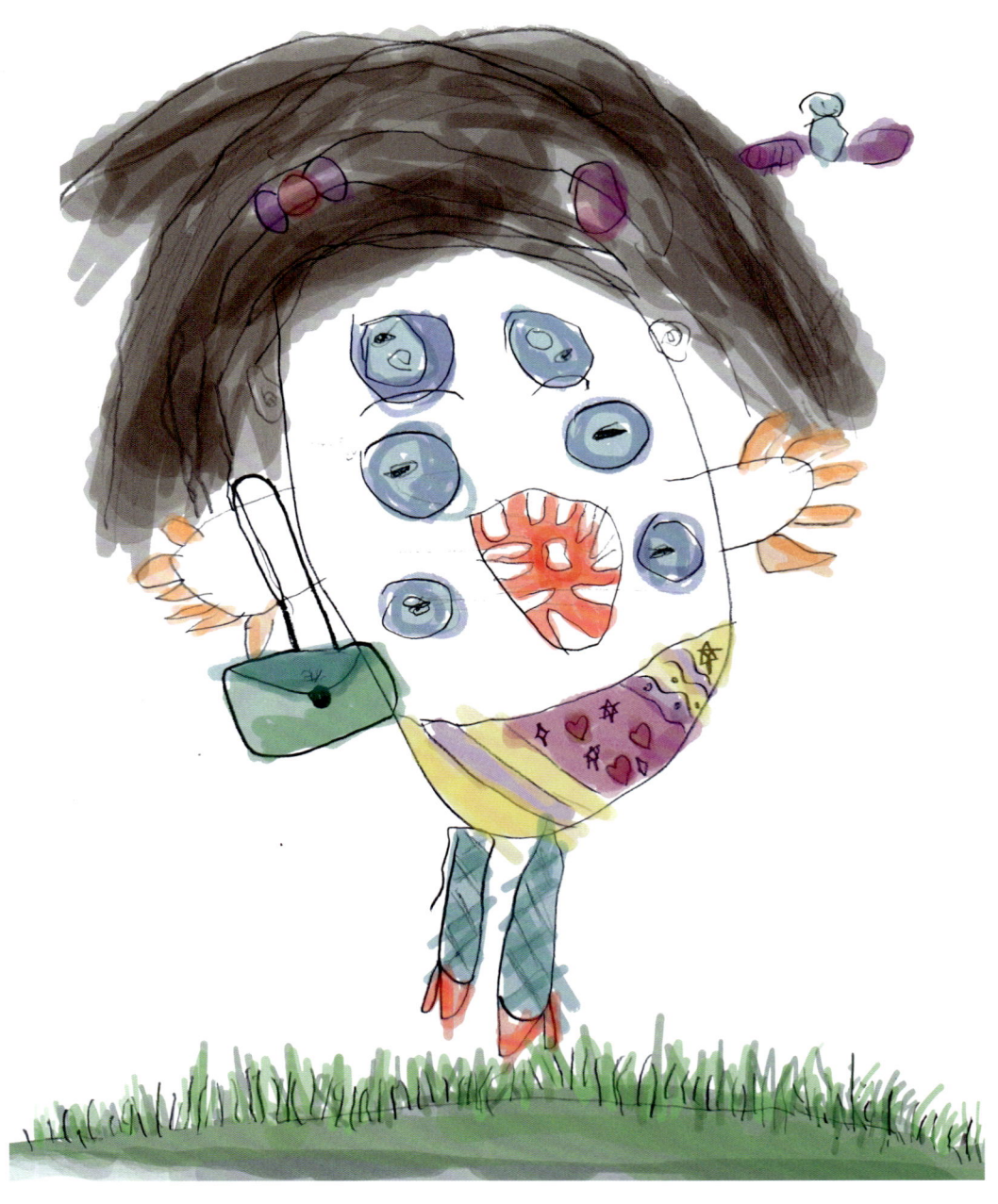

My beautiful mom

—Felipa, age five

You are SO beautiful.
You look nothing like yourself.

—Olive, age six

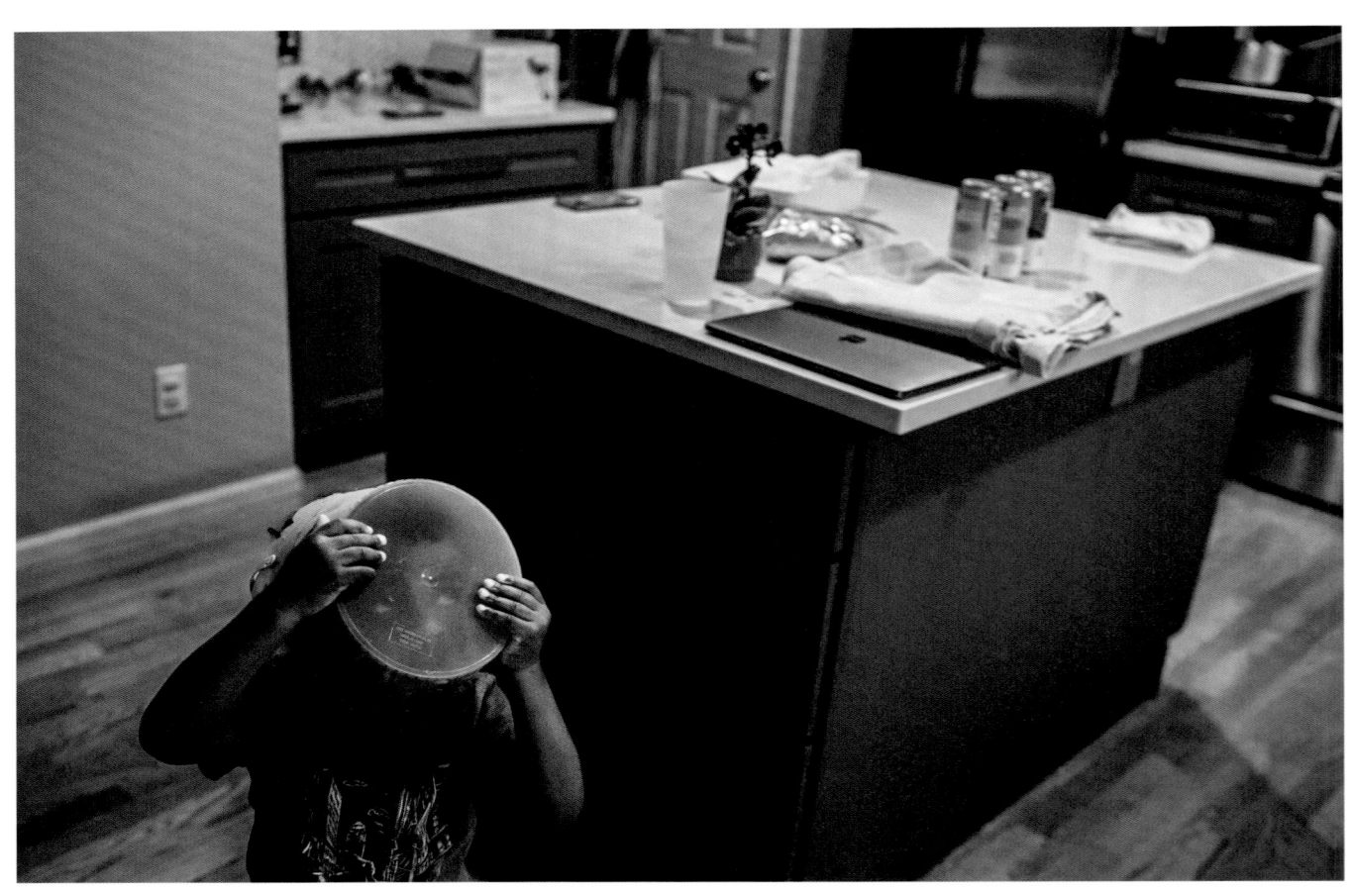

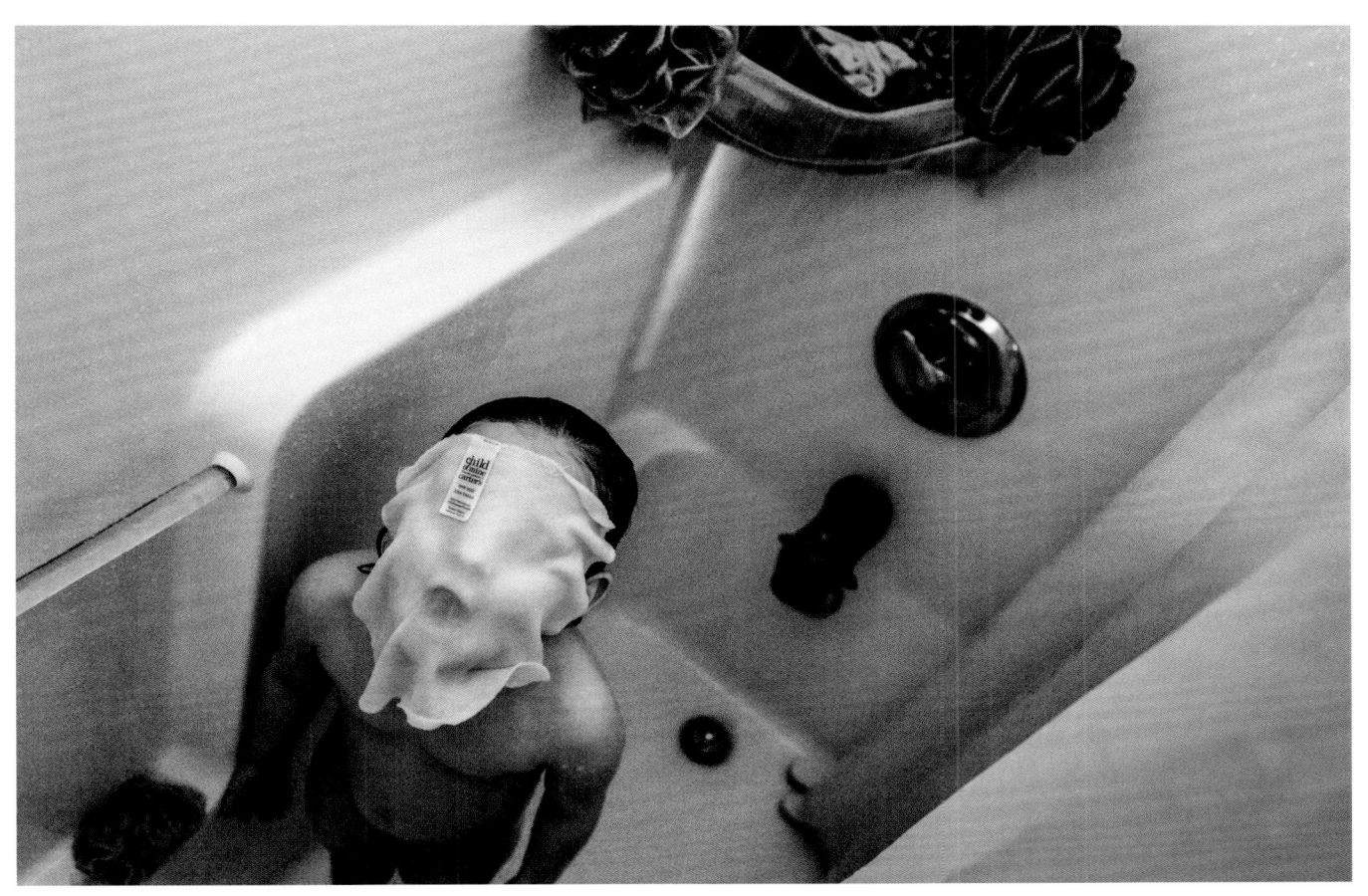

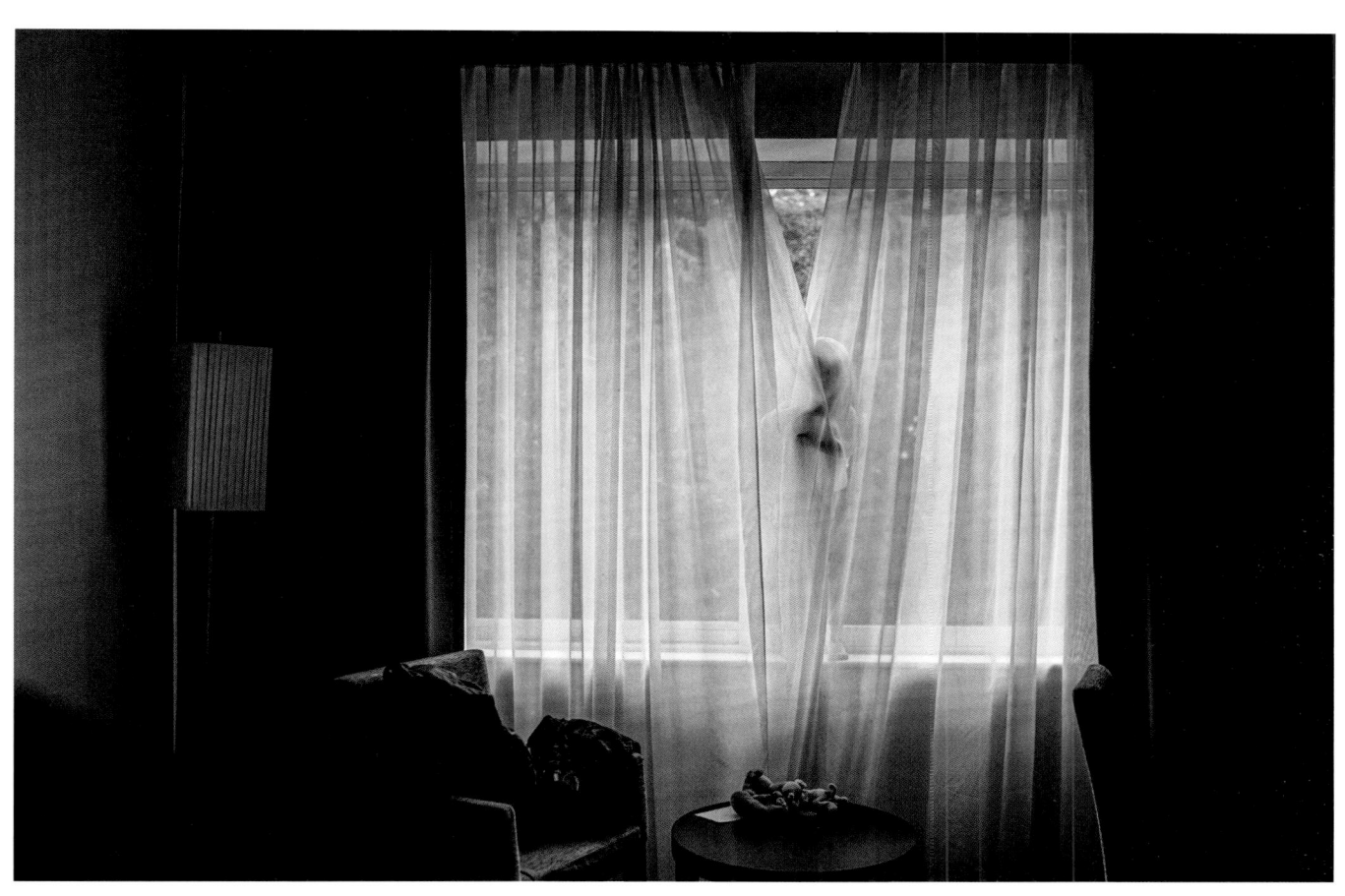

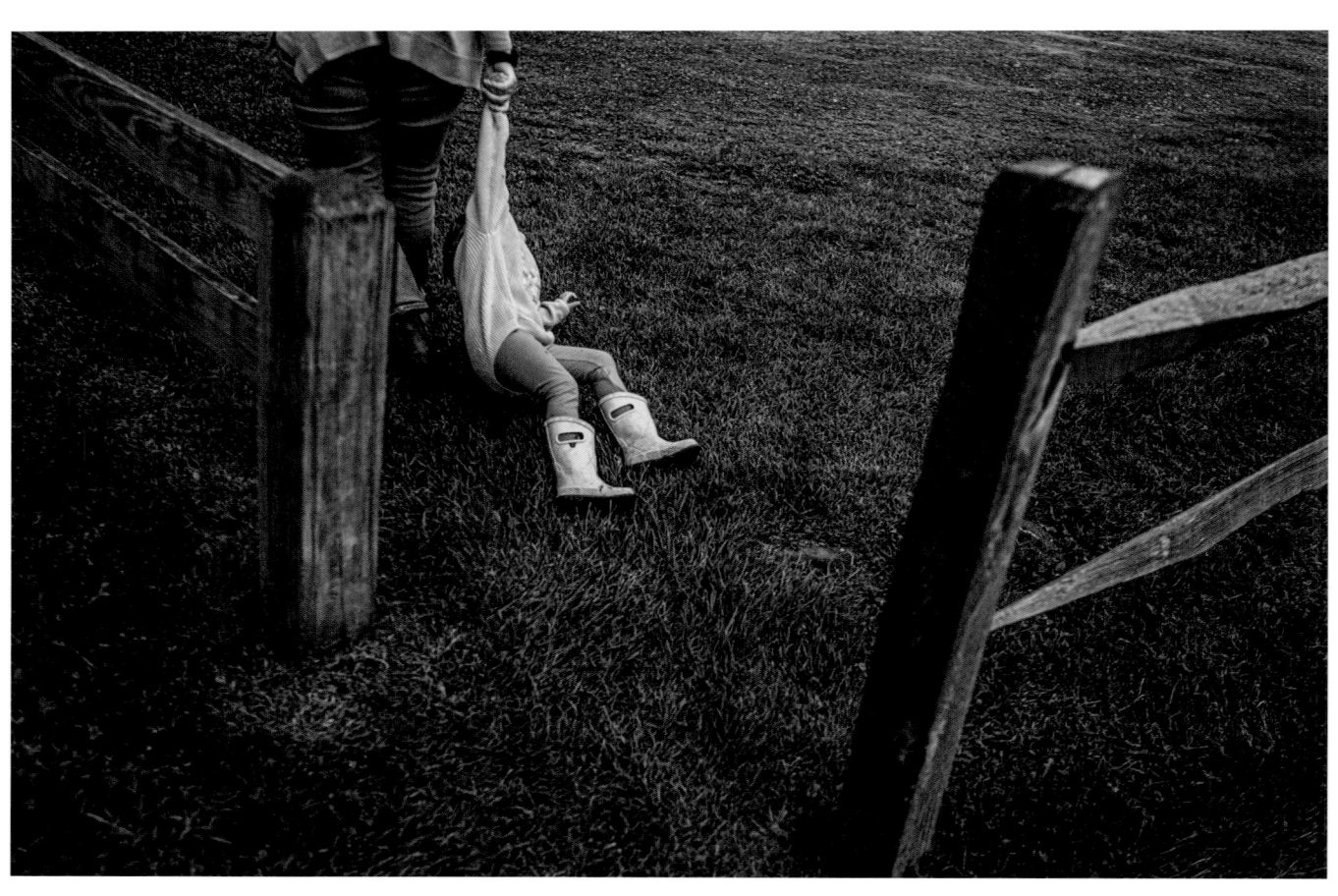

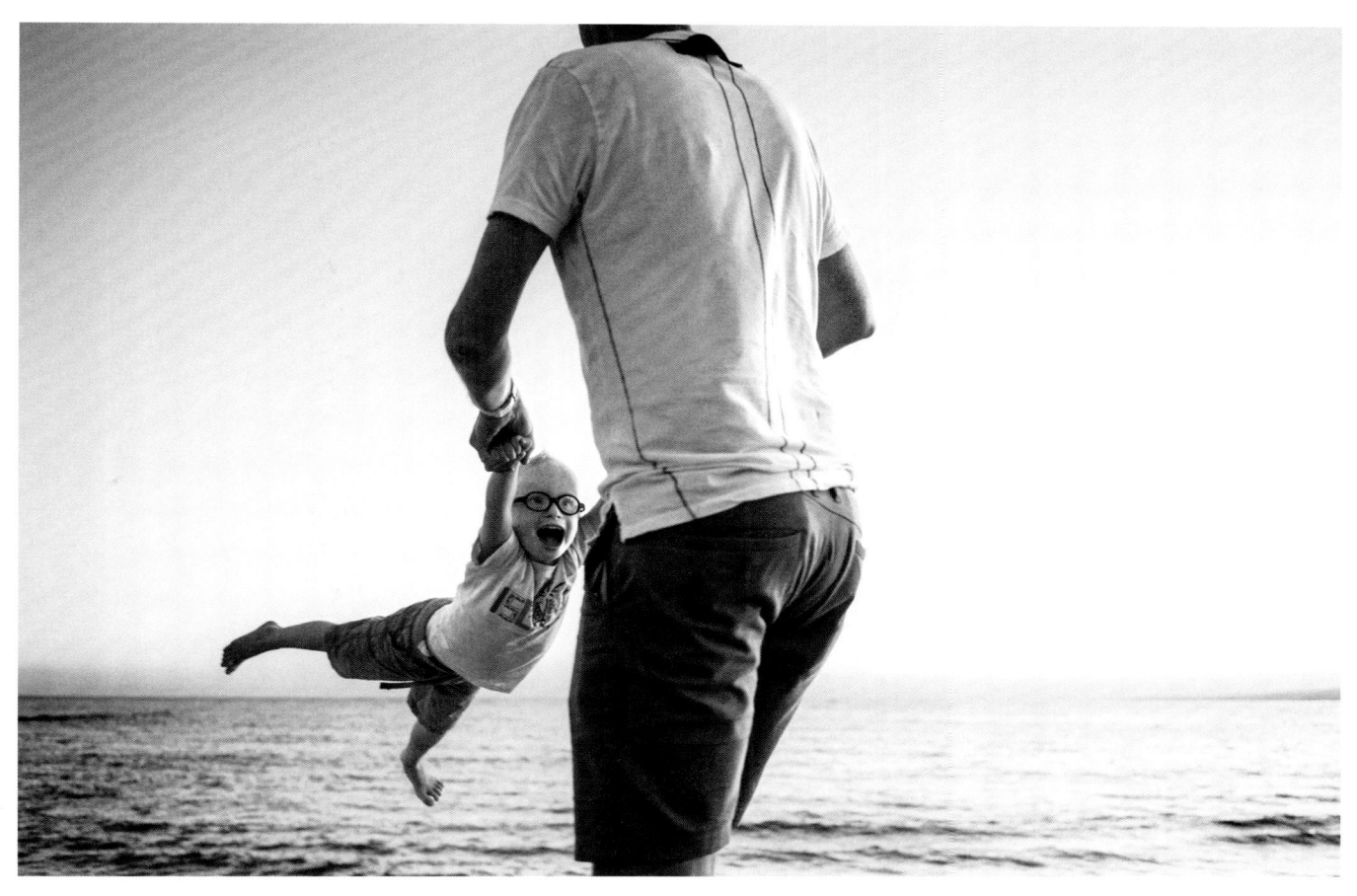

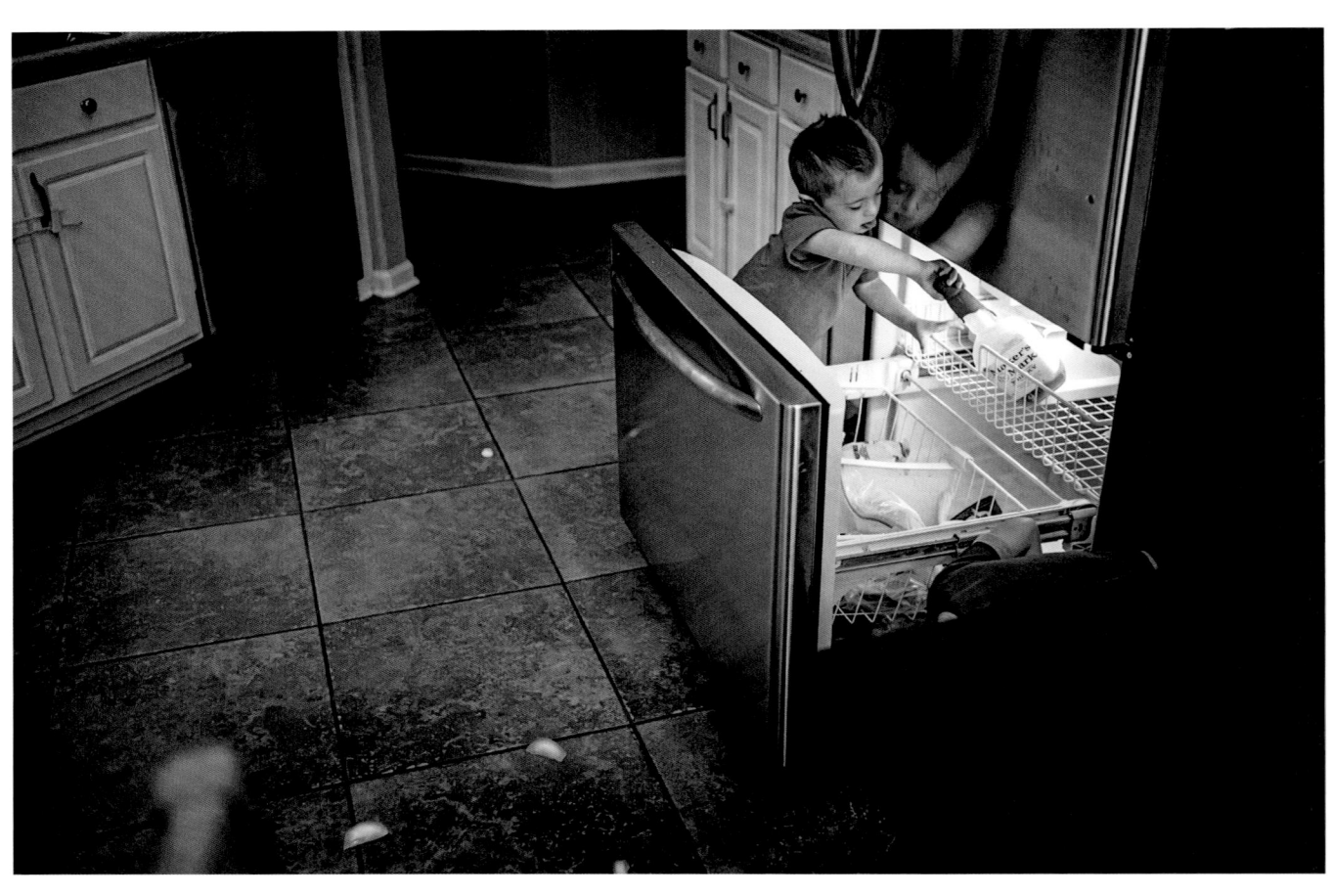

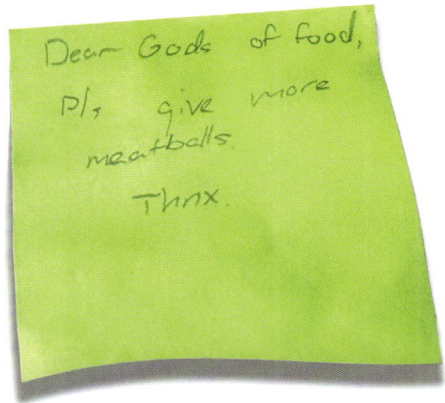

I have been packing lunch . . .

—Joe Newman

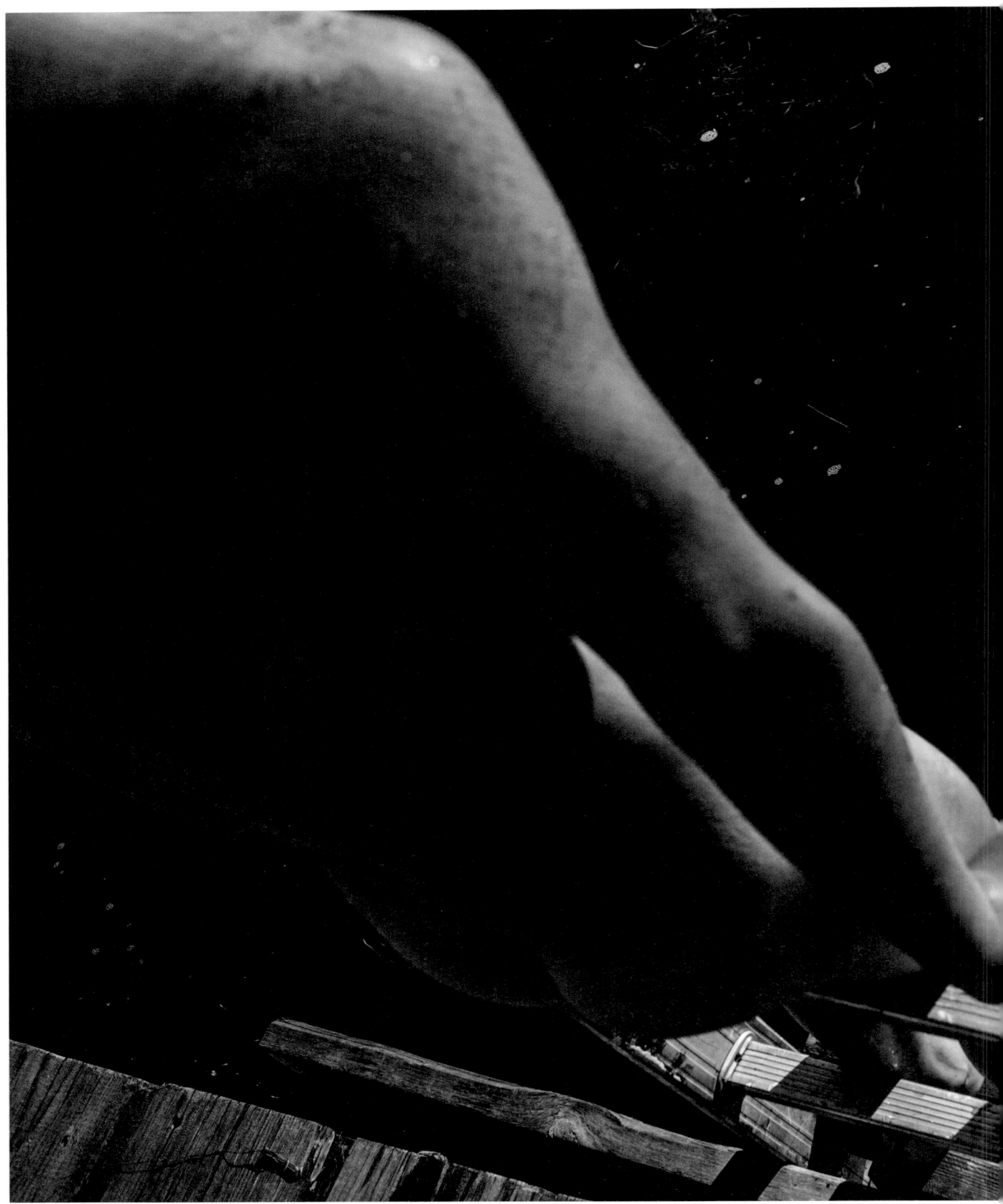

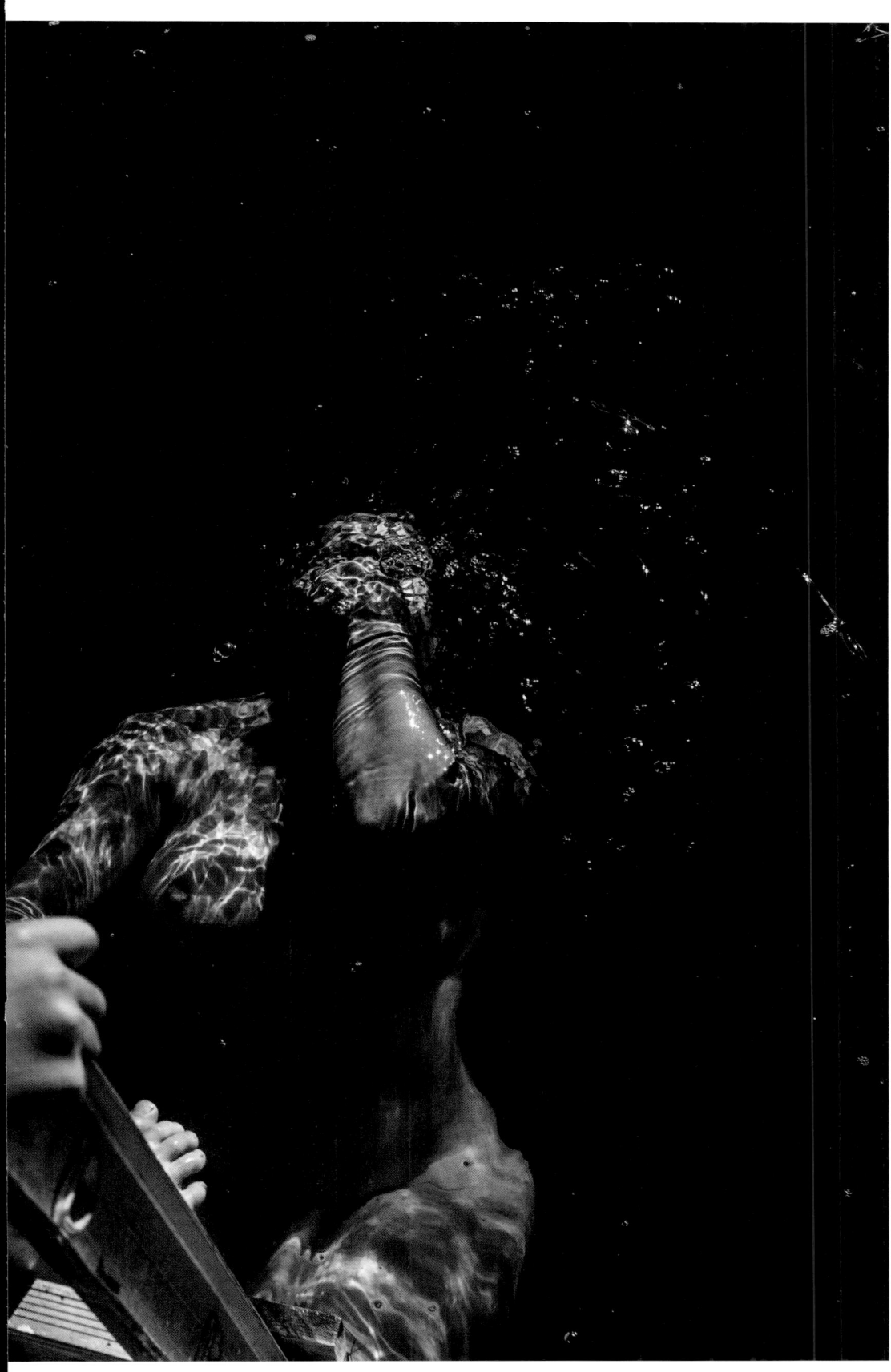

*Conversations with a
three-year-old*

Anna: Call me
    Louisa, Mama.

Me: But your name
    is Anna.

Anna: Call me Louisa
    anyway!

Me: When you are a
    mother and have
    a daughter you can
    name her Louisa.

Anna: Nooo! I don't
    want to become a
    mother! That's too
    exhausting!

—Juliane Sassmann

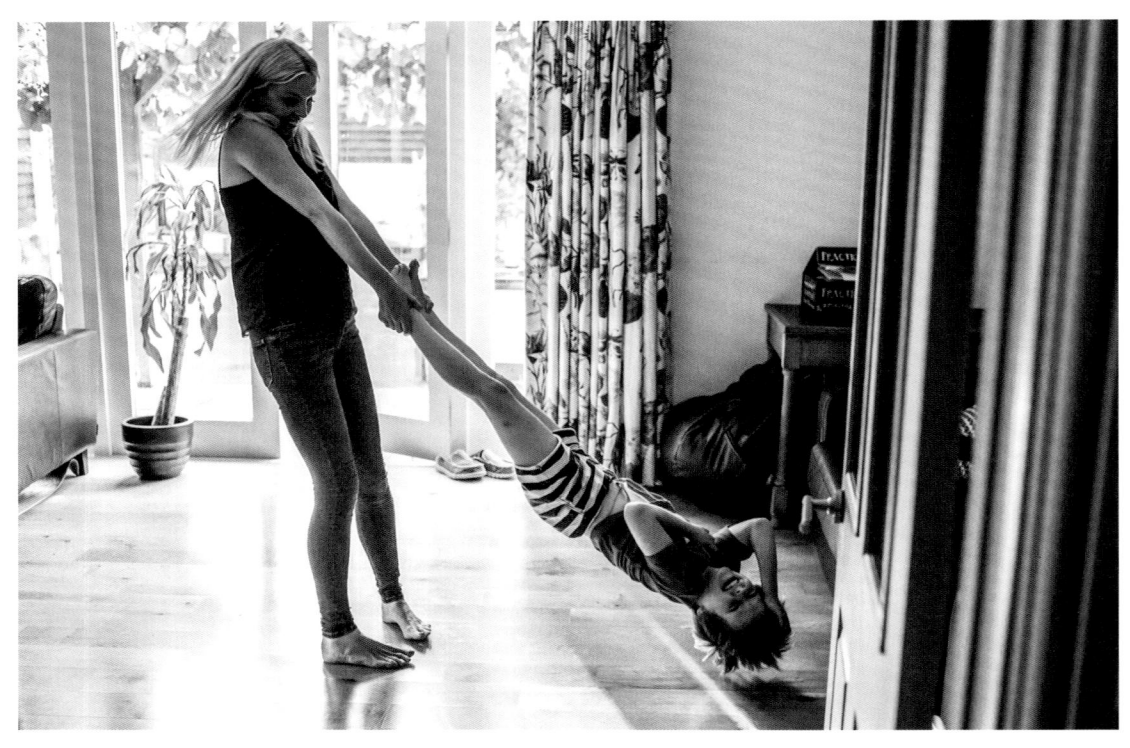

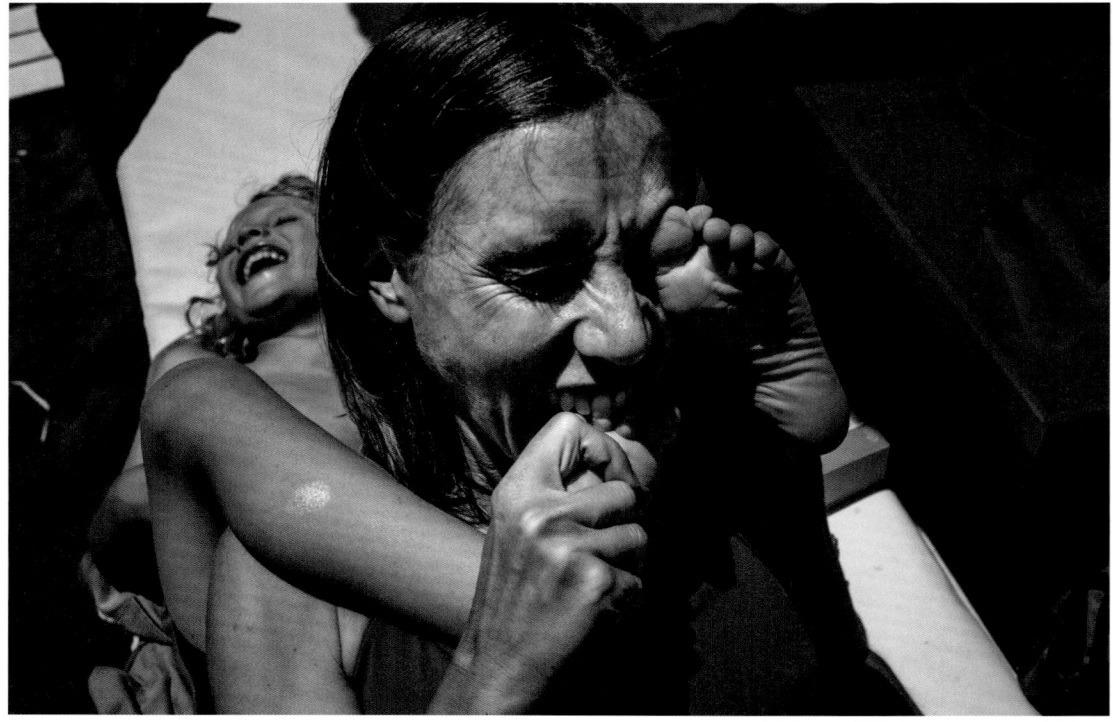

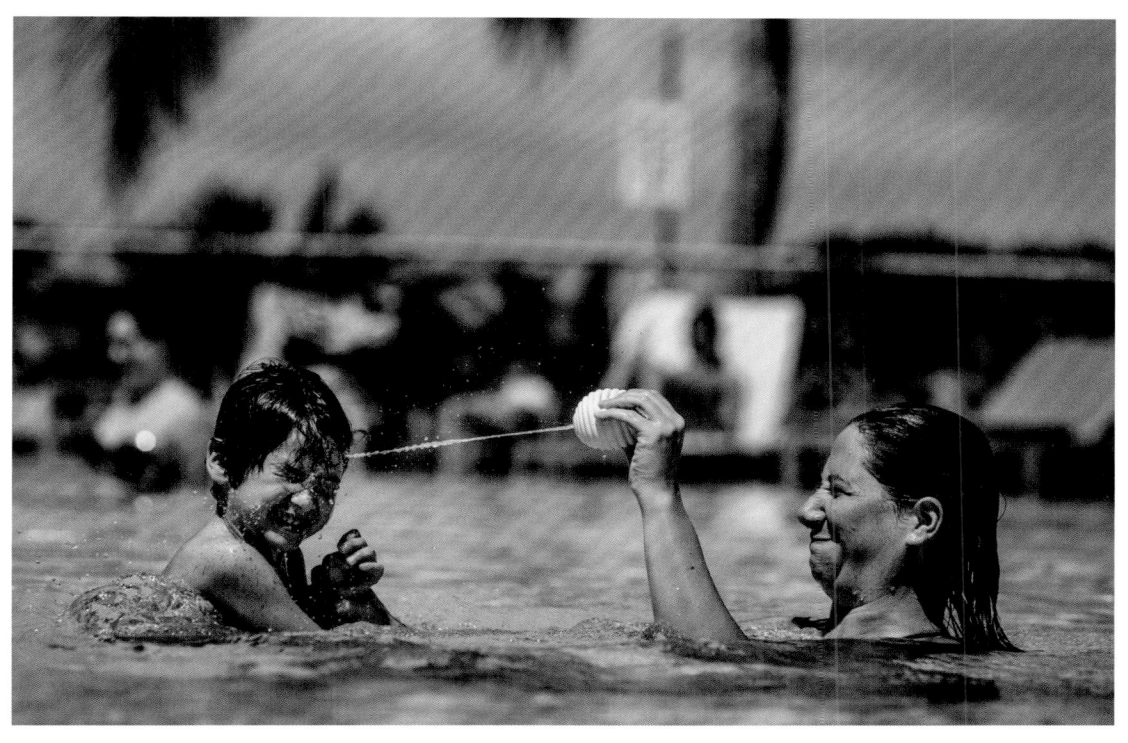

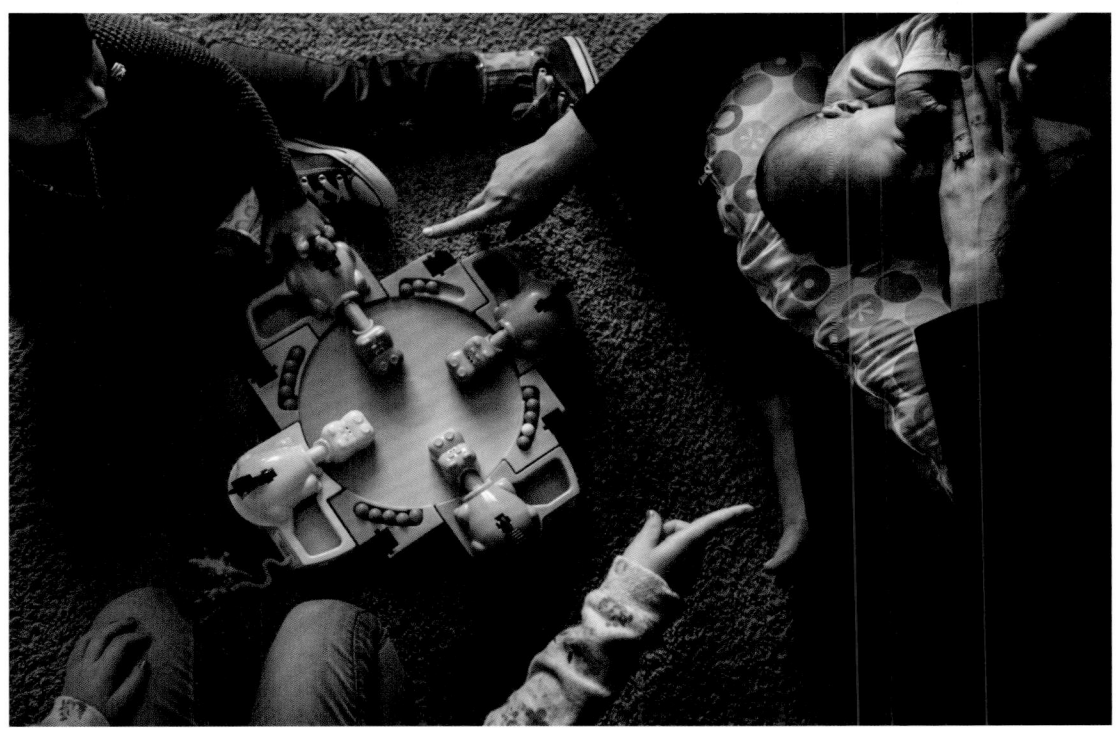

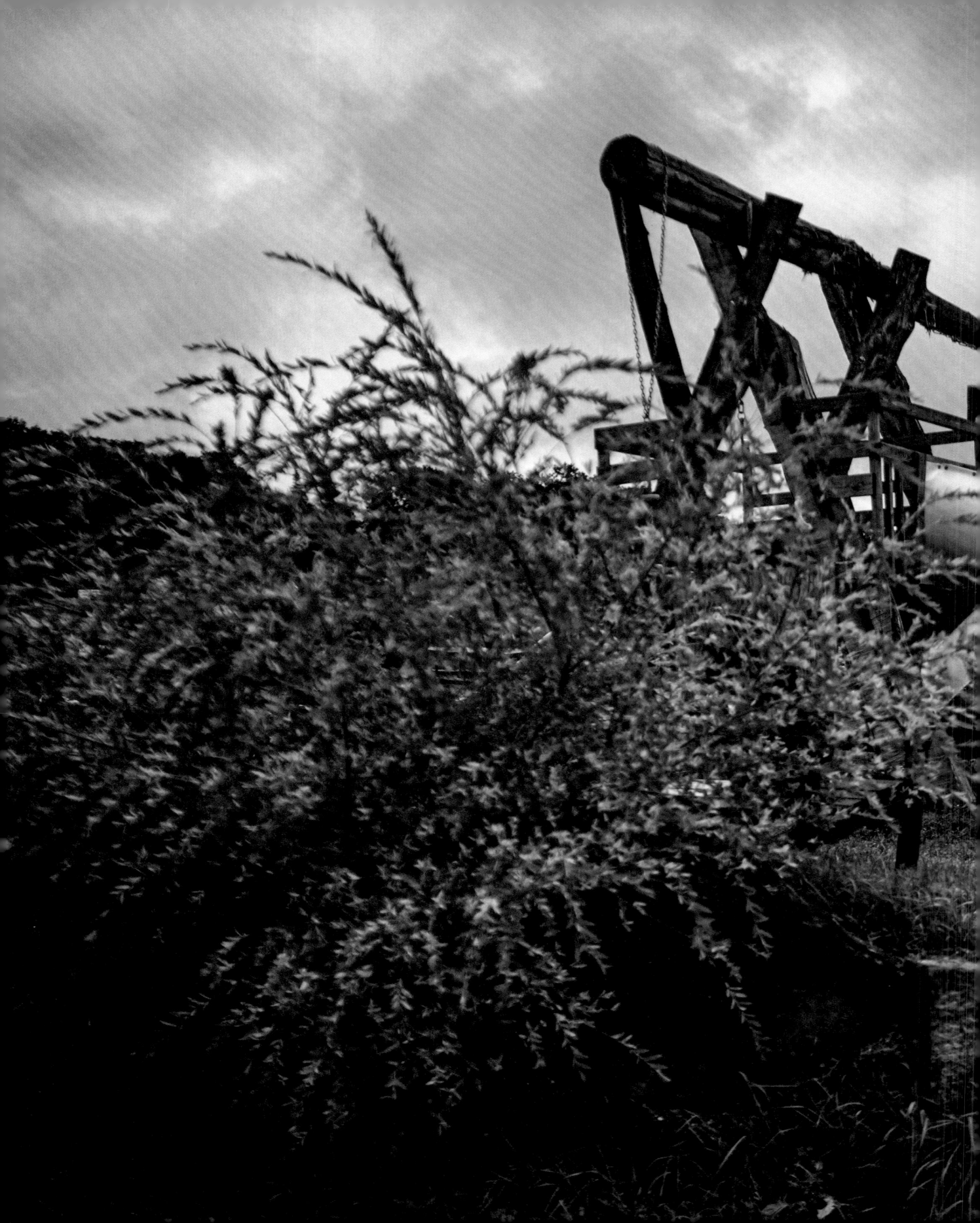

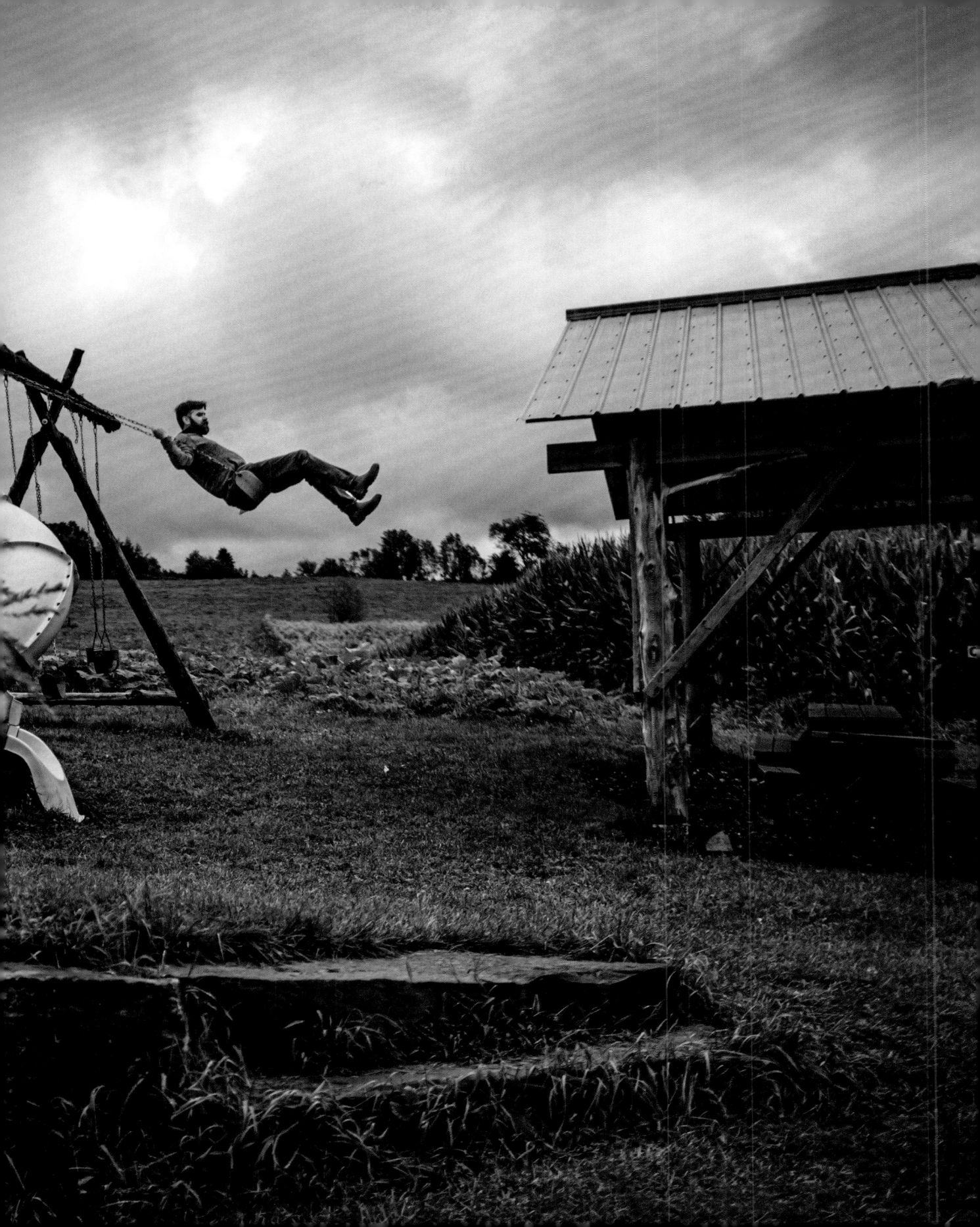

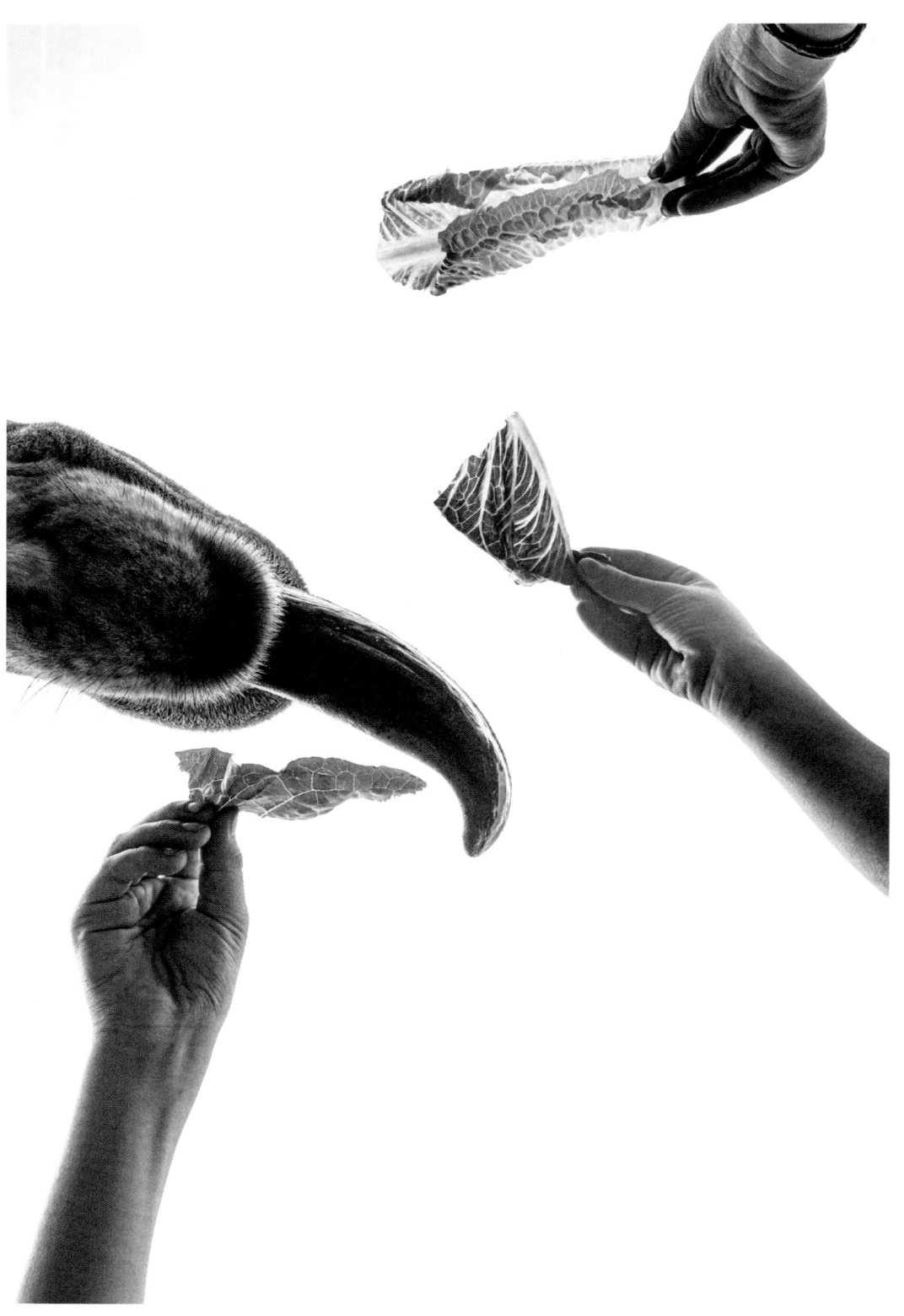

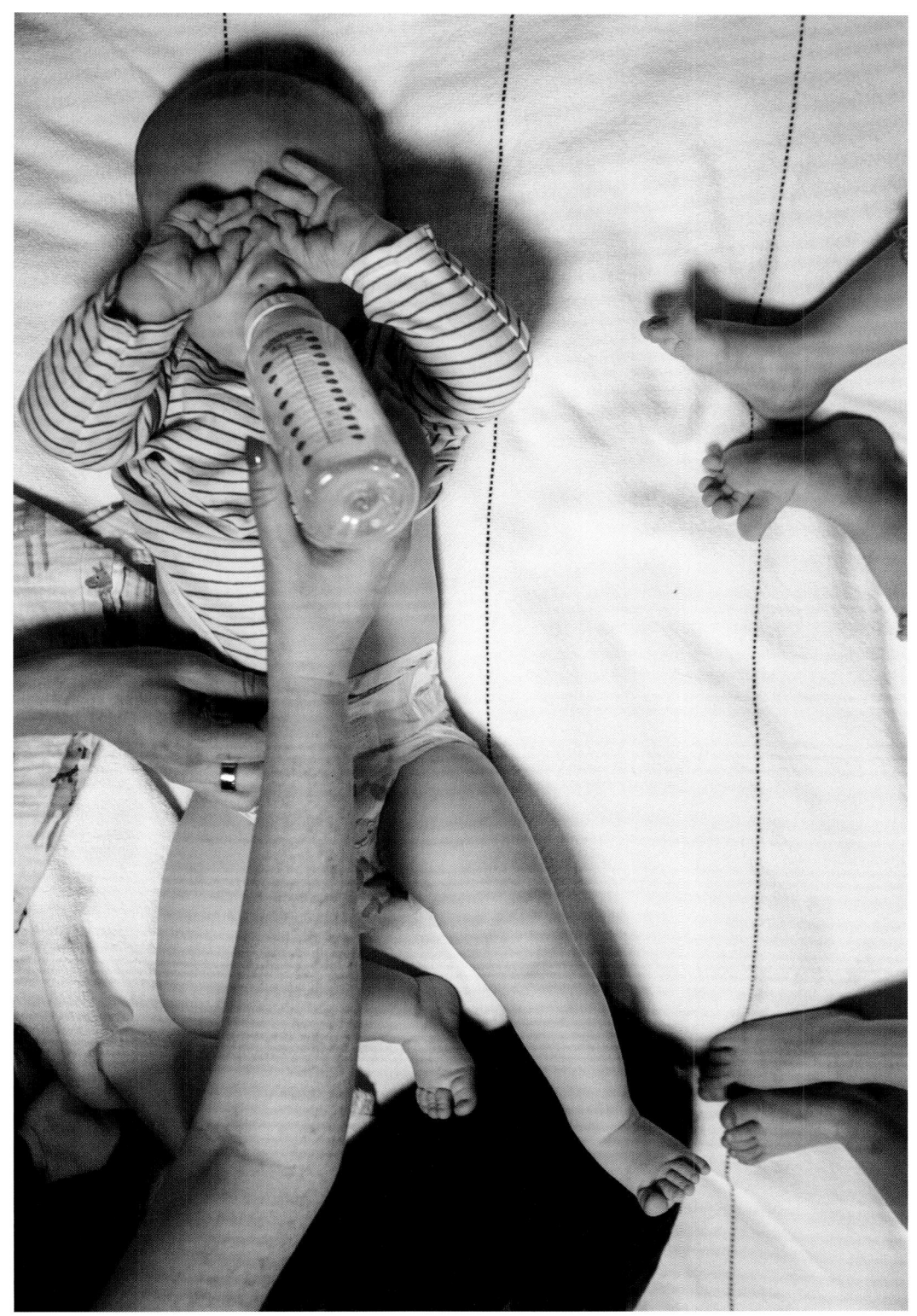

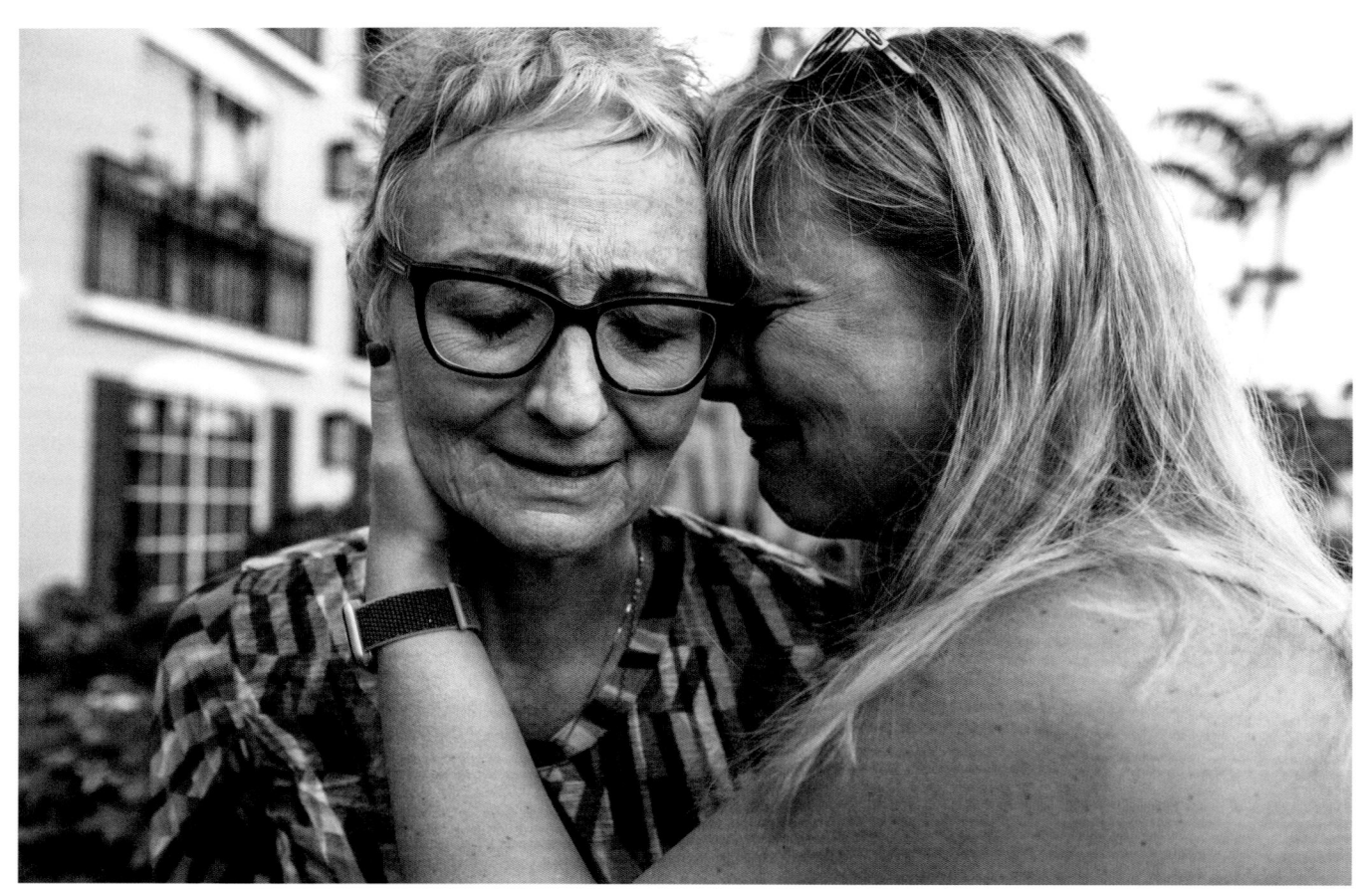

The most beautiful moments in a relationship are when we let go of the roles we assume . . .

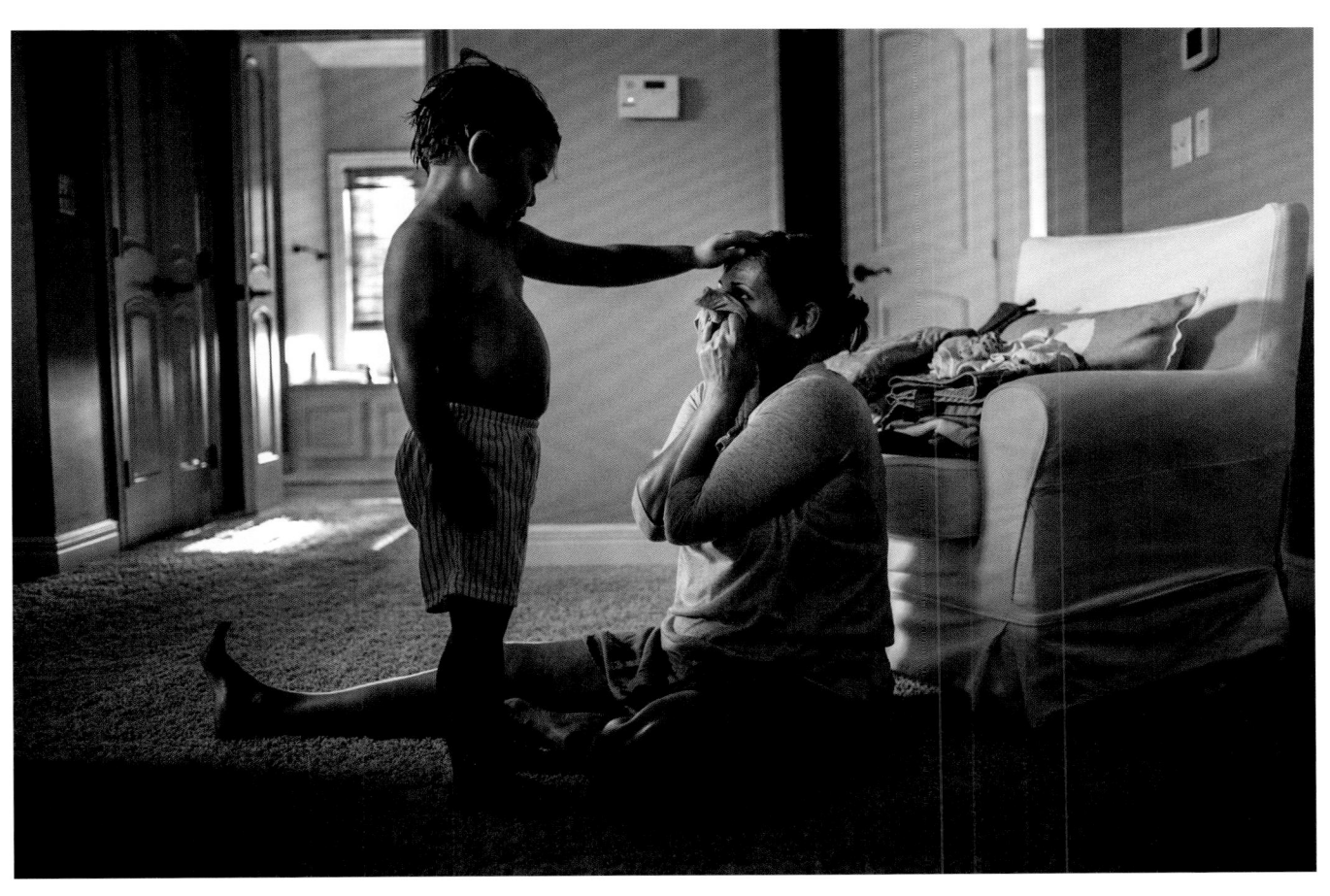

and just be human for someone else.

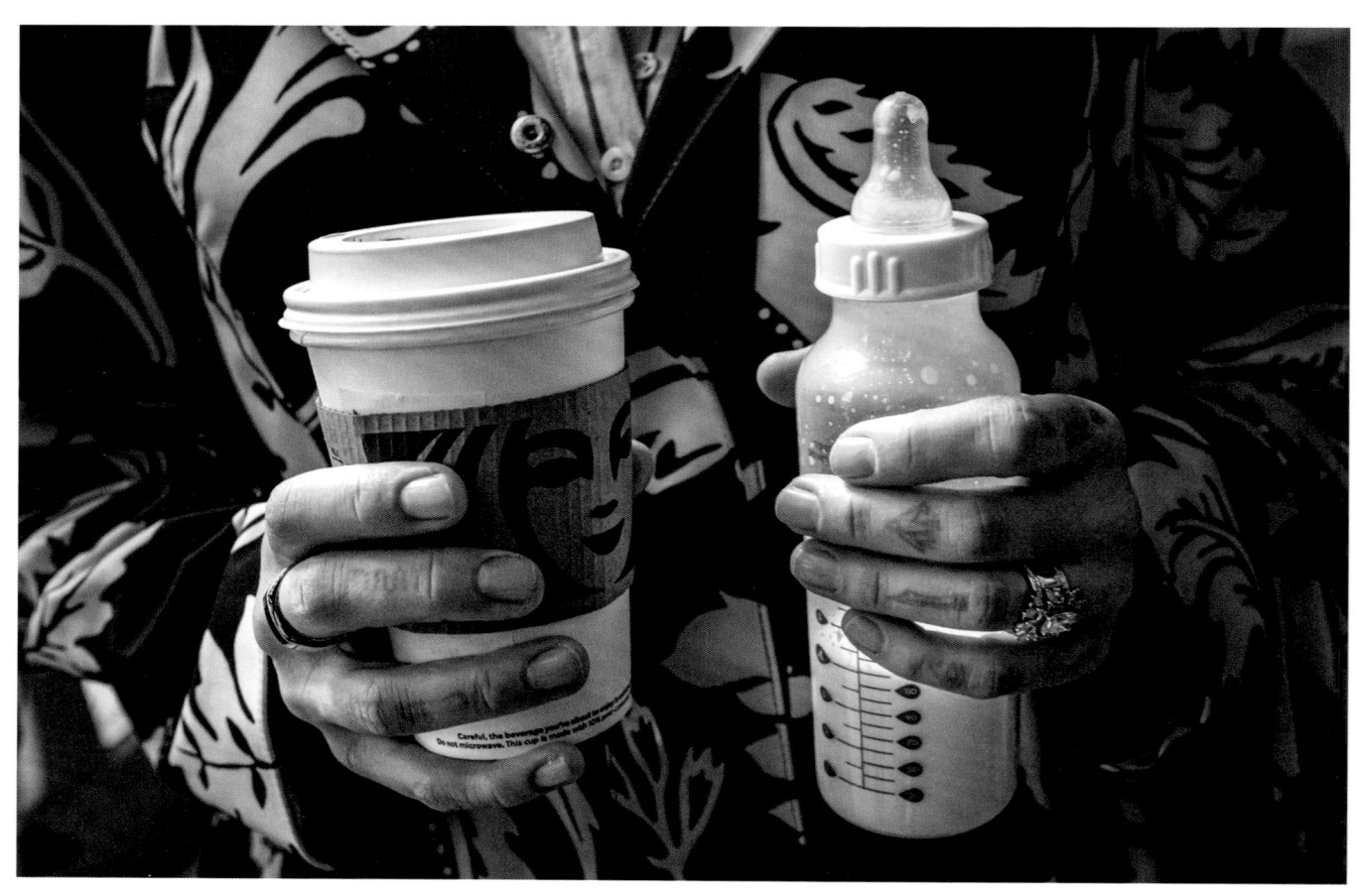

Don't be afraid of laughing gas. Sometimes you will see tiny men on the walls.
And they are made of lights.

—Benjamin, age five

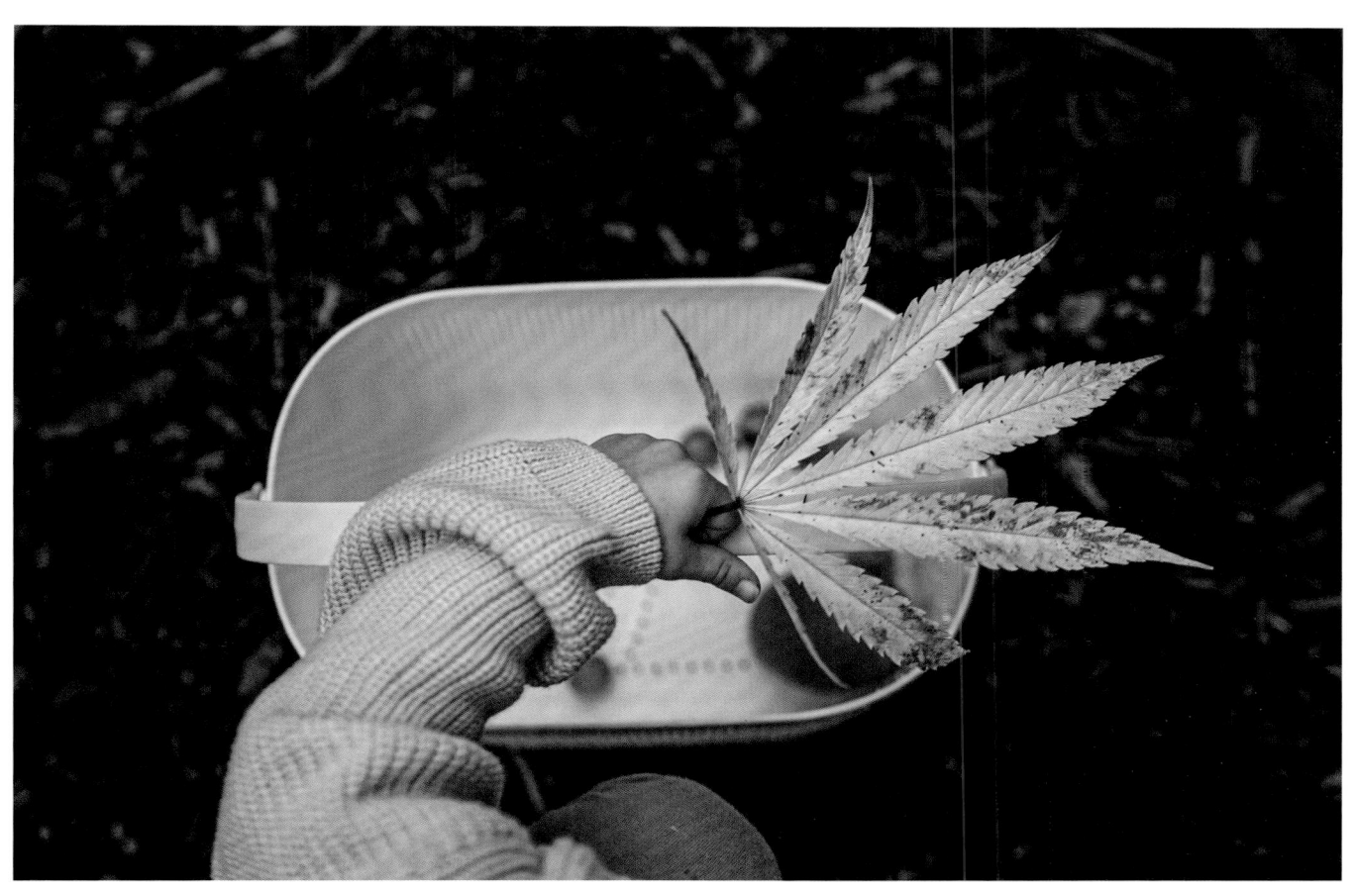

Can I have that medicine that inhibits my pain receptors?

—Arthur, age seven

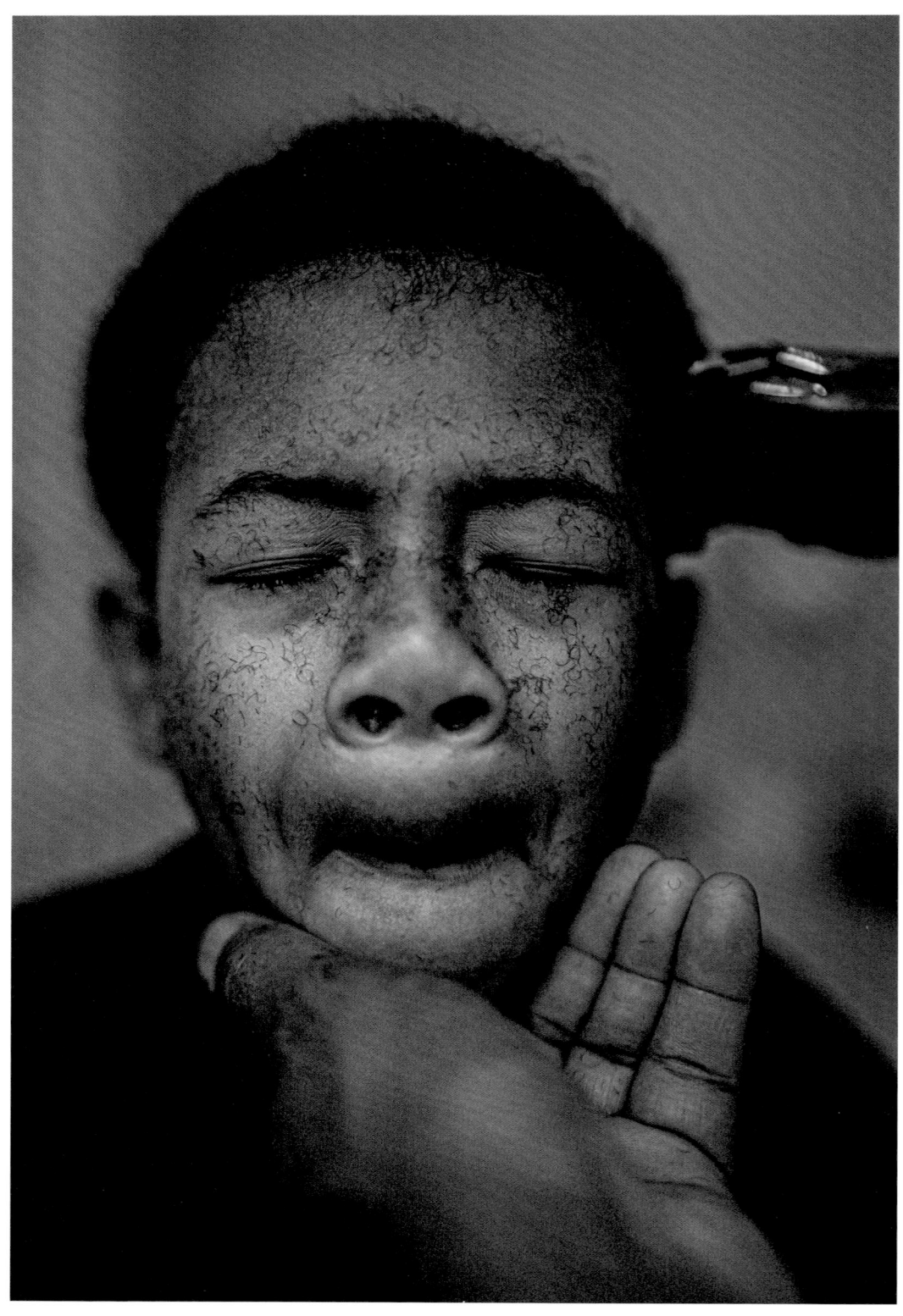

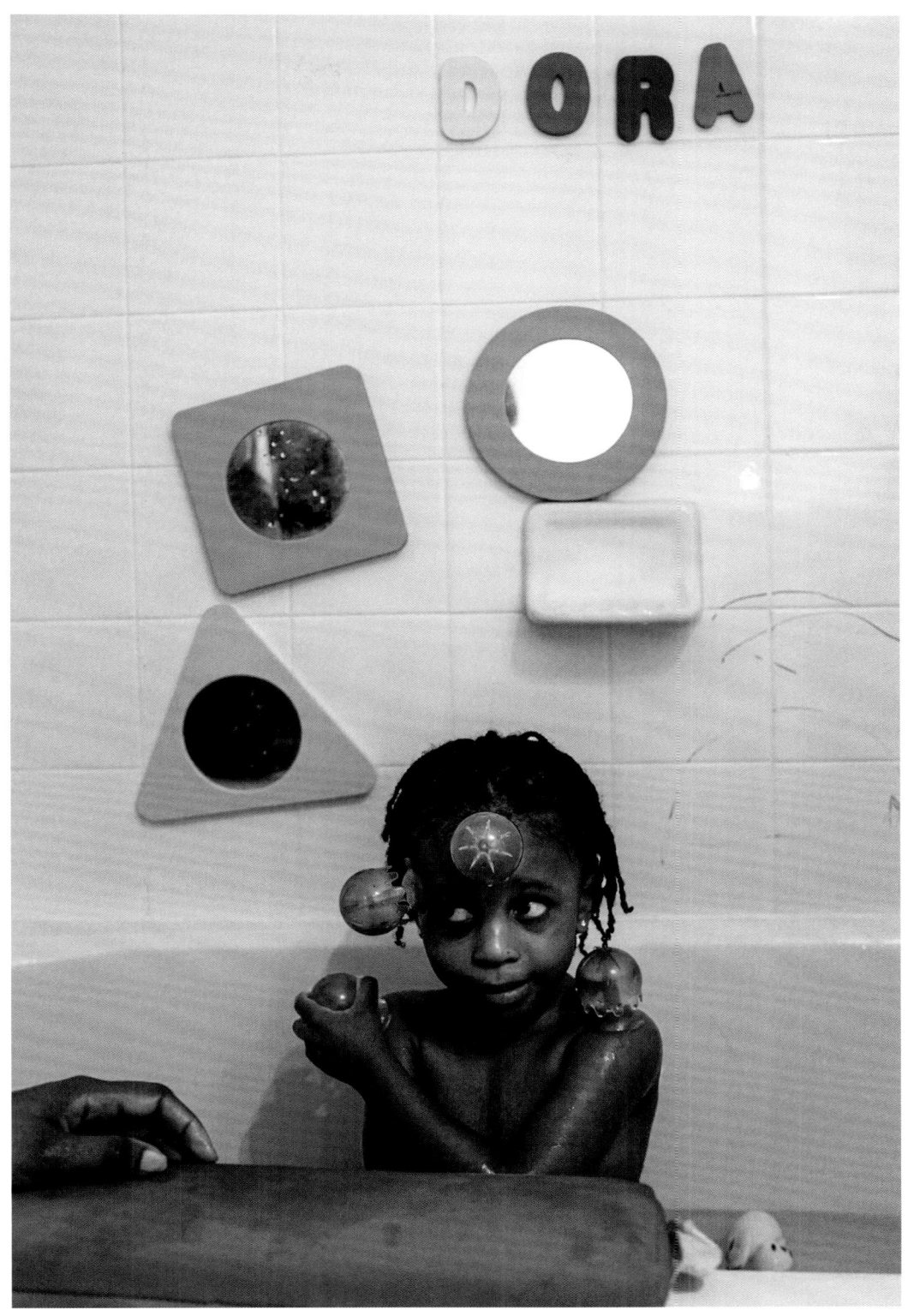

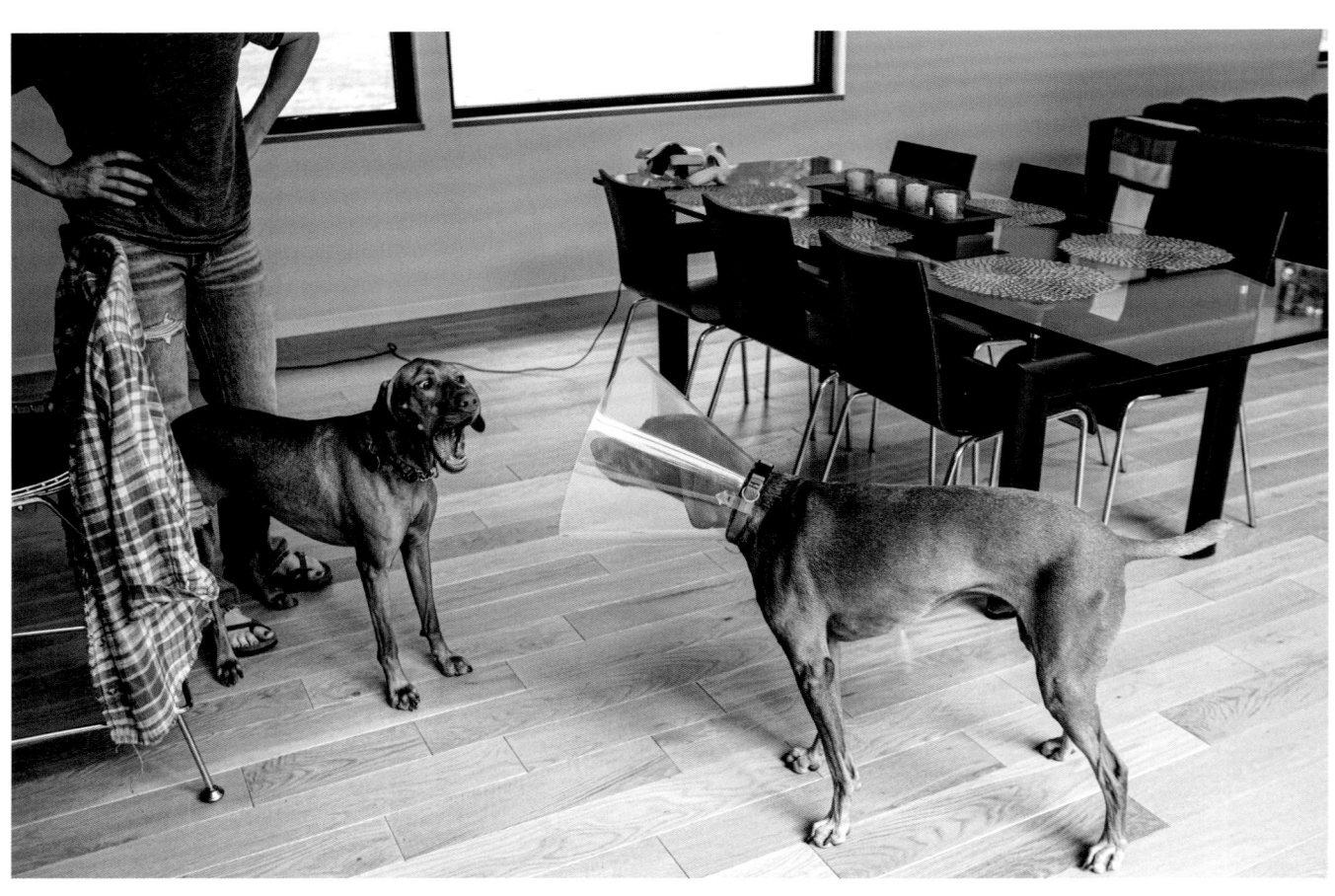

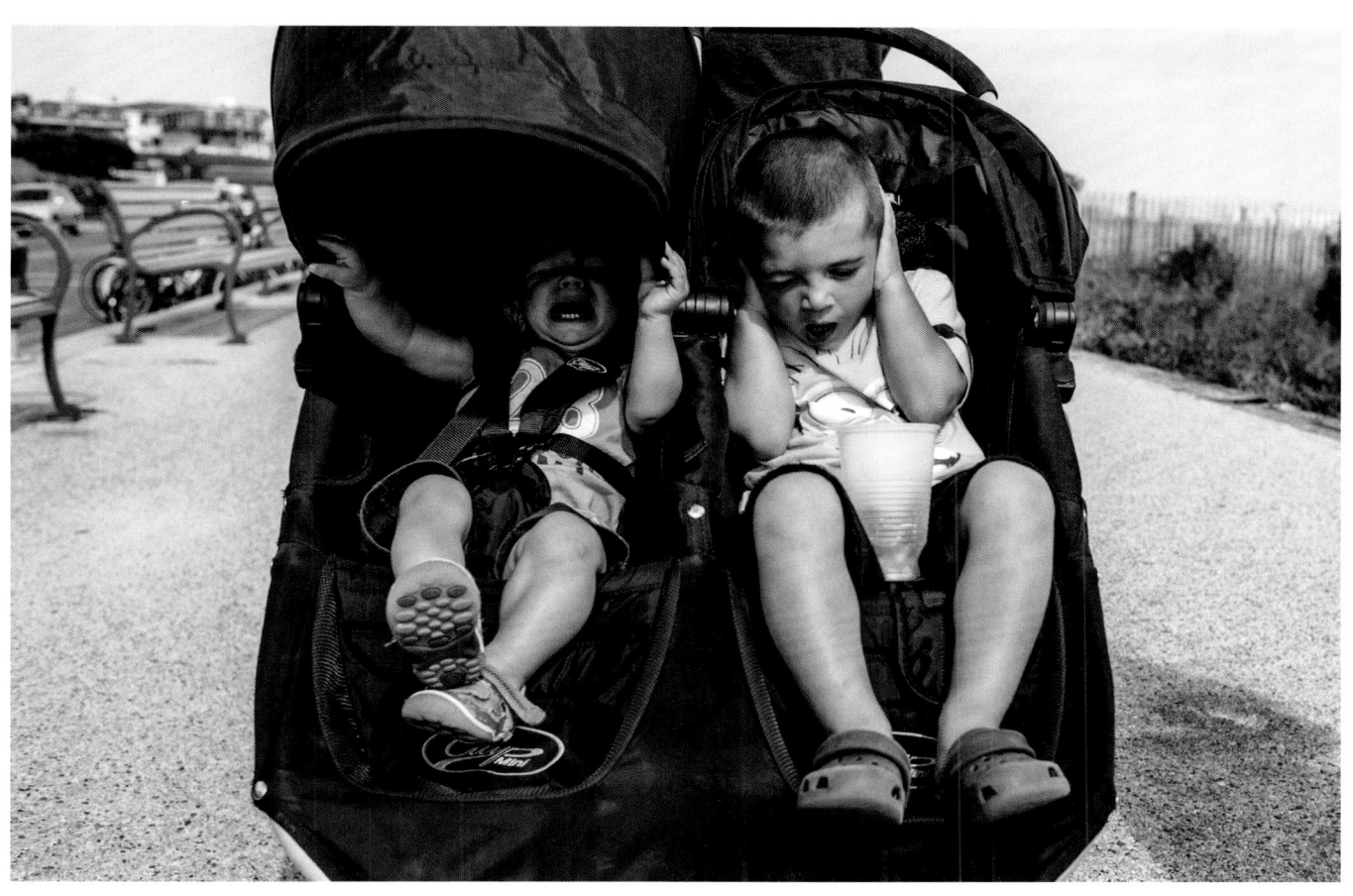

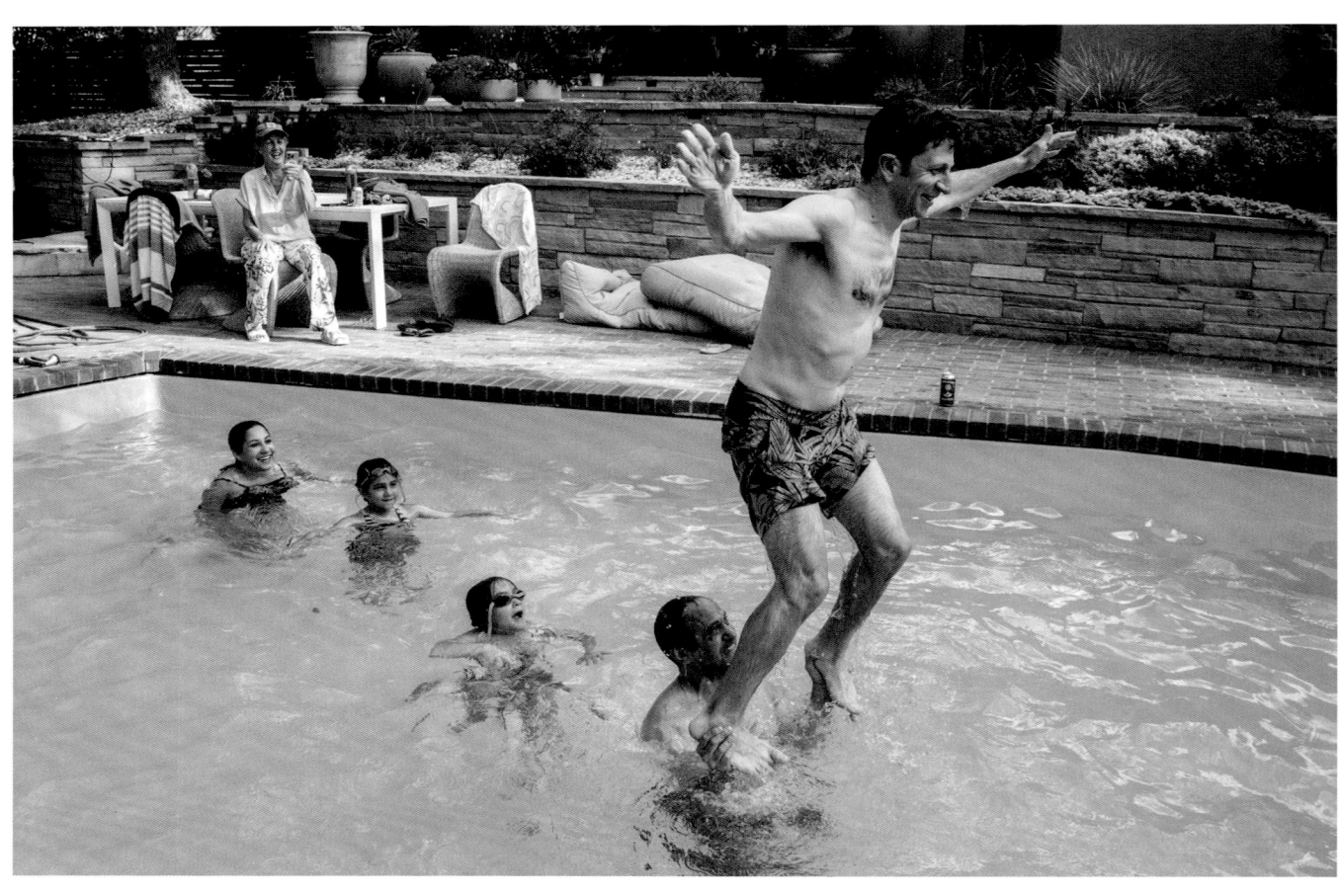

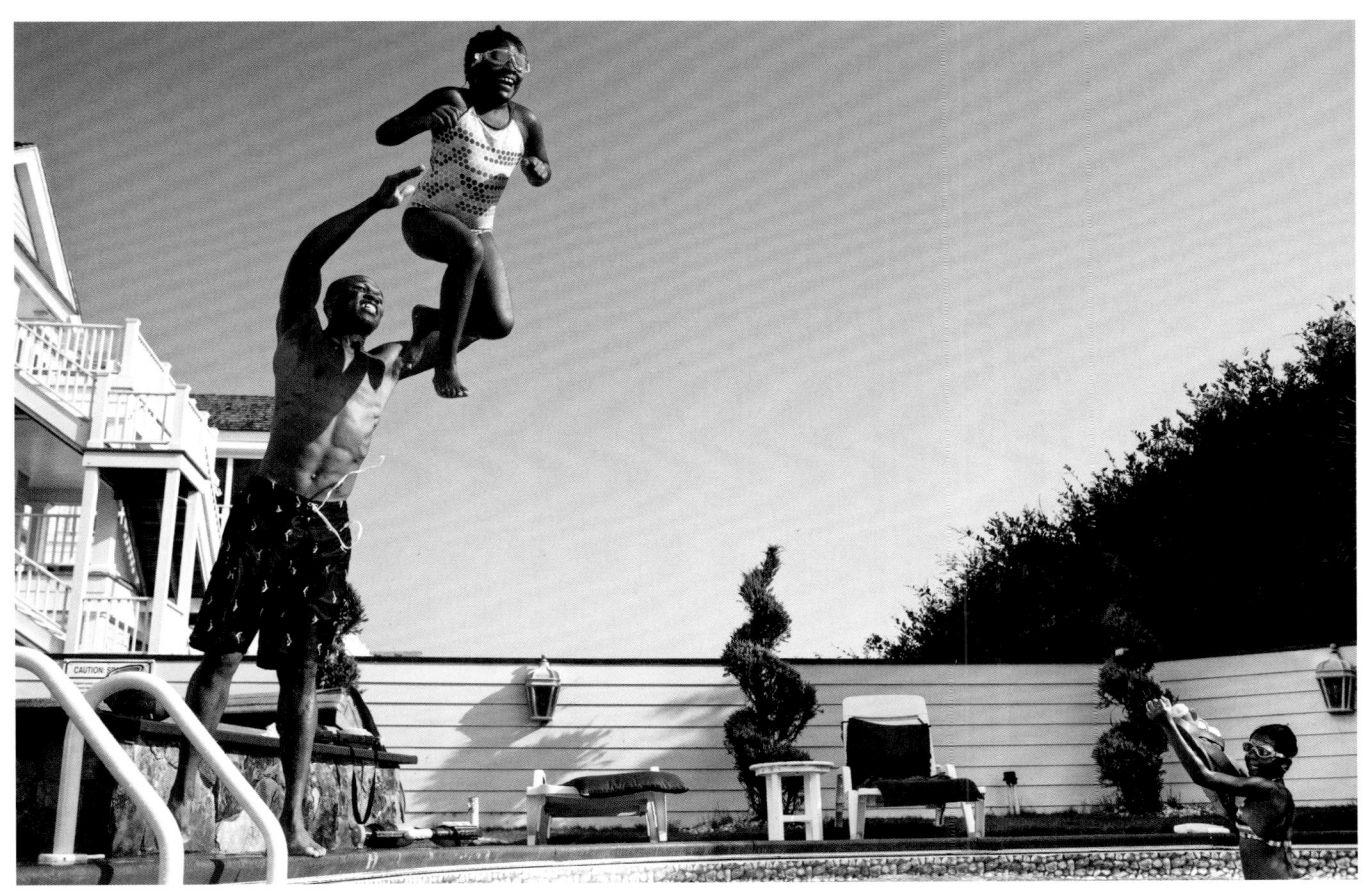

Advice on being a dad: That every win, no matter how small or personal, should be celebrated. Take more pictures, give more hugs, be grateful every day you get to witness this little garden of yours and the seeds you've planted grow and thrive and flower in the sunshine and rain and snow and wind. You cannot protect them from everything, but you can talk to them and prepare them. Sometimes your wife just wants you to listen and eat the ice cream and nod your head and empathize and hate the boss or that coworker along with her. Introduce them to the things you love. Not so that they will love them, but so they can know you better and eventually love you fuller.

—Jerry Henderson

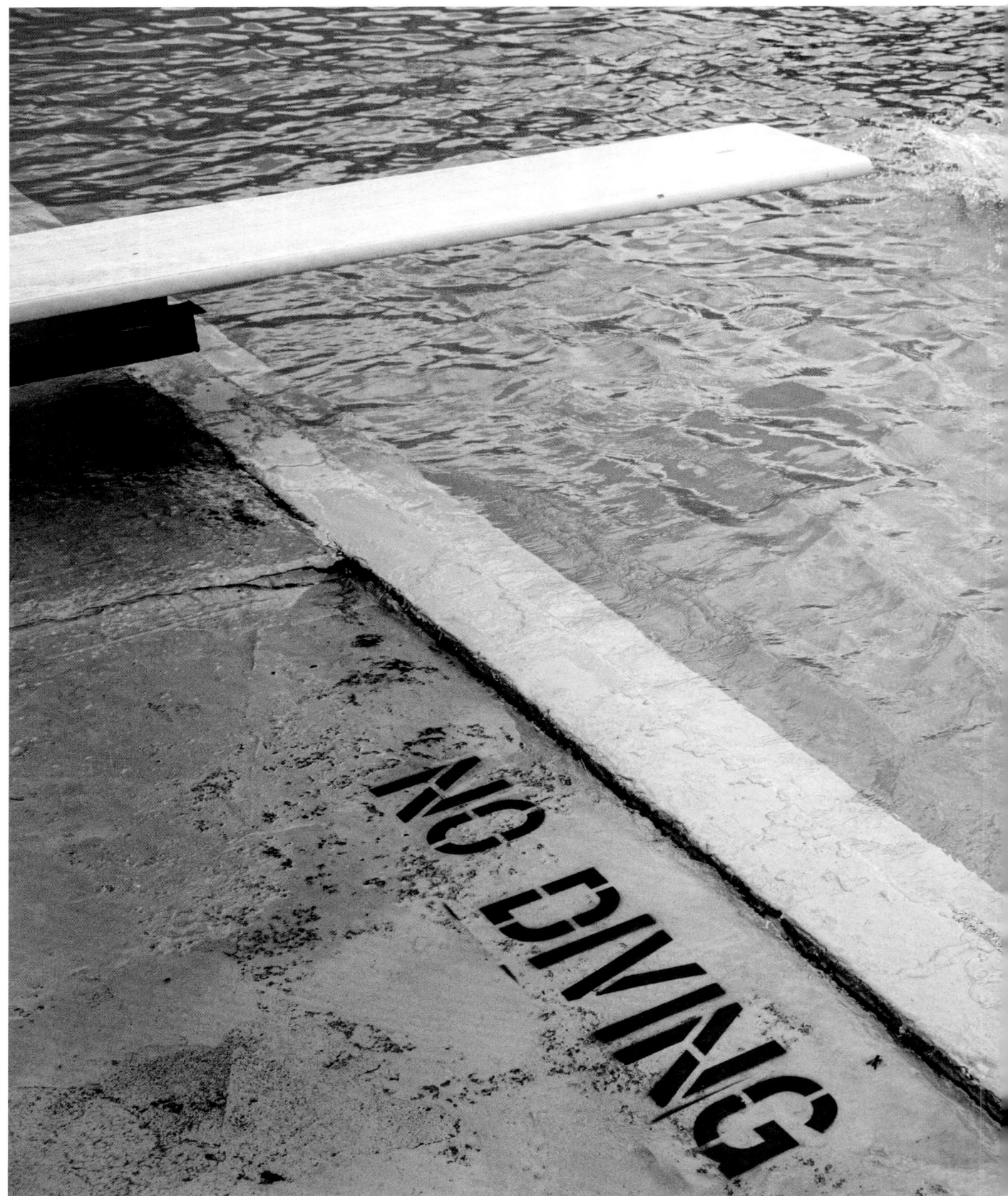

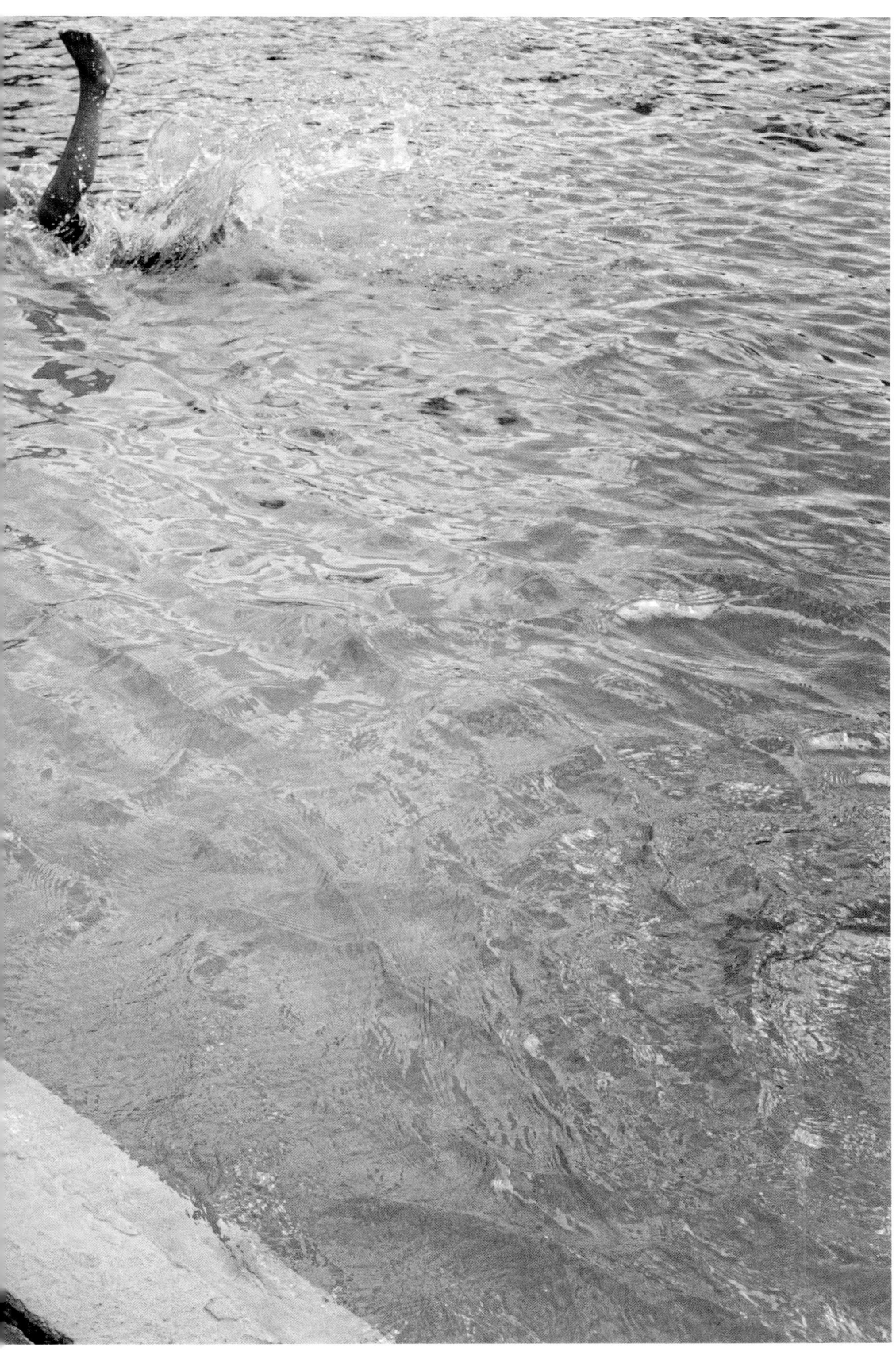

Things I didn't
know about parent-
hood? Something
is always wet.

—Marie O'Mahony

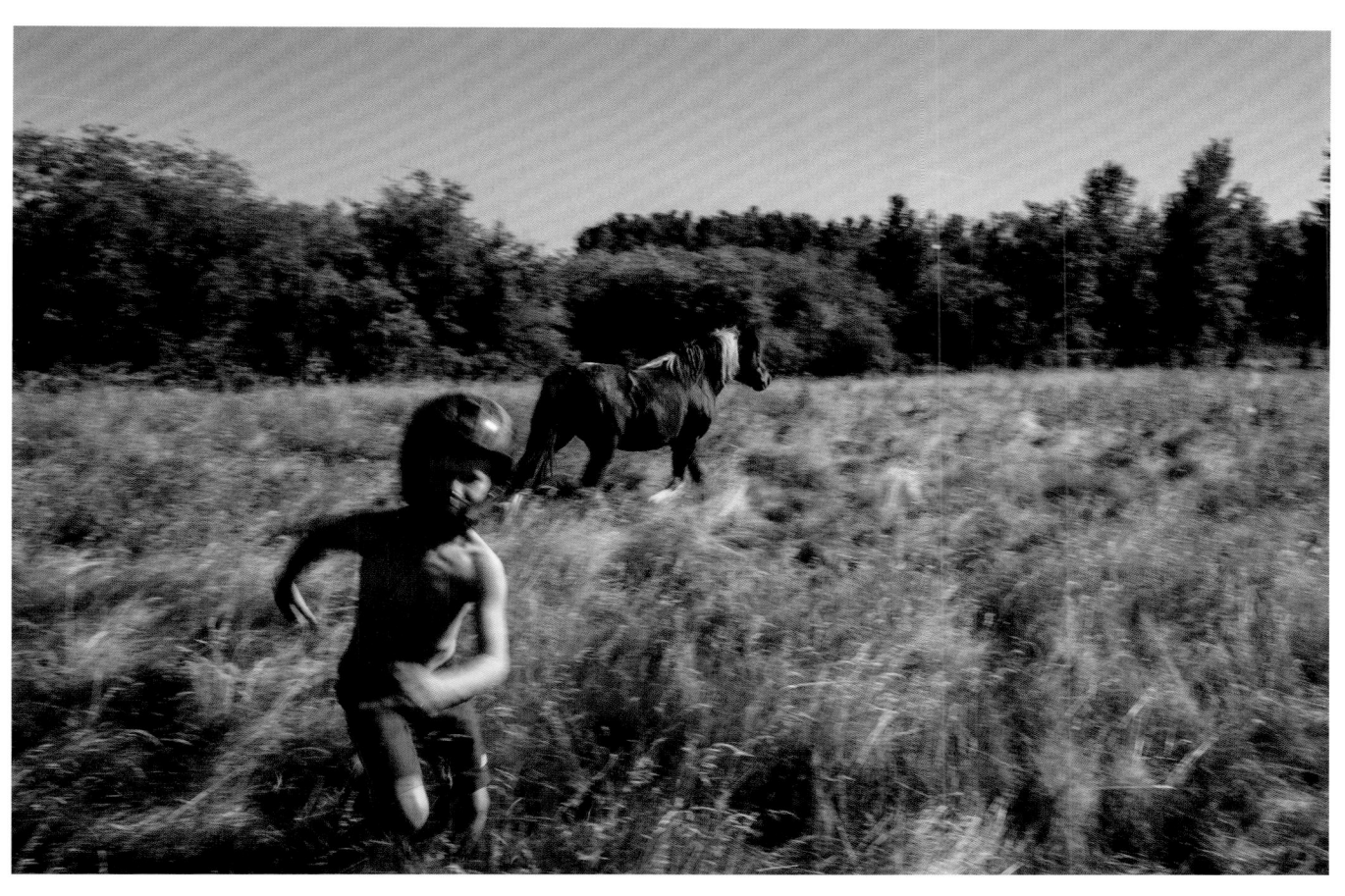

My sketchy parenting advice:

Default to "yes" instead of "no." Let them experience life. Reserve "no" for real dangers.

—Joel Carter

Introduce your children to the idea of death as early as possible. It is an inevitable part of life, so they will learn about it eventually; delaying their understanding does them no good. I think about it like a box in your head. Kids won't fully understand the finality of death when you first talk to them about it. But if you introduce the idea early (give them the box), when they are older and do understand the finality of death, they at least have a box in which to place that uncomfortable knowledge. Otherwise they learn about the concept of death and the finality of it in one fell swoop. That can be difficult.
—Nolan Johnson

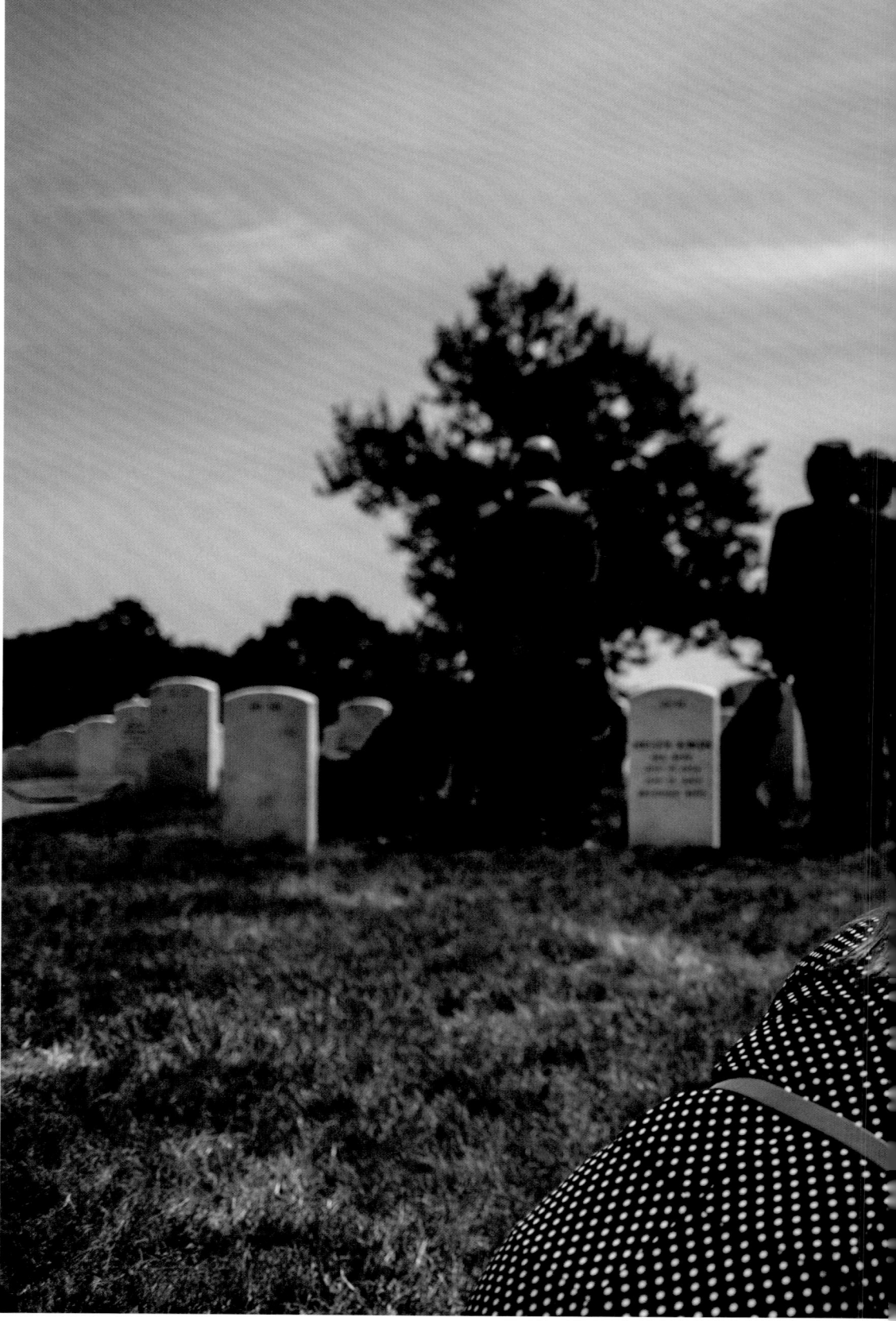

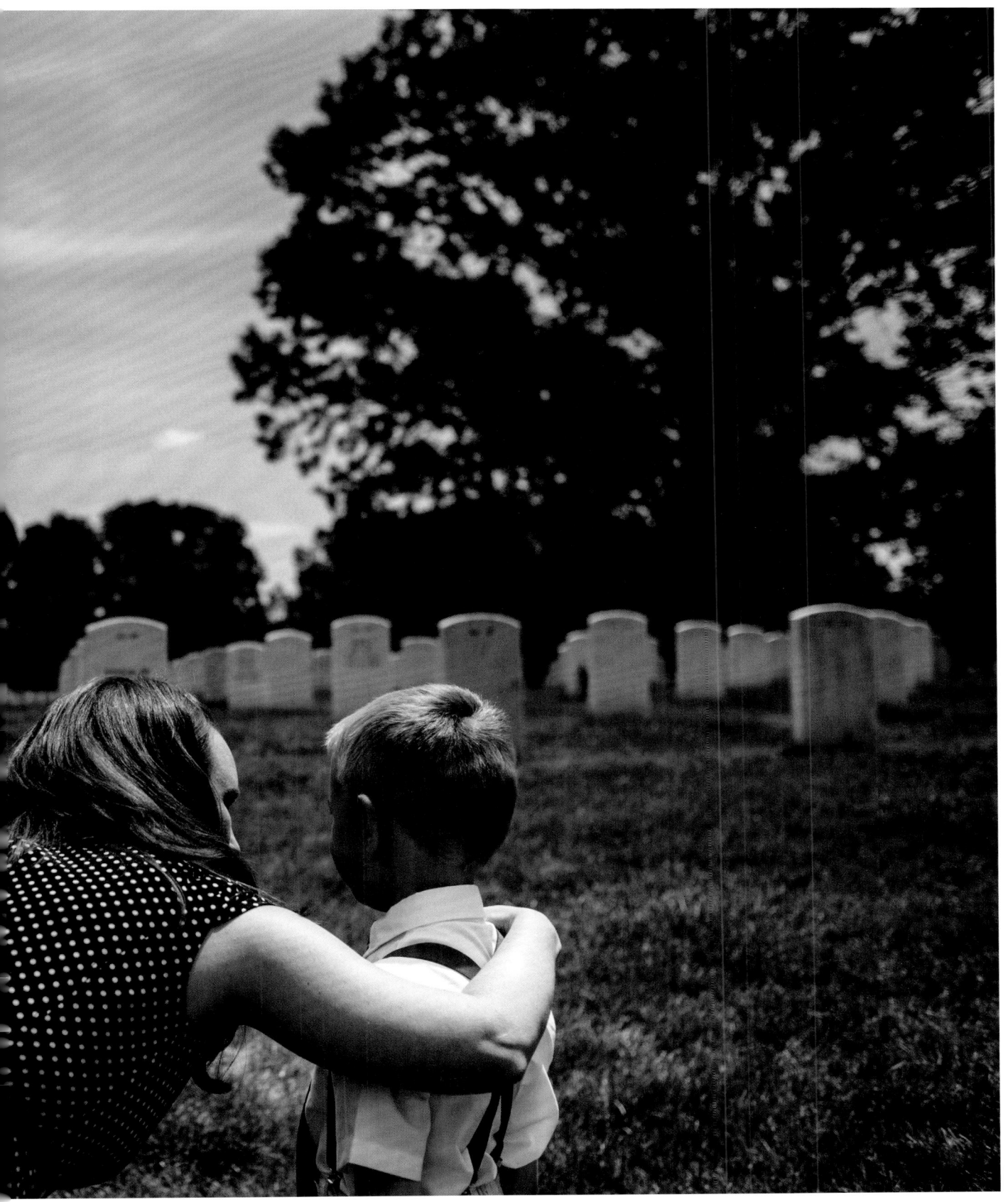

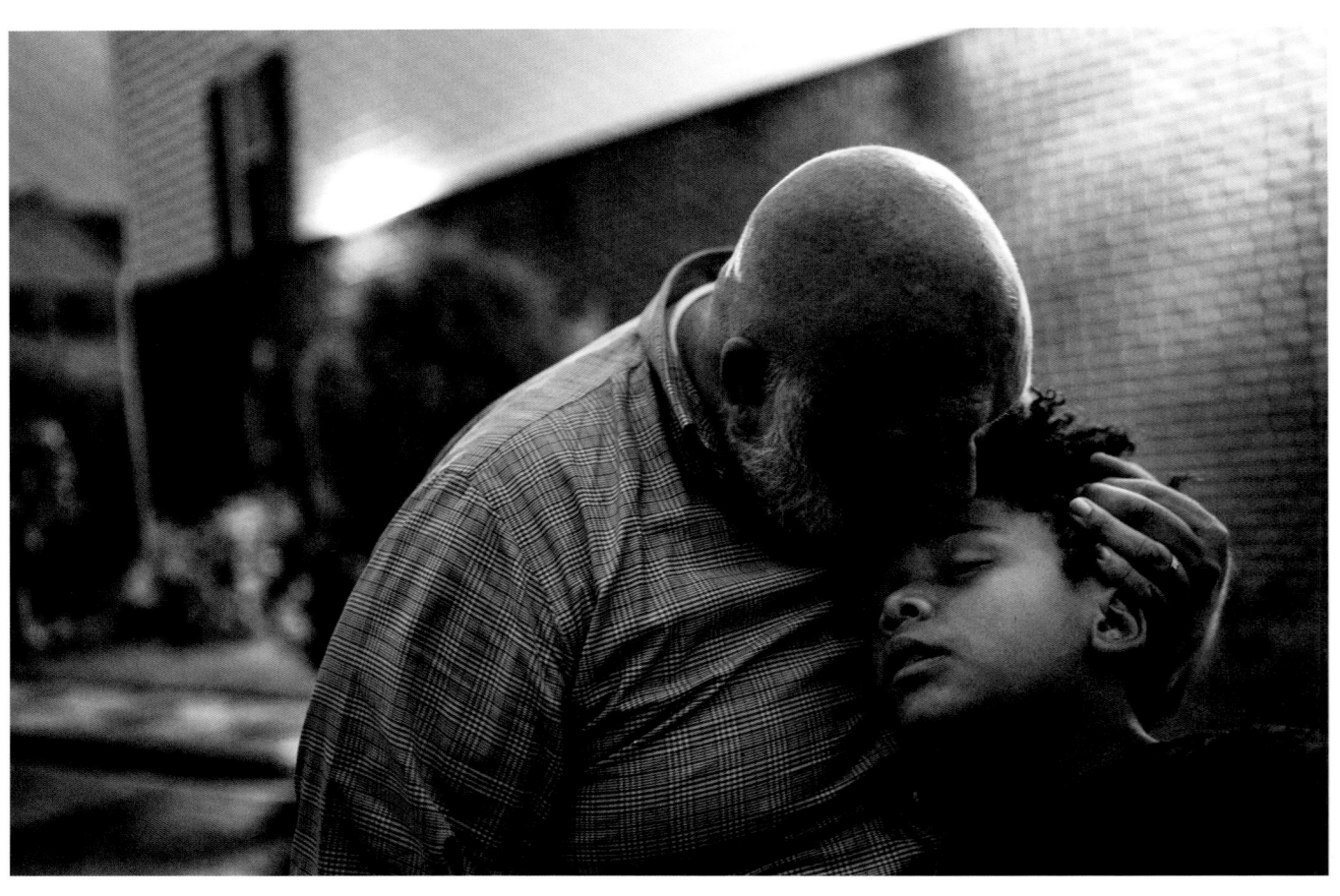

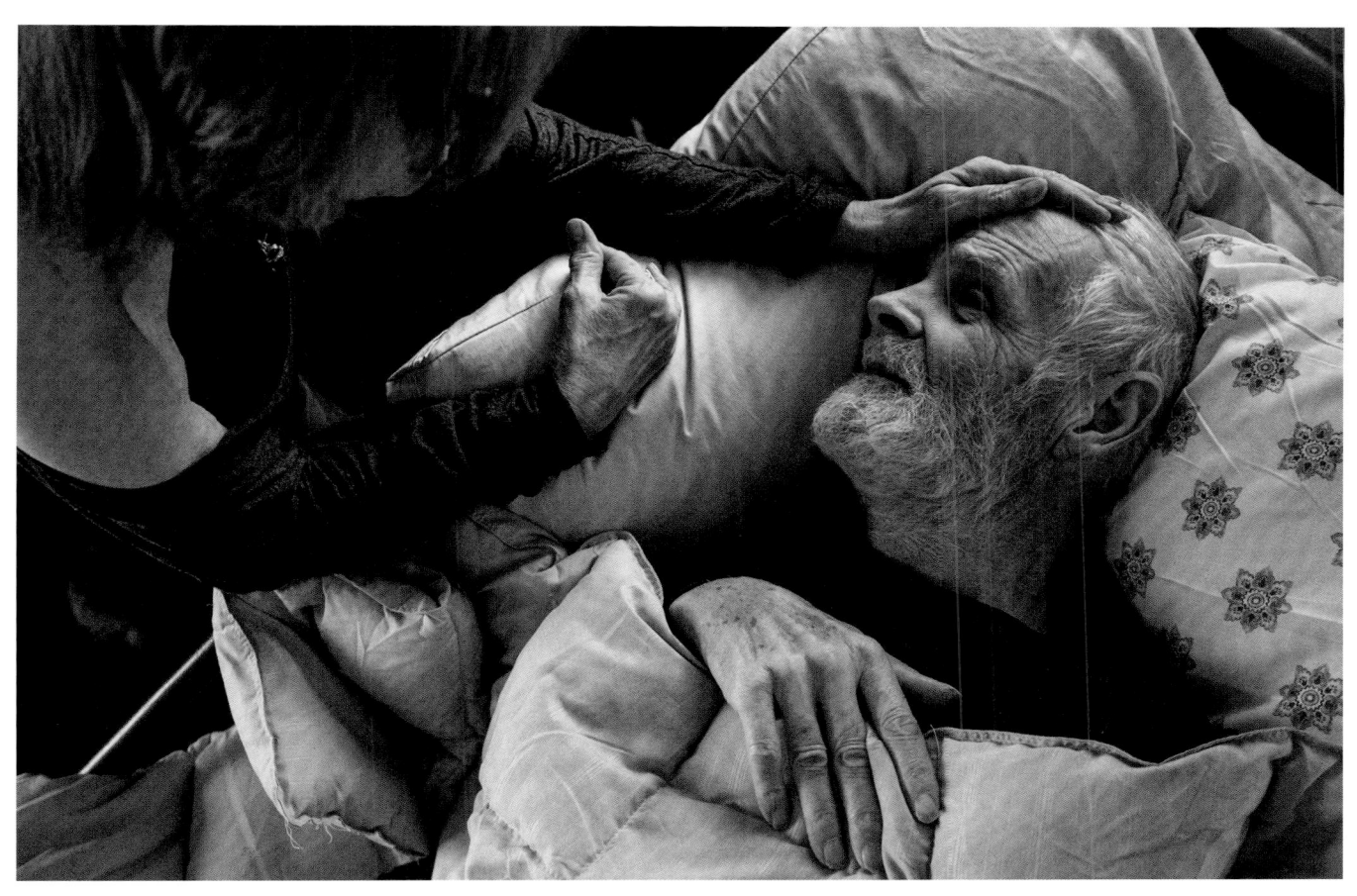

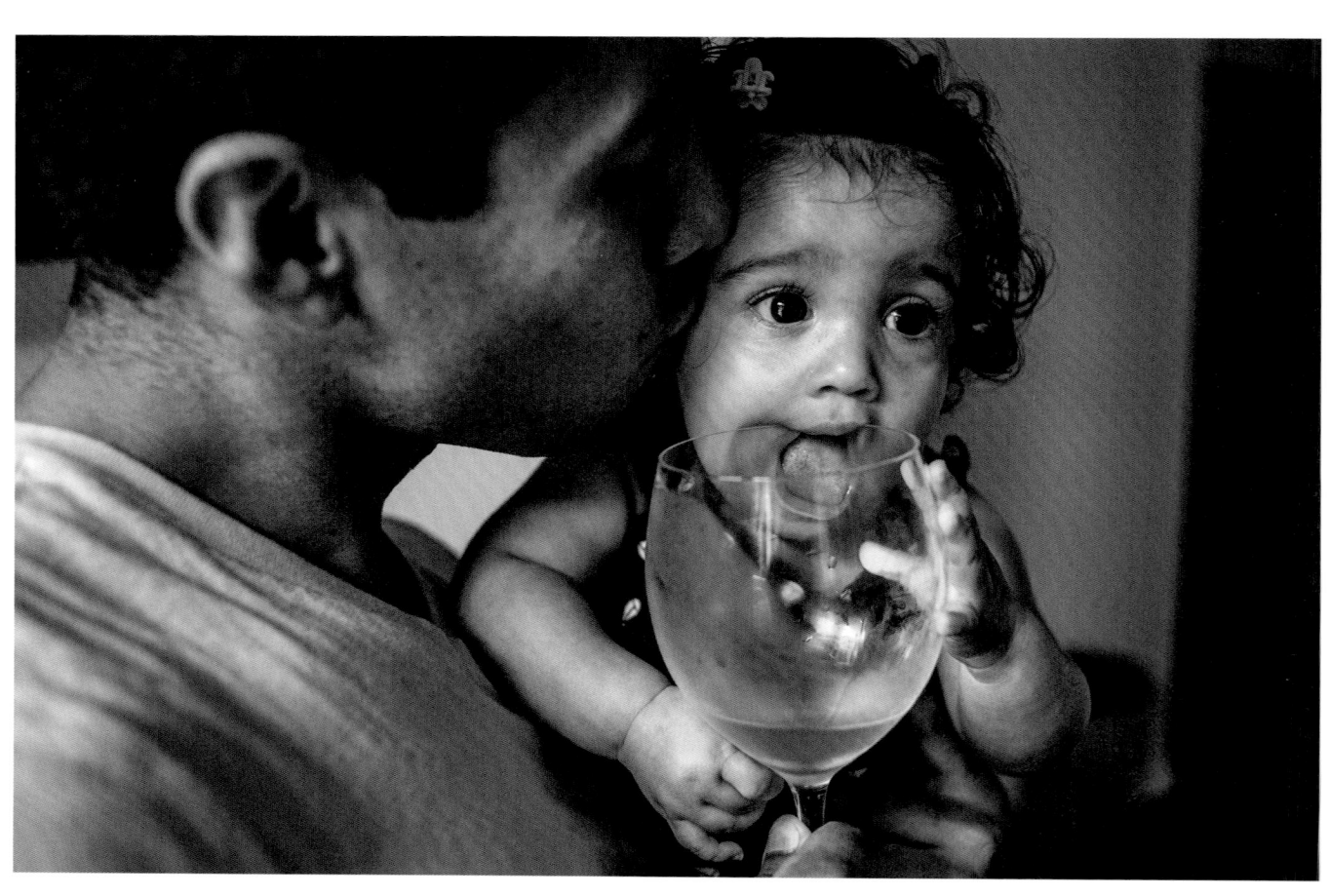

FOOLPROOF HICCUP REMEDY:

1. Fill a pint glass with water.

2. Grab a straw.

3. Using your fingers, seal your ears by applying pressure to the tragus.

4. Drink the entire glass of water through the straw.

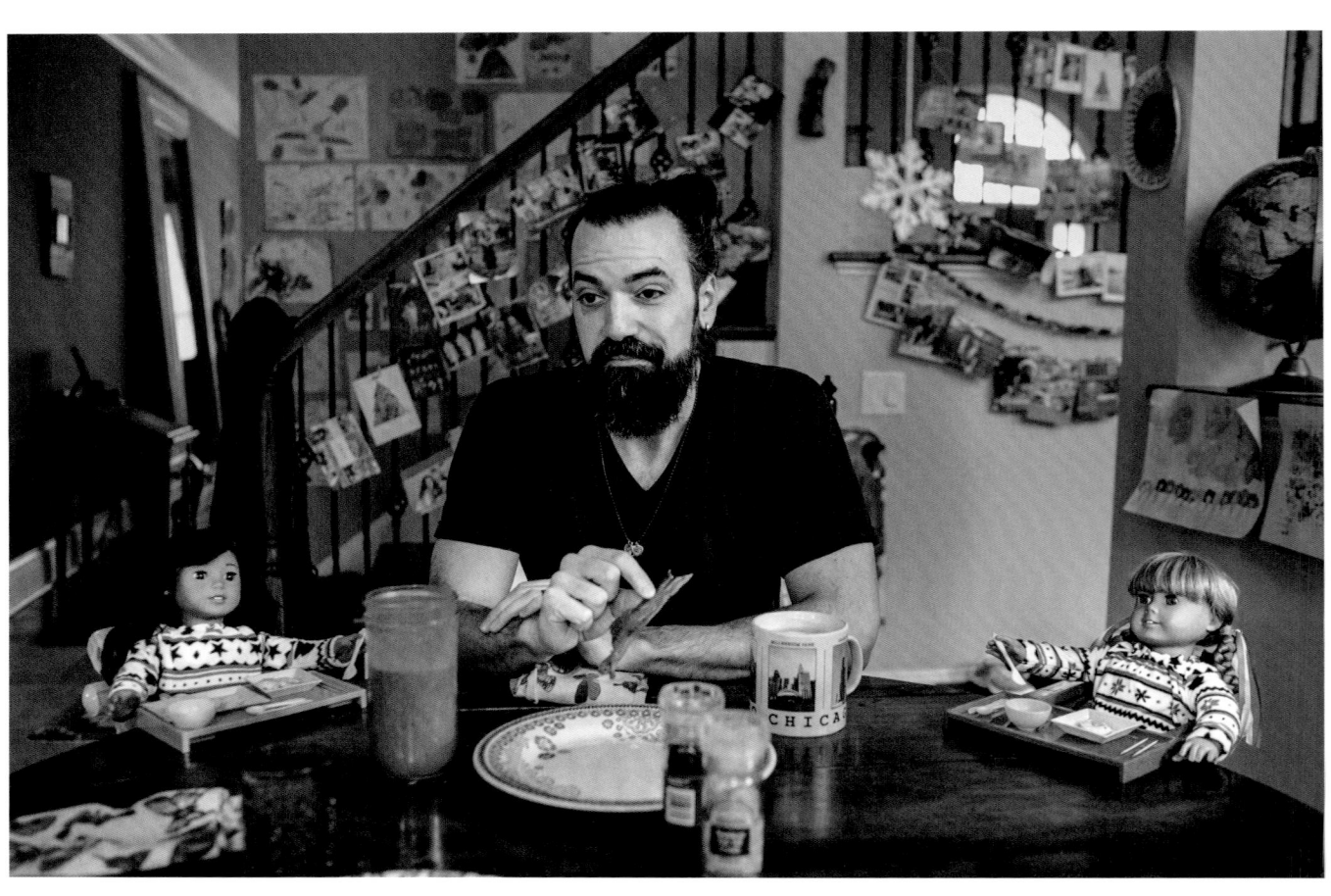

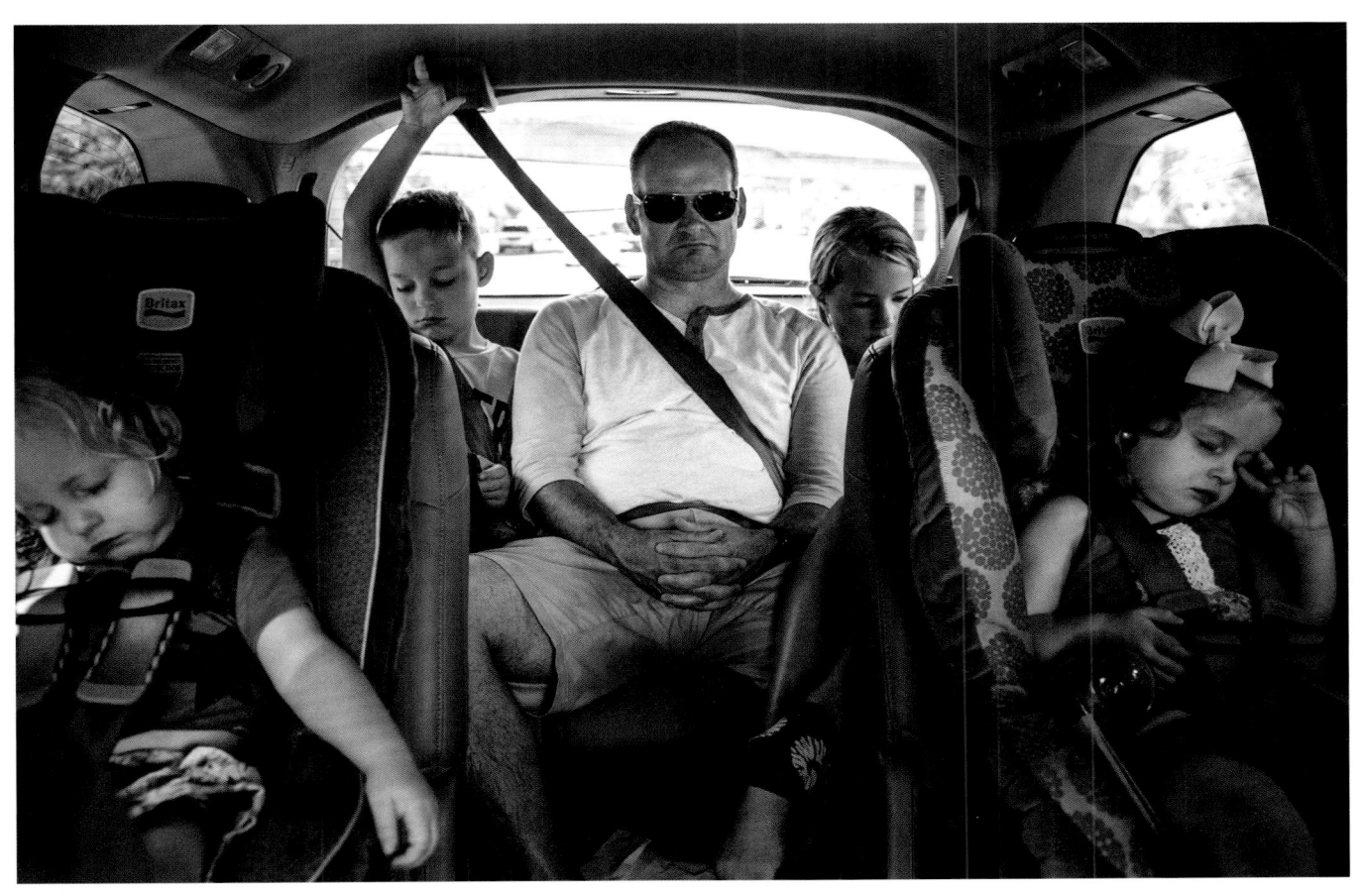

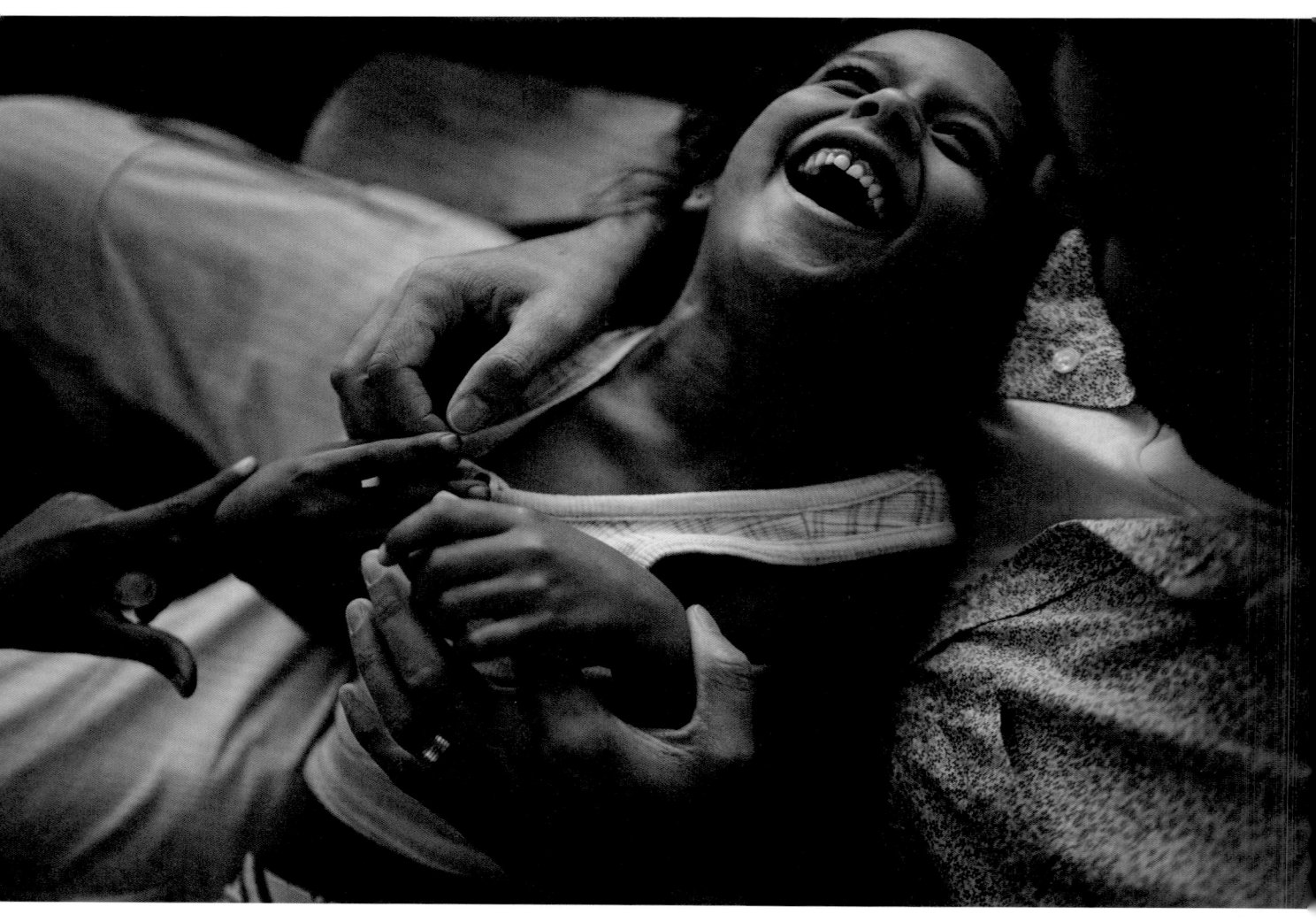

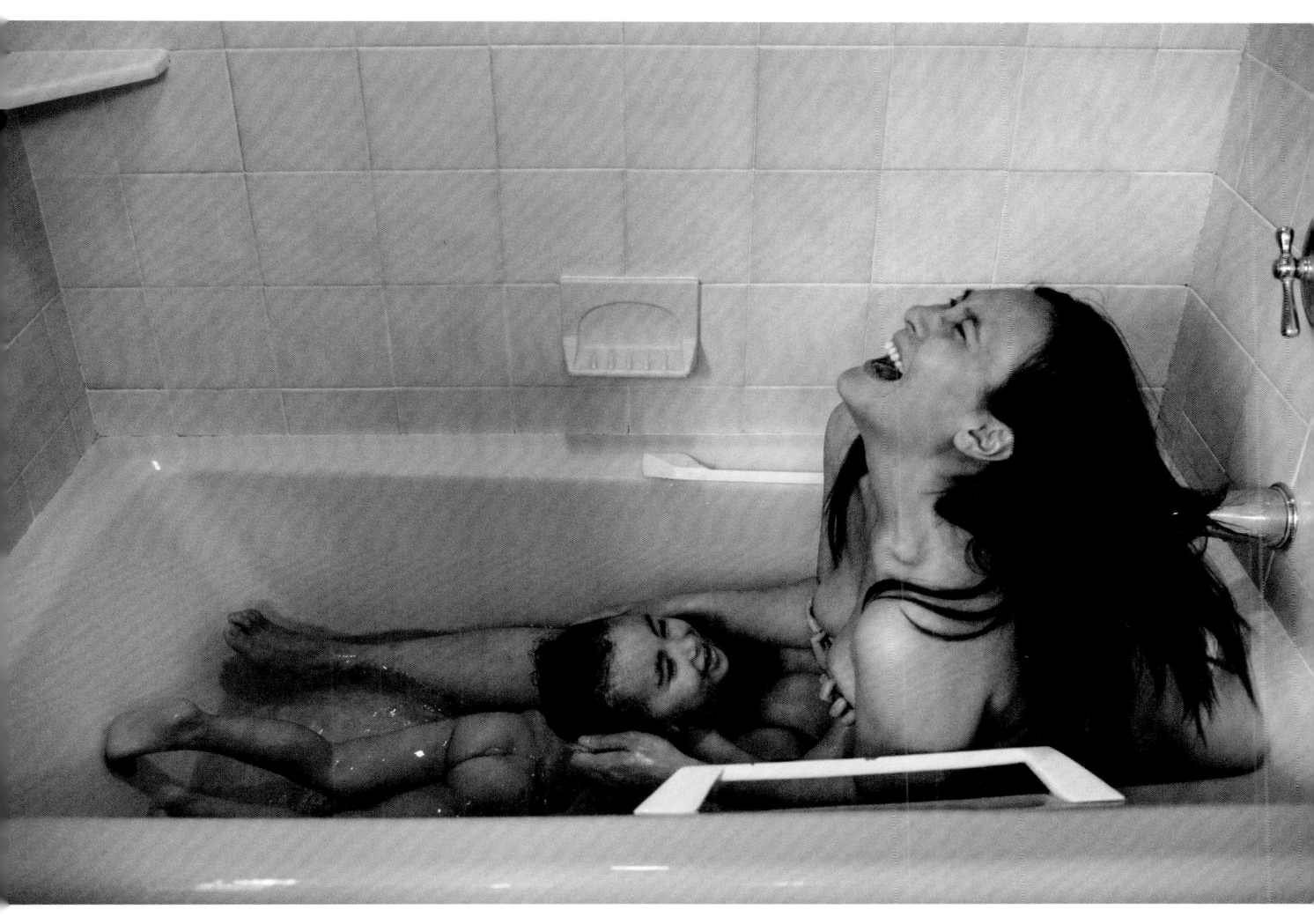

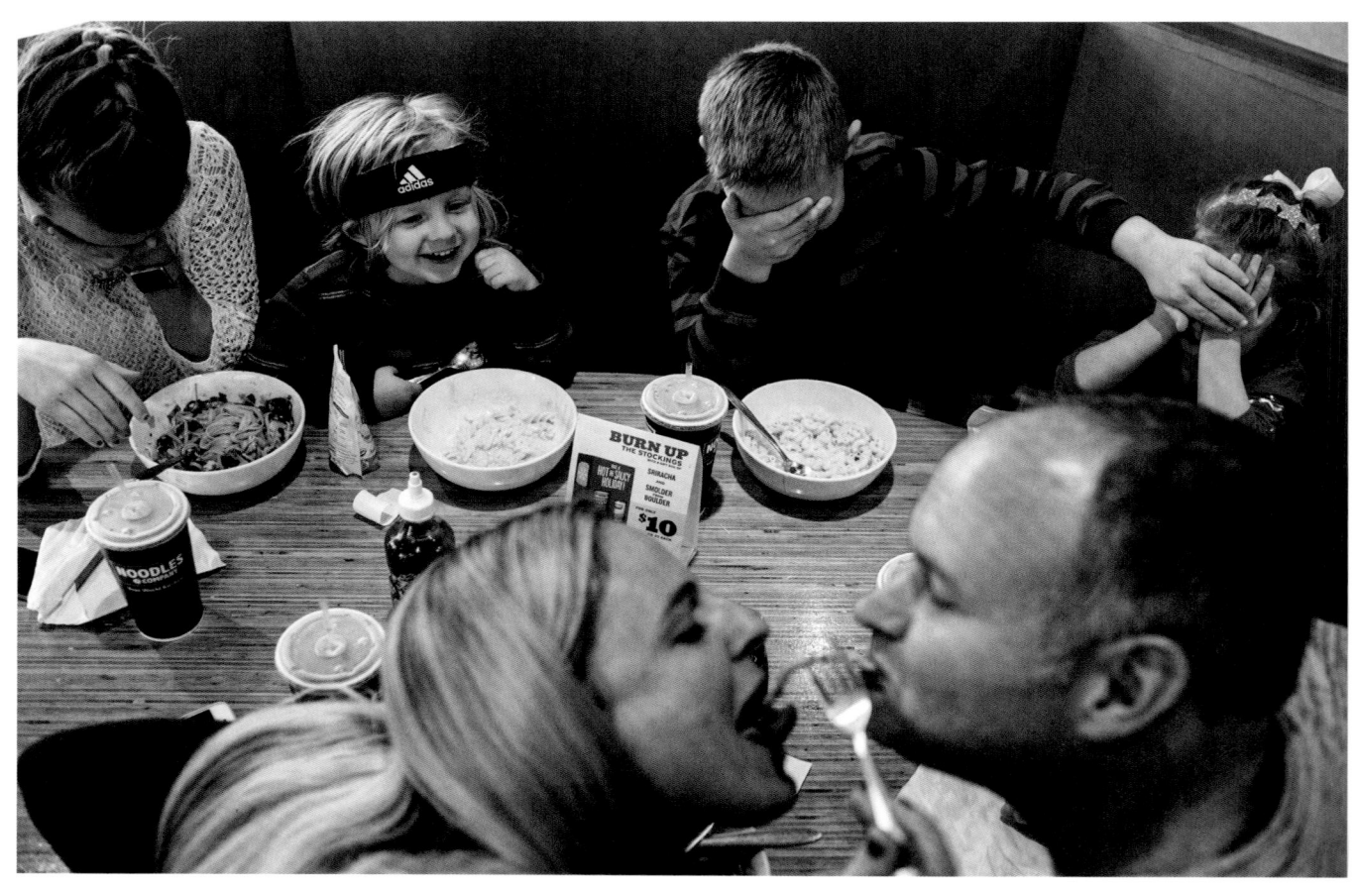

Oh, by the way, I know how babies are made, and I can't believe you did that to dad THREE TIMES. It's disgusting.

—Ben, age nine

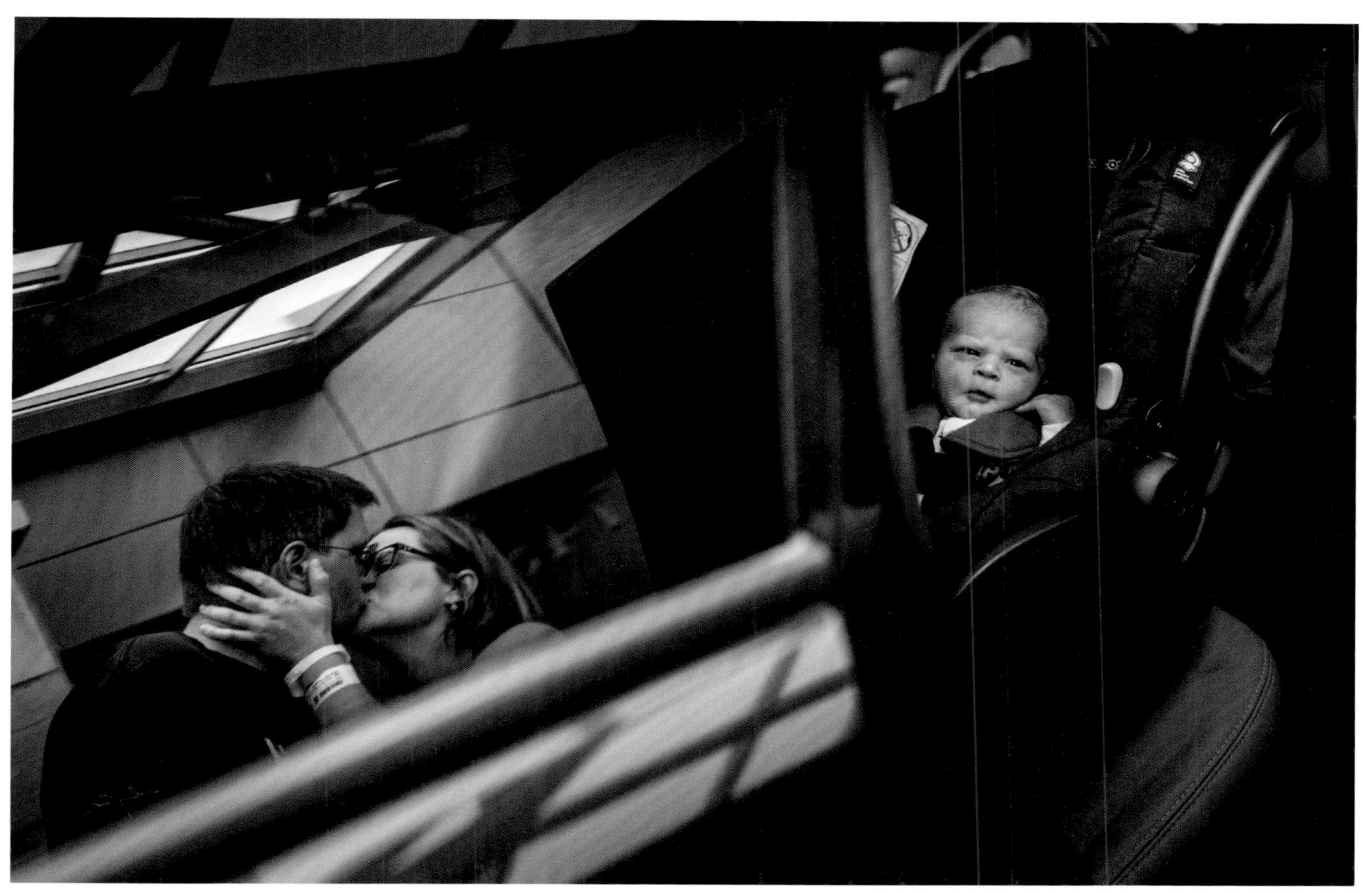

When his little brother started crawling and licking his Legos my three-year-old son asked:
"Mom, can we bring him back, and can I get a cat instead?"
—Julia Rose-Greim

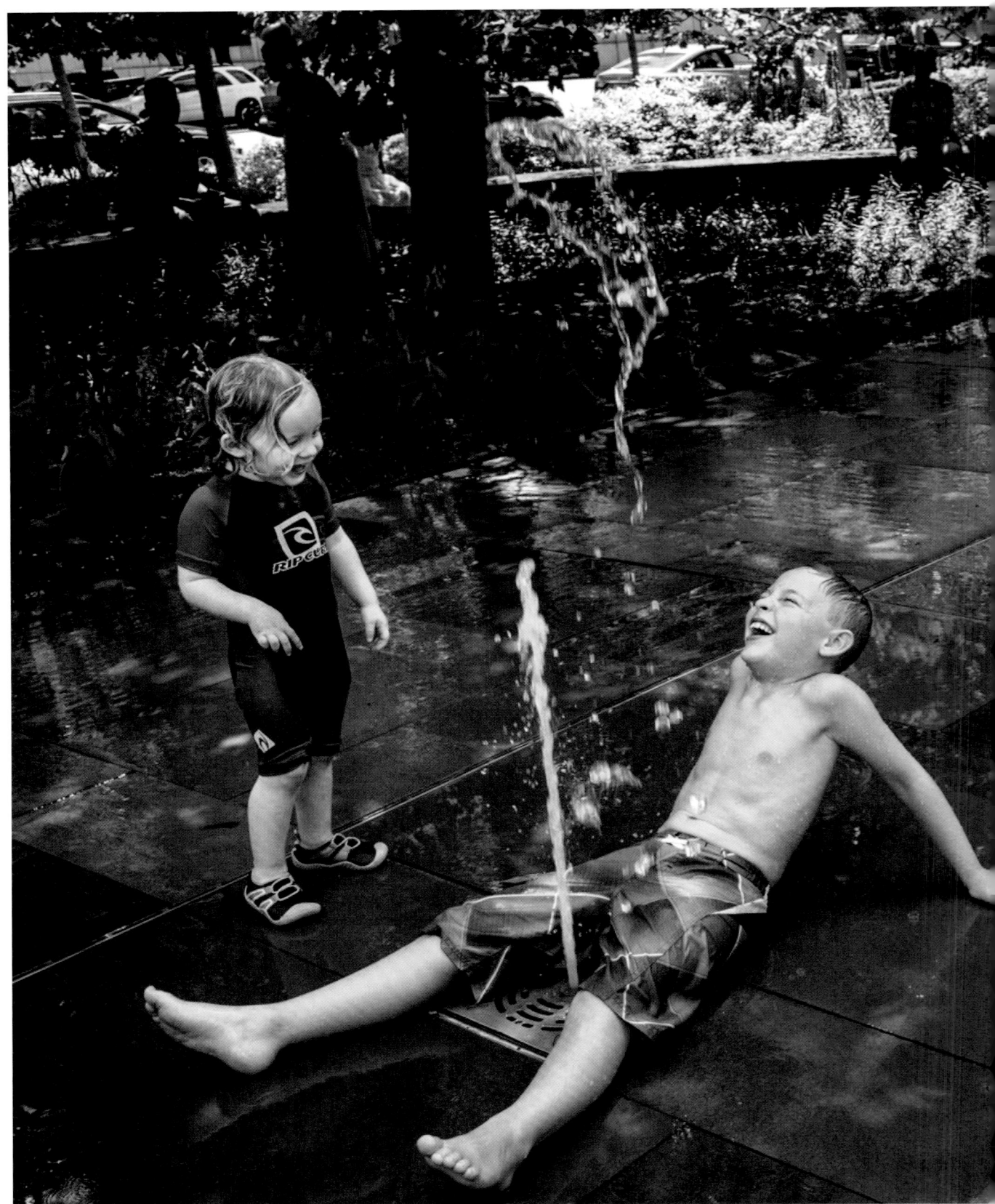

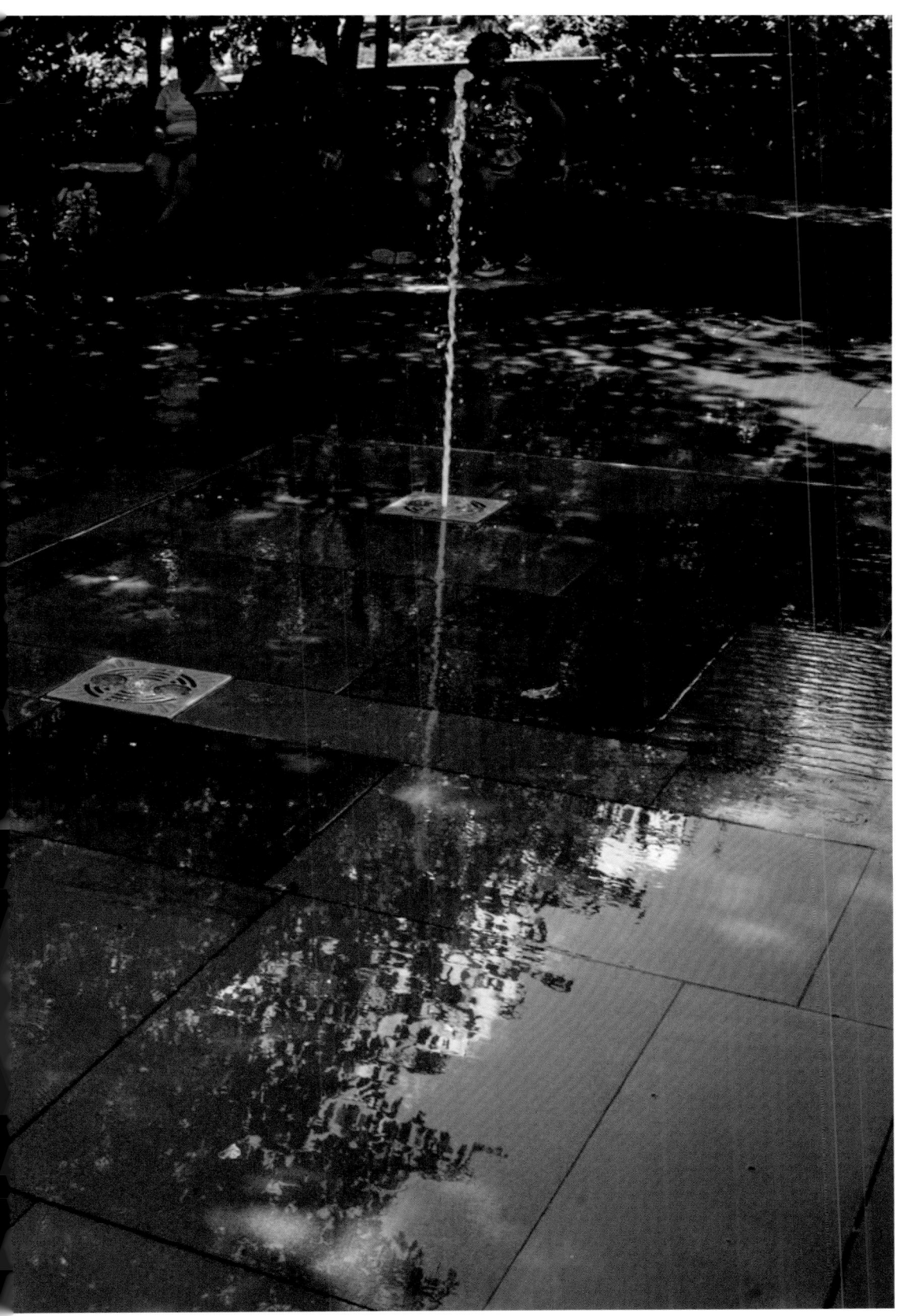

I asked my (then) twelve-year-old daughter, Abby, if she had a crush on a boy in her class. Her response: "Ew. No! Boys are annoying. And they have herpes."

—Danielle Santoro MacInnes

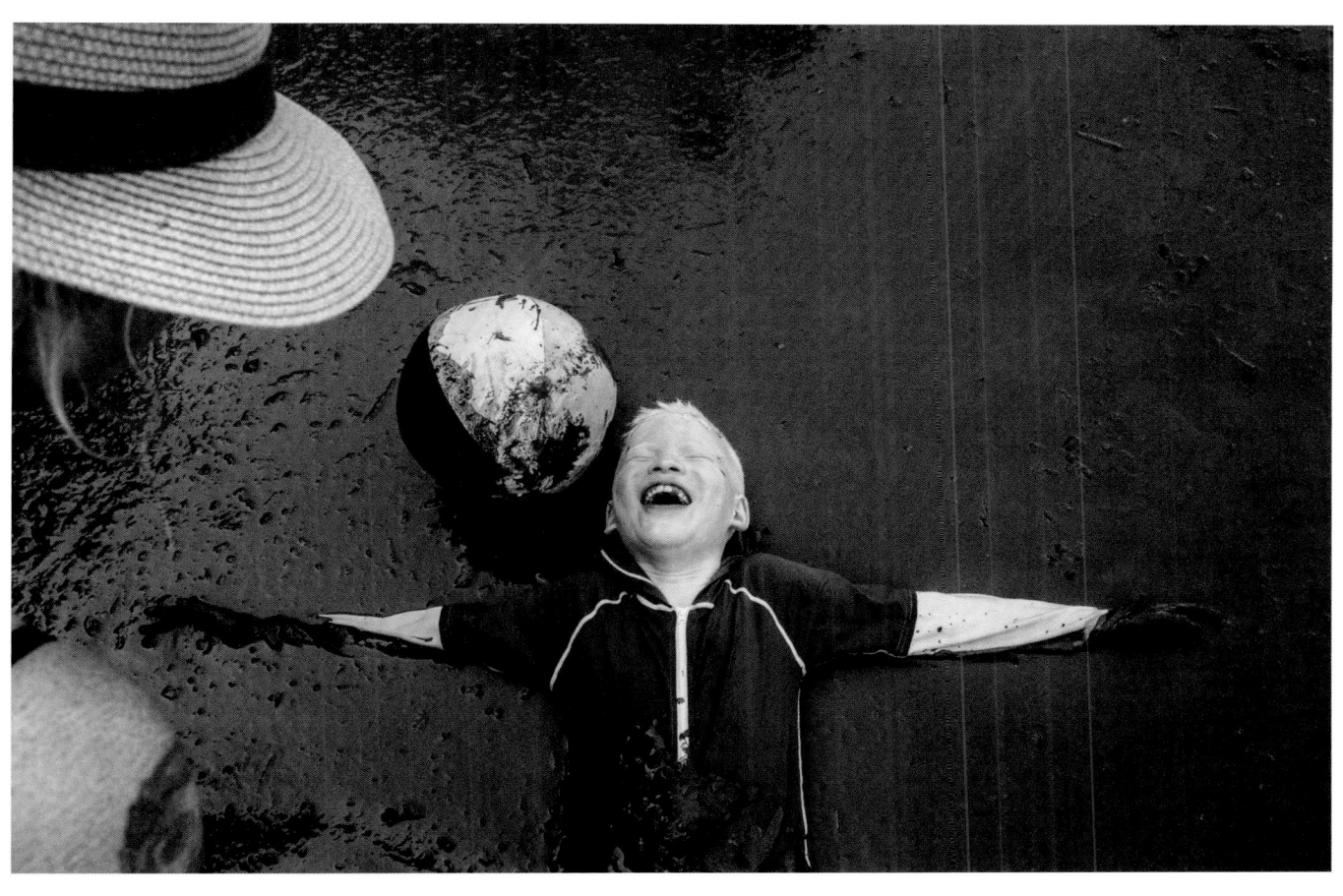

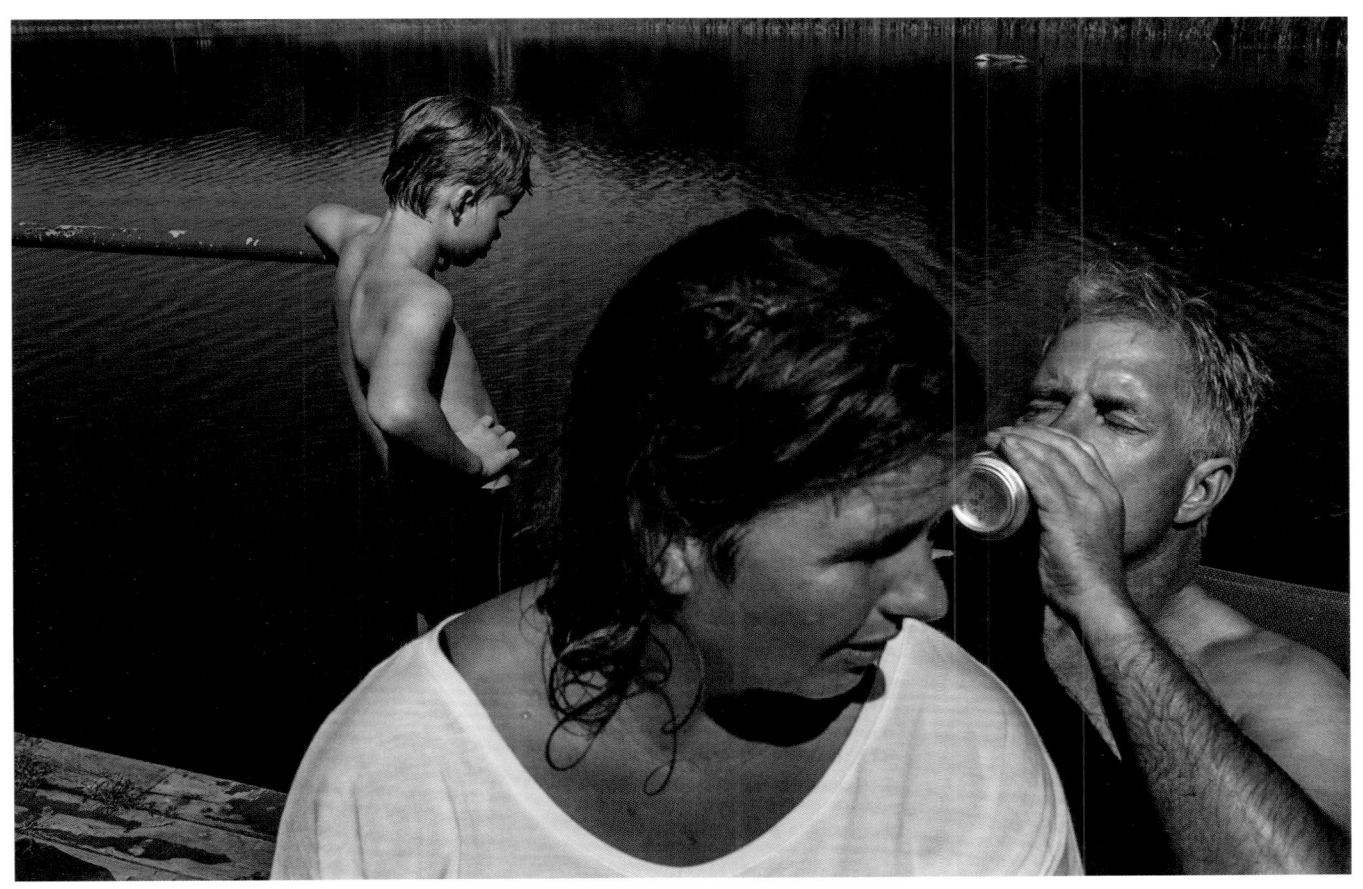

Admitting you are wrong to your child, regardless of their age, is not a sign of weakness. It validates their perspective, empowers them to critically think, and gives you as a parent a chance to reflect and correct going forward.

—Lee Kamenitz

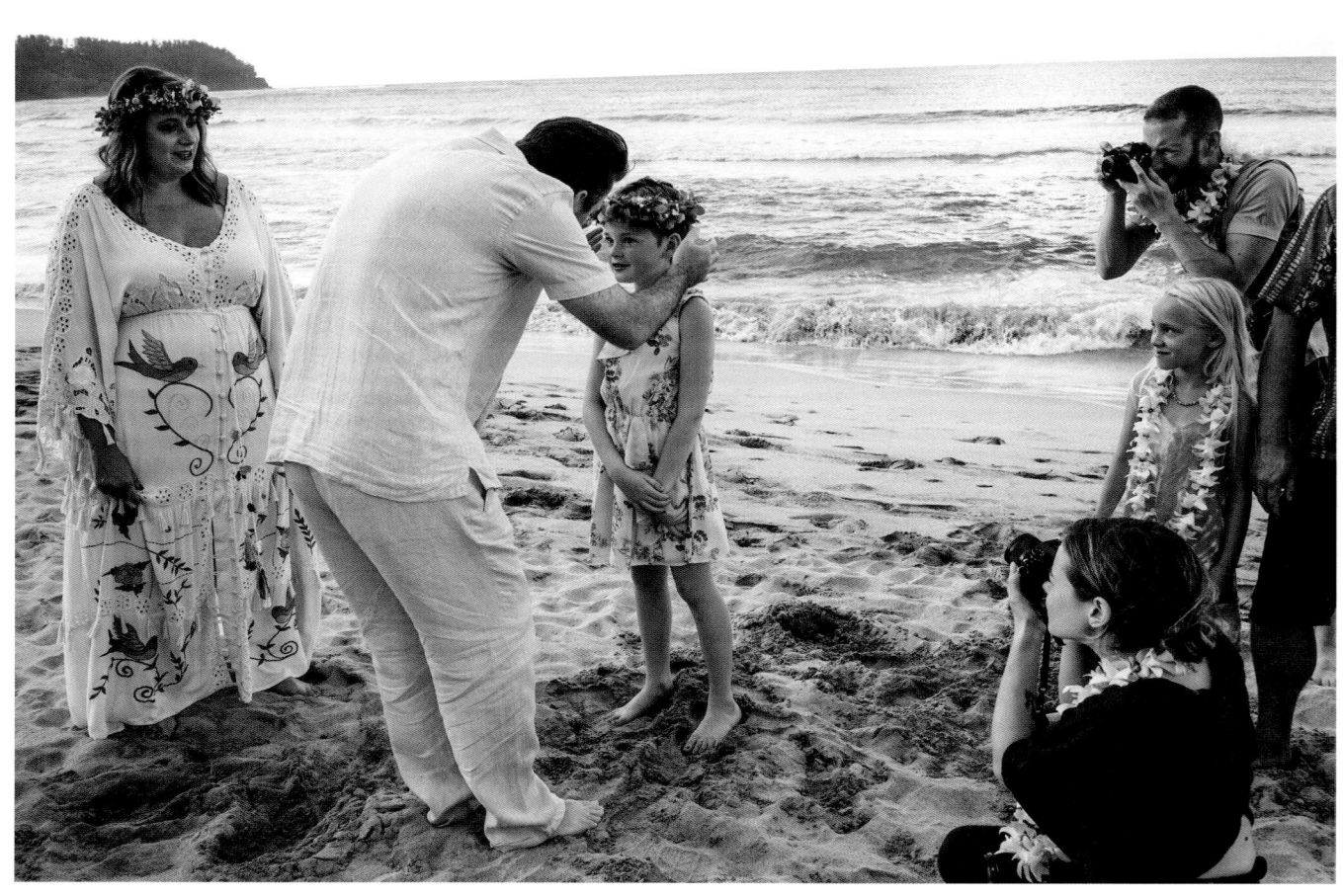

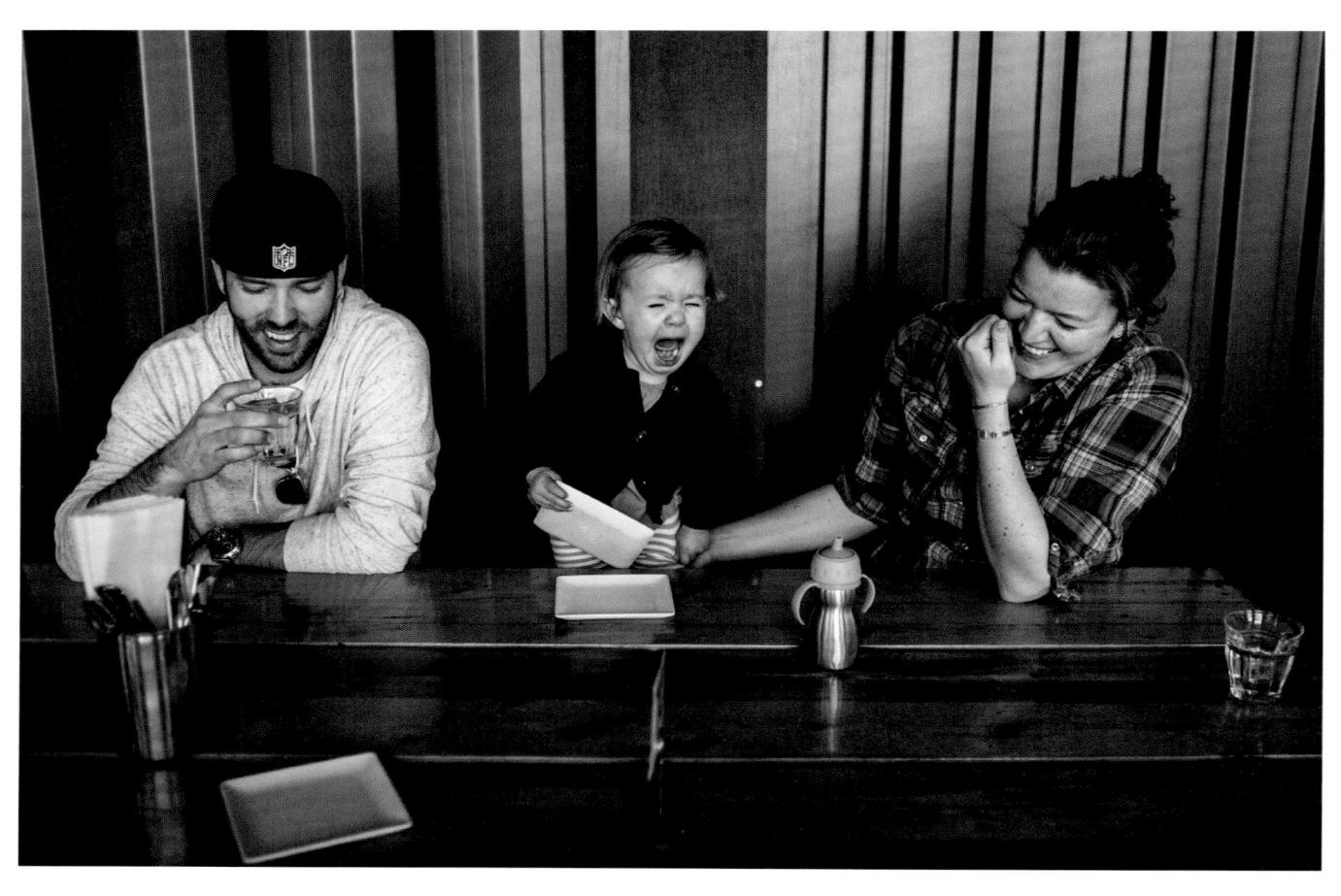

DADDY ATE THE PIZZA CRUST I WAS GOING TO THROW OUT!!!
—Byrdie Mae, age three

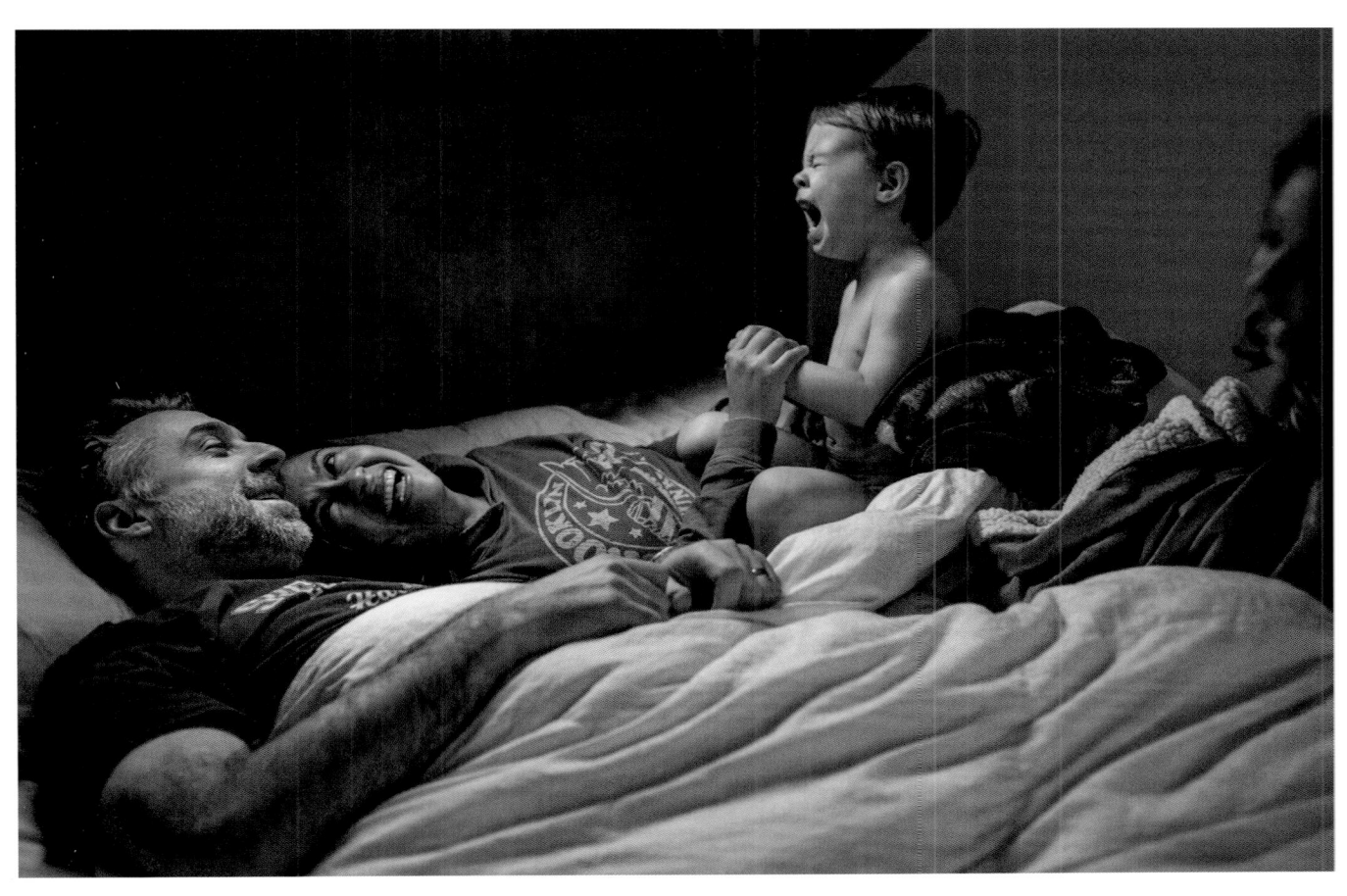

MOM! DAD THINKS I'M HIS SON!
—James, age three

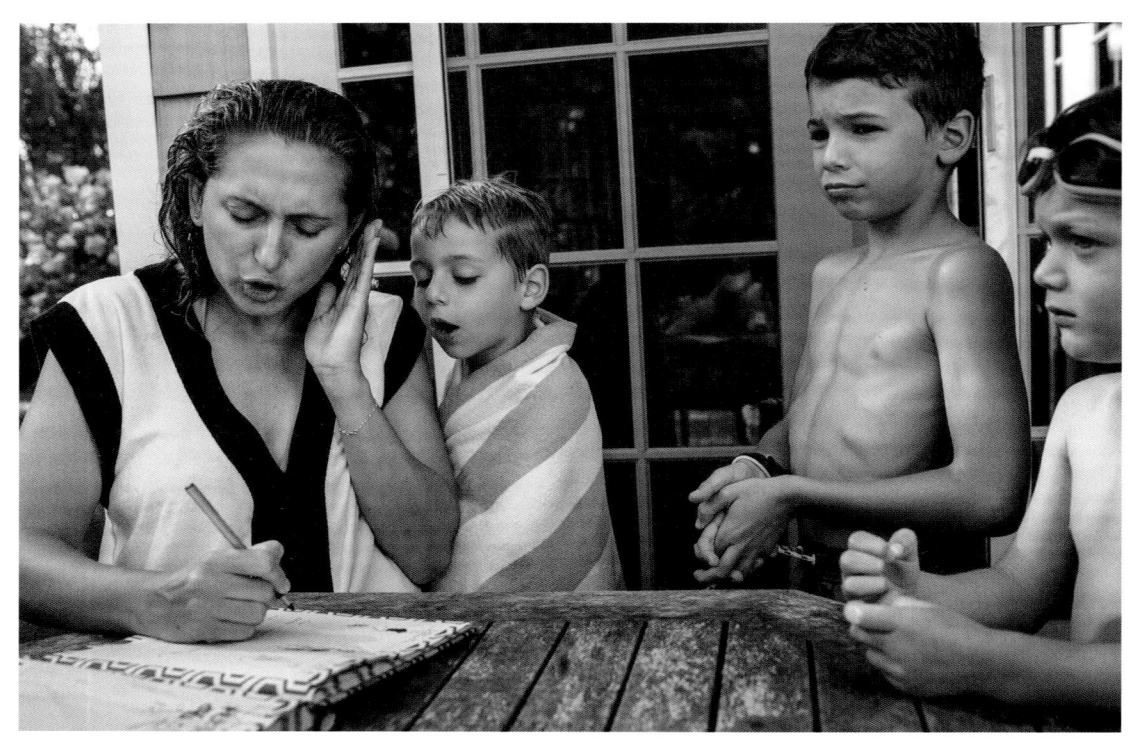

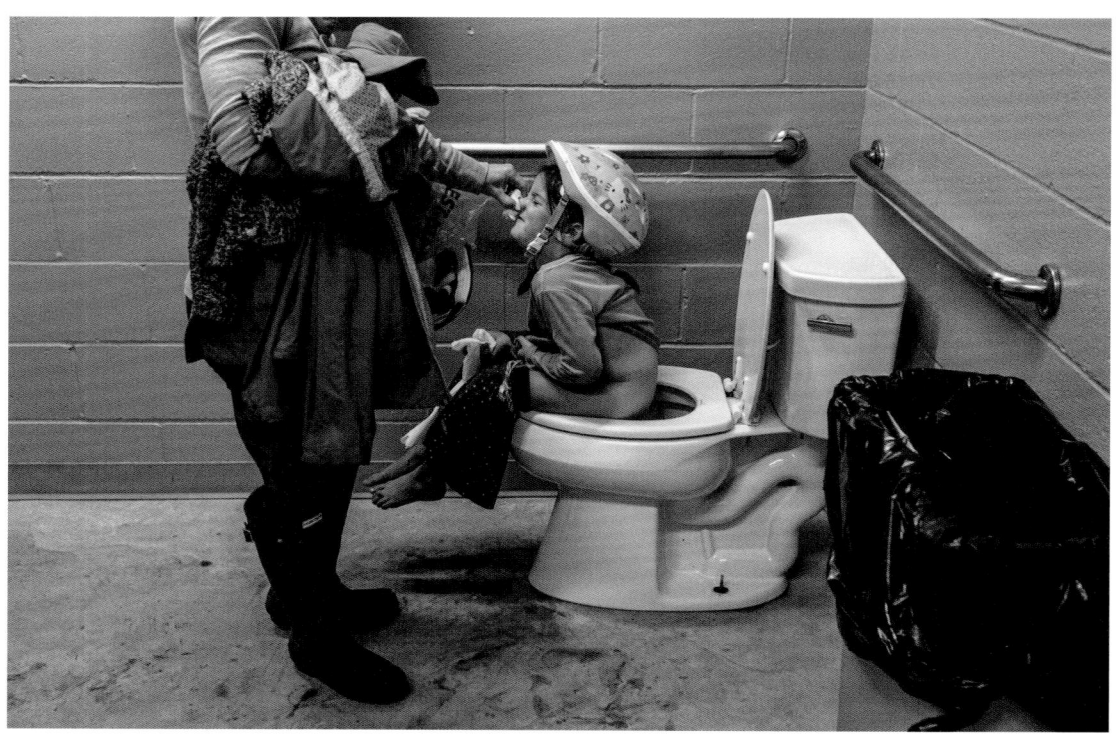

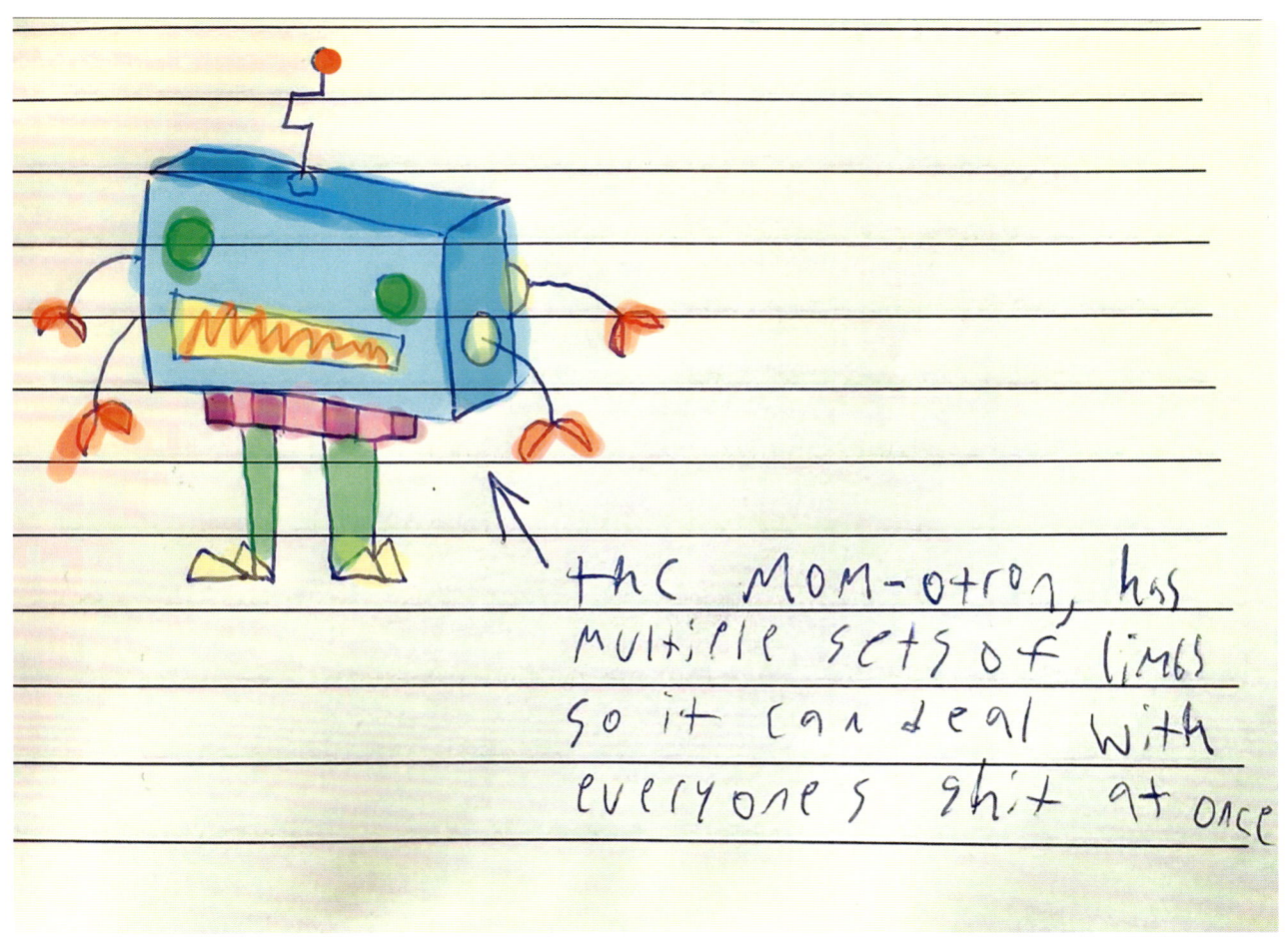

the Mom-otron, has multiple sets of limbs so it can deal with everyones shit at once

THE MOM-OTRON. Has multiple sets of limbs so it can deal
with everyone's shit at once.

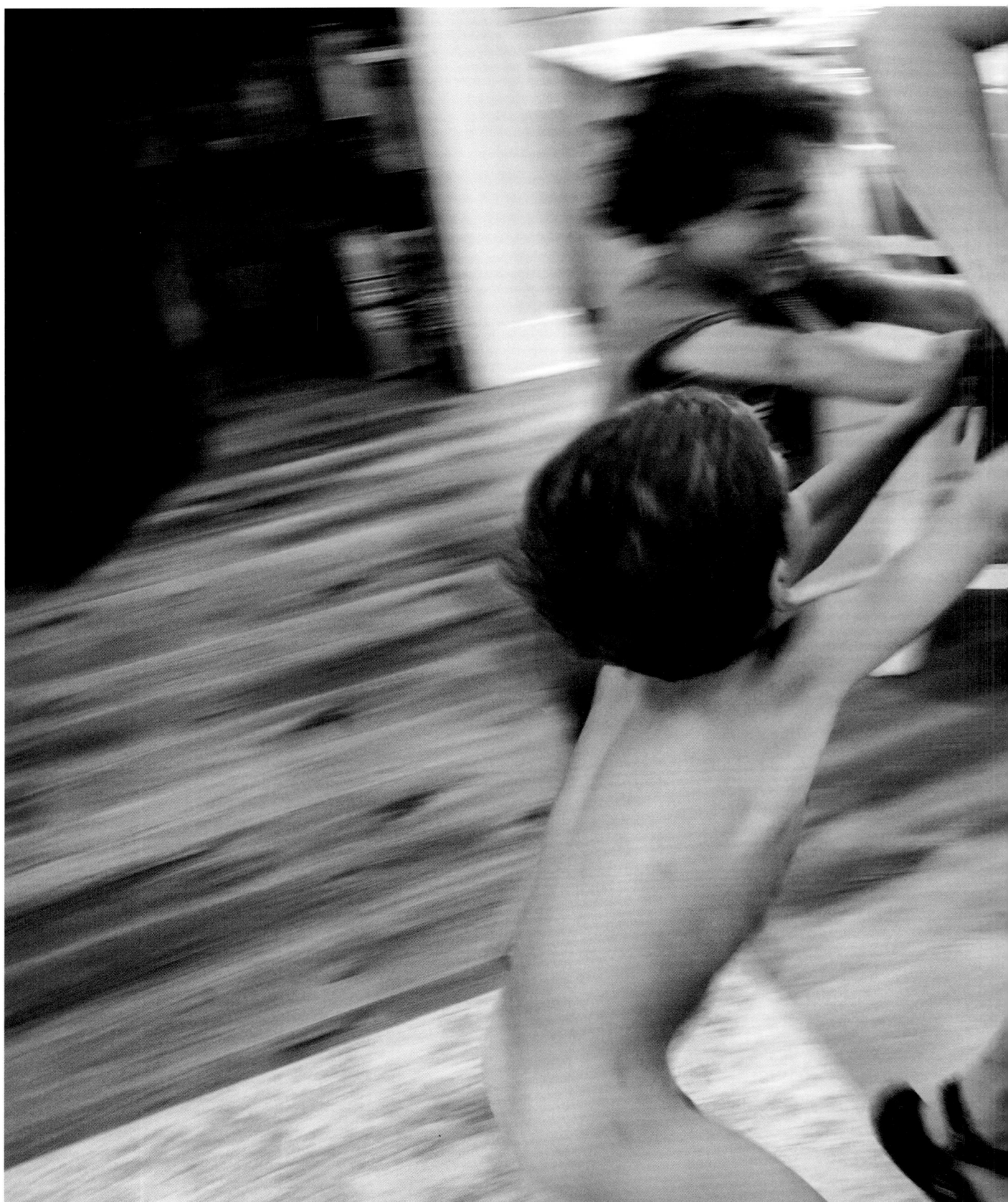

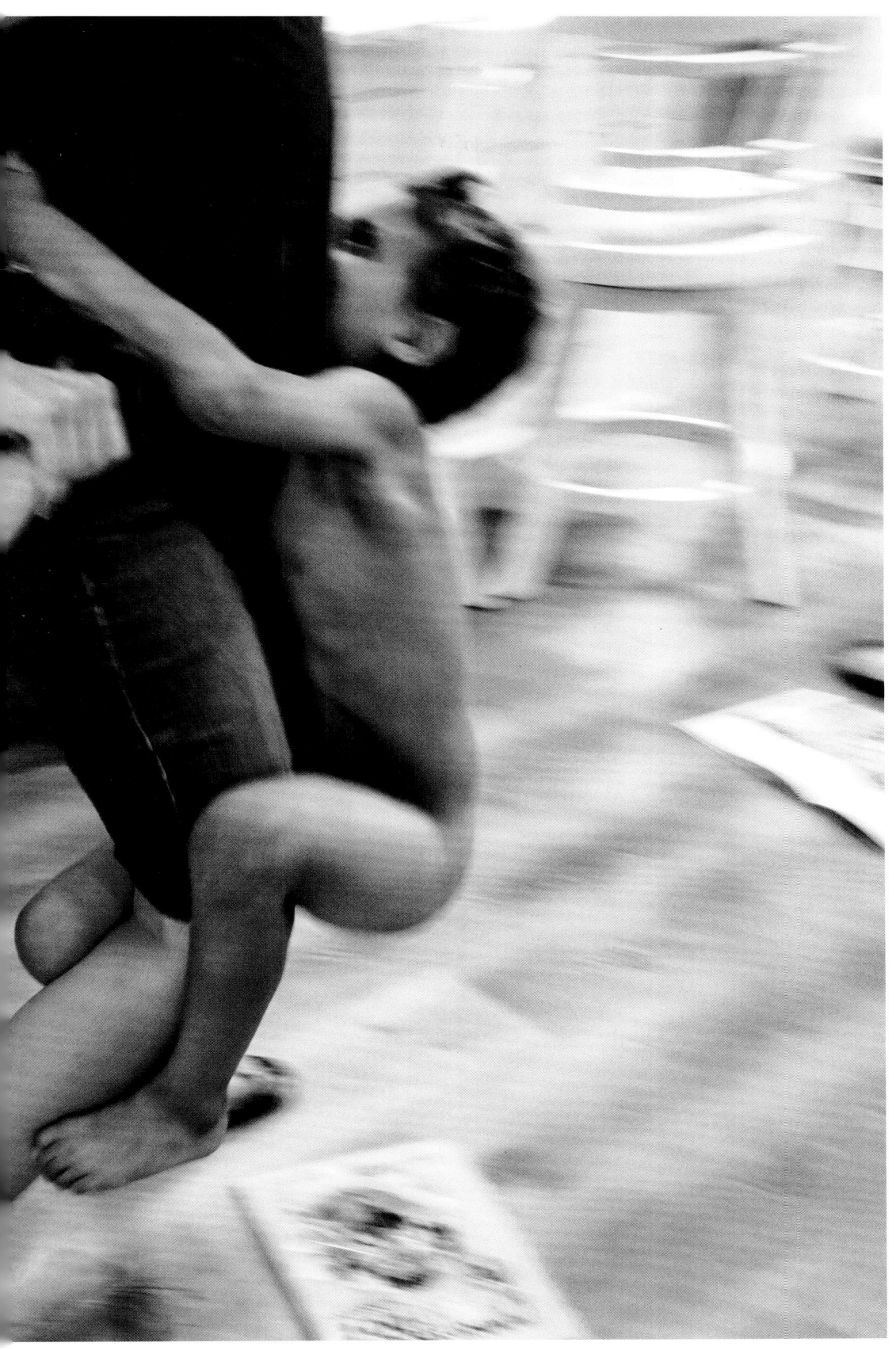

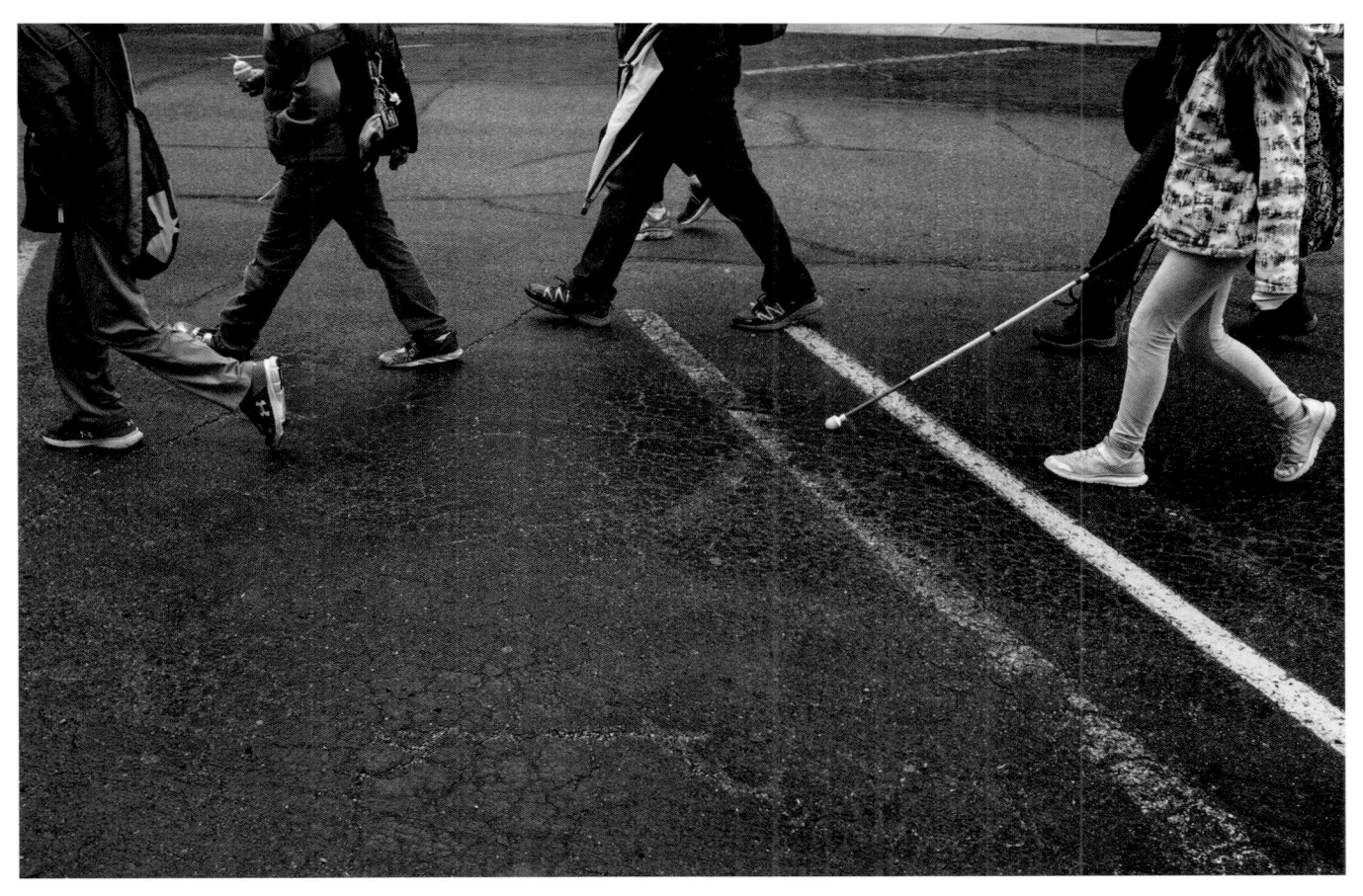

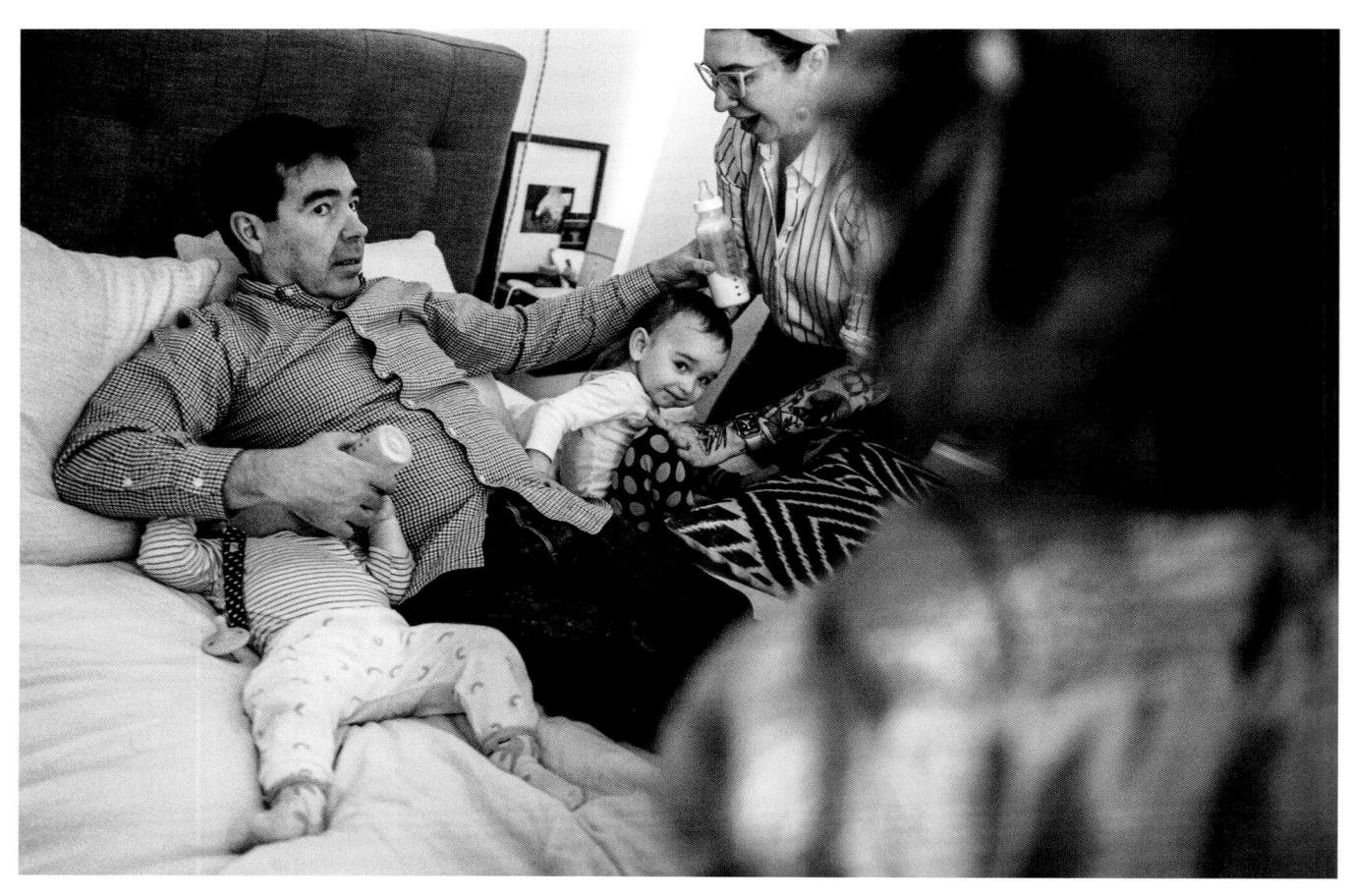

I was just really excited to be getting laid; I didn't think about the kids part.

—Sterling, fifty-seven (first-time dad of one- and two-year-olds)

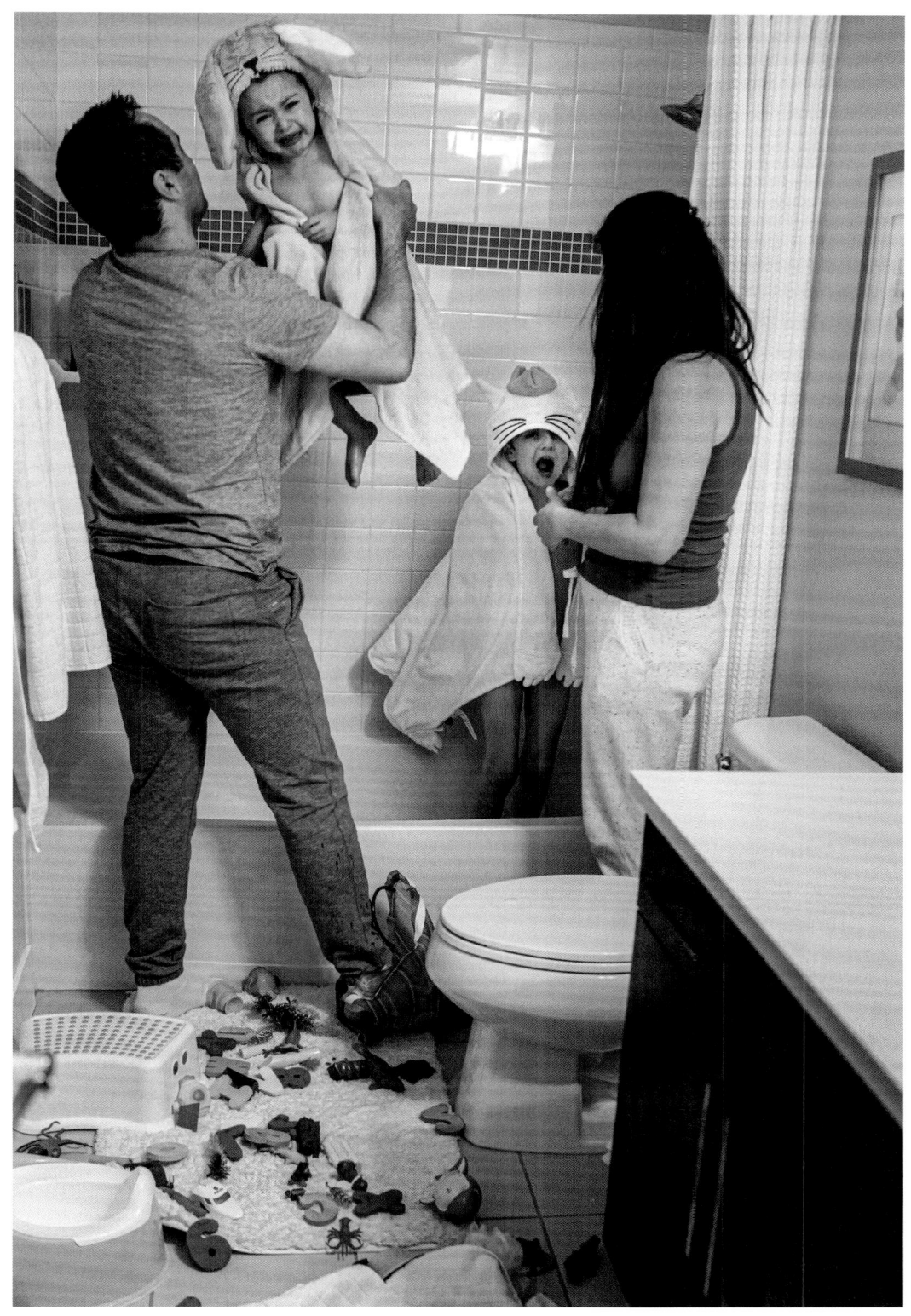

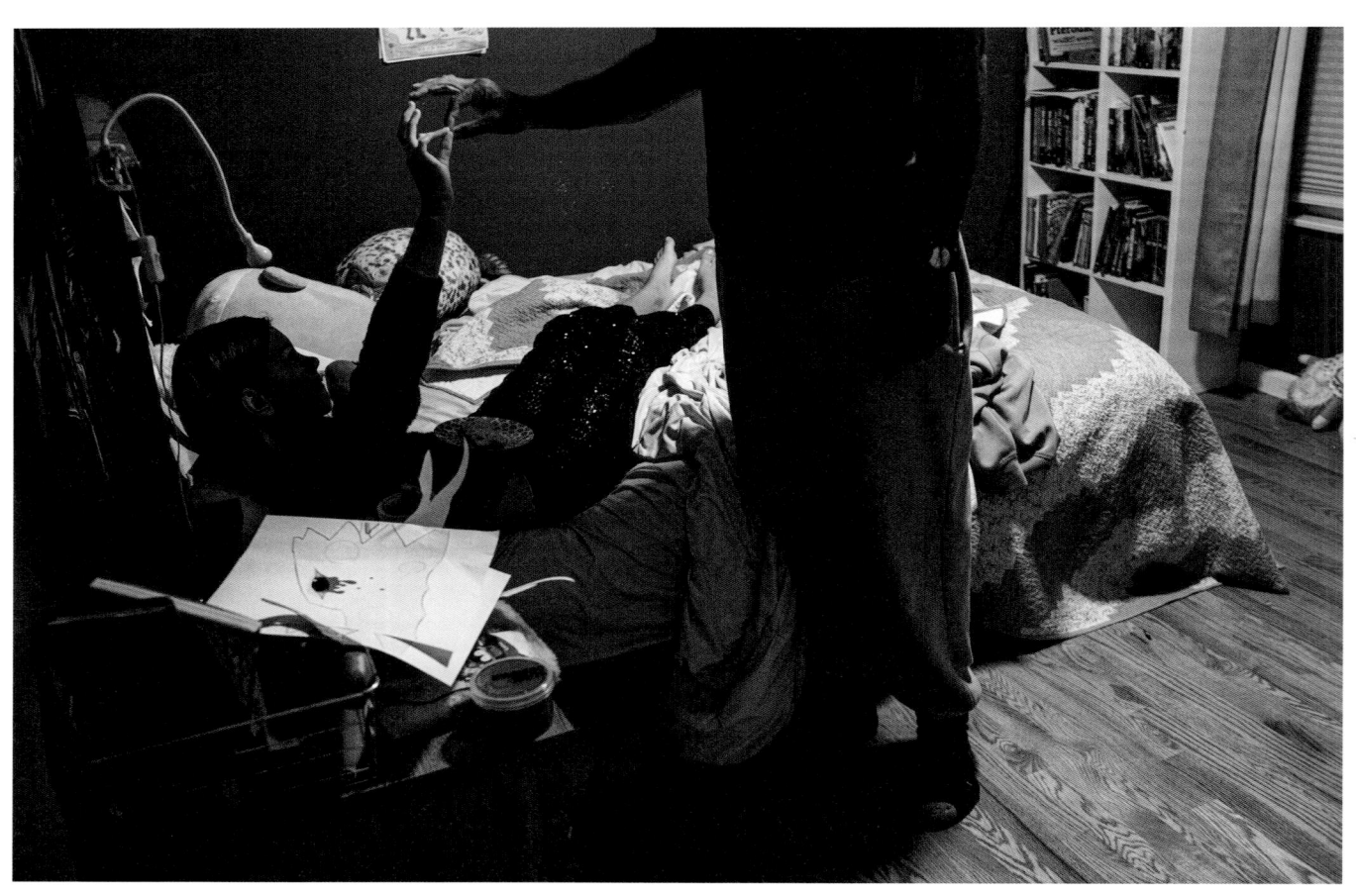

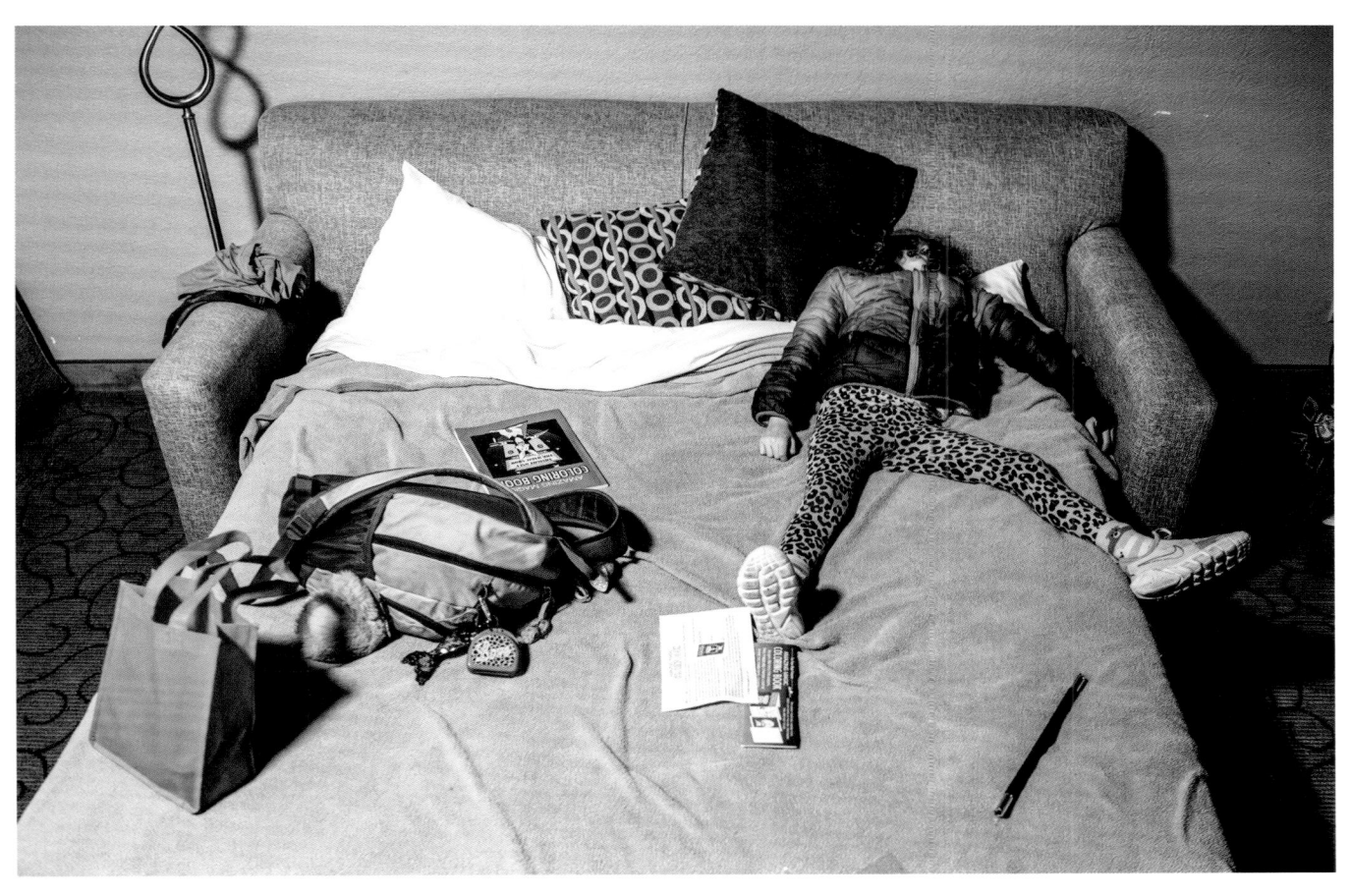

Nico, age eight: Mama, you're the best mom in the world.

Max, age ten: Yeah, you are.

Owen, age six: Eh, you're okay. I mean, there are probably better moms out there.

—Stephanie Deyo Mitsakos

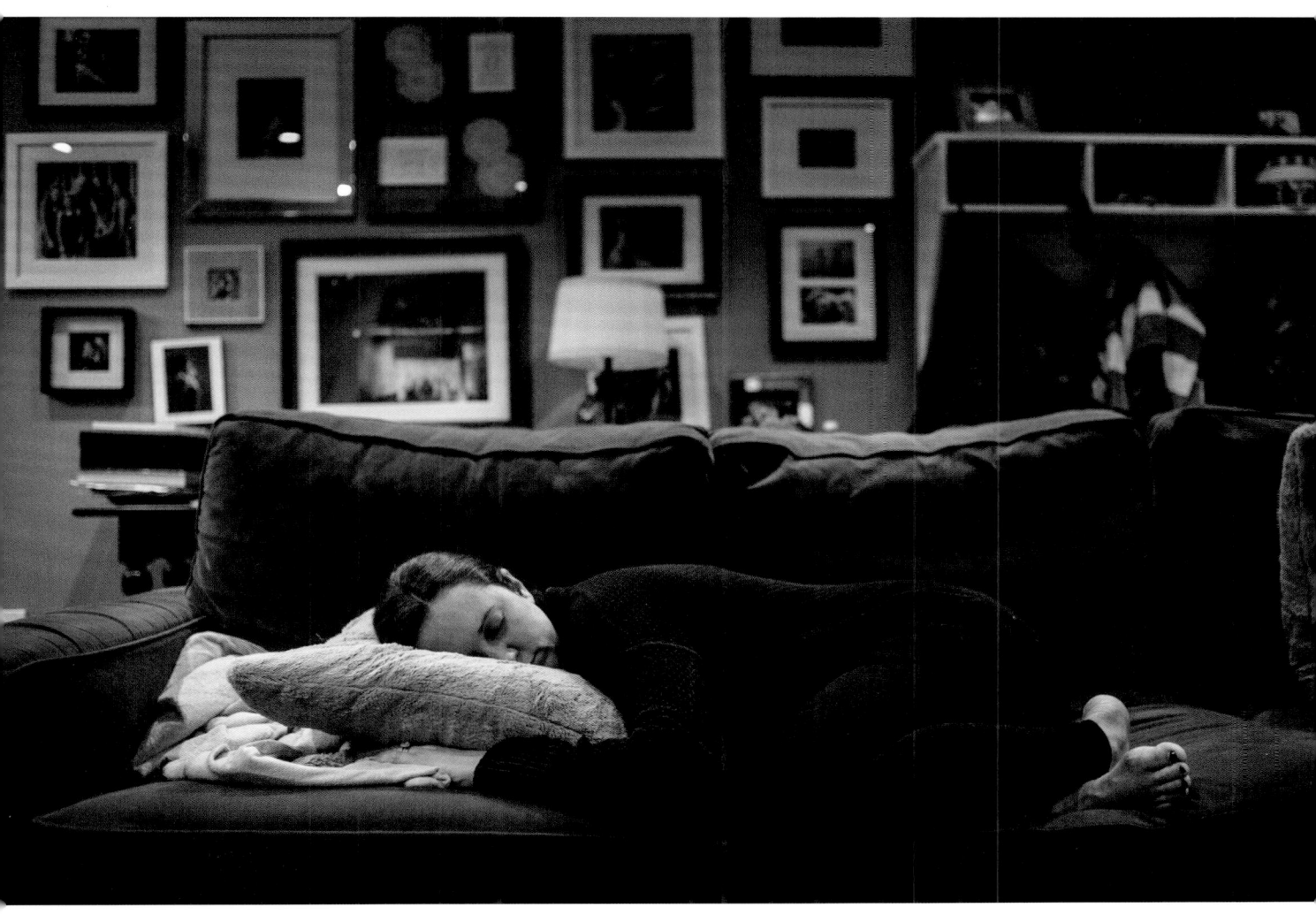

MAKE YOUR OWN

DUST JACKET

SUPPLIES NEEDED

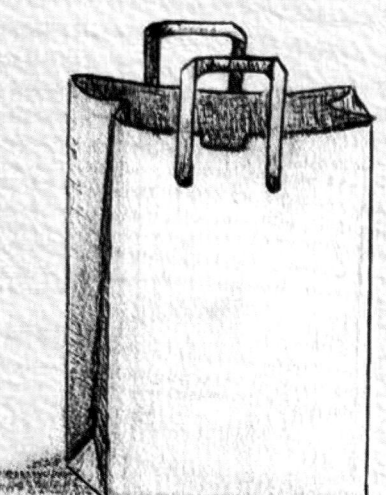

**1.
BROWN PAPER
SHOPPING BAG**

*one from a
grocery store
works best in
terms of size
and thickness*

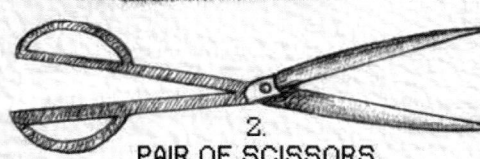

**2.
PAIR OF SCISSORS**

*IMPORTANT NOTE: any scissors
will work however, if you value
your life do NOT use your
mother's sacred sewing scissors*

**3.
CRAYONS
MARKERS
PAINT & BRUSHES,
ETC**

*the most important
part of this process
is decorating your
dust jacket. make
sure you have a
variety of art
supplies to create
your own cover*

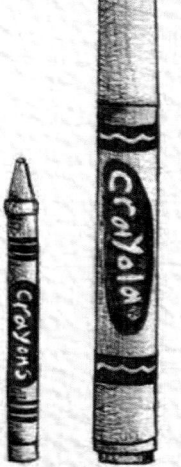

INSTRUCTIONS

Prepare the Bag

Cut the bag along one side seam and the bottom to lay it flat, turning it into a single large sheet.

Make sure the printed side of the bag is facing up (this will be the inside of your dust jacket).

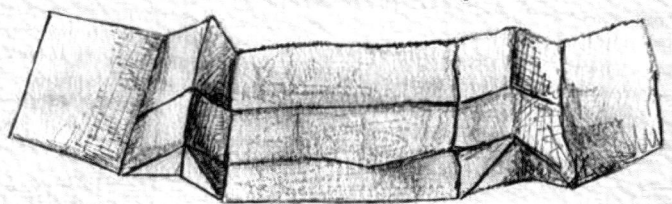

Measure the Book

Place the book in the center of the flattened bag. With the book closed, fold the top and bottom edges of the paper over the book's top and bottom edges to create a snug fit.

Press the folds firmly and crease them.

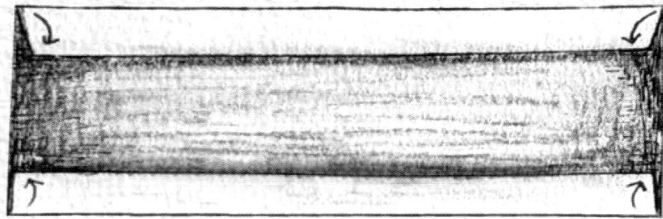

Create the Flaps

Fold the excess paper on the left and right sides around the book cover to form the flaps.
Slide the front and back covers of the book into these flaps to secure the jacket in place.

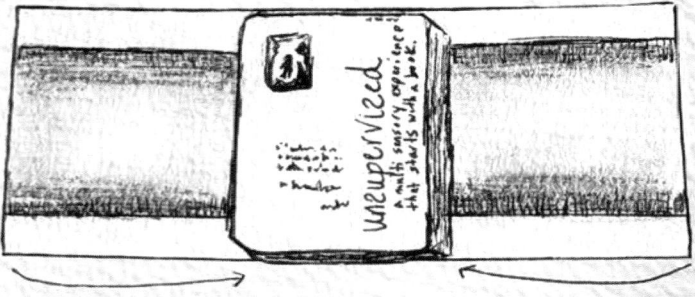

If you and your family create a one-of-a-kind dust jacket, share it with other book owners through the app!

ACKNOWLEDGMENTS

It was a Thursday. I managed to stuff the entire pile of third-quarter vocabulary tests in my bag before racing out the door, following behind twenty-three tiny pairs of what the South foolishly calls "tennis shoes." I guarantee you not a single one of these tiny people played tennis. It was my day for bus duty, a responsibility I was unaware of when accepting my position at G.H. Reid Elementary School. It was not fun. Not fun at all. Especially in torrential rain, fighting a four-day snot fest during the last month of school. After escorting the final group of soggy bus riders, I poured my drenched, virus-infested self into my car. Oh, my car. A 1999 Volkswagen Jetta, plus one medical tape–wrapped stick shift, minus one sound-buffering essential muffler. The perfect combination for any twenty-nine-and-a-half-year-old mousey blonde, white-privileged, drinks mimosas on Sundays while listening to Ani DiFranco, system-bucking first-grade teacher. I had made a decision. After engaging in a 173-minute-long conversation with a predictable, nonthreatening, probably gets "friend-zoned" on the regular Outer Banks family beach photographer a few weekends prior, I, too, wanted to cash in on a potential $40K/season per year. More money in twelve weeks than I made in an entire school year? Yes. That was going to happen. Despite questioning if I had a severe sinus infection, tuberculosis, or maybe just one too many Parliament Lights at the late-night teacher event Tuesday, I was making the three-hour drive down to Southern Shores to interview for a roommate position. I remember my heart racing as I made a right into the unlit driveway. I could see a warm, ambient glow filling a screen porch where two women were sitting in wooden rocking chairs. I buried my face into four aloe-laced Kleenex, discharged enough green boogers to fill an eagle's nest, then exited the car.

The conversation was intense, yet comfortable. While we were three strangers, my potential new roommate and her ride-or-die sidekick felt totally familiar. There was past roommate interrogation coupled with banter regarding what life is like living on a small island. We discovered life overlaps, including friends that attended UVA and working in the wedding industry. I was provided a tour of the secluded space for rent that sat on the north side of the house on the first floor, a small living room, medium-sized bedroom, and private bathroom. I unloaded my extra-full nasal cavities approximately seventeen more times during the hour-long experience, which resulted in subtle facial reactions of increasing concern and disgust from my hoping-to-be new friends. Before having to climb back into my car, drive three hours back home to Richmond, and photograph a ten-hour wedding the next day, I extended my hand in jest, to thank them both for meeting me despite my horrifying illness. I expressed, multiple times, my sincere interest in fulfilling the position for a "young, professional, female to share a home for the summer season." The entire drive home I tried to send good energy out the half-opened driver's side manual crank window. "PLEASE PICK ME PLEASE PICK ME PLEASE PICK ME."

That was the last night I wasn't Sara's new roommate. I got the call the next morning. And it changed my life forever. If it had not been for Sara placing an ad on Craigslist, I would never be writing an acknowledgment page for my own photography book. She became my agent, my manager, my number-one hype lady, "before we had a cool term for it." She recommended me to EVERY SINGLE guest who stayed in one of the properties she managed. She pushed me on every bride, whether they already had a photographer or not. She single-handedly carved a path straight through every grain of sand until I was turning work away. I will NEVER be able to fully thank Sara for everything, especially being the very best friend to me and godmother to my daughter. I miss you every day; what I wouldn't give to have you by my side the day this book launches. I'd mortify you in less than three minutes, and you'd enjoy every moment of it.

I'm not sure how I could ever thank, well, EVERYONE. It's nearly impossible.

To Daylight. Ursula and Michael. I feel like I've had a lot of "almosts" in my career. This is one of only two "big breaks" I've been given. I know it was definitely a risk to add me to the client list; my gratitude is immeasurable. I know that each and every strand of patience has been tested through this process, working with me. I am just super appreciative that you never gave up, and that you continued to believe in me. I cannot wait to do all I can to make it worth it in the end!

To each and every family who has invited me into their life to be messy in front of. To be chaotic in front of. To be emotional and complicated and unpredictable in front of. It has been the utmost honor to share breathing air with you. I am forever indebted to you for reminding me of why we are all fumbling around this giant flying rock in the atmosphere every day, especially when everything feels just so hard at times. I know, unequivocally so, that I am a better person today because of everything you have all taught me.

To every parent online who has generously shared their thoughts, advice, children's quotes, and drawings with me. Without your contributions, this book would absolutely NOT be as engaging, entertaining, or endearing. I hope to find endless ways to celebrate you all, not just those small few that made it to print.

To the children. All the children who will one day realize that who you are RIGHT now will be your constant compass in the future. My hope is that this book will make you smile, laugh, ask questions, make art, feel brave, ask for more hugs, feel no shame when you cry in public, search for meaning, fly paper airplanes, and remember that every NO in life is simply one step closer to the YES you are ultimately working towards. You inspire me to keep trying over and over and over again, even when I get bored, distracted, or in trouble.

Amelia, the only person I've had to change a flight for. Thank you for continuing to love me despite an unfortunate pre-wedding bleach incident and ten-year photo delivery wait. Twenty-six years flew by, and still, you're my GO-TO car-ride call.

Raquita, my long-lost twin. I would not have survived the last four years without you. IT IS NOT POSSIBLE. Thank you for never asking, always reaching. I'm so grateful for you, to you, because of you. And to be an honorary Henderson is the biggest gift; your entire family is embedded in my flesh.

Jason and Charmi, yes. All of it. My forever bookends when shit gets tough and I'm flailing. For always loving and accepting me, never judging or shaming me. For teaching me how to be a better businessperson, white person, human person. For checking me and practicing patience, my gratitude for you both extends far beyond the Continental Divide. Oh, and Charmi, thanks for my kid!

Kelly, Lauren, and Heidi. Giant, squishy, awkward, clumsy, emphatic love. You are my safe space whether all together or one at a time. You are the epitome of authenticity and integrity. I'm a far better mother because of the graceful guidance you've shared. A million and forty-five thousand thank-yous just scratches the wrinkly surface.

To the "sorority," I cannot imagine what the last twenty-three years would look like if Dee had never come over to Matt's at 5:15 p.m. instead of going home. There are few people with whom I feel completely and utterly comfortable being me. Like, the hottest of messes me. It's you three, the ones that make me laugh the hardest. From getting caught admiring a Dad-Stranger in a gold glass frame, falling down stairs making all the condiments rain, confusing mythical beasts with corn and bean mixtures, Guinness chugs, and nameless cheap wine by the pitcher. Swimming with bull sharks, dining with card sharks, dating dog stealers, and butt beads at Easter. I LOVE YOU FOR EVERYTHING.

Jenna and Tristan, there will never be enough minutes in the day or pages in a book to thank you adequately. You continue to inspire me, "the biggest undiscovered talents in the world." I would not have been able to make this book without the love and support from you both; endless gratitude. From champagne at 7 a.m., chickens in a hot tub, failed phony phone calls, naked spas, barreling down hills off the highway to hang with a colony of sea lions, missed photos, a million photos, the DFAs and dissolution of the DFAs, mean people, beautiful people . . . I can't remember all the moments my heart will never forget. I love you immensely, unendingly so.

Bethie. My biggest cheerleader. My ride or "let's get the fuck out of here." My BPF. First there was Sara. Then there was you. How on EARTH has it been seventeen years since our candlelit, outdoor, mountain-cave, pizza date? Some of the most formative moments of my entire life include you. Thank you for always being there, before I even have a moment to ask. Around the world and back again, one of the best decisions I have ever made was reaching out to a stranger and saying, "I don't have any friends, would you like to be mine?" I love you the most.

Winni. There are very few women I have met in my life that have ever shown up the way that you have. Without ever having to ask, you will just show up at my door when I need someone the most. You will send a text when I feel like I'm the only one left on the planet. You intentionally make time to meet me right where I am. THANK YOU for your undying support, for your pompoms, your late-night chats, adventuring, friendship, photos, food, feedback. Thank you for everything you bring to my life; my family and I are elevated versions of ourselves simply by having the honor of sharing space with you. xo.

Kristen. Thank GOD Molly convinced me that it was totally OK to hire another seven, nine, or two. Ha, I can't begin to envision what my life would look like if the three had actually shown up for her second interview. You have been one of the best surprises the Universe has ever gifted to me. Truly. Your patience, grace, generosity, thoughtfulness, and friendship have kept me balanced the last few years. And in the last year? You've been the life preserver preventing me from drowning. I would not be writing this page without you in my life, and I am committed to spending the rest of my time here making sure you know just how incredibly important you are in the world. Forever indebted to you.

Molly. I never, ever, would've been able to predict that six years after meeting in a professional manner that we would magically become family. And by family, I mean both falling in love with men who shoved their youngest sister into the laundry shoot and sent her plummeting to the first floor for FUN, when they were both still in the single digits, growing up together in Memphis. I have accepted that part of my life's journey is learning how to navigate hard life stuff, piled onto one another, every day or so, relentlessly, until one day it stops. And I feel incredible peace. And it's super silent. Because . . . I'm dead. I am certain that you entered my sphere to encourage me when I laugh deliriously at the absurdity of the life experience. You bring something so beautiful, gentle, and genuine to my life that I seem sacred in nature.

To my parents, all three of them . . . thank you for all of the lessons. The mistakes. The laughs. The tears. The consequences and praise. Thank you so very much for supporting every creative endeavor and artistic adventure. Thank you for modeling how to remain friends despite broken love stories. Mostly, thank you for being you, so that I could become me, every part of me that is now poured into these pages.

To the Magdovitz family, I could not be more grateful for each one of you. My entire life I have imagined what it would be like to experience a part of my identity that was absent from my upbringing through adulthood. Each one of you has become new threads that have helped sew my spirit whole. For the very first time. I treasure each moment I get to learn more and more lessons on what is truly important in life.

Joan and Carl, I could write an entire book around the gratitude I have for you both as humans and as my bonus parents for the last decade. I will simply say, thank you so much for loving me unconditionally when you never were expected to.

Greg. Who would've ever imagined that twenty-three years after meeting, dating each other's friends, marriages, divorces, deaths, births . . . that you and I would be tethered to one another through the most magical human being on the planet. There is no one else in the entire world I would choose to be the father of our daughter. She reflects all your very best parts back into the world and reminds me every day how to become a better person. You gave me the very best gift I will ever receive, the privilege to be Byrdie Mae's mom. And to Jenna, as a mom you try to read all the books, listen to all the podcasts, ask all the questions, and do all the research. No one truly prepares you for one of the biggest fears: "What happens to my kid if I die?" You coming into Greg's life, slowly but surely, just . . . took it away. I don't ever wonder who will hold her aching body after her first heartbreak, rub her back as she vomits through her first hangover, push her forward after her first major failure, or simply make space for me to be remembered daily, if I die. I know that YOU will do that. And in thinking about that, you will whether or not my life ends suddenly or before any of us are ready. Thank you for being a part of our family and the very best bonus mom to my daughter.

Mitch. I seem to have an endless stream of words to fill silent spaces, pauses, breaths. In this moment, the attempt to adequately sum up what you mean to me in less than ten sentence is simply impossible. In the last three years you have proven me wrong time and time again. You've stayed. By my side. Through . . . everything. I am a more empathetic, humble, courageous, vulnerable, whole person because of your love and support. I would never have finished this project without having you by my side. Thank you for being my most favorit*e person. That you for encouraging me to cry, to weep, to wail. Thank you for meeting me where I am, not where I've been or where I hope to go. Most importantly, thank you for laughing with me every day, especially when it's much easier to give up and run away. I love you from a space inside that I did not know existed, the part of me that was waiting forty-five years to awaken. Maximus + Karen 4ever, or until one of us bites it.

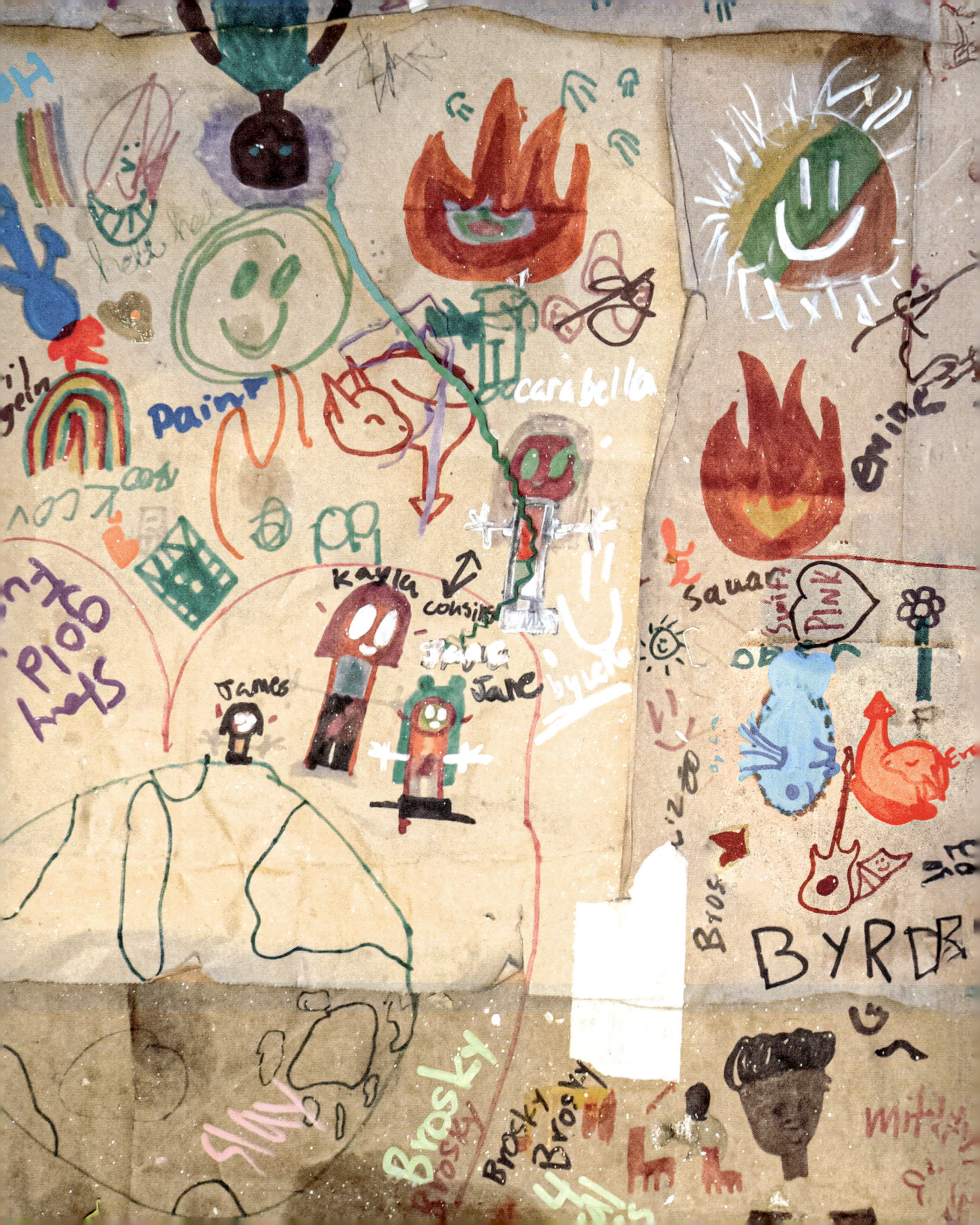